The Nineteenth Century is the second volume to appear in the Laurel British Drama series, which will present the outstanding plays of that country from medieval times to the present. In this volume the significant plays of the nineteenth century have been collected. Included also are essays on each by noted critics or by the authors themselves, which give fresh insight into the works.

Robert W. Corrigan is Professor of Dramatic Literature and Dean of the New York University School of the Arts. He has taught drama at several colleges, including Carnegie Institute of Technology, where he was Andrew Mellon Professor and Head of the Department of Drama. Professor Corrigan was the founder and first editor of the TULANE DRAMA REVIEW and has also edited numerous books on the theatre, including THE MODERN THEATRE, THEATRE IN THE 20TH CENTURY, CHEKHOV: SIX PLAYS, THE LAUREL CLASSICAL DRAMA series (5 vols. Laurel Editions), and the NEW THEATRE OF EUROPE series (Delta Books).

LAUREL BRITISH DRAMA:

The Nineteenth Century

Edited, with an Introduction by
ROBERT W. CORRIGAN

For Fred
   with great affection

Published by Dell Publishing Co., Inc.
750 Third Avenue, New York, N.Y. 10017
Copyright © 1967, by Dell Publishing Co., Inc.
Laurel ® TM 674623, Dell Publishing Co., Inc.
All rights reserved
First printing—June 1967
Printed in the United States of America

ACKNOWLEDGMENTS:

"The Art of Acting" by Dion L. Boucicault: Reprinted from
   PAPERS ON ACTING published by Hill and Wang, Inc., by
   permission of Columbia University.
"A Stage Play" by W. S. Gilbert: Reprinted from PAPERS ON
   PLAYMAKING published by Hill and Wang, Inc., by per-
   mission of Columbia University.
"An Old New Play and a New Old One" by George Bernard
   Shaw: Reprinted from DRAMATIC OPINIONS AND ES-
   SAYS, Vol. I by permission of The Public Trustee and The
   Society of Authors.
"Arms and The Man" by George Bernard Shaw: Reprinted by
   permission of The Public Trustee and The Society of Authors.
"The Making of a Dramatist" by Eric Bentley: Reprinted by
   permission of the author.
"The Unimportance of Being Oscar" by Mary McCarthy: Re-
   printed from SIGHTS AND SPECTACLES: THEATRE
   CHRONICLES by Mary McCarthy by permission of Farrar,
   Straus and Giroux, Inc., Copyright 1947 by Mary McCarthy.

contents

Melodrama and the Popular Tradition
in the Nineteenth-Century
British Theatre

Throughout all of England's long and illustrious theatrical history, one period—the nineteenth century—is invariably dismissed by critics and historians of theatre as unworthy of their effort and attention. Examining the stage histories, one finds pretty much the same recurring pattern: a scant mention will be made of the century's vigorous but allegedly meaningless theatricality; somewhat more space will be devoted to the numerous nondramatic entertainments which emerged during most of the second half of the century; and the lion's share of attention will be given to those actor-managers who dominated the British theatre at that time because they believed so firmly in their right to remake plays to serve their own narcissistic ends. But compared to the glories of the Elizabethan theatre, the wit and style of the Restoration, the balance and nobility of the Augustan age, and the probing, questioning, and rebellious spirit of the twentieth-century playwrights, the British drama of the nineteenth century is quickly passed over as little more than so much tinsel. This, say the critics with an air of superiority, was the age of melodrama! And since we all know that melodrama deals with externals, is simplistic in its attitudes, is sensational and sentimental in its effects, and—worst of all—appeals to the lowest level of public taste, the less said about it by serious-minded people the better. Fortunately, during the past few years, the myopic nature of this prejudicial view of one of the theatre's oldest forms has been vigorously and intelligently exposed. So the time is ripe for a reconsideration of melodrama, and particularly of that manifestation of it which flourished in the nineteenth-century British theatre.

THE BASIC CHARACTERISTICS OF MELODRAMA

All drama is built upon catastrophe (literally, a shift in

direction)—any event which overturns the previously existing order or system of things. As such, catastrophe is itself
devoid of moral meanings, and is equally capable of
producing joy and happiness or sadness and grief depending upon the context in which it occurs. The first important
characteristic of melodrama, and it is this which finally
distinguishes it from all other dramatic forms, is the fact
that all the significant "catastrophic" events which occur
are caused by forces outside the protagonists. *King Lear*
and *The Duchess of Malfi* have many things in common,
but, because Lear is clearly brought low by the dividedness
of his own nature while the Duchess in spite of her inner
conflicts, is ultimately destroyed by external forces, we
consider Shakespeare's play a tragedy and Webster's a
melodrama. The same distinction can be found in classical
Greek drama: certainly there is as much suffering in *The
Trojan Women* as in *Oedipus The King*—probably more;
but because the King of Thebes is responsible for his own
suffering in a way that the victimized women of Troy are
not, we correctly believe that the difference between the
two dramas is one of kind and not degree. Making these
distinctions is not just academic nit-picking or an exercise
in pedantic labeling. Rather it is the insistence that tragedy
and melodrama are two fundamentally different structures
of experience, and each must be considered on its own
terms.

Perhaps we could make these distinctions clearer by
temporarily dropping the term "melodrama" (which has
acquired so many negative connotations) and using in its
place the "drama of disaster." Disaster in its purest form
means "that which happens because of the stars," and as
such it is an apt metaphor for the unhappiness and suffering that come to men from without—i.e., from nature,
society, or other individuals. It should be pointed out,
however, that the literal meaning of "disaster" does not
have such negative connotations. Plays as diverse as
Euripides' *Helen* and Shaw's *You Never Can Tell* have
disastrous but happy resolutions. One of the most interesting characteristics of nineteenth-century melodrama is the
ready willingness with which the playwrights alternated
painful and fortunate events of disaster.) Such unhappy
events can be just as painful and as capable of moving us
as are the events of tragedy, but they are profoundly

different. Unlike tragedy, in the drama of disaster the protagonist(s) is a victim who is acted upon; his moral quality is not essential to the event, and his suffering does not imply an inevitable related guilt—in fact, there need not be any meaningful relation between the suffering of the protagonist and the cause and nature of the disastrous event.

This probably accounts for the overriding tone of paranoia which informs melodrama. When catastrophic events occur in our lives for which we are not responsible and over which we have no control, we cannot help but feel persecuted by a blind, meaningless, and hence absurd fate. Try as we may to fabricate rational explanations for such catastrophes, there is always the hovering shadow of the boogeyman. This fact does much to account for melodrama's strong hold on the imagination—particularly the popular imagination—and it also explains the overpowering sense of reality that the form of melodrama engenders even when on the surface it seems so patently unreal. For melodrama's greatest achievement is its capacity to give direct objective form to our irrational fears. Why else the compelling appeal of Richard III or Iago, Dracula or Frankenstein? Because these characters have been endowed with the authentic power and energy of irrational fear. Why else the great popularity of horror movies at midnight? Because our most savage superstitions, our most neurotic fantasies, our most grotesque childhood imaginings are given uninhibited, yet harmless, expression. Even the wild and threatening landscape in which most melodramatic actions are set enhances this paranoiac effect. All of these elements prompted Eric Bentley to write in his most important book, *The Life of the Drama* (New York: Atheneum, 1964): "The success of a melodramatist will always depend primarily upon his power to feel and project fear."

But this paranoiac aspect of the melodramatic vision is related to another quality which is almost unique to this form. Invariably, whenever people discuss melodrama, it doesn't take very long for the subject of "ham acting" to come up. In fact, every account of the nineteenth-century theatre moves to this point very quickly and dwells on it almost *ad nauseam*. Historians are only too ready to quote remarks such as Henry Labouchere's:

An actor must, in order to win popularity, have mannerisms, and the more peculiar they are, the greater will be his popularity. No one can for a moment suppose that Mr. Irving could not speak distinctly and progress about the stage after the manner of human beings, and stand still without balancing to and fro like a bear in a cage, if he pleased. Yet, had he done all this he would—notwithstanding that there is a touch of real genius about his acting sometimes—never have made the mark he has. He is, indeed, to the stage what Lord Beaconsfield was to politics. . . . Were Mr. Irving at present to abate his peculiarities, his fervent worshippers would complain that their idol was sinking into the commonplace.

Or Martin Harvey's response when he was reproached for altering texts:

My game is acting, and not necessarily the exploitation of literature. Material is chosen because it gives opportunities to practise my art—the art of acting.

Or finally Henry Irving's own account of the function of the stage:

To the common, indifferent man, immersed as a rule in the business and socialities of daily life, it brings visions of glory and adventure, of emotion, of broad human interest. To all it uncurtains a world, not that in which they live and yet not other than it, a world in which interest is heightened and yet the conditions of truth are observed, in which the capabilities of men and women are seen developed without losing their consistency to nature, and developed with a curious and wholesome fidelity to simple and universal instincts of clear right and wrong.

There is no doubt about it, melodrama—like its twin sister in music, opera—is a grandiose theatrical style. In fact, the characters of melodrama conceive of themselves constantly in histrionic terms; the source of their vitality and appeal is visceral and not intellectual. But a strongly marked style doesn't emerge without a cause. All literature of disaster, from Homer to Hemingway, deals with man alive in a universe of danger. The realm of disaster, as we have just indicated, is one dominated by irrational fears; it also encourages self-pity. As long ago as Aristotle we knew that, whenever we shift from feeling sorry for pain received to fear of pain given, we move from the sense of disaster toward the tragic sense. In melodrama neither the characters nor the audience make such a shift, with the result that the dominant *style* (as opposed, but nonetheless related, to the underlying *tone* of paranoia) is one of grandiloquent self-pity. This combination is alien to us today— at least when we go to the theatre—for reasons which I will discuss presently, but it is at the core of every successful melodrama from *Iphigenia at Aulis* to *Under the Gaslight*.

Before going any further, it would probably be appropriate to say something about the word "melodrama" itself. The word is Greek in origin, its literal meaning being "music drama" or "song drama," and it referred to those parts of the ancient festivals which included choral songs and dances. However, the modern usage of the word was first introduced by the French in 1772 and Rousseau applied it *(le mélodrame)* to his *Pygmalion* (1775), a *scène lyrique*, in which a character expresses action through speech and dumb show to the accompaniment of music. As a form it was introduced to the British theatre by Guilbert de Pixérécourt, the leading French melodramatist, whose influence on nineteenth-century British theatre was incalculable. But such historical facts can be misleading and possibly can distort our understanding of the basic form. The late eighteenth- and early nineteenth-century French innovations only underscore what has always been true about melodrama. The music was used to heighten the mood of irrationality and impending disaster which already existed in the scripts themselves. Thus the music fulfilled the function of a film score (say of *Spellbound*) rather than the more explicitly thematic function of Shakespeare's songs. For instance, the stage directions of Thomas Holcroft's *The Tale of Mystery* (1802), one of the first important English melodramas, contain such instructions as "Music to express discontent and alarm . . . Threatening music . . . Violent distracted music

. . . Music of painful remorse." Or for another example, in
C. P. Thompson's *The Shade* (1829) a single chord is
used:

> SHADE [*points to the ruined cloister*]: Blondel—
> there thy friend was foully murdered! [*Music in a
> chord.*] Blood for blood! [*Chord more terrific.*] Re-
> venge! [*Chord—thunder.*]

As we read such passages, they seem laughable; but
Hollywood and the television networks would collapse
without musical scores very similar to them. Music was
one of the chief devices to achieve the visceral effects of
melodrama.

It is for these reasons that, from the theatre's earliest
beginnings, the basic plot form of melodrama has been
the good guys versus the bad guys. However, it is a more
sophisticated structure than such a simple formulation of
it may seem to indicate, and it has been consciously used
by such "tragic" dramatists as Euripides, Shakespeare,
Webster, Ibsen, Tolstoy, Synge, and O'Neill, to name but a
few. In the structure of melodrama, as Robert Heilman
has described so persuasively in his article, "Tragedy and
Melodrama: Speculations on Generic Form" (*The Texas
Quarterly,* Summer, 1960), "man is essentially *'whole.'*"
Professor Heilman goes on to point out that such wholeness is morally neutral and implies neither greatness nor
moral perfection; rather it indicates an absence of the kind
of inner conflict which is so significant that it *must* claim
our first attention. (The protagonist of melodrama may be
humanly incomplete, indeed he usually is; but his incom-
pleteness is not the issue of the drama.) Wholeness, then,
is the central structural characteristic of melodrama.
And whether he win or lose, the action of melodrama is
essentially that of undivided protagonist facing an outer
conflict. The issue is not self-knowledge and the reordering
of one's relationship to the universe (as it is in tragedy),
but rather the maintenance of self in a hostile world and
the reordering of one's relations with others. For this
reason the resolution of the melodramatic conflict is
always clear-cut and simple: the protagonist is engaged
in a conflict which finally is either won or lost. The resolution of tragedy, on the other hand, is always complex and

ambiguous: in his struggle with necessity man always wins in the losing and loses in the winning.

Traditionally, then, melodrama has been dismissed as second rate because it lacks tragedy's broader moral dimension. However, even if tragedy is accorded a greater significance on these grounds, it should be hastily added that the very fact that the majority of the plays ever written has been melodrama, underscores a basic truth of the human condition: most of the crises and conflicts in which each of us have engaged in our daily lives lack tragedy's moral dimension as well. Melodrama is the form which expresses our human reality as we experience it most of the time, a fact which Robert Louis Stevenson knew well when he wrote:

> There is a vast deal in life where the interest turns, not upon what a man shall choose to do, but on how he manages to do it; not on the passionate slips and hesitations of the conscience, but on the problems of the body and of the practical intelligence, in clean open-air adventure, the shock of arms or the diplomacy of life. This is the realm of melodrama.

THE NINETEENTH CENTURY AND THE MODALITY OF MELODRAMA

While it is true, then, that the structure and spirit of melodrama is as old as the theatre itself, we, nonetheless—and quite correctly—think of the nineteenth century as *the* Age of Melodrama. This was particularly so in England. Somehow the characteristics of melodrama seem to be a true reflection of both the vast number of social changes that took place during the period and also of the sturdy Victorian morality which maintained itself—at least until the very last years of the century—like a Gibraltar in the midst of those changes. Melodrama, as we pointed out, is a simplification and an idealization of human experience in dramatic terms, and thus for Victorian audiences it was both an escape from an often harsh reality and also a projection of reality as it ought to be. But its chief appeal is that—then as now—one always knows where one is in melodrama. Moral principles are clearly established, and so, too, are the rules of proper conduct (factors which in large measure explain the stereotyped characters and rigid

moral distinction which are so characteristic of the form).
Motives and psychological explanations were irrelevant, at
least until Ibsenism hit the country in the '90's, because
to the Victorian mind actions were believed to speak for
themselves and were readily and easily judged. In melodrama, as in no other dramatic form, the wages of sin are
death. The action may be full of violence, but these terrible
catastrophes are all accepted as billboards along the highway to ultimate happiness, the triumph of virtue, and the
defeat of a clearly recognizable evil. English audiences
knew this, and their pleasure was in large measure due to
their knowledge that no matter how dire the circumstances,
all would turn out right.

But as important as the Victorian morality is to an
understanding of the nineteenth-century British theatre, it
is an inadequate explanation, since, in truth, Victorianism
was not so much a causal force as it was symptomatic of a
broader revolution of thought and sensibility which was
sweeping over all of Europe.

The nineteenth century is almost unique in the history
of Western culture in that the dominant concerns of its
most advanced and profound thinkers and its most sensitive and expressive artists corresponded so closely with the
needs, attitudes, and tastes of the public at large. As I said,
such a close relationship has seldom existed in history. We
know that Socrates and Euripides probably came as close
as any to revealing the tonalities of Greece at the end of
the fifth century B.C., but we also know that each of them
was not very popular in his own time. Shakespeare's
unique genius was, among other things, that he spoke to
all levels of people in a highly stratified society. But during
his lifetime he was not regarded so highly by the intel-
ligentsia as was Ben Jonson. The great dramatists—and the
philosophers as well—of the seventeenth and eighteenth
centuries wrote for relatively small and specialized aristocratic audiences, and therefore their works reveal very
little to us about popular taste. But in the nineteenth
century—at least for a good part of it, and especially in
England—there is an almost direct correspondence between the great revolutions of thought, the major trends
in the arts, and the life and conditions of the majority of
the population. In short, not only was melodrama the pre-
vailing form of popular entertainment, it was the dominant

modality of all nineteenth-century British life and thought.

No one has written more brilliantly on this subject than has Wylie Sypher in his superb essay, "Aesthetic of Revolution: The Marxist Melodrama," and because his ideas apply so directly to my present point, I quote the following extensive passage from his essay to support it:

> The thesis that melodrama is a characteristic mode of nineteenth century thought and art becomes clearer when we attempt to identify contrasting modalities in the eighteenth and twentieth centuries. Although the eighteenth century played its own incidental melodrama, we may say that the characteristic mode of enlightened thought and art was the mental fiction— those abstract and summary concepts erected inside the mind and harmoniously adjusted to each other within the rationalized order of Nature. These mental fictions were the substructure of the distinctive eighteenth-century performances in every direction: the rights of man, the literary rules, the state of nature, the deistic world order, the coherent Newtonian universe with its fictions of absolute space and absolute time, the perfectability of mankind, the theoretical codes of the encyclopedists, the generalizations of the heroic couplet, the regularity of the sonata, the balances of Augustan and Georgian architecture, the precise articulations of the formal garden, the nobility of the savage, the simple economic motives of enlightened self-interest. All these modes of the eighteenth-century mind could enlist the emotions, and often did; yet their substratum was the purely intellectual construct, the beautiful and coherent simplification that was not dramatized because it stood detached, without opposition or polarity, as an absolute assumption or idea, and because it was not animated or mythologized. The eighteenth-century sensibility moved freely and remotely in the clear atmosphere of the mental fiction.
>
> Also in contrast to the nineteenth-century melodrama, the authentic twentieth-century modality has abandoned the "event" and the theatrical act. We bear with us a sense of the conditional, of interrelationships, that the nineteenth century did not. We can-

not isolate events. Our interpretation is less personal.
We are more scientific and sceptical. For us the universe is denser—a continuum, in fact, without the
vacuums and intermissions necessary to distinguish the
individual events. Our recognition of complexities is so
involved that we cannot with assurance locate an
event in its isolated status; we cannot separate it
from its antecedents and contexts. Our novels have
fewer emphatic moments and are devoted to close in-
terconnections, uninterrupted impressions, multiple
approaches. As Whitehead has put it, the whole is
part of every event, and every event occurs only
within the structure of the whole. Thus an event is for
us a hypothetical occasion. Indeed, we have so far
abandoned the melodramatic view that we have
often withdrawn to impersonal, abstract representation of our perceptions. The disintegrations of cubism
suggest our pictorial view. By a determined analysis
or "destruction" of the object we reduce it to a study
of intimate and manifold relationships, a fragmenta-
tion within a continuum of forms until the definition
of the "subject" remains equivocal. In narrative the
disintegration began as early as Chekhov, and has
continued within Proust, Joyce, Stein, and Woolf.
Melodrama has become, for us, an inappropriate and
incredible modality.

But

. . . for the nineteenth century the modality is melodrama, the oversimplification into polarities and
oppositions that may be animated by emphatic in-
stances. To the nineteenth-century mind the very
iron laws of science operate with melodramatic fatalism—the pressure of population against subsistence,
the dynamics of supply and demand and the wages
fund, the struggle for existence in a nature red in
tooth and claw, the unalterable majestic course of
matter and force mythologized by Hardy and the
biologist Haeckel, the brooding malign policies of
Egdon Heath and the awesome tyranny of power in
geology and physics, with men and generations of

men sealed within the grim and dusty hills of the Mongolian desert.

All this is melodrama, not tragedy; and certainly not science. The view of the world as a diagram of polar forces encourages not only a melodramatic ethics (the strong and the weak, the hard and the soft, the good and the bad) but also emotive history and emotive science, which, as Huxley confidently assumed, can satisfy the spiritual longings of man. . . . By a confusion of categories the inevitabilities of matter and motion and political economy assume a moral sanction, just as in melodrama chance assumes the tenor of poetic justice, just as the impersonal "naturalism" of Zola and Ibsen always moves toward moral conclusions. The world becomes a theatre of tensions between abstractions. Melodrama has become social, if not cosmic. . . . Therefore the aesthetic category of melodrama becomes a modality of the nineteenth-century mind, which emancipated itself only with difficulty from oversimplified premises, a fatalism theatrically effective, and a displacement of moral responses into the universe. The declamatory language, the violent and symbolic gestures, the animation of polar opposites to the point of caricature are evidence of a psychic crisis. . . . Melodrama cannot admit exceptions, for they would immediately involve the action too deeply within the context of actuality and trammel the gesture. The types must behave with a decorum of extremes; the resolution must be vividly schematic. The tensions must concentrate toward a last overwhelming tableau, a final stasis beyond which one must not think. The aesthetic values of melodrama are the values of crisis, the event accepted as consummation.*

MELODRAMA AND THE POPULAR TRADITION

Clearly, the emergence of melodrama as the dominant dramatic form in the nineteenth-century English theatre

* Wyle Sypher, "Aesthetic of Revolution: The Marxist Melodrama," *The Kenyon Review,* Vol. X, No. 3 (Summer, 1948), pp. 431–44. This excerpt is quoted by permission of the author.

corresponds directly to the rise of a new and significantly different audience. We tend to forget that a century ago the theatre was the only form of popular entertainment. In the decade between 1850 and 1860 the number of theatres built throughout the country was doubled, and in the middle of the sixties, in London alone, 150,000 would be attending the theatre on any given day. Only when we realize that the theatre was to Victorian England what television is to us today will we be able to comprehend both its wide appeal and its limited artistic achievements. Because of the industrial revolution a new audience was created which demanded entertainment. Neither the Augustan theatre nor the bourgeois theatre which had emerged by the end of the eighteenth century could meet this demand. Shakespeare was too literary (unless he was hoked up), and the efforts of serious writers to write for the theatre were rejected because they in no way satisfied this new audience which came to the theatre to escape the drabness and squalor of everyday life. As a result the theatre became increasingly both anti-aristocratic and anti-middle class. And when Archer introduced Ibsen and the "new" drama, it was aimed not at the dominant popular audience, but rather was for those serious-minded people who had been driven out of the theatre two decades earlier. We cannot appreciate the achievements of the nineteenth-century British theatre unless we understand the contradictions inherent in this divorce. (The split between serious and popular theatre is still very much with us today. However, the advent of film and TV make it less significant now than it once was.)

We can see some of them most clearly in the plays of Dion Boucicault (1820?–1890). This eccentric Irishman (who significantly was given the name of Dionysius) was one of the first commercially successful dramatists of the century. He began his career as an actor and before he died he is reported to have written, translated, adapted, or cribbed better than 400 plays. Boucicault started at the top—his first produced play, *London Assurance,* was an immediate hit when it opened in 1841—and he stayed there for half a century. This continuing success was in some measure due to his ability to fashion spine-tingling plots, many of them dramatizations of the latest crimes which were reported in the mass-circulation newspapers which were coming into being at the same time, but probably more important was his imaginative use of spectacular theatrical effects. The popular imagination has always loved spectacle and Britain's first "mass" audience was emerging at the very time that the theatre was discovering radically new production techniques. Boucicault exploited them to the limit. He used the new machinery and lighting instruments to create everything from earth-consuming holocausts to giant floods. There is something paradoxical in all of this; Boucicault's use of these stage techniques led to the development of more and more realistic effects for a drama that was becoming increasingly unrealistic. This paradox is at the core of one of the contradictions inherent in the divorce mentioned above. Because of his use of these techniques, no one did more than Boucicault to bring the popular audience into the theatre, and at the same time drive out the old establishment. But in developing these very realistic techniques he provided the means for the serious naturalistic playwrights to recapture the theatre from the melodramatists some forty to fifty years later—and thus make the split between the serious and the popular even wider.

A similar contradiction can be found in the acting of the time. It is certainly true that throughout most of the century the star actors dominated the English theatre. And no star in this constellation came close to approaching the brightness of Henry Irving. Every aspect of production was subordinated to the will and the talents of this stage colossus, who was the first British subject ever to be knighted because of his acting prowess. To support Irving and the other lead actors, the stock company was developed, and this kind of organization, with its character types and set roles, corresponded beautifully to the aesthetic and moral stereotypes of melodrama. But one need only read Gordon Craig's description of Irving's sensitive and psychologically motivated acting in his production of *The Bells* (see p. 113) or recall that most of Shaw's plays have casts modeled on a traditional stock company to realize that the new serious theatre got much of both its force and technique from this earlier approach to acting.

William Gilbert, Arthur Wing Pinero, and Oscar Wilde are transitional figures. They cannot be properly called

melodramatists nor were they a part of the Ibsenite revolt
which dominated the new serious theatre. Gilbert was too
cynical, Pinero too serious-minded, and Wilde too witty
to write melodrama. But each of them used as his point of
departure the structure and attitudes of this form which
they scorned. And as the plays in this volume attest, their
work is much closer in every respect to Boucicault and
Lewis than it is to the achievements of Ibsen, Strindberg,
Hauptmann, or Chekhov. (Even Wilde's *The Importance
of Being Earnest*, which has an almost parthenogenetic
quality to it, is actually based on Gilbert's only non-
musical script—*Engaged* (1881)—which was in turn based
on a melodrama of the sixties.)

But it is in the work of Shaw that we see the contradictions most clearly. No one attacked the old-fashioned
melodrama more violently than did the master of St.
Ayot. In his early reviews of the nineties and in numerous
prefaces and plays he was vitriolic in his abuse and
parody of this kind of drama "which pandered to the
lowest and worst elements of mankind." And yet as Eric
Bentley has pointed out (and convincingly substantiated),
Shaw is the "supreme melodramatist." For all of G.B.S.'s
moral, philosophical and social concerns, his plays can be
successfully produced only if they are approached melodramatically. As Bentley puts it, "If Shaw hated the morals
of melodrama—the projection upon the world of our
irresponsible narcissistic fantasies—he loved its manners."
Once when Granville-Barker was having trouble with a
production of *Androcles and the Lion,* Shaw gave him this
advice: "Remember that it's Italian opera."

A final contradiction, this too involving Shaw: as I said
earlier, melodrama was the most appropriate and most
expressive form of the Victorian drawing room. It was the
true social reflection of its times. Shaw as a playwright,
essayist, and Fabian social reformer attacked violently
and eloquently every manifestation of Victorian morality
and manners. He was, in short, opposed to the modalities
of melodrama. But as a writer, his protests notwithstanding,
he was totally dependent upon the stability and values of
the Victorian drawing room. Even in his diatribes against
it, Shaw counted on the drawing room; it was his cosmos
as much as the Olympian deities or the Great Chain of
Being was the cosmos for an Athenian or an Elizabethan

dramatist. And when, in *Heartbreak House,* Shaw finally acknowledged the collapse of this sturdy edifice, something collapsed in his plays as well. He achieved some great moments after 1920, but his sense of structure was gone and it was never to be restored. Thus, while Shaw and his colleagues were trying to create a new theatre—a theatre free from the moral flabbiness and psychological simplifications of nineteenth-century melodrama—they succeeded only so long as they could incorporate the morality of Victorianism and the methods of melodrama into their protest.

THE DECLINE OF THE THEATRE AS A POPULAR ART

In the passage which I quoted earlier, we can recall how Wylie Sypher distinguishes between the modalities of melodrama and the atonalities of the twentieth century. I quite agree with both his description and analysis, and yet in one all-important regard there is something a little misleading about his argument. There is no doubt about it that the Victorian drawing room, its sturdy morality and all, has collapsed and in its demise all the easy absolutes and eternal ideals that we associate with it went, too. But melodrama was not one of the victims. It may have left the serious theatre (to the theatre's great loss), but it has never died. In the twentieth century, we once again—at least until now—have had a situation where serious art, public attitudes, and popular taste seldom correspond. So the theatre consorts with the enemies of melodrama: a psychological concern for motives, the sense of alienation and loss and the chaos of a fragmented people, the ambiguities of guilt and responsibility, antiheroism, and dry irony. Amidst such deep concerns, melodrama with its direct emotional appeal and simplified external structure seems superficial, cheap, and even irrelevant.

But, as I indicated earlier, melodrama never ever completely disappears because of the need of the popular imagination to draw rigid moral distinctions. So long as people want to escape into a world that is not their own, so long as they want thrills and tender emotions, so long as they want things to come out right, so long as they want to empathize with heroes who are directly associated with readily identifiable values to which they can aspire, for so long there will always be a place for melodrama. And if serious artists, concerned with revealing the truth about reality, do not provide these things too, the large majority of the people will go where they can be found. When the theatre rejected melodrama—as it has in this century—it lost its popular audience, first to the movies, and now more recently to television. (Both of these media are superbly suited to melodrama since they are so well equipped to provide the combination of effective sound and music and the rapid series of short scenes and quick radical changes which are so characteristic of the form.) In fact, interestingly enough, what's happening to films today in this regard is very similar to what happened to the theatre earlier. As TV takes over the realm of melodrama, the film is becoming "serious art." "Film," they say, "is where the action's really at." The foreign film, the independent filmmakers, the underground are showing life as it really is, and are thus capturing the new audiences, the kind of intelligent people that the serious theatre used to attract in the early days of the movies. If this is so, and it may well be, then even the plays of Ionesco, Genet, Beckett, Pinter, and Arden have a relationship to the theatre that is very similar to that of those contemporary painters whose work hangs in the Museum of Modern Art.

All of this is a far cry from the British theatre of the nineteenth century. But then our theatre of today, too, is a far distance from that theatre which you will in part discover in this book. But our life and our needs are not. The next time you turn on the television to watch *The Man From Uncle* or *Bonanza* or whatever else happens to make it on the ratings this year (and the consumption rate in the nineteenth-century theatre was much higher than on TV today), remember that your counterpart of a hundred years ago would have been going to see the latest hit at the Prince of Wales Theatre and he would be doing it for the same reasons and to satisfy the same longings.

New York City
Autumn 1966   ROBERT W. CORRIGAN

Dion L. Boucicault (1820?–1890)
London Assurance

A COMEDY IN FIVE ACTS

The Art of Acting

BY DION L. BOUCICAULT

Ladies and gentlemen, I feel very much flattered indeed to see before me such an assembly, and more particularly as I have seen on the plan that it is mainly composed of my fellow members and colleagues of our own profession. I am glad that they have so great an interest in questions that we are about to-day to discuss. I am not going to give you a lecture in any sense, much less to keep you to hear me speak on every form of acting. Nobody could do that in an hour, or an hour and a quarter. All of you know that perfectly well. All I have to do to-day is to explain how acting can be taught, and I hope you will agree with me, before I end, that this is the way acting should be taught. There was, you are aware, a few weeks ago, a lively discussion with regard to the establishment of a permanent school. There was one project that was put forward by members of our own profession. I say of our own profession, because I know I am addressing actors and actresses, my colleagues, and my fellow students. That project was dropped, suspended, put aside, because certain good patrons of the drama had organised another project and pushed it forward with a great deal of energy. During this discussion certain influential members of the public press —graciously taking, as they have always done, great interest in the art dramatic—in their editorials pronounced their opinion that acting could not be taught; that it was not an art at all; that it was a gift; that it was the effusion of enthusiasm; that, in point of fact, actors, like poets, were born, not made. Now that appeared to me to place our art below that of a handicraft, for no art becomes respectable or respected until its principles, its tenets, and its precepts are recognised, methodised, and housed in a system. If it be said that we cannot teach a man to be a genius, that we cannot teach him to be talented, that is simply a fact; but

I ask you in any art what great men, like, for example, Michelangelo, Landseer, Murillo, would have existed if some kind of art had not preceded them by which they learned the art of, say, mixing colours, the principles of proportion, and the principles of perspective. Where would Shakespeare have been if he had accidentally and unfortunately been born in some remote region at the plow-tail, where there was not within his reach the drama school of Stratford-on-Avon? He would have perished at the plow-tail and have been buried in a furrow, and we should never have known it. You must absolutely have principles in all arts. You cannot produce your own thoughts, your own feelings, unless you have some principles as some guide, some ground. I am not an eloquent man. I am an actor, an author, one who is in the habit of giving speech to others and supplying speeches for others, rather than delivering speeches myself.

Now, you know in all good wine-growing countries the best of the produce is exported. That is the reason why you get such very bad wine when you are there. Well, this is, as I have said, a large subject. I cannot do more in an hour than just skim the surface. I can, as Newton said, but wander on the shore of the great ocean and pick up the shells. I can but give you enough to make you understand what our art is, its philosophic principles; that a good actor is not due to accident, that a man is not born to be an actor unless he is trained.

You know that in Paris acting is taught. You are aware also that actors and authors are in the habit on the stage of teaching the actors how the characters they have drawn should be played. I allude, for example, to the great Mr. T. W. Robertson, one of the greatest productions of our age, who has revolutionised the drama of his period. That man was in the habit of teaching and conveying his ideas to actors on the stage, and as to how the parts should be rendered. I may also refer to M. Sardou in Paris, who, it is notorious, does the same thing, as well as many of the stage-managers of the present day. Alexandre Dumas is known to be constantly doing the same thing. I may refer also to Mr. Gilbert, the author, who does the same thing, and so stamps the character that that character is entirely new, and one that you have never seen before. You know that all active managers, such as Mr. Irving, Mr. Wilson

Barrett, Mr. Bancroft, Mr. Hare, Mr. Kendal, all teach the younger actors and actresses how to play their parts. They are obliged to do so in the present condition of affairs, because there is no school in the provinces to lick the novices into shape and to teach them the ground of their art, how to walk and how to talk—that is, to teach them acting.

Acting is not mere speech! It is not taking the dialogue of the author and giving it artistically, but sometimes not articulately. Acting is to perform, to be the part; to be it in your arms, your legs; to be what you are acting; to be it all over, that is acting. The subject of acting may be divided into the voice for the treatment of the production; the expression of feature or gesture. I call gesture that action of the body above the waist—the arms, the neck, the head, and the bust. The carriage is that action of the body which is below the waist.

Then there is the study of character. Now, there is no speechifying in that. It has nothing to do with dialogue, it has nothing to do with posture. It applies practically to that portion of the profession with which you have to do before you begin anything of the sort. Now, with regard to the voice, the secret of being heard is not a loud voice. I am not now speaking with a loud voice, yet I hope I am heard all over this place. ["*Yes.*"] Thank you. Now I will tell you why. Because I have practised speaking articulately. Every syllable of every word is pronounced, and, as far as I can, every consonant and every vowel is pronounced. That is the secret of speaking plainly, speaking easily, and being heard over a large assembly. Now it is the vowel which gives support, and value, and volume to the consonant. When you want to give strong expression it is the consonant you go at, and not the vowel; but when you want to be expressive, when you want to be agreeable, you go at your vowel.

The next thing a young actor has got to do is to measure his breath. Usually he gets anxious, he gasps, he takes breath in the wrong place, he expands his breath in the beginning of the phrase, or too much of it, and when he gets to the end of it he has got no more; the consequence is he is pumped out. All young actors fall off in the end of their phrases, and all go down in consequence. The first fault of a young public speaker is that he begins with a great rush, and then falls in the distance. The next thing for the young actor to study will be the letters *l, m, n,* and *r,* the four liquids in the alphabet—the four letters out of which you cannot possibly compose an unmusical word. You may tumble them about in any way you please, but you cannot use those four letters without giving sweetness to the remaining consonants as a consequence, if you give them their due value. What have you English people done? One thing that you have done is that you have abolished the letter *r.* There is no more splendid letter in the whole alphabet than the letter *r.* Some people pronounce it like *w.* That is a misfortune that they cannot help. But the majority of you, and I dare say a great number of you, who are now laughing at those who pronounce it like *w* do not pronounce it at all. Some of you pronounce it as if it was an *h,* and when you are speaking of the Egyptian war you say "the Egyptian wah!" and you say "that is rathah!" when you mean "rather," and "mothah," when you mean "mother"; whereas there are no such words in the English language. I am now speaking the straight and simple truth, and I hope nobody will be offended.

Then another fault of young actors and actresses is that they condense their words. Words having three syllables they put into two. For "syllable" they will say "syllble," and for "appetite" they say "apptite." They do not say "A Limited Liability Company," but "A Limted Libility Compny." That is the modern way of pronouncing the English language. People have a habit of clipping their words. This is bad for the stage. I do not know whether it is a contemporary fashion outside it. An old stager holds great stress on all the letters in order that he shall maintain the standard of purity and the proper pronunciation of the English language. There is another fault that young actors and actresses have, and that is that they pronounce vowels wrongly. They pronounce the letter *i* sometimes like *oi,* and sometimes *a-eh.* They talk of "Moi oie" or "Ma-eh a-eh"; yet neither of those is the pronounciation of *i* in the English language. In the better theatres and theatres of the first class, actors are kept in check in this respect, because the acting managers are educated men, and therefore prevent actors from doing so; but when I go to theatres of a second class I hear the English language pronounced in a way that—well, if the audience are of my opinion I should express myself very loudly. Now, there are young people who go upon the stage sometimes who are inclined to think they cannot get on because their voices are so weak, and so they are discouraged. I will give you an instance of what I mean. About twenty-two years ago I was producing a play at the Adelphi Theatre. It was *The Colleen Bawn*. In the last act a young lady played a part where she had only about three lines to utter in one of the conversations. The young lady was sweet and interesting-looking, and I went up to her and said, "My dear young lady, do speak a little louder, you cannot be heard." I tried to persuade her, but it was hopeless. I said, "A little louder, please, try." At last she burst into tears as she said, "I am trying." I went to the leader of the orchestra and said, "Do you hear this lady speak?" They hesitated, but I pressed them, when they said, "No, we do not." She subsided, and went down. One of her relations came to me the next morning and said, "I am sorry you are troubled with my relation on the stage; pray do not encourage her to go on, she will never succeed; she had much better do something else." Well, I thought so too, but three years afterwards I found that young lady playing a leading part in *The Colleen Bawn*. I also found her playing a leading juvenile part in a piece at the Olympic Theatre, and holding her own by the side of the best actors, and now she possesses one of the sweetest, most sympathetic, and best voices that I ever heard on the stage in any country. It was one of the most charming organs for perfection and sweetness that to my recollection I have ever heard. That was done by practice and self-tuition. Her name is Miss Lydia Foote.

I must now go to a subject of a rather delicate nature, and that is really the first of my subject—the voice. You know there are certain voices on the stage—you are perfectly aware of this—that the actor does not use off the stage; that are exclusively confined to tragedy. It is not the actor's ordinary voice. The idea is that the tragedian never has to use his own voice. Why? What is the reason? Before this century the great French tragedians before Talma and the great English tragedians before Kean used their treble voice—the tea-pot style. They did it as if they played on the flute. Then came the period when the tragedian played his part on the bouble bass *so*. [*The speaker imitated a very deep bass amid much laughter*.] There was no reason for it. Now we perform that part in the present age in what is called the medium voice. The reason is this. It is the transcendental drama tragedy. When I call it transcendental I mean unreal, poetic, to distinguish it from the realistic or the drama of ordinary life. The transcendental drama assumes that the dialogues are uttered by beings larger than life, who express ideas that no human being could pour out. The actor has accustomed himself to feel that he is in a different region, and therefore he feels if he uses his ordinary voice it might jar on the transcendental effect. I have fought out this very question with the great tragedians in France; and it seemed as if the tragedians were afraid of destroying the delicate illusion of the audience, who are sent about four hundred years back, as if they were living with people whom they had never seen and had no knowledge of. The consequence is those characters are too big for any ordinary human being, and the actor tries to make his manner and his voice correspond.

I will now leave the question of voice, and go to the question of gesture. Now gesture on the stage must be distinct and deliberate. When you look at a person you do not turn your eye, but you turn your whole head. If you want to point, do *that* [*with the arm straight out from the shoulder*]—the action must go from the shoulder. Every novice does *that*—[*pointing with finger only*]—particularly little women. If you have to shake your head, it must be full. Now, there is one cardinal rule—no, I will not say that, because in the theatre there is no such thing as a cardinal rule. Great men and great women often make the greatest effects by inverting the well-known rule; but the rule is that all gesture should precede slightly the words that it is to impress or to illustrate. If I am making an address to heaven I raise my arms first *so* [*illustrating*]— "By heaven!" The gesture indicates slightly to the mind what is going to be given in words, and the words complete that idea and satisfy the mind of the audience. If I were to say "By heaven!" *so* [*raising the arms after words*], that is comic, is it not? If I were to say to you "Now, look here," that is right [*the action of the hand preceding the words*]; but if I say, "Now, look here" [*the action following the words*], that would be wrong. Then, no one except in doubt and in very exceptional circumstances puts his hand to his head. It is a bad habit, or it is a bad gesture. It is only called in when the man is in trouble, or, as old Kean

did it, in despair. It is very exceptional. Of course great
men may do these sorts of things, just as a great painter
puts characters in attitudes that are wrong, but which are
right in him. Why in the attitude of appeal do you put
your hands up *so?* Because you want them. You cannot
appeal *that* way [*with the palms downwards*]. Why in dep-
recation do you put your hands downwards? You cannot
do it *that* way [*the palms upwards*]. Common sense will
tell you that many of these little matters are matters that
depend upon philosophy. They are so simple, so clear, and
distinct, that you laugh at them. But do you know they are
not generally known? The actor picks up these things by
degrees on the stage. Rules are scattered about the stage
and transmitted, gipsy-like, in our vagrant life from one
generation to another; but do you know that sometimes it
is ages before they are learned, and that an actor has to go
on picking up these things one by one? Do you know how
many years an actor is in doing that? What was Irving doing antecedent to 1870? He had been several years on the
stage. I first met Mr. Irving in 1866, in Manchester. He
happened, very fortunately for me, to have been selected
to play a part in a piece of mine which was first produced
there. He played it, and I said at once, "Here is the man,
here is somebody!" A short time afterwards I said to him,
"Why are not you in London?" He said, "Because I cannot get there." I said, "Oh, that is very simple; I am going
to produce this piece in London, and I shall make it an
absolute condition that you play this part." Therefore he
came in 1866. Now from 1866 to 1870 what were you
about? Were you stone blind that you did not know him?
No, it was not your fault. During all that time he had been
gathering together, painfully and laboriously, all these arts
of his profession, and while he was gathering them he
could not, till he got them together, be sure of his art. He
had not that internal power which should have enabled him
to know the stage so as to take his stand upon the stage and
possess you! When he felt that he could do it he did it, but
not before.

But that is a digression from gesture. Now, I will say
a word as to superfluous gesture, and I would say, Let the
gesture be exactly such as pertains to what you say, so as
to help the meaning, and no more. Do not use *gesticles*—
little gestures—that is, fidgety. The audience are very much

alive to gesture, and if they see you constantly on the stage, and find that your gestures mean nothing, they will pay you no further attention. Gesture is not a small thing. Ask the man in the House of Commons! Ask the man speaking after-dinner speeches! and they will tell you. That the knowledge of it is necessary is quite clear from the way he puts his hands into his pockets, or down on the table, or anything or anywhere, simply because nothing interferes with a man so much as not having learned the appropriate gesture. Now, in gesture you will observe that when the face is delivered to the public in the ordinary way in which an actor acts you see two cheeks, two eyes, the whole of the mouth, and the whole of the nose, but the gesture is foreshortened; but in profile you see half a face, one eye, one half of the mouth, and one half of the nose, but then the gestic assistance becomes powerful. So [*full face*], the gesture is weak; so [*profile*], the gesture is strong.

Then, gesture must be subordinate to the spectator himself. All things in this art must be subordinate to that. It is a sort of picture. Therefore, the arm farthest from the audience must, as a general rule, go up. These, you will say, are slight rules; but still they will jar on the audience occasionally if they are not followed. I beg to observe, as far as I have gone, these are not altogether rules that apply to the stage. They apply to oratory. They belong to the pulpit, they belong to the bar, and they belong to the House of Commons. If they did not, they would not be true. They do not belong to one more than another. Now, there is a very important thing about gesture which we will call byplay—that is, the gestures that are used while another person is speaking, so that the recipient, by receiving the speech from the stage, may transmit its effect to the audience. That is a very delicate process, and one that is very difficult for a novice to understand and perform; but he should know, if he is properly instructed, how to keep that gesture to listen to the principal actor, for if he does not do so he will not convey it to the audience, and he may conclude: "If his speech has no effect upon me it will not have any effect upon them."

Another thing is, do not let your gesture be too short. It seems that some cannot give the appropriate gesture. They say, "Go away!" [*with a quick gesture*]. They cannot rest long enough in a gesture. You do not know how long you can rest upon a good one. It tires you, but it will not tire the spectator. He does not like it, and does not understand that quick change. Then you should very rarely reach across your own body. Everything that is strictly natural is not always right. If I were in a room I should take my hat from this table with my right hand and turn, but here I should turn my back on the audience if I do so, therefore I take it *so* [*with the left hand, and passing it to the right*] when I am going out, although I have no right to take it in my left hand naturally. I could say a good deal more upon gesture, but I am afraid I am keeping you here too long. [*"No, no!" and cheers.*]

Now let us go to posture and to character. I now come to a most important fact. I am going to ask you what has become of the lost art of walking? Some waddle, some roll, and some toddle; but there is but one man in five hundred —nay, in one thousand—that really walks. Examine the Greek friezes, where the lines of persons are represented in the true attitude of a person walking. Nowadays on the stage, or in the street, you will find the action is totally different, and I will explain it. There are some southern Spaniards who still possess the lost art, and some Arabs do. I will tell you why presently. Let me explain the process. The English and French walk with their knees never brought straight. That is ungraceful, and not a proper method of walking. Walking means a stride with the foot from one position to another. That is the art of walking. If that stride is taken properly it is a walk. One reason for this is the modern walker is not accustomed to bend the foot, but unless those joints can play you cannot walk. The leg must be brought back into a perfectly straight position, because the walk is made by propulsion from one position to another. The leg is thrown forward, but should never be kicked out, but as the leg advances the propulsion is like that of the Greek friezes. The right leg is forward, or if the left is forward the right is always straight. The foot is brought perfectly level with the ground. The foot must not be dragged as some actors do it. There is no elasticity in it that way. I have not the slightest intention to be personal to anybody. The foot being brought forward slowly and level with the ground, the shoulders are kept back and the body is perfectly perpendicular.

Now, how is that to be obtained? I will tell you. If you

place a pad on the head, and if you place on the pad a weight of say thirty or forty pounds—oh, you can bear sixty pounds without any trouble; you do not know what power there is in the backbone—that obliges you to carry your weight strictly over the backbone and to hold your head up; the head and neck immediately assume a uniform and erect attitude. The weight being where it is, the whole body assumes a perfect attitude and the arms drop in the right place. If you attempt to walk, the legs must be kept cleanly and clearly underneath, the body must be kept perfectly straight, and you can walk—a little stiffly, perhaps, because if you do not you will fall. When you get into the habit of carrying anything on the head you will walk with ease and grace under it. That is why the Arabs walk so well, because they are in the habit of carrying things on their heads. That is, perhaps, the reason the Greeks walk so well, because they were likely to carry something *in* their heads.

Now, in walking let us study some living thing. You know that some birds are noticeable for their grace; and you will find that with animals like those of the feline tribe there is at the middle of the walk a very slight pause. The walk is not continuous and continual, but there is a pause in the middle. You will also find that birds of a certain class walk in that way. That also adds grace to the movement; and you will find when you carry a weight of that kind upon your head you will feel when you get to the centre of the step that you make a slight pause, and this habit cultivates that peculiar touch of grace which is essential to an exceedingly graceful and full walk. Some ladies have it naturally, and it is always better if these things come not by art, but by nature. Then, again, the leg farthest from the audience should be always farther forward than the other. Starting for a walk, you should commence it with the off leg. If you kneel on the stage, kneel on the knee next the audience. These are ordinary facts that we should all know.

Now, when you walk backwards and forwards, do not turn upon the ball of your foot in turning round; but, when you come to the end of the walk, it is more dignified to take one step and bring your foot back, and then take the movement back again. A lady, if she attempts to do it, walks on the tail of her own dress. She is obliged, therefore, to be more graceful. Then measure your distance.

Novices always fall short, or turn back; but good actors, by habit, render this impossible. A good actress gets to the table, if she wants to get to it, without difficulty. In the old style, actors used to have a number of tricks on the stage, which, fortunately, recent tragedians have abolished. One of these was what was called "taking the step." Your Richard and Macbeth could not act except in a circle; but then they made a point of taking the stage [*the speaker walked rapidly across the stage*], and that was the cue to applaud! When the performer had given a remarkable speech, and when he came to its point, he walked into one of the corners. It was impossible in the palaces of the kind and elsewhere for the performers to get into the corners, especially a lady, therefore he did not continue to cultivate a habit which was not only so unnatural, but so inartistic.

Another trick which comedians as well as tragedians used in taking an exit was to commence the speech in this way, "So, my Lord, I take my leave," and then go to the other side of the stage and finish it. This was equally conventional; the actor would reserve the last three or four words of his scene, and, walking to the side, would turn and speak those words "to take him off." So that twenty or thirty years ago an actor often said, "Would you give me a few words to take me off?" They could not get off the stage!

I think I have said enough on that branch of the subject, so that I may leave that in order to leave a little room for that part of the subject which relates to the study of character. Now, the great fault of young actors in the present day, novices particularly, before they go on the stage, is to imagine, when they have got the words into their heads, that all is done. That is not all. A child could do that, because it has a much better memory than a grown-up man —much better memory. Young actors think when they know the part they know the work. But it is not the getting of the words into your head, it is the getting them out again. He goes on the stage, dresses nicely, parts his hair properly, and provides himself with patent-leather boots; but, if he does not study character, it is no use. You may look the thing very nicely; but the audience will discount that in a very few minutes. The question is whether you can do it. I am sorry to say that the young actors of the present day do not give so much attention to the inside of the subject as they ought to do.

The first lesson an actor has to learn is, not to speak. It is to learn to walk on the stage, stand still, and walk off again. That appears very simple, but it is very difficult. When he walks on the stage he fixes his attention on what is said and what is done on the scene, never removing it to follow the speakers. But his part is to listen, and if he can perform that part well—that is, the part of a good listener —he will have achieved a progress in his art that many very favourite and prominent actors have never yet achieved. That one lesson alone, if it is perfectly learned, will actuate his whole career. He will never forget it, and it will be one reason of his success. Now, the finer part of the acting is to obtain an effect, not altogether by what is given you to speak, but by listening to what another person speaks, and by its effect upon you, by continuing your character while the other man is speaking. Your performance on the stage by that byplay may not be as great at his, but still it prepares the audience for the scene; the gesture helps the tone. The effect is exhibited on the actor who listens, and from him on the rest of the audience, if the beginner allows his mind to be employed in this manner it has this effect, his mind is no longer in attendance upon his arms; that terrible egotism, that vanity sickness that we call stage fright, he is relieved of nearly altogether. He cannot help feeling it because he rushes into it in consequence of the great pains he is at to obtain a judgment that is of value for its sweetness, and is acutely feared for its censure. If the man fixes his mind upon some other object, if the mind is over *there,* not *here* on himself, ease will naturally follow, because he is naturally there as a listener. That is his first lesson; when he has accomplished this he must come to the study of character.

To the young beginner I would say, when you go upon the stage do not be full of yourself, but be full of your part. That is mistaking vanity for genius, and is the fault of many more than perhaps you are aware of. If actors' and actresses' minds be employed upon themselves, and not on the character they wish and aspire to perform, they never really get out of themselves. Many think they are studying their character when they are only studying themselves. They get their costume, they put it on, see how it fits, they cut and contrive it, but all that is not studying their character, but their costume. Actors and actresses frequently come to me and say, "Have you any part that will fit me?" They never dream of saying, "Have you any part that I can fit? that I can expand myself or contract myself into; that I can put myself inside of; that I, as a Protean, can shape myself into, even alter my voice and everything that nature has given to me, and be what you have contrived? I do not want you to contrive like a tailor to fit me." That is what is constantly happening.

Now, I will give you an example of what happens when a new play is brought into the theatre. It is usually read in the green-room. I do not think that is a good plan. My experience, which extends to forty years, is that actors listen to the parts that others have to play, but never to their own, and are dissatisfied. "Oh, yes," says Smith, "I have a fine part but look at Jones." Jones, grumbling, says, "Oh, yes; I suppose I shall do something with it; but see how it falls off in the last act. Miss Popkins has the best part." Miss Popkins is the leading woman. She comes and says, "Mr. Boucicault, I do object to be the mother of Miss Brown, whom I knew as a leading actress when I was a child." Then Miss Brown comes to me the following day full of anxiety, and, taking me aside, says, "What am I to wear?" I say, "Study your character." She still says, "What am I to wear?" and "Can I change between the second and third acts?" Then I am button-holed by Mr. Smith, who says, "Please, what is your idea about my wig?" This is not the study of character. It is jealousy of the other parts, and not their own.

It was not so forty years ago. They had their faults, many of them, but they did not constitute costume and make-up as the study of character, which it is not. I will tell you what did happen forty years ago. I was producing a comedy in which Mr. Farren, the father of the gentleman who so ably bears the same name (old Farren), played a leading part. He did not ask what he was going to wear, but he came to me, and said, "Who did you draw this party from; had you any type?" I said, "Yes, I had," and mentioned the names of two old fogies who, at that time, were well known in London society. One he knew, the other he did not. He went and studied Sir Harcourt Courtly, and he studied by the speediest method, for the study was absolutely and literally out of the mouth of the man himself. That will give you an idea how they studied character.

Once Mr. Mathews came to me and said, "Do you know Dazzle?" I said, "Yes." He said, "Do you know really a good type?" "Yes, I do." "Will you kindly let me see him?" I said, "I am in some difficulty, for if he thought I was going to put him on the stage he would shoot me, and I do not want that, but I can describe him." "Very well," he said, "what sort of a man is he?" I described him exactly. I said, "The other day I was standing on the hearth rug, and a mutual friend, a young plunger, came in in a great state of excitement and announced to us that a distant relative had left him £10,000. Dazzle looked at the ceiling and said, 'If I had only £10,000! Bless me! I should be having £20,000 a year for six months.'" From that he understood immediately what the character was.

That is the way to study character, to get at the bottom of human nature, and I am happy to say that, amongst some young actors who have come out within the last ten or fifteen years, I have seen a natural instinct for the study of character and for the drawing of character most admirably, and much more faithfully than they drew it twenty or thirty years ago. There is a study of character that we may call good and true that has been accomplished within the last fifteen or sixteen years.

Now, I will say something by way of anecdote to show how utterly unnecessary it is for you to bother your minds so much about your dress. I was producing *The Shaughraun* in New York. I generally had enough to employ my time. I get the actors and actresses to study their characters, and generally leave myself to the last. But the last morning before the play was produced I saw my dresser hobbling about, but afraid to come to the stage. At last he said, "Have you thought of your costume?" I said I had not done any such thing. It was about three o'clock in the afternoon, and I had to play about seven o'clock in the evening. I went upstairs and said, "Have you got a red coat?" "Yes; we have got a uniform red hunting coat." "Oh, that is of no use!" "We have got one that was used in *She Stoops to Conquer*." That was brought, but it had broad lapels and looked to belong to about one hundred and fifty years ago. "Oh!" said the man, "there is an old

coat that was worn by Mr. Beckett as Goldfinch." When he
came to that it reached all down to my feet, and was too
long in the sleeves. So I cut them off with a big pair of
shears, and by the shears and the scissors I got some sort
of a fit. Then I got an old hunting cap, a pair of breeches,
and sent for some old boots that cost about 2s. 6d. and
did not fit me, and that is how I came on the stage. The
editor of one of the newspapers said, "Where on earth did
you get that extraordinary costume from?"

Believe me, I mention these circumstances simply to show
that the study of character should be from the inside; not
from the outside! Great painters, I am told, used to draw
a human figure in the nude form, and, when they were
proposing to finish their pictures, to paint the costumes;
then the costumes came right. That is exactly how an actor
ought to study his art. He ought to paint his character in
the nude form and put the costume on the last thing.

Now, let me give this particular advice to all persons going on the stage. Many of you are already on the stage, but
others may be going on. Having arrived at the conclusion
as to what your line is going to be, always try to select those
kinds of characters and the line that is most suited and
more nearly conforms to your own natural gifts. Nature
knows best. If you happen to have a short, sharp face, a
hard voice, an angular figure, you are suited for the intellectual characters of the drama, such as Hamlet and so
forth. If you are of a soft, passionate nature—if you have
a soft voice and that sort of sensuous disposition which
seems to lubricate your entire form, your limbs, so that
your movements are gentle and softer than others—then
this character is fitted for a Romeo or an Othello. You
will find, if you look back at the records of actors, there
are few great actors that have shone in the two different
lines, the intellectual and the sensual drama. Kemble can
do Hamlet, but he could not do Othello. Kean could do
Othello, but he could not do Hamlet. The one was passionate and sensual, the other was an intellectual, a noble,
grand actor.

Now, after you have made this preliminary study you
will recollect that in every great character there are three
characters really. We are all free men, in one sense, speaking, of course, of our inner life; but we have three characters. First there is the man by himself—as he is to

himself—as he is to his God. That is one man, the inner
man, as he is when alone; the unclothed man. Then there
is the native man, the domestic man, as he is to his family. Still there is a certain amount of disguise. He is not as
he is to other men. Then there is the man as he stands
before the world at large; as he is outside in society. Those
are the three characters. They are all in the one man, and
the dramatist does not know his business unless he
puts them into one character. Look at Hamlet in his solilo-
quies: he is passionate, he is violent, he is intemperate in
himself, he knows his faults and lashes his own weakness.
But he has no sooner done that than Horatio comes on the
stage with a few friends. Horatio is the mild, soft, gentle
companion; with his arm around his neck, Hamlet forgets
the other man; he gets a little on, but he is the same man to
Horatio as he is to his mother, when he gets her in the
closet. But when he encounters the world at large, he is
the Prince! the condescending man! You have seen Hamlet
played, and if you watched closely, you have seen those
three phases of his character have been given on this
stage! So it is in nearly all characters—comic or otherwise.
You will find that the three characters always combine in
the man.

This should be studied to be preserved. It is one of the
charms of comedy, as all dramatists know very well how to
employ. Take, for instance, where the woman is the
affected woman of society. Something occurs to break her
down, and she is bound to break down; the audience immediately recognise it, because they recognise the true
woman. The truth comes out, and they do not like affectation; they prefer nature. When Pauline, in *The Lady of
Lyons,* carries on the proud woman—that is, the woman of
society—as she falls in love she struggles for what? To
maintain the woman of society. During the struggle the
audience watch with intensest interest whilst they gradually see her breaking down. Eventually, crash! and the true
woman bursts out. There you see the preservation of
those two characters. The observation of the three characters is one secret of the true and the highest form of the
dramatic art, and the dramatist, if he would be true to
nature and to his art, must carry them out. Now, it may
be said that these things are not altogether high art. They
may not be high art, but the high art rests on them. You

cannot get on without them. They are the pedestals on which the statue rests. They are as necessary to the great picture as they are to the life they represent.

Now, ladies and gentlemen, I have kept you a long time. All I say now is that I have to give you most heartily and conscientiously, as an old man, an old dramatist, and an old actor, this advice. Whatever is done by an actor let it be done with circumspection, without anxiety or hurry, remembering that vehemence is not passion, that the public will feel and appreciate when the actor is not full of himself, but when he is full of his character, with that deliberation without slowness, that calmness of resolution without coldness, that self-possession without overweening confidence, which should combine in the actor so as to give grace to comic and importance to tragic presence. The audience are impressed with the unaffected character of one who moves forward with a fixed purpose, full of momentous designs. He expresses a passion with which they will sympathise, and radiates a command which they will obey.

Now, ladies and gentlemen, I have detained you here longer than I intended. I thank you very sincerely for the kindness with which you have attended to me. I do not know that I have given you anything very valuable, but I hope you will think that I have given you sufficient, and more than sufficient, to help you to study this, the art of acting, although it is simply a bit of a very great deal that can be taught to the young actor, who should be taught if he is to approach perfection in the period of probation which he has to go through. Let us give him the sound principles of his art. Do not let us leave the managers to be obliged to take the most ignorant people, and have to do here on the stage what should be done elsewhere. Let them be properly and fairly prepared and brought into such a position as to be able to do some of the minor parts of the drama which they profess to follow. If you believe anything I have said is good and worthy of your attention, and that I have not employed your hour foolishly and infructuously, then I will ask you to be kind enough to help me to thank Mr. Irving for his very great kindness in giving me this stage, and you the free use of this house, this afternoon, so that we may *collogue* together. I will ask you to be kind enough to say that you thank Mr.

Irving, and to help me to thank Mr. Stoker and other gentlemen of this house, who have gone through an immense deal of trouble (more than I can explain) in putting me in a position so as to be able to address so brilliant and so kind an audience.

TO
CHARLES KEMBLE
This comedy (with his kind permission) is dedicated
by his fervent admirer and humble servant
Dion L. Boucicault

First performed at Covent Garden Theatre, March 4, 1841.

CHARACTERS

Sir Harcourt Courtly
Max Harkaway
Charles Courtly
Mr. Spanker
Dazzle
Mark Meddle
Cool (valet)
Simpson (butler)
Martin
Lady Gay Spanker
Grace Harkaway
Pert

The Scene lies in London and Gloucestershire in 1841.
Time—Three days.

SCENE ONE

An ante-room in Sir Harcourt Courtley's house in Belgrave Square.

[*Enter Cool.*]

Cool. Half-past nine, and Mr. Charles has not yet returned:
I am in a fever of dread. If his father happen to rise
earlier than usual on any morning, he is sure to ask
first for Mr. Charles. Poor deluded old gentleman—he
little thinks how he is deceived. [*Enter Martin, lazily.*]
Well, Martin, he has not come home yet?

Martin. No; and I have not had a wink of sleep all night
—I cannot stand this any longer; I shall give warning.
This is the fifth night Mr. Courtly has remained out,
and I am obliged to stand at the hall window to watch
for him.

Cool. You know if Sir Harcourt is aware that we connived
at his son's irregularities, we should all be discharged.

Martin. I have used up all my common excuses on his
duns.—"Call again," "Not at home," and "Send it
down to you," won't serve any more; and Mr. Crust,
the wine-merchant, swears he will be paid.

Cool. So they all say. Why, he has arrests out against him
already. I've seen the fellows watching the door—
[*Loud knock and ring heard.*]—there he is, just in
time—quick, Martin, for I expect Sir William's bell
every moment—[*Bell rings.*]—and there it is. [*Exit
Martin, slowly.*] Thank heaven! he will return to college to-morrow, and his heavy responsibility will be
taken off my shoulders. A valet is as difficult a post to
fill properly as that of prime minister. [*Exit.*]

Young Courtly [*without*]. Hollo!

Dazzle [*without*]. Steady!

[*Enter Young Courtly and Dazzle.*]

Young Courtly. Hollo-o-o!

Dazzle. Hush! what are you about, howling like a Hottentot. Sit down there, and thank heaven you are in Belgrave Square, instead of Bow Street.

Young Courtly. D——d—damn Bow Street.

Dazzle. Oh, with all my heart!—you have not seen as much of it as I have.

Young Courtly. I say—let me see—what was I going to say?—oh, look here—[*He pulls out a large assortment of knockers, bell-pulls, etc., from his pocket.*] There! dam'me! I'll puzzle the two-penny postmen,—I'll deprive them of their right of disturbing the neighborhood. That black lion's head did belong to old Vampire, the money-lender, this bell-pull to Miss Stitch, the milliner.

Dazzle. And this brass griffin—

Young Courtly. That! Oh, let me see—I think—I twisted that off our own hall-door as I came in, while you were paying the cab.

Dazzle. What shall I do with them?

Young Courtly. Pack 'em in a small hamper, and send 'em to the sitting magistrate with my father's compliments; in the mean time, come into my room, and I'll astonish you with some Burgundy.

[*Re-enter Cool.*]

Cool. Mr. Charles—

Young Courtly. Out! out! not at home to any one.

Cool. And drunk—

Young Courtly. As a lord.

Cool. If Sir Harcourt knew this, he would go mad, he would discharge me.

Young Courtly. You flatter yourself; that would be no proof of his insanity.—[*To Dazzle.*] This is Cool, sir, Mr. Cool; he is the best liar in London—there is a pungency about his invention, and an originality in his equivocation, that is perfectly refreshing.

Cool [*aside*]. Why, Mr. Charles, where did you pick him up?

Young Courtly. You mistake, he picked *me* up.

[*Bell rings.*]

Cool. Here comes Sir Harcourt—pray do not let him see you in this state.

Young Courtly. State! what do you mean? I am in a beautiful state.

Cool. I should lose my character.

Young Courtly. That would be a fortunate epoch in your life, Cool.

Cool. Your father would discharge me.

Young Courtly. Cool, my dad is an old ass!

Cool. Retire to your own room, for heaven's sake, Mr. Charles.

Young Courtly. I'll do so for my own sake. [*To Dazzle.*] I say, old fellow, [*staggering*] just hold the door steady while I go in.

Dazzle. This way. Now then!—take care! [*Helps him into the room.*]

[*Enter Sir Harcourt Courtly in an elegant dressing-gown, and Greek scull-cap and tassels, etc.*]

Sir Harcourt. Cool, is breakfast ready?

Cool. Quite ready, Sir Harcourt.

Sir Harcourt. Apropos. I omitted to mention that I expect Squire Harkaway to join us this morning, and you must prepare for my departure to Oak Hall immediately.

Cool. Leave town in the middle of the season, Sir Harcourt? So unprecedented a proceeding!

Sir Harcourt. It is. I confess it, there is but one power could effect such a miracle,—that is divinity.

Cool. How!

Sir Harcourt. In female form, of course. Cool, I am about to present society with a second Lady Courtly; young —blushing eighteen;—lovely! I have her portrait; rich! I have her banker's account;—an heiress, and a Venus!

Cool. Lady Courtly could be none other.

Sir Harcourt. Ha! ha! Cool, your manners are above your station.—Apropos, I shall find no further use for my brocaded dressing-gown.

Cool. I thank you, Sir Harcourt; might I ask who the fortunate lady is?

Sir Harcourt. Certainly; Miss Grace Harkaway, the niece of my old friend, Max.

Cool. Have you never seen the lady, sir?

Sir Harcourt. Never—that is, yes—eight years ago. Having been, as you know, on the continent for the last seven years, I have not had the opportunity of paying my devoirs. Our connection and betrothal was a very extraordinary one. Her father's estates were contiguous to mine;—being a penurious, miserly, *ugly* old scoundrel, he made a market of my indiscretion, and supplied my extravagance with large sums of money on mortgages, his great desire being to unite the two properties. About seven years ago, he died—leaving Grace, a girl, to the guardianship of her uncle, with this will:—if, on attaining the age of nineteen, she would consent to marry me, I should receive those deeds, and all his property, as her dowry. If she refused to comply with this condition, they should revert to my heir-presumptive or apparent.—She consents.

Cool. Who would not?

Sir Harcourt. I consent to receive her 15,000*l.* a year.

Cool [*aside*]. Who would not?

Sir Harcourt. So prepare, Cool, prepare;—but where is my boy, where is Charles?

Cool. Why—oh, he is gone out, Sir Harcourt; yes, gone out to take a walk.

Sir Harcourt. Poor child! A perfect child in heart—a sober, placid mind—the simplicity and verdure of boyhood, kept fresh and unsullied by any contact with society. Tell me, Cool, at what time was he in bed last night?

Cool. Half-past nine, Sir Harcourt.

Sir Harcourt. Half-past nine! Beautiful! What an original idea! Reposing in cherub slumbers, while all around him teems with drinking and debauchery! Primitive sweetness of nature! No pilot-coated, bear-skinned brawling!

Cool. Oh, Sir Harcourt!

Sir Harcourt. No cigar-smoking—

Cool. Faints at the smell of one.

Sir Harcourt. No brandy and water bibbing—

Cool. Doesn't know the taste of anything stronger than barley-water.

Sir Harcourt. No night parading—

Cool. Never heard the clock strike twelve, except at noon.

Sir Harcourt. In fact, he is my son, and became a gentleman by right of paternity. He inherited my manners.

[*Enter Martin.*]

Martin. Mr. Harkaway!

[*Enter Max Harkaway.*]

Max. Squire Harkaway, fellow, or Max Harkaway, another
time. [*Martin bows, and exit.*] Ah! Ha! Sir Harcourt,
I'm devilish glad to see ye! Gi' me your fist. Dang it
but I'm glad to see ye! Let me see. Six—seven years,
or more, since we have met. How quickly they have
flown!

Sir Harcourt [*throwing off his studied manner*]. Max, Max!
Give me your hand, old boy.—[*Aside.*] Ah! he *is* glad
to see me. There is no fawning pretense about that
squeeze. Cool, you may retire.

[*Exit Cool.*]

Max. Why, you are looking quite rosy.

Sir Harcourt. Ah! ah! rosy! Am I too florid?

Max. Not a bit; not a bit.

Sir Harcourt. I thought so.—[*Aside.*] Cool said I had put
too much on.

Max. How comes it, Courtly, that you manage to retain
your youth? See, I'm as grey as an old badger, or a
wild rabbit; while you are—are as black as a young
rook. I say, whose head grew your hair, eh?

Sir Harcourt. Permit me to remark that all the beauties of
my person are of home manufacture. Why should
you be surprised at my youth? I have scarcely thrown
off the giddiness of a very boy—elasticity of limb—
buoyancy of soul! Remark this position—[*Throws
himself into an attitude.*] I held that attitude for ten
minutes at Lady Acid's last *réunion,* at the express
desire of one of our first sculptors, while he was
making a sketch of me for the Apollo.

Max [*aside*]. Making a butt of thee for their gibes.

Sir Harcourt. Lady Sarah Sarcasm started up, and, pointing
to my face, ejaculated, "Good gracious! Does not Sir
Harcourt remind you of the countenance of Ajax, in
the Pompeian portrait?"

Max. Ajax—humbug!

Sir Harcourt. You are complimentary.

Max. I'm a plain man, and always speak my mind. What's
in a face or figure? Does a Grecian nose entail a good
temper? Does a waspish waist indicate a good heart?
Or, do oily perfumed locks necessarily thatch a well-
furnished brain?

Sir Harcourt. It's an undeniable fact,—*plain* people always
praise the beauties of the *mind.*

Max. Excuse the insinuation; I had thought the first Lady
Courtly had surfeited you with beauty.

Sir Harcourt. No; she lived fourteen months with me, and
then eloped with an intimate friend. Etiquette compelled me to challenge the seducer; so I received satisfaction—and a bullet in my shoulder at the same
time. However, I had the consolation of knowing
that he was the handsomest man of the age. She did
not insult me, by running away with a d——d ill-
looking scoundrel.

Max. That certainly was flattering.

Sir Harcourt. I felt so, as I pocketed the ten thousand
pounds damages.

Max. That must have been a great balm to your sore honor.

Sir Harcourt. It was—Max, my honor would have died
without it; for on that year the wrong horse won the
Derby—by some mistake. It was one of the luckiest
chances—a thing that does not happen twice in a
man's life—the opportunity of getting rid of his wife
and his debts at the same time.

Max. Tell the truth, Courtly! Did you not feel a little
frayed in your delicacy?—your honor, now? Eh?

Sir Harcourt. Not a whit. Why should I? I married *money*,
and I received it—virgin gold! My delicacy and honor
had nothing to do with hers. The world pities the be-
reaved husband, when it should congratulate. No,—
the affair made a sensation, and I was the object.
Besides, it is vulgar to make a parade of one's feelings,
however acute they may be: impenetrability of countenance is the sure sign of your highly-bred man of
fashion.

Max. So, a man must, therefore, lose his wife and his
money with a smile,—in fact, every thing he possesses
but his temper.

Sir Harcourt. Exactly,—and greet ruin with *vive la baga-
telle!* For example,—your modish beauty never dis-
composes the shape of her features with convulsive
laughter. A smile rewards the *bon mot,* and also shows
the whiteness of her teeth. She never weeps impromp-
tu,—tears might destroy the economy of her cheek.
Scenes are vulgar,—hysterics obsolete: she exhibits a
calm, placid, impenetrable lake, whose surface is reflection, but of unfathomable depth,—a statue, whose

life is hypothetical, and not a *prima facie* fact.

Max. Well, give me the girl that will fly at your eyes in an argument, and stick to her point like a fox to his own tail.

Sir Harcourt. But etiquette! Max,—remember etiquette!

Max. Damn etiquette! I have seen a man who thought it sacrilege to eat fish with a knife, that would not scruple to rise up and rob his brother of his birthright in a gambling-house. Your thorough-bred, well-blooded heart will seldom kick over the traces of good feeling. That's my opinion, and I don't care who knows it.

Sir Harcourt. Pardon me,—etiquette is the pulse of society, by regulating which the body politic is retained in health. I consider myself one of the faculty in the art.

Max. Well, well; you are a living libel upon common sense, for you are old enough to know better.

Sir Harcourt. Old enough! What do you mean? Old! I still retain all my little juvenile indiscretions, which your niece's beauties must teach me to discard. I have not sown my wild oats yet.

Max. Time you did, at sixty-three.

Sir Harcourt. Sixty-three! Good God!—forty, 'pon my life! forty, next March.

Max. Why, you are older than I am.

Sir Harcourt. Oh! you are old enough to be my father.

Max. Well, if I am, I am; that's etiquette, I suppose. Poor Grace! how often I have pitied her fate! That a young and beautiful creature should be driven into wretched splendor, or miserable poverty!

Sir Harcourt. Wretched! wherefore? Lady Courtly wretched! Impossible!

Max. Will she not be compelled to marry you, whether she likes you or not?—a choice between you and poverty. [*Aside.*] And hang me if it isn't a tie!—*But* why do you not introduce your son Charles to me? I have not seen him since he was a child. You would never permit him to accept any of my invitations to spend his vacation at Oak Hall,—of course, we shall have the pleasure of his company now.

Sir Harcourt. He is not fit to enter society yet. He is a studious, sober boy.

Max. Boy! Why, he's five-and-twenty.

Sir Harcourt. Good gracious! Max,—you will permit me to know my own son's age,—he is not twenty.

Max. I'm dumb.

Sir Harcourt. You will excuse me while I indulge in the process of dressing.—Cool! [*Enter Cool.*] Prepare my toilet. [*Exit Cool.*] That is a ceremony, which, with me, supersedes all others. I consider it a duty which every gentleman owes to society—to render himself as agreeable an object as possible—and the least compliment a mortal can pay to nature, when she honors him by bestowing extra care in the manufacture of his person, is to display her taste to the best possible advantage; and so, *au revoir.* [*Exit.*]

Max. That's a good soul—he has his faults, and who has not? Forty years of age! Oh, monstrous!—but he does look uncommonly young for sixty, spite of his foreign locks and complexion.

[*Enter Dazzle.*]

Dazzle. Who's my friend, with the stick and gaiters, I wonder—one of the family—the governor maybe.

Max. Who's this? Oh, Charles—is that you, my boy? How are you? [*Aside.*] This is the *boy.*

Dazzle [*aside*]. He knows me—he is too respectable for a bailiff. [*Aloud.*] How are you?

Max. Your father has just left me.

Dazzle [*aside*]. The devil he has! He's been dead these ten years. Oh! I see, he thinks I'm young Courtly. [*Aloud.*] The honor you would confer upon me, I must unwillingly disclaim,—I am not Mr. Courtly.

Max. I beg pardon—a friend, I suppose.

Dazzle. Oh, a most intimate friend—a friend of years—distantly related to the family—one of my ancestors married one of his. [*Aside.*] Adam and Eve.

Max. Are you on a visit here?

Dazzle. Yes. Oh! yes. [*Aside.*] Rather a short one, I'm afraid.

Max [*aside*]. This appears a dashing kind of fellow—as he is a friend of Sir Harcourt's, I'll invite him to the wedding. [*Aloud.*] Sir, if you are not otherwise engaged, I shall feel honored by your company at my house, Oak Hall, Gloucestershire.

Dazzle. Your name is—

Max. Harkaway—Max Harkaway.

Dazzle. Harkaway—let me see—I ought to be related to the Harkaways, somehow.

Max. A wedding is about to come off—will you take a part on the occasion?

Dazzle. With pleasure! any part, but that of the husband.

Max. Have you any previous engagement?

Dazzle. I was thinking—eh! why, let me see. [*Aside.*] Promised to meet my tailor and his account to-morrow; however, I'll postpone that. [*Aloud.*] Have you good shooting?

Max. Shooting! Why, there's no shooting at this time of the year.

Dazzle. Oh! I'm in no hurry—I can wait till the season, of course. I was only speaking precautionally—you have good shooting?

Max. The best in the country.

Dazzle. Make yourself comfortable!—Say no more—I'm your man—wait till you see how I'll murder your preserves.

Max. Do you hunt?

Dazzle. Pardon me—but will you repeat that? [*Aside.*] Delicious and expensive idea!

Max. You ride?

Dazzle. Anything! Everything! From a blood to a broomstick. Only catch me a flash of lightning, and let me get on the back of it, and dam'me if I wouldn't astonish the elements.

Max. Ha! ha!

Dazzle. I'd put a girdle round about the earth, in very considerable less than forty minutes.

Max. Ah! ha! We'll show old Fiddlestrings how to spend the day. He imagines that Nature, at the earnest request of Fashion, made summer days long for him to saunter in the Park, and winter nights, that he might have good time to get cleared out at hazard or at whist. Give me the yelping of a pack of hounds before the shuffling of a pack of cards. What state can match the chase in full cry, each vying with his fellow which shall be most happy? A thousand deaths fly by unheeded in that one hour's life of ecstasy. Time to outrun, and Nature seems to grudge our bliss by making the day so short.

Dazzle. No, for then rises up the idol of my great adoration.

Max. Who's that?

Dazzle. The bottle—that lends a lustre to the soul!—When the world puts on its night-cap and extinguishes the sun—then comes the bottle! Oh, mighty wine! Don't ask me to apostrophise. Wine and love are the only two indescribable things in nature; but I prefer the wine, because its consequences are not entailed, and are more easily got rid of.

Max. How so?

Dazzle. Love ends in matrimony, wine in soda water.

Max. Well, I can promise you as fine a bottle as ever was cracked.

Dazzle. Never mind the bottle, give me the wine. Say no more; but, when I arrive, just shake one of my hands, and put the key to the cellar into the other, and if I don't make myself intimately acquainted with its internal organization—well, I say nothing,—time will show.

Max. I foresee some happy days.

Dazzle. And I some glorious nights.

Max. It mustn't be a flying visit.

Dazzle. I despise the word—I'll stop a month with you.

Max. Or a year or two.

Dazzle. I'll live and die with you!

Max. Ha! ha! Remember Max Harkaway, Oak Hall, Gloucestershire.

Dazzle. I'll remember—fare ye well. [*Max is going.*] I say, holloa!—Tallyho-o-o-o!

Max. Yoicks!—Tallyho-o-o-o! [*Exit.*]

Dazzle. There I am—quartered for a couple of years at the least. The old boy wants somebody to ride his horses, shoot his game, and keep a restraint on the morals of the parish: I'm eligible. What a lucky accident to meet young Courtly last night! Who could have thought it?—Yesterday, I could not make certain of a dinner, except at my own proper peril; to-day, I would flirt with a banquet.

[*Enter Young Courtly.*]

Young Courtly. What infernal row was that? Why, [*seeing Dazzle*] are you here still?

Dazzle. Yes. Ain't you delighted? I'll ring, and send the servant for my luggage.

Young Courtly. The devil you will! Why, you don't mean to say you seriously intend to take up a permanent residence here? [*He rings bell.*]

Dazzle. Now, that's a most inhospitable insinuation.

Young Courtly. Might I ask your name?

Dazzle. With a deal of pleasure—Richard Dazzle, late of the Unattached Volunteers, vulgarly entitled the Dirty Buffs.

[*Enter Martin.*]

Young Courtly. Then, Mr. Richard Dazzle, I have the honor of wishing you a very good morning. Martin, show this gentleman the door.

Dazzle. If he does, I'll kick Martin out of it.—No offence. [*Exit Martin.*] Now, sir, permit me to place a dioramic view of your conduct before you. After bringing you safely home this morning—after indulgently waiting, whenever you took a passing fancy to a knocker or bell-pull—after conducting a retreat that would have reflected honor on Napoleon—you would kick me into the street, like a mangy cur: and that's what you call gratitude. Now, to show you how superior I am to petty malice, I give you an unlimited invitation to my house—my country house—to remain as long as you please.

Young Courtly. Your house!

Dazzle. Oak Hall, Gloucestershire,—fine old place—for further particulars see roadbook; that is, it *nominally* belongs to my old friend and relation, Max Harkaway; but I'm privileged. Capital old fellow—say, shall we be honored?

Young Courtly. Sir, permit me to hesitate a moment. [*Aside.*] Let me see—I go back to college to-morrow, so I shall not be missing; tradesmen begin to dun— [*Enter Cool.*] I hear thunder; here is shelter ready for me.

Cool. Oh, Mr. Charles, Mr. Solomon Isaacs is in the hall, and swears he will remain till he has arrested you!

Young Courtly. Does he!—sorry he is so obstinate—take him my compliments, and I will bet him five to one he will not.

Dazzle. Double or quits, with my kind regards.

Cool. But, sir, he has discovered the house in Curzon Street; he says he is aware the furniture, at least, belongs to you, and he will put a man in immediately.

Young Courtly. That's awkward—what's to be done?

Dazzle. Ask him whether he couldn't make it a woman.

Young Courtly. I must trust that to fate.

Dazzle. I will give you my acceptance, if it will be of any use to you; it is of none to me.

Young Courtly. No, sir; but in reply to your most generous and kind invitation, if you be in earnest, I shall feel delighted to accept it.

Dazzle. Certainly.

Young Courtly. Then off we go—through the stables—down the mews, and so slip through my friend's fingers.

Dazzle. But, stay, you must do the polite; say farewell to him before you part. Damn it, don't cut him!

Young Courtly. You jest!

Dazzle. Here, lend me a card. [*Courtly gives him one.*] Now, then, [*writes*] "Our respects to Mr. Isaacs—sorry to have been prevented from seeing him."—Ha! ha!

Young Courtly. Ha! ha!

Dazzle. We'll send him up some game.

Young Courtly [*to Cool*]. Don't let my father see him. [*Exeunt.*]

Cool. What's this?—"Mr. Charles Courtly, P.P.C., returns thanks for obliging inquiries." [*Exit.*]

SCENE ONE

The lawn before Oak Hall, a fine Elizabethan mansion; a drawing-room is seen through large French windows at the back. Statues, urns, and garden chairs about the stage.

[*Enter Pert and James.*]

Pert. James, Miss Grace desires me to request that you will watch at the avenue, and let her know when the squire's carriage is seen on the London road.

James. I will go to the lodge. [*Exit.*]

Pert. How I do long to see what kind of a man Sir Harcourt Courtly is! They say he is sixty; so he must be old, and consequently ugly. If I was Miss Grace, I would rather give up all my fortune and marry the man I liked, than go to church with a stuffed eel-skin. But taste is everything,—she doesn't seem to care whether he is sixty or sixteen; jokes at love; prepares for matrimony as she would for dinner; says it is a necessary evil, and what can't be cured must be endured. Now, I say this is against all nature; and she is either no woman, or a deeper one than I am, if she prefers an old man to a young one. Here she comes! looking as cheerfully as if she was going to marry Mr. Jenks! my Mr. Jenks! whom nobody won't lead to the halter till I have that honor.

[*Enter Grace from the drawing-room.*]

Grace. Well, Pert? any sign of the squire yet?

Pert. No, Miss Grace; but James has gone to watch the road.

Grace. In my uncle's letter he mentions a Mr. Dazzle, whom he has invited; so you must prepare a room for him. He is some friend of my husband that is to be, and my uncle seems to have taken an extraordinary predilection for him. Apropos! I must not forget to have a bouquet for the dear old man when he arrives.

Pert. The dear old man! Do you mean Sir Harcourt?

Grace. Law! no, my uncle, of course. [*Plucking flowers.*] What do I care for Sir Harcourt Courtly?

Pert. Isn't it odd, Miss, you have never seen your intended, though it has been so long since you were betrothed?

Grace. Not at all; marriage matters are conducted now-a-days in a most mercantile manner; consequently a previous acquaintance is by no means indispensable. Besides, my *prescribed* husband has been upon the continent for the benefit of his—property! They say a southern climate is a great restorer of consumptive estates.

Pert. Well, Miss, for my own part, I should like to have a good look at my bargain before I paid for it; 'specially when one's life is the price of the article. But why, ma'am do you consent to marry in this blind-man's-buff sort of manner? What would you think if he were not quite so old?

Grace. I should think he was a little younger.

Pert. I should like him all the better.

Grace. That wouldn't I. A young husband might expect affection and nonsense, which 'twould be deceit in me to render; nor would he permit me to remain with my uncle.—Sir Harcourt takes me with the incumbrances on his estate, and I shall beg to be left among the rest of the live stock.

Pert. Ah, Miss! but some day you might chance to stumble over *the* man,—what could you do then?

Grace. Do! beg *the* man's pardon, and request *the* man to pick me up again.

Pert. Ah! you were never in love, Miss?

Grace. I never was, nor will be, till I am tired of myself and common sense. Love is a pleasant scape-goat for a little epidemic madness. I must have been inoculated in my infancy, for the infection passes over poor me in contempt.

[*Enter James.*]

James. Two gentlemen, Miss Grace, have just alighted.

Grace. Very well, James. [*Exit James.*] Love is pictured as a boy; in another century they will be wiser, and paint him as a fool, with cap and bells, without a thought above the jingling of his own folly. Now, Pert, remember this as a maxim,—A woman is always in love with one of two things.

Pert. What are they, Miss?

Grace. A man, or herself—and I know which is the most profitable. [*Exit.*]

Pert. I wonder what my Jenks would say, if I was to ask him. Law! here comes Mr. Meddle, his rival, contemporary solicitor, as he calls him,—a nasty, prying, ugly wretch—what brings him here? He comes puffed with some news. [*Retires.*]

[*Enter Meddle, with a newspaper.*]

Meddle. I have secured the only newspaper in the village— my character as an attorney-at-law depended on the monopoly of its information.—I took it up by chance, when this paragraph met my astonished view: [*Reads.*] "We understand that the contract of marriage so long in abeyance on account of the lady's minority, is about to be celebrated, at Oak Hall, Gloucestershire, the well-known and magnificent mansion of Maxmilian Harkaway, Esq., between Sir Harcourt Courtly, Baronet, of fashionable celebrity, and Miss Grace Harkaway, niece to the said Mr. Harkaway. The preparations are proceeding on the good old English style." Is it possible! I seldom swear, except in a witness box, but damme, had it been known in the village, my reputation would have been lost; my voice in the parlor of the Red Lion mute, and Jenks, a fellow who calls himself a lawyer, without more capability than a broomstick, and as much impudence as a young barrister, after getting a verdict, by mistake; why, he would actually have taken the Reverend Mr. Spout by the button, which is now my sole privilege. Ah! here is Mrs. Pert; couldn't have hit upon a better person. I'll cross-examine her— Lady's maid to Miss Grace, confidential purloiner of second-hand silk—a *nisi prius* of her mistress—Ah! sits on the woolsack in the pantry, and dictates the laws of kitchen etiquette.—Ah! Mrs. Pert, good morning; permit me to say,—and my word as a legal character is not unduly considered—I venture to affirm, that you look a—quite like the—a—

Pert. Law! Mr. Meddle.

Meddle. Exactly like the law.

Pert. Ha! indeed; complimentary, I confess; like the law; tedious, prosy, made up of musty paper. You sha'n't have a long suit of me. Good morning! [*Going.*]

Meddle. Stay, Mrs. Pert; don't calumniate my calling, or disseminate vulgar prejudices.

Pert. Vulgar! you talk of vulgarity to me! you, whose sole employment is to sneak about like a pig, snouting out the dust-hole of society, and feeding upon the bad ends of vice! you, who live upon the world's iniquity; you miserable specimen of a bad six-and-eightpence!

Meddle. But, Mrs. Pert—

Pert. Don't but me, sir; I won't be butted by any such low fellow.

Meddle. This is slander; an action will lie.

Pert. Let it lie; lying is your trade. I'll tell you what, Mr. Meddle: if I had my will, I would soon put a check on your prying propensities. I'd treat you as the farmers do the inquisitive hogs.

Meddle. How?

Pert. I would ring your nose. [*Exit.*]

Meddle. Not much information elicited from that witness. Jenks is at the bottom of this. I have very little hesitation in saying, Jenks is a libellous rascal; I heard reports that he was undermining my character here, through Mrs. Pert. Now I'm certain of it. Assault is expensive; but I certainly will put by a small weekly stipendium, until I can afford to kick Jenks.

Dazzle [*outside*]. Come along; this way!

Meddle. Ah! whom have we here? Visitors; I'll address them.

[*Enter Dazzle.*]

Dazzle. Who's this, I wonder; one of the family? I must know him. [*To Meddle.*] Ah! how are ye?

Meddle. Quite well. Just arrived?—ah!—um!—Might I request the honor of knowing whom I address?

Dazzle. Richard Dazzle, Esquire; and you—

Meddle. Mark Meddle, Attorney-at-law.

[*Enter Young Courtly.*]

Dazzle. What detained you?

Young Courtly. My dear fellow, I have just seen such a woman!

Dazzle [*aside*]. Hush! [*Aloud.*] Permit me to introduce you
　　to my very old friend, Meddle. He's a capital fellow;
　　know him.

Meddle. I feel honored. Who is your friend?

Dazzle. Oh, he? What, my friend? Oh! Augustus Hamilton.

Young Courtly. How d'ye do? [*Looking off.*] There she is
　　again!

Meddle [*looking off*]. Why, that is Miss Grace.

Dazzle. Of course, Grace.

Young Courtly. I'll go and introduce myself.

[*Dazzle stops him.*]

Dazzle [*aside*]. What are you about? would you insult my
　　old friend, Puddle, by running away? [*Aloud.*] I say,
　　Puddle, just show my friend the lions, while I say
　　how d'ye do to my young friend, Grace. [*Aside.*]
　　Cultivate his acquaintance. [*Exit.—Young Courtly
　　looks after him.*]

Meddle. Mr. Hamilton, might I take the liberty?

Young Courtly [*looking off*]. Confound the fellow!

Meddle. Sir, what did you remark?

Young Courtly. She's gone! Oh, are you here still, Mr.
　　Thingomerry Puddle?

Meddle. Meddle, sir, Meddle, in the list of attorneys.

Young Courtly. Well, Muddle, or Puddle, or whoever you
　　are, you are a bore.

Meddle [*aside*]. How excessively odd! Mrs. Pert said I
　　was a pig; now I'm a boar! I wonder what they'll
　　make of me next.

Young Courtly. Mr. Thingamy, will you take a word of
　　advice?

Meddle. Feel honored.

Young Courtly. Get out.

Meddle. Do you mean to—I don't understand.

Young Courtly. Delighted to quicken your apprehension.
　　You are an ass, Puddle.

Meddle. Ha! ha! another quadruped! Yes; beautiful—
　　[*Aside.*] I wish he'd call me something libellous: but
　　that would be too much to expect.—[*Aloud.*] Any-
　　thing else?

Young Courtly. Some miserable, pettifogging scoundrel!

Meddle. Good! ha! ha!

Young Courtly. What do you mean by laughing at me?

Meddle. Ha! ha! ha! excellent! delicious!

Young Courtly. Mr. ——— are you ambitious of a kicking?

Meddle. Very, very—Go on—kick—go on.

Young Courtly [*looking off*]. Here she comes! I'll speak to her.

Meddle. But, sir—sir—

Young Courtly. Oh, go to the devil! [*He runs off.*]

Meddle. There, there's a chance lost—gone! I have no hesitation in saying that, in another minute, I should have been kicked; literally kicked—a legal luxury. Costs, damages, and actions rose up like sky-rockets in my aspiring soul. With golden tails reaching to the infinity of my hopes, [*looking*]—they are coming this way, Mr. Hamilton in close conversation with Lady Courtly that is to be. Crim. Con.—Courtly versus Hamilton—damages problematical—Meddle, chief witness for plaintiff—guinea a day—professional man! I'll take down their conversation verbatim. [*He retires behind a bush.*]

[*Enter Grace, followed by Young Courtly.*]

Grace. Perhaps you would follow your friend into the dining-room; refreshment after your long journey must be requisite.

Young Courtly. Pardon me, madam; but the lovely garden and the loveliness before me is better refreshment than I could procure in any dining-room.

Grace. Ha! Your company and compliments arrive together.

Young Courtly. I trust that a passing remark will not spoil so welcome an introduction as this by offending you.

Grace. I am not certain that anything you could say would offend me.

Young Courtly. I never meant—

Grace. I thought not. In turn, pardon me, when I request you will commence your visit with this piece of information: I consider compliments impertinent, and sweetmeat language fulsome.

Young Courtly. I would condemn my tongue to a Pythagorean silence if I thought it could attempt to flatter.

Grace. It strikes me, sir, that you are a stray bee from the hive of fashion; if so, reserve your honey for its proper cell. A truce to compliments.—You have just arrived *from town*, I apprehend.

Young Courtly. This moment I left mighty London, under the fever of a full season, groaning with the noisy pulse of wealth and the giddy whirling brain of fashion. Enchanting, busy London! how have I prevailed on myself to desert you! Next week the new ballet comes out,—the week after comes Ascot.— Oh!

Grace. How agonizing must be the reflection.

Young Courtly. Torture! Can you inform me how you manage to avoid suicide here? If there was but an opera, even, within twenty miles! We couldn't get up a rustic ballet among the village girls? No?—ah!

Grace. I am afraid you would find that difficult. How I contrive to support life I don't know—it is wonderful —but I have not precisely contemplated suicide yet, nor do I miss the opera.

Young Courtly. How can you manage to kill time?

Grace. I can't. Men talk of killing time, while time quietly kills them. I have many employments—this week I devote to study and various amusements—next week to being married—the following week to repentance, perhaps.

Young Courtly. Married!

Grace. You seem surprised; I believe it is of frequent occurrence in the metropolis.—Is it not?

Young Courtly. Might I ask to whom?

Grace. A gentleman who has been strongly recommended to me for the situation of husband.

Young Courtly. What an extraordinary match! Would you not consider it advisable to see him, previous to incurring the consequences of such an act?

Grace. You must be aware that fashion says otherwise. The gentleman swears eternal devotion to the lady's fortune, and the lady swears she will outvie him still. My lord's horses, and my lady's diamonds, shine through a few seasons, until a seat in Parliament, or the continent, stares them in the face; then, when thrown upon each other for resources of comfort, they begin to quarrel about the original conditions of the sale.

Young Courtly. Sale! No! that would be degrading civilization into Turkish barbarity.

Grace. Worse, sir, a great deal worse; for there at least they do not attempt concealment of the barter; but

here, every London ball-room is a marriage mart—
young ladies are trotted out, while the mother, father,
or chaperone plays auctioneer, and knocks them down
to the highest bidder,—young men are ticketed up
with their fortunes on their backs,—and Love, turned
into a dapper shopman, descants on the excellent
qualities of the material.

Young Courtly. Oh! that such a custom could have ever
emanated from the healthy soil of an English heart!

Grace. No. It never did—like most of our literary dandy-
isms and dandy literature, it was borrowed from the
French.

Young Courtly. You seem to laugh at love.

Grace. Love! why, the very word is a breathing satire upon
a man's reason—a mania, indigenous to humanity—
nature's jester, who plays off tricks upon the world,
and trips up common sense. When I'm in love, I'll
write an almanac, for very lack of wit—prognosticate
the sighing season—when to beware of tears—about
this time, expect matrimony to be prevalent! Ha! ha!
Why should I lay out my life in love's bonds upon the
bare security of a man's word?

[*Enter James.*]

James. The Squire, madam, has just arrived, and another
gentleman with him.

Grace [*aside*]. My intended, I suppose. [*Exit James.*]

Young Courtly. I perceive you are one of the railers
against what is termed the follies of high life.

Grace. No, not particularly; I deprecate all folly. By what
prerogative can the west-end mint issue absurdity,
which, if coined in the east, would be voted vulgar?

Young Courtly. By a sovereign right—because it has
Fashion's head upon its side, and that stamps it
current.

Grace. Poor Fashion, for how many sins hast thou to
answer! The gambler pawns his birth-right for fashion
—the *roué* steals his friend's wife for fashion—each
abandons himself to the storm of impulse, calling it
the breeze of fashion.

Young Courtly. Is this idol of the world so radically
vicious?

Grace. No; the root is well enough, as the body was, until
it had outgrown its native soil; but now, like a mighty

giant lying over Europe, it pillows its head in Italy,
its heart in France, leaving the heels alone its sole
support for England.

Young Courtly. Pardon me madam, you wrong yourself
to rail against your own inheritance—the kingdom to
which loveliness and wit attest your title.

Grace. A mighty realm, forsooth,—with milliners for
ministers, a cabinet of coxcombs, envy for my
homage, ruin for my revenue—my right of rule depending on the shape of a bonnet or the sit of a
pelisse, with the next grand noodle as my heir-
apparent. Mr. Hamilton, when I am crowned, I shall
feel happy to abdicate in your favor. [*Curtseys and
exit.*]

Young Courtly. What did she mean by that? Hang me if
I can understand her—she is evidently not used to
society. Ha!—takes every word I say for infallible
truth—requires the solution of a compliment, as if
it were a problem in Euclid. She said she was about to
marry, but I rather imagine she was in jest. 'Pon my
life, I feel very queer at the contemplation of such
an idea—I'll follow her. [*Meddle comes down.*] Oh!
perhaps this booby can inform me something about
her. [*Meddle makes signs at him.*] What the devil is
he at!

Meddle. It won't do—no—ah! um—it's not to be done.

Young Courtly. What do you mean?

Meddle [*points after Grace*]. Counsel retained—cause to
come off!

Young Courtly. Cause to come off!

Meddle. Miss Grace is about to be married.

Young Courtly. Is it possible?

Meddle. Certainly. If *I* have the drawing out of the deeds—

Young Courtly. To whom?

Meddle. Ha! hem! Oh, yes! I dare say—Information being scarce in the market, I hope to make mine valuable.

Young Courtly. Married! married!

Meddle. Now I shall have another chance.

Young Courtly. I'll run and ascertain the truth of this from
Dazzle. [*Exit.*]

Meddle. It's of no use: he either dare not kick me, or he

can't afford it—in either case, he is beneath my notice. Ah! who comes here?—can it be Sir Harcourt Courtly himself? It can be no other. [*Enter Cool.*] Sir, I have the honor to bid you welcome to Oak Hall and the village of Oldborough.

Cool [*aside*]. Excessively polite. [*Aloud.*]—Sir, thank you.

Meddle. The township contains two thousand inhabitants.

Cool. Does it! I am delighted to hear it.

Meddle [*aside*]. I can charge him for that—ahem—six and eightpence is not much—but it is a beginning. [*Aloud.*] If you will permit me, I can inform you of the different commodities for which it is famous.

Cool. Much obliged—but here comes Sir Harcourt Courtly, my master and Mr. Harkaway—any other time I shall feel delighted.

Meddle. Oh! [*Aside.*] Mistook the man for the master. [*He retires up.*]

[*Enter Max and Sir Harcourt.*]

Max. Here we are at last. Now give ye welcome to Oak Hall, Sir Harcourt, heartily!

Sir Harcourt [*languidly*]. Cool, assist me. [*Cool takes off his furred cloak and gloves; gives him white gloves and a white handkerchief.*]

Max. Why, you require unpacking as carefully as my best bin of port. Well, now you are decanted, tell me, what did you think of my park as we came along?

Sir Harcourt. That it would never come to an end. You said it was only a stone's throw from your infernal lodge to the house; why, it's ten miles at least.

Max. I'll do it in ten minutes any day.

Sir Harcourt. Yes, in a steam carriage. Cool, perfume my handkerchief.

Max. Don't do it. Don't! perfume in the country! why, it's high treason in the very face of Nature; 'tis introducing the robbed to the robber. Here are the sweets from which your fulsome essences are pilfered, and libelled with their names,—don't insult them, too.

Sir Harcourt [*to Meddle*]. Oh! cull me a bouquet, my man!

Max [*turning*]. Ah, Meddle! how are you? This is Lawyer Meddle.

Sir Harcourt. Oh! I took him for one of your people.

Meddle. Ah! naturally—um—Sir Harcourt Courtly, I

have the honor to congratulate—happy occasion approaches. Ahem! I have no hesitation in saying this *very* happy occasion approaches.

Sir Harcourt. Cool, is the conversation addressed towards me?

Cool. I believe so, Sir Harcourt.

Meddle. Oh, certainly! I was complimenting you.

Sir Harcourt. Sir, you are very good; the honor is undeserved; but I am only in the habit of receiving compliments from the fair sex. Men's admiration is so damnably insipid.

Meddle. I had hoped to make a unit on that occasion.

Sir Harcourt. Yes, and you hoped to put an infernal number of ciphers after your unit on that and any other occasion.

Meddle. Ha! ha! very good. Why, I did hope to have the honor of drawing out the deeds; for, whatever Jenks may say to the contrary, I have no hesitation in saying—

Sir Harcourt [*putting him aside*]. [*To Max.*] If the future Lady Courtly be visible at so unfashionable an hour as this, I shall beg to be introduced.

Max. Visible! Ever since six this morning, I'll warrant ye. Two to one she is at dinner.

Sir Harcourt. Dinner! Is it possible? Lady Courtly dine at half-past one P.M.!

Meddle. I rather prefer that hour to peck a little my—

Sir Harcourt. Dear me! who was addressing you?

Meddle. Oh! I beg pardon.

Max. Here, James! [*Calling. Enter James.*] Tell Miss Grace to come here directly. [*Exit James.*] Now prepare, Courtly, for, though I say it, she *is*—with the exception of my bay mare, Kitty—the handsomest thing in the country. Considering she is a biped, she is a wonder! Full of blood, sound wind and limb, plenty of bone, sweet coat, in fine condition, with a thoroughbred step, as dainty as a pet greyhound.

Sir Harcourt. Damme, don't compare her to a horse!

Max. Well, I wouldn't, but she's almost as fine a creature, —close similarities.

Meddle. Oh, very fine creature! Close similarity amounting to identity.

Sir Harcourt. Good gracious, sir! What can a lawyer know about women!

Meddle. Everything. The consistorial court is fine study of the character, and I have no hesitation in saying that I have examined more women than Jenks, or—

Sir Harcourt. Oh, damn Jenks!

Meddle. Sir, thank you. Damn him again, sir, damn him again!

[*Enter Grace.*]

Grace. My dear uncle!

Max. Ah, Grace, you little jade, come here.

Sir Harcourt [*eyeing her through his glass*]. Oh, dear! she is a rural Venus! I'm astonished and delighted.

Max. Won't you kiss your old uncle? [*He kisses her.*]

Sir Harcourt [*draws an agonizing face*]. Oh!—ah—um!— N'importe!—my privilege in embryo—hem! It's very tantalizing, though.

Max. You are not glad to see me; you are not. [*Kissing her.*]

Sir Harcourt. Oh; no, no! [*Aside.*] That is too much. I shall do something horrible presently, if this goes on. [*Aloud.*] I should be sorry to curtail any little ebullition of affection; but—ahem! May I be permitted?

Max. Of course you may. There, Grace, is Sir Harcourt, your husband that will be. Go to him, girl.

Sir Harcourt. Permit me to do homage to the charms, the presence of which have placed me in sight of Paradise.

[*Sir Harcourt and Grace retire. Enter Dazzle.*]

Dazzle. Ah! old fellow, how are you?

Max. I'm glad to see you! Are you comfortably quartered, yet, eh?

Dazzle. Splendidly quartered! What a place you've got here! Here, Hamilton. [*Enter Young Courtly.*] Permit me to introduce my friend, Augustus Hamilton. [*Aside.*] Capital fellow! drinks like a sieve, and rides like a thunder-storm.

Max. Sir, I'm devilish glad to see you. Here, Sir Harcourt, permit me to introduce to you—

Young Courtly. The devil!

Dazzle [*aside*]. What's the matter?

Young Courtly [*aside*]. Why, that is my governor, by Jupiter!

Dazzle [*aside*]. What, old Whiskers? you don't say that!

Young Courtly [*aside*]. It is; what's to be done now?

Max. Mr. Hamilton, Sir Harcourt Courtly, Mr. Hamilton.

Sir Harcourt. Hamilton! Good gracious! God bless me!— why, Charles, is it possible?—why, Max, that's my son!

Young Courtly [*aside*]. What shall I do!

Max. Your son!

Grace. Your son, Sir Harcourt! have you a son as old as that gentleman!

Sir Harcourt. No—that is—a—yes,—not by twenty years —a—Charles, why don't you answer me, sir?

Young Courtly [*aside to Dazzle*]. What shall I say?

Dazzle [*aside*]. Deny your identity.

Young Courtly [*aside*]. Capital! [*Aloud.*] What's the matter, sir?

Sir Harcourt. How came you down here, sir?

Young Courtly. By one of Newman's—best fours—in twelve hours and a quarter.

Sir Harcourt. Isn't your name Charles Courtly?

Young Courtly. Not to my knowledge.

Sir Harcourt. Do you mean to say that you are usually called Augustus Hamilton?

Young Courtly. Lamentable fact—and quite correct.

Sir Harcourt. Cool, is that my son?

Cool. No, sir—it is not Mr. Charles—but is very like him.

Max. I cannot understand all this.

Grace [*aside*]. I think I can.

Dazzle [*aside to Young Courtly*]. Give him a touch of the indignant.

Young Courtly. Allow me to say, Sir What-d'ye-call-'em Hartly—

Sir Harcourt. Hartly, sir! Courtly, sir! Courtly!

Young Courtly. Well, Hartly, or Court-heart, or whatever your name may be, I say your conduct is—a—a—, and were it not for the presence of this lady, I should feel inclined—to—to—

Sir Harcourt. No, no, that can't be my son,—he never would address me in that way.

Max. What is all this?

Sir Harcourt. Sir, your likeness to my son Charles is so astonishing, that it, for a moment—the equilibrium of my etiquette—'pon my life, I—permit me to request your pardon.

Meddle [*to Sir Harcourt*]. Sir Harcourt, don't apologize, don't—bring an action. I'm witness.

Sir Harcourt. Some one take this man away.

[*Enter James.*]

James. Luncheon is on the table, sir.

Sir Harcourt. Miss Harkaway, I never swore before a lady in my life—except when I promised to love and cherish the late Lady Courtly, which I took care to preface with an apology,—I was compelled to the ceremony, and consequently not answerable for the language—but to that gentleman's identity I would have pledged—my hair.

Grace [*aside*]. If that security were called for, I suspect the answer would be—no effects. [*Exeunt Sir Harcourt and Grace.*]

Meddle [*to Max*]. I have something very particular to communicate.

Max. Can't listen at present. [*Exit.*]

Meddle [*to Dazzle and Young Courtly*]. I can afford you information, which I—

Dazzle. Oh, don't bother!

Young Courtly. Go to the devil!

[*Exeunt.*]

Meddle. Now, I have no hesitation in saying that is the height of ingratitude.—oh—Mr. Cool—can you oblige me? [*Presents his account.*]

Cool. Why, what is all this?

Meddle. Small account *versus* you—to giving information concerning the last census of the population of Oldborough and vicinity, six and eightpence.

Cool. Oh, you mean to make me pay for this, do you?

Meddle. Unconditionally.

Cool. Well, I have no objection—the charge is fair—but remember, I am a servant on board wages,—will you throw in a little advice gratis—if I give you the money?

Meddle. Ahem!—I will.

Cool. A fellow has insulted me. I want to abuse him—what terms are actionable?

Meddle. You may call him anything you please, providing there are no witnesses.

Cool. Oh, may I? [*Looks round*]—then you rascally, pettifogging scoundrel!

Meddle. Hallo!

Cool. You mean—dirty—disgrace to your profession.

Meddle. Libel—slander—

Cool. Aye, but where are your witnesses?

Meddle. Give me the costs—six and eight pence.

Cool. I deny that you gave me information at all.

Meddle. You do!

Cool. Yes, where are your witnesses? [*Exit.*]

Meddle. Ah—damme! [*Exit.*]

SCENE ONE

A morning-room in Oak Hall, French windows opening to the lawn.

[*Max and Sir Harcourt seated on one side, Dazzle on the other; Grace and Young Courtly are playing chess at back. All dressed for dinner.*]

Max [*aside to Sir Harcourt*]. What can I do?

Sir Harcourt. Get rid of them civilly.

Max. What, turn them out, after I particularly invited them to stay a month or two?

Sir Harcourt. Why, they are disreputable characters; as for that young fellow, in whom my Lady Courtly appears so particularly absorbed,—I am bewildered—I have written to town for my Charles, my boy—it certainly is the most extraordinary likeness—

Dazzle. Sir Harcourt, I have an idea—

Sir Harcourt. Sir, I am delighted to hear it.—[*Aside.*] That fellow is a swindler.

Max. I met him at your house.

Sir Harcourt. Never saw him before in all my life.

Dazzle [*crossing to Sir Harcourt*]. I will bet you five to one that I can beat you three out of four games at billiards, with one hand.

Sir Harcourt. No, sir.

Dazzle. I don't mind giving you ten points in fifty.

Sir Harcourt. Sir, I never gamble.

Dazzle. You don't! Well, I'll teach you—easiest thing in life—you have every requisite—good temper.

Sir Harcourt. I have not, sir.

Dazzle. A long-headed, knowing old buck.

Sir Harcourt. Sir! [*They go up conversing with Max.*]

Grace. Really, Mr. Hamilton, you improve.—A young man

pays us a visit, as you half intimate, to escape inconvenient friends—that is complimentary to us, his hosts.

Young Courtly. Nay, that is too severe.

Grace. After an acquaintanceship of two days, you sit down to teach me chess, and domestic economy at the same time.—Might I ask where you graduated in that science—where you learned all that store of matrimonial advice which you have obliged me with?

Young Courtly. I [imbibed] it, madam, from the moment I beheld you, and having studied my subject *con amore,* took my degrees from your eyes.

Grace. Oh, I see you are a Master of Arts already.

Young Courtly. Unfortunately, no—I shall remain a bachelor—till you can assist me to that honor. [*Sir Harcourt comes down—aside to Dazzle.*] Keep the old boy away.

Dazzle [*aside*]. How do you get on?

Young Courtly [*aside*]. Splendidly!

Sir Harcourt. Is the conversation strictly confidential?— or might I join?

Dazzle [*taking his arm*]. Oh, not in the least, my dear sir— we were remarking that rifle shooting was an excellent diversion during the summer months.

Sir Harcourt [*drawing himself up*]. Sir, I was addressing—

Dazzle. And I was saying what a pity it was I couldn't find any one reasonable enough to back his opinion with long odds—come out on the lawn, and pitch up your hat, and I will hold you ten to one I put a bullet into it every time, at forty paces.

Sir Harcourt. No, sir—I consider you—

Max. Here, all of you—look, here is Lady Gay Spanker coming across the lawn at a hand gallop!

Sir Harcourt [*running to the window*]. Bless me, the horse is running away!

Max. Look how she takes that fence! there's a seat.

Sir Harcourt. Lady Gay Spanker—who may she be?

Grace. Gay Spanker, Sir Harcourt? My cousin and dearest friend—you *must* like her.

Sir Harcourt. It will be my devoir, since it is your wish— though it will be a hard task in your presence.

Grace. I am sure she will like you.

Sir Harcourt. Ha! ha! I flatter myself.

Young Courtly. Who, and what is she?

Grace. Glee, glee made a living thing—Nature in some frolic mood shut up a merry devil in her eye, and, spiting Art, stole joy's brightest harmony to thrill her laugh, which peals out sorrow's knell. Her cry rings loudest in the field—the very echo loves it best, and, as each hill attempts to ape her voice, earth seems to laugh that it made a thing so glad.

Max. Ay, the merriest minx I ever kissed.

[*Lady Gay laughs without.*]

Lady Gay [*without*]. Max!

Max. Come in, you mischievous puss.

[*Enter James.*]

James. Mr. Adolphus and Lady Gay Spanker.

[*Enter Lady Gay, fully equipped in riding habit, etc.*]

Lady Gay. Ha! ha! Well, Governor, how are ye? I have been down five times, climbing up your stairs in my long clothes. How are you, Grace, dear? [*Kisses her.*] There, don't fidget, Max. And there—[*kisses him*]—there's one for you.

Sir Harcourt. Ahem!

Lady Gay. Oh, gracious, I didn't see you had visitors.

Max. Permit me to introduce—Sir Harcourt Courtly, Lady Gay Spanker. Mr. Dazzle, Mr. Hamilton—Lady Gay Spanker.

Sir Harcourt [*aside*]. A devilish fine woman!

Dazzle [*aside to Sir Harcourt*]. She's a devilish fine woman.

Lady Gay. You mustn't think anything of the liberties I take with my old papa here—bless him!

Sir Harcourt. Oh, no! [*Aside.*] I only thought I should like to be in his place.

Lady Gay. I am so glad you have come, Sir Harcourt. Now we shall be able to make a decent figure at the heels of a hunt.

Sir Harcourt. Does your ladyship hunt?

Lady Gay. Ha! I say, Governor, does my ladyship hunt? I rather flatter myself that I do hunt! Why, Sir Harcourt, one might as well live without laughing as without hunting. Man was fashioned expressly to fit a horse. Are not hedges and ditches created for leaps? Of course! And I look upon foxes to be one of the most blessed dispensations of a benign Providence.

Sir Harcourt. Yes, it is all very well in the abstract: I tried it once.

Lady Gay. Once! Only once?

Sir Harcourt. Once, only once. And then the animal ran away with me.

Lady Gay. Why, you would not have him walk!

Sir Harcourt. Finding my society disagreeable, he instituted a series of kicks, with a view to removing the annoyance; but aided by the united stays of the mane and tail, I frustrated his intentions. His next resource, however, was more effectual, for he succeeded in rubbing me off against a tree.

Max and Lady Gay. Ha! ha! ha!

Dazzle. How absurd you must have looked with your legs and arms in the air, like a shipwrecked tea-table.

Sir Harcourt. Sir, I never looked absurd in my life. Ah, it may be very amusing in relation, I dare say, but very unpleasant in effect.

Lady Gay. I pity you, Sir Harcourt: it was criminal in your parents to neglect your education so shamefully.

Sir Harcourt. Possibly; but be assured I shall never break my neck awkwardly from a horse, when it might be accomplished with less trouble from a bedroom window.

Young Courtly [*aside*]. My dad will be caught by this she-Bucephalus tamer.

Max. Ah! Sir Harcourt, had you been here a month ago, you would have witnessed the most glorious run that ever swept over merry England's green cheek—a steeple-chase, sir, which I intended to win, but my horse broke down the day before. I had a chance, notwithstanding, and but for Gay here, I should have won. How I regretted my absence from it! How did my filly behave herself, Gay?

Lady Gay. Gloriously, Max! gloriously! There were sixty horses in the field, all mettle to the bone; the start was a picture—away we went in a cloud—pell-mell—helter-skelter—the fools first, as usual, using themselves up—we soon passed them—first your Kitty, then my Blueskin, and Craven's colt last. Then came the tug—Kitty skimmed the walls—Blueskin flew o'er

the fences—the Colt neck and neck, and half a mile
to run—at last the Colt baulked a leap and went wild.
Kitty and I had it all to ourselves—she was three
lengths ahead as we breasted the last wall, six feet,
if an inch, and a ditch on the other side. Now, for the
first time, I gave Blueskin his head—ha! ha!—Away
he flew like a thunderbolt—over went the filly—I over
the same spot, leaving Kitty in the ditch—walked the
steeple, eight miles in thirty minutes, and scarcely
turned a hair.

All. Bravo! Bravo!

Lady Gay. Do you hunt?

Dazzle. Hunt! I belong to a hunting family. I was born on
horseback and cradled in a kennel! Aye, and I hope I
may die with a whoo-whoop!

Max [*to Sir Harcourt*]. You must leave your town habits
in the smoke of London: here we rise with the lark.

Sir Harcourt. Haven't the remotest conception when that
period is.

Grace. The man that misses sunrise loses the sweetest part
of his existence.

Sir Harcourt. Oh, pardon me; I have seen sunrise frequently after a ball, or from the window of my travelling
carriage, and I always considered it disagreeable.

Grace. I love to watch the first tear that glistens in the
opening eye of morning, the silent song the flowers
breathe, the thrilly choir of the woodland minstrels,
to which the modest brook trickles applause;—these,
swelling out the sweetest chord of sweet creation's
matins, seem to pour some soft and merry tale into
the daylight's ear, as if the waking world had dreamed
a happy thing, and now smiled o'er the telling of it.

Sir Harcourt. The effect of a rustic education! Who could
ever discover music in a damp foggy morning, except
those confounded waits, who never play in tune, and
a miserable wretch who makes a point of crying
coffee under my window just as I am persuading myself to sleep; in fact, I never heard any music worth
listening to, except in Italy.

Lady Gay. No? then you never heard a well-trained English
pack, full cry.

Sir Harcourt. Full cry!

Lady Gay. Aye! there is harmony, if you will. Give me the

trumpet-neigh; the spotted pack just catching scent. What a chorus is their yelp! The view-hallo, blent with a peal of free and fearless mirth! That's our English music,—match it where you can.

Sir Harcourt [*aside*]. I must see about Lady Gay Spanker.

Dazzle [*aside to Sir Harcourt*]. Ah, would you—

Lady Gay. Time then appears as young as love, and plumes as swift a wing. Away we go! The earth flies back to aid our course! Horse, man, hound, earth, heaven!— all—all—one piece of glowing ecstasy! Then I love the world, myself, and every living thing,—a jocund soul cries out for very glee, as it could wish that all creation had but one mouth that I might kiss it!

Sir Harcourt [*aside*]. I wish I was the mouth!

Max. Why, we will regenerate you, baronet! But Gay, where is your husband?—Where is Adolphus!

Lady Gay. Bless me, where is my Dolly?

Sir Harcourt. You are married, then?

Lady Gay. I have a husband somewhere, though I can't find him just now. Dolly, dear! [*Aside to Max.*] Governor, at home I always whistle when I want him.

[*Enter Spanker.*]

Spanker. Here I am,—did you call me, Gay?

Sir Harcourt [*eyeing him*]. Is that your husband?

Lady Gay [*aside*]. Yes, bless his stupid face, that's my Dolly.

Max. Permit me to introduce you to Sir Harcourt Courtly.

Spanker. How d'ye do? I—ah!—um! [*Appears frightened.*]

Lady Gay. Delighted to have the honor of making the acquaintance of a gentleman so highly celebrated in the world of fashion.

Spanker. Oh, yes, delighted, I'm sure—quite—very, so delighted—delighted! [*Gets quite confused, draws on his glove, and tears it.*]

Lady Gay. Where have you been Dolly?

Spanker. Oh, ah, I was just outside.

Max. Why did you not come in?

Spanker. I'm sure I didn't—I don't exactly know, but I thought as—perhaps—I can't remember.

Dazzle. Shall we have the pleasure of your company to dinner?

Spanker. I always dine—usually—that is, unless Gay remains.

Lady Gay. Stay dinner, of course; we came on purpose to stop three or four days with you.

Grace. Will you excuse my absence, Gay?

Max. What! what! Where are you going? What takes you away?

Grace. We must postpone the dinner till Gay is dressed.

Max. Oh, never mind,—stay where you are.

Grace. No, I must go.

Max. I say you sha'n't! I will be king in my own house.

Grace. Do, my dear uncle;—you shall be king, and I'll be your prime minister,—that is, I will rule, and you shall have the honor of taking the consequences. [*Exit.*]

Lady Gay. Well said, Grace; have your own way; it is the only thing we women ought to be allowed.

Max. Come, Gay, dress for dinner.

Sir Harcourt. Permit me, Lady Gay Spanker.

Lady Gay. With pleasure,—what do you want?

Sir Harcourt. To escort you.

Lady Gay. Oh, never mind, I can escort myself, thank you, and Dolly too;—come, dear!

Sir Harcourt. Au revoir!

Spanker. Ah, thank you! [*Exit awkwardly.*]

Sir Harcourt. What an ill-assorted pair!

Max. Not a bit! She married him for freedom, and she has it; he married her for protection, and he has it.

Sir Harcourt. How he ever summoned courage to propose to her, I can't guess.

Max. Bless you, he never did. She proposed to him! She says he would, if he could; but as he couldn't, she did for him. [*Exeunt, laughing.*]

[*Enter Cool with a letter.*]

Cool. Mr. Charles, I have been watching to find you alone. Sir Harcourt has written to town for you.

Young Courtly. The devil he has!

Cool. He expects you down to-morrow evening.

Dazzle. Oh! he'll be punctual. A thought strikes me.

Young Courtly. Pooh! Confound your thoughts! I can think of nothing but the idea of leaving Grace, at the very moment when I had established the most—

Dazzle. What if I can prevent her marriage with your Governor?

Young Courtly. Impossible!

Dazzle. He's pluming himself for the conquest of Lady Gay

Spanker. It will not be difficult to make him believe she accedes to his suit. And if she would but join in the plan—

Young Courtly. I see it all. And do you think she would?

Dazzle. I mistake my game if she would not.

Cool. Here comes Sir Harcourt!

Dazzle. I'll begin with him. Retire, and watch how I'll open the campaign for you.

[*Young Courtly and Cool retire. Enter Sir Harcourt.*]

Sir Harcourt. Here is that cursed fellow again.

Dazzle. Ah, my dear old friend!

Sir Harcourt. Mr. Dazzle.

Dazzle. I have a secret of importance to disclose to you. Are you a man of honor? Hush! don't speak; you are. It is with the greatest pain I am compelled to request you, as a gentleman, that you will shun studiously the society of Lady Gay Spanker!

Sir Harcourt. Good gracious! Wherefore, and by what right, do you make such a demand?

Dazzle. Why, I am distantly related to the Spankers.

Sir Harcourt. Why, damme, sir, if you don't appear to be related to every family in Great Britain!

Dazzle. A good many of the nobility claim me as a connection. But, to return—she is much struck with your address; evidently, she laid herself out for display.

Sir Harcourt. Ha! you surprise me!

Dazzle. To entangle you.

Sir Harcourt. Ha! ha! why, it did appear like it.

Dazzle. You will spare her for my sake; give no encouragement; if disgrace come upon my relatives, the Spankers, I should never hold up my head again.

Sir Harcourt [*aside*]. I shall achieve an easy conquest, and a glorious. Ha! ha! I never remarked it before; but this is a gentleman.

Dazzle. May I rely on your generosity?

Sir Harcourt. Faithfully. [*Shakes his hand.*] Sir, I honor and esteem you; but, might I ask, how came you to meet our friend, Max Harkaway, in my house in Belgrave Square?

[*Re-enter Young Courtly. Sits on sofa at back.*]

Dazzle. Certainly. I had an acceptance of your son's for one hundred pounds.

Sir Harcourt [*astonished*]. Of my son's? Impossible!

Dazzle. Ah, sir, fact! he paid a debt for a poor, unfortunate man—fifteen children—half-a-dozen wives—the devil knows what all.

Sir Harcourt. Simple boy!

Dazzle. Innocent youth, I have no doubt; when you have the hundred convenient, I shall feel delighted.

Sir Harcourt. Oh! follow me to my room, and if you have the document, it will be happiness to me to pay it. Poor Charles! good heart!

Dazzle. Oh, a splendid heart! I dare say. [*Exit Sir Harcourt.*] Come here; write me the bill.

Young Courtly. What for?

Dazzle. What for? why, to release the unfortunate man and his family, to be sure, from jail.

Young Courtly. Who is he?

Dazzle. Yourself.

Young Courtly. But I haven't fifteen children!

Dazzle. Will you take your oath of that?

Young Courtly. Nor four wives.

Dazzle. More shame for you, with all that family. Come, don't be obstinate; write and date it back.

Young Courtly. Ay, but where is the stamp?

Dazzle. Here they are, of all patterns. [*Pulls out a pocketbook.*] I keep them ready drawn in case of necessity, all but the date and acceptance. Now, if you are in an autographic humor, you can try how your signature will look across half a dozen of them;—there write—exactly—you know the place—across—good—and thank your lucky stars that you have found a friend at last, that gives you money and advice. [*Takes paper and exit.*]

Young Courtly. Things are approaching to a climax; I must appear *in propria persona*—and immediately—but I must first ascertain what are the real sentiments of this riddle of a woman. Does she love me? I flatter myself.—By Jove, here she comes—I shall never have such an opportunity again!

[*Enter Grace.*]

Grace. I wish I had never seen Mr. Hamilton. Why does every object appear robbed of the charm it once presented to me? Why do I shudder at the contemplation of this marriage, which, till now, was to me a subject of indifference? Am I in love? In love!—if I am, my

past life has been the work of raising up a pedestal
to place my own folly on—I—the infidel—the railer!

Young Courtly. Meditating upon matrimony, madam?

Grace [*aside*]. He little thinks he was the subject of my
meditations! [*Aloud.*] No.

Young Courtly [*aside*]. I must unmask my battery now.

Grace [*aside*]. How foolish I am—he will perceive that I
tremble—I must appear at ease. [*A pause.*]

Young Courtly. Eh! ah! um!

Grace. Ah! [*They sink into silence again. Aside.*] How very
awkward!

Young Courtly [*aside*]. It is a very difficult subject to begin. [*Aloud.*] Madam—ahem—there was—is—I mean
—I was about to remark—a—[*Aside.*] Hang me if it
is not a very slippery subject. I must brush up my
faculties; attack her in her own way. [*Aloud.*] Sing!
oh, muse.—[*Aside.*] Why, I have made love before
to a hundred women!

Grace [*aside*]. I wish I had something to do, for I have
nothing to say.

Young Courtly. Madam—there is—a subject so fraught
with fate to my future life, that you must pardon my
lack of delicacy, should a too hasty expression mar
the fervent courtesy of its intent. To you, I feel aware,
I must appear in the light of a comparative stranger.

Grace [*aside*]. I know what's coming.

Young Courtly. Of you—I know perhaps too much for my
own peace.

Grace [*aside*]. He *is* in love.

Young Courtly. I forget all that befell before I saw your
beauteous self: I seem born into another world—my
nature changed—the beams of that bright face falling
on my soul, have, from its chaos, warmed into life
the flowrets of affection, whose maiden odors now
float toward the sun, pouring forth on their pure
tongue a mite of adoration, midst the voices of a
universe. [*Aside.*] That's something in her own style.

Grace. Mr. Hamilton!

Young Courtly. You cannot feel surprised—

Grace. I am more than surprised. [*Aside.*] I am delighted.

Young Courtly. Do not speak so coldly.

Grace. You have offended me.

Young Courtly. No, madam; no woman, whatever her

state, can be offended by the adoration even of the
meanest; it is myself whom I have offended and deceived—but still I ask your pardon.

Grace [*aside*]. Oh! he thinks I'm refusing him. [*Aloud.*]
I am not exactly offended, but—

Young Courtly. Consider my position—a few days—and
an insurmountable barrier would have placed you
beyond my wildest hopes—you would have been my
mother.

Grace. I should have been your mother! [*Aside.*] I thought
so.

Young Courtly. No—that is, I meant Sir Harcourt Courtly's bride.

Grace [*with great emphasis*]. Never!

Young Courtly. How! never! may I then hope?—you turn
away—you would not lacerate me by a refusal?

Grace [*aside*]. How stupid he is!

Young Courtly. Still silent! I thank you, Miss Grace—I
ought to have expected this—fool that I have been
—one course alone remains—farewell!

Grace [*aside*]. Now he's going.

Young Courtly. Farewell forever! [*Sits.*] Will you not speak
one word? I shall leave this house immediately—I
shall not see you again.

Grace. Unhand me, sir, I insist.

Young Courtly [*aside*]. Oh! what an ass I've been! [*Rushes
up to her, and seizes her hand.*] Release this hand?
Never! never! [*Kissing it.*] Never will I quit this hand!
it shall be my companion in misery—in solitude—
when you are far away.

Grace. Oh! should any one come! [*Drops her handkerchief;
he stoops to pick it up.*] For heaven's sake, do not
kneel.

Young Courtly [*kneels*]. Forever thus prostrate, before my
soul's saint, I will lead a pious life of eternal adoration.

Grace. Should we be discovered thus—pray, Mr. Hamilton—pray—pray.

Young Courtly. Pray! I am praying; what more can I do?

Grace. Your conduct is shameful.

Young Courtly. It is. [*Rises.*]

Grace. And if I do not scream, it is not for your sake—
that—but it might alarm the family.

Young Courtly. It might—it would. Say, am I wholly in-
    different to you? I entreat one word—I implore you
    —do not withdraw your hand—[*She snatches it away
    —he puts his round her waist.*]—you smile.
Grace. Leave me, dear Mr. Hamilton!
Young Courtly. Dear! Then I am dear to you; that word
    once more; say—say you love me!
Grace. Is this fair?
[*He catches her in his arms, and kisses her. Enter Lady
    Gay Spanker.*]
Lady Gay. Ha! oh!
Grace. Gay! destruction! [*Exit.*]
Young Courtly. Fizgig! The devil!
Lady Gay. Don't mind me—pray, don't let me be any
    interruption!
Young Courtly. I was just—
Lady Gay. Yes, I see you were.
Young Courtly. Oh! madam, how could you mar my bliss,
    in the very ecstasy of its fulfilment?
Lady Gay. I always like to be in at the death. Never drop
    your ears; bless you, she is only a little fresh—give
    her her head, and she will outrun herself.
Young Courtly. Possibly; but what am I to do?
Lady Gay. Keep your seat.
Young Courtly. But in a few days she will take a leap
    that must throw me—she marries Sir Harcourt Court-
    ly.
Lady Gay. Why, that is awkward, certainly; but you can
    challenge him, and shoot him.
Young Courtly. Unfortunately, that is out of the question.
Lady Gay. How so?
Young Courtly. You will not betray a secret, if I inform
    you?
Lady Gay. All right—what is it?
Young Courtly. I am his son.
Lady Gay. What—his son? But does he not know you?
Young Courtly. No. I met him here, by chance, and faced
    it out. I never saw him before in my life.
Lady Gay. Beautiful!—I see it all—you're in love with
    your mother, that should be—your wife, that will be.
Young Courtly. Now, I think I could distance the old
    gentleman, if you will but lend us your assistance.
Lady Gay. I will, in anything.

Young Courtly. You must know, then, that my father, Sir Harcourt, has fallen desperately in love with you.

Lady Gay. With me!—[*Utters a scream of delight.*]—That is delicious!

Young Courtly. Now, if you only could—

Lady Gay. Could!—I will. Ha! ha! I see my cue. I'll cross his scent—I'll draw him after me. Ho! ho! won't I make love to him? Ha!

Young Courtly. The only objection might be Mr. Spanker, who might—

Lady Gay. No, he mightn't—he's no objection. Bless him, he's an inestimable little character—you don't know him as well as I do, I dare say—ha! ha! [*Dinner-bell rings.*] Here they come to dinner. I'll commence my operations on your Governor immediately. Ha! ha! how I shall enjoy it!

Young Courtly. Be guarded!

[*Enter Max Harkaway, Sir Harcourt, Dazzle, Grace and Spanker.*]

Max. Now, gentlemen—Sir Harcourt, do you lead Grace.

Lady Gay. I believe Sir Harcourt is engaged to me. [*Takes his arm.*]

Max. Well, please yourselves.

[*They file out, Max first, Young Courtly and Grace, Sir Harcourt coquetting with Lady Gay, leaving Dazzle, who offers his arm to Spanker.*]

SCENE ONE

A handsome drawing-room in Oak Hall, chandeliers, tables with books, drawings, etc.

[*Grace and Lady Gay discovered. Servant handing coffee.*]

Grace. If there be one habit more abominable than another, it is that of the gentlemen sitting over their wine; it is a selfish, unfeeling fashion, and a gross insult to our sex.

Lady Gay. We are turned out just when the fun begins. How happy the poor wretches look at the contemplation of being rid of us.

Grace. The conventional signal for the ladies to withdraw is anxiously and deliberately waited for.

Lady Gay. Then I begin to wish I were a man.

Grace. The instant the door is closed upon us, there rises a roar!

Lady Gay. In celebration of their short-lived liberty, my love; rejoicing over their emancipation.

Grace. I think it very insulting, whatever it may be.

Lady Gay. Ah! my dear, philosophers say that man is the creature of an hour—it is the dinner hour, I suppose.

[*Loud noise. Cries of "A song, a song."*]

Grace. I am afraid they are getting too pleasant to be agreeable.

Lady Gay. I hope the squire will restrict himself; after his third bottle, he becomes rather voluminous. [*Cries of "Silence."*] Some one is going to sing. [*Jumps up.*] Let us hear!

[*Spanker is heard to sing.*]

Grace. Oh, no, Gay, for heaven's sake!

Lady Gay. Oho! ha! ha! why, that is my Dolly. [*At the conclusion of the verse.*] Well, I never heard my Dolly sing before! Happy wretches, how I envy them!

[*Enter James, with a note.*]

James. Mr. Hamilton has just left the house for London.

Grace. Impossible!—that is, without seeing—that is—

Lady Gay. Ha! ha!

Grace. He never—speak, sir!

James. He left, Miss Grace, in a desperate hurry, and this note, I believe, for you. [*Presenting a note on a salver.*]

Grace. For me! [*She is about to snatch it, but restraining herself, takes it coolly. Exit James.*] [*Reads.*] "Your your manner during dinner has left me no alternative but instant departure; my absence will release you from the oppression which my society must necessarily inflict on your sensitive mind. It may tend also to smother, though it can never extinguish, that indomitable passion, of which I am the passive victim. Dare I supplicate pardon and oblivion for the past? It is the last request of the self-deceived, but still loving

AUGUSTUS HAMILTON."

[*Puts her hand to her forehead and appears giddy.*]

Lady Gay. Hallo, Grace! what's the matter?

Grace [*recovering herself*]. Nothing—the heat of the room.

Lady Gay. Oh! what excuse does he make? particular unforeseen business, I suppose?

Grace. Why, yes—a mere formula—a—a—you may put it in the fire. [*She puts it in her bosom.*]

Lady Gay [*aside*]. It is near enough to the fire where it is.

Grace. I'm glad he's gone.

Lady Gay. So am I.

Grace. He was a disagreeable, ignorant person.

Lady Gay. Yes; and so vulgar.

Grace. No, he was not at all vulgar.

Lady Gay. I mean in appearance.

Grace. Oh! how can you say so; he was very *distingué*.

Lady Gay. Well, I might have been mistaken, but I took him for a forward, intrusive—

Grace. Good gracious, Gay! he was very retiring—even shy.

Lady Gay [*aside*]. It's all right. *She* is in love,—blows hot and cold, in the same breath.

Grace. How can you be a competent judge? Why, you
   have not known him more than a few hours—while
   I—I—

Lady Gay. Have known him two days and a quarter! I
   yield—I confess, I never was, or will be, so intimate
   with him as you appeared to be! Ha! ha!

[*Loud noise of argument. The folding-doors are thrown
   open. Enter the whole party of gentlemen apparently
   engaged in warm discussion. They assemble in knots,
   while the servants hand coffee, etc., Max, Sir Harcourt, Dazzle, and Spanker, together.*]

Dazzle. But my dear sir, consider the position of the two
   countries under such a constitution.

Sir Harcourt. The two countries! What have they to do
   with the subject?

Max. Everything. Look at their two legislative bodies.

Spanker. Ay, look at their two legislative bodies.

Sir Harcourt. Why, it would inevitably establish universal
   anarchy and confusion.

Grace. I think they are pretty well established already.

Spanker. Well, suppose it did, what has anarchy and confusion to do with the subject?

Lady Gay. Do look at my Dolly; he is arguing—talking
   politics—'pon my life he is. [*Calling.*] Mr. Spanker,
   my dear!

Spanker. Excuse me, love, I am discussing a point of importance.

Lady Gay. Oh, that is delicious; he must discuss that to
   me.—[*She goes up and leads him down; he appears
   to have shaken off his gaucherie; she shakes her head.*]
   Dolly! Dolly!

Spanker. Pardon me, Lady Gay Spanker, I conceive your
   mutilation of my sponsorial appellation derogatory
   to my *amour propre.*

Lady Gay. Your what? Ho! ho!

Spanker. And I particularly request that, for the future, I
   may not be treated with that cavalier spirit which does
   not become your sex, nor your station, your ladyship.

Lady Gay. You have been indulging till you have lost the
   little wit nature dribbled into your unfortunate little
   head—your brains want the whipper-in—you are not
   yourself.

Spanker. Madam, I am doubly myself; and permit me to inform you, that unless you voluntarily pay obedience to my commands, I shall enforce them.

Lady Gay. Your commands!

Spanker. Yes, madam; I mean to put a full stop to your hunting.

Lady Gay. You do! ah! [*Aside.*] I can scarcely speak from delight. [*Aloud.*] Who put such an idea into your head, for I am sure it is not an original emanation of your genius?

Spanker. Sir Harcourt Courtly, my friend; and now, mark me! I request, for your own sake, that I may not be compelled to assert my a—my authority, as your husband. I shall say no more than this—if you persist in this absurd rebellion—

Lady Gay. Well?

Spanker. Contemplate a separation. [*He looks at her haughtily, and retires.*]

Lady Gay. Now I'm happy! My own little darling, inestimable Dolly, has tumbled into a spirit, somehow. Sir Harcourt, too! Ha! ha! he's trying to make him ill-treat me, so that his own suit may thrive.

Sir Harcourt [*advances*]. Lady Gay!

Lady Gay. Now for it.

Sir Harcourt. What hours of misery were those I passed, when, by your secession, the room suffered a total eclipse.

Lady Gay. Ah! you flatter.

Sir Harcourt. No, pardon me, that were impossible. No, believe me, I tried to join in the boisterous mirth, but my thoughts would desert to the drawing-room. Ah! how I envied the careless levity and cool indifference with which Mr. Spanker enjoyed your absence.

Dazzle [*who is lounging in a chair*]. Max, that Madeira is worth its weight in gold; I hope you have more of it.

Max. A pipe, I think.

Dazzle. I consider a magnum of that nectar, and a meerschaum of kanaster, to consummate the ultimatum of all mundane bliss. To drown myself in liquid ecstasy, and then blow a cloud on which the enfranchised soul could soar above Olympus.—Oh!

[*Enter James.*]

James. Mr. Charles Courtly!

Sir Harcourt. Ah, now, Max, you must see a living apology
for my conduct. [*Enter Young Courtly, dressed very
plainly.*] Well, Charles, how are you? Don't be afraid.
There, Max, what do you say now?

Max. Well, this is the most extraordinary likeness.

Grace [*aside*]. Yes—considering it is the original. I am not
so easily deceived!

Max. Sir, I am delighted to see you.

Young Courtly. Thank you, sir.

Dazzle. Will you be kind enough to introduce me, Sir
Harcourt?

Sir Harcourt. This is Mr. Dazzle, Charles.

Young Courtly. Which? [*Looking from Mr. Spanker to
Dazzle.*]

Sir Harcourt [*to Lady Gay*]. Is not that refreshing? Miss
Harkaway—Charles, this is your mother, or rather
will be.

Young Courtly. Madam, I shall love, honor, and obey you
punctually. [*Takes out a book, sighs, and goes up
reading.*]

[*Enter James.*]

Sir Harcourt. You perceive. Quite unused to society—
perfectly ignorant of every conventional rule of life.

James. The Doctor and the young ladies have arrived.
[*Exit.*]

Max. The young ladies—now we must to the ball—I make
it a rule always to commence the festivities with a
good old country dance—a rattling Sir Roger de
Coverly; come, Sir Harcourt.

Sir Harcourt. Does this antiquity require a war-whoop in
it?

Max. Nothing but a nimble foot and a light heart.

Sir Harcourt. Very antediluvian indispensables! Lady Gay
Spanker, will you honor me by becoming my pre-
ceptor?

Lady Gay. Why, I am engaged—but [*aloud*] on such a
plea as Sir Harcourt's, I must waive all obstacles.

Max. Now, Grace, girl—give your hand to Mr. Courtly.

Grace. Pray, excuse me, uncle—I have a headache.

Sir Harcourt [*aside*]. Jealousy! by the gods.—Jealous of
my devotions at another's fame! [*Aloud.*] Charles, my
boy! amuse Miss Grace during our absence. [*Exit
with Lady Gay.*]

Max. But don't you dance, Mr. Courtly!

Young Courtly. Dance, sir!—I never dance—I can procure exercise in a much more rational manner—and music disturbs my meditations.

Max. Well, do the gallant. [*Exit.*]

Young Courtly. I never studied that Art—but I have a Prize Essay on a Hydrostatic subject, which would delight her—for it enchanted the Reverend Doctor Pump, of Corpus Christi.

Grace [*aside*]. What on earth could have induced him to disfigure himself in that frightful way!—I rather suspect some plot to entrap me into a confession.

Young Courtly [*aside*]. Dare I confess this trick to her? No! Not until I have proved her affection indisputably.—Let me see—I must concoct. [*He takes a chair, and, forgetting his assumed character, is about to take his natural free manner.—Grace looks surprised.—He turns abashed.*] Madam, I have been desired to amuse you.

Grace. Thank you.

Young Courtly. "The labor we delight in, physics pain." I will draw you a moral, ahem! Subject, the effects of inebriety!—which, according to Ben Jonson—means perplexion of the intellects, caused by imbibing spirituous liquors.—About an hour before my arrival, I passed an appalling evidence of the effects of this state—a carriage was overthrown—horses killed—gentleman in a helpless state, with his neck broken—all occasioned by the intoxication of the post-boy.

Grace. That is very amusing.

Young Courtly. I found it edifying—nutritious food for reflection—the expiring man desired his best compliments to you.

Grace. To me—

Young Courtly. Yes.

Grace. His name was—

Young Courtly. Mr. Augustus Hamilton.

Grace. Augustus! Oh! [*Affects to faint.*]

Young Courtly [*aside*]. Huzza!

Grace. But where, sir, did this happen?

Young Courtly. About four miles down the road.

Grace. He must be conveyed here.

[*Enter servant.*]

Servant. Mr. Meddle, madam.

[*Enter Meddle*.]

Meddle. On very particular business.

Grace. The very person. My dear sir!

Meddle. My dear madam!

Grace. You must execute a very particular commission for me immediately. Mr. Hamilton has met with a frightful accident on the London road, and is in a dying state.

Meddle. Well! I have no hesitation in saying, he takes it uncommonly easy—he looks as if he was used to it.

Grace. You mistake: that is not Mr. Hamilton, but Mr. Courtly, who will explain everything, and conduct you to the spot.

Young Courtly [*aside*]. Oh! I must put a stop to all this, or I shall be found out.—[*Aloud*.] Madam, that were useless; for I omitted to mention a small fact which occurred before I left Mr. Hamilton—he died.

Grace. Dear me! Oh, then we needn't trouble you, Mr. Meddle. Hark! I hear they are commencing a waltz— if you will ask me—perhaps your society and conversation may tend to dispel the dreadful sensation you have aroused.

Young Courtly [*aside*]. Hears of my death—screams out— and then asks me to waltz! I am bewildered! Can she suspect me? I wonder which she likes best—me or my double? Confound this disguise—I must retain it —I have gone too far with my dad to pull up now.— At your service, madam.

Grace [*aside*]. I will pay him well for this trick! [*Exeunt*.]

Meddle. Well, if that is not Mr. Hamilton, scratch me out with a big blade, for I am a blot—a mistake upon the rolls. There is an error in the pleadings somewhere, and I will discover it.—I would swear to his identity before the most discriminating jury. By the bye, this accident will form a capital excuse for my presence here. I just stepped in to see how matters worked, and—stay—here comes the bridegroom elect —and, oh! in his very arms, Lady Gay Spanker! [*Looks round*.] Where are my witnesses? Oh, that some one else were here! However, I can retire and get some information, eh—Spanker versus Courtly—

damages—witness. [*Gets into an arm-chair, which he turns round.*]

[*Enter Sir Harcourt, supporting Lady Gay.*]

Sir Harcourt. This cool room will recover you.

Lady Gay. Excuse my trusting to you for support.

Sir Harcourt. I am transported! Allow me thus ever to support this lovely burden, and I shall conceive that Paradise is regained. [*They sit.*]

Lady Gay. Oh! Sir Harcourt, I feel very faint.

Sir Harcourt. The waltz made you giddy.

Lady Gay. And I have left my salts in the other room.

Sir Harcourt. I always carry a flacon, for the express accommodation of the fair sex. [*Producing a smelling-bottle.*]

Lady Gay. Thank you—ah! [*She sighs.*]

Sir Harcourt. What a sigh was there!

Lady Gay. The vapor of consuming grief.

Sir Harcourt. Grief? Is it possible, have you a grief? Are you unhappy? Dear me!

Lady Gay. Am I not married?

Sir Harcourt. What a horrible state of existence!

Lady Gay. I am never contradicted, so there are none of those enlivening, interest[ing] little differences, which so pleasingly diversify the monotony of conjugal life, like spots of verdure—no quarrels, like oases in the desert of matrimony—no rows.

Sir Harcourt. How vulgar! what a brute!

Lady Gay. I never have anything but my own way; and he won't permit me to spend more than I like.

Sir Harcourt. Mean-spirited wretch!

Lady Gay. How can I help being miserable?

Sir Harcourt. Miserable! I wonder you are not in a lunatic asylum, with such unheard-of barbarism!

Lady Gay. But worse than all that!

Sir Harcourt. Can it be out-heroded?

Lady Gay. Yes, I could forgive that—I do—it is my duty. But only imagine—picture to yourself, my dear Sir Harcourt, though I, the third daughter of an Earl, married him out of pity for his destitute and helpless situation as a bachelor with ten thousand a year—conceive, if you can—he actually permits me, with the most placid indifference, to flirt with any old fool I may meet.

Sir Harcourt. Good gracious! miserable idiot!

Lady Gay. I fear there is an incompatibility of temper, which renders a separation inevitable.

Sir Harcourt. Indispensable, my dear madam! Ah! had I been the happy possessor of such a realm of bliss—what a beatific eternity unfolds itself to my extending imagination! Had another man but looked at you, I should have annihilated him at once; and if he had the temerity to speak, his life alone could have expiated his crime.

Lady Gay. Oh, an existence of such a nature is too bright for the eye of thought—too sweet to bear reflection.

Sir Harcourt. My devotion, eternal, deep—

Lady Gay. Oh, Sir Harcourt!

Sir Harcourt [*more fervently*]. Your every thought should be a separate study,—each wish forestalled by the quick apprehension of a kindred soul.

Lady Gay. Alas! how can I avoid my fate?

Sir Harcourt. If a life—a heart—were offered to your astonished view by one who is considered the index of fashion—the vane of the *beau monde,*—if you saw him at your feet, begging, beseeching your acceptance of all, and more than this, what would your answer—

Lady Gay. Ah! I know of none so devoted!

Sir Harcourt. You do! [*Throwing himself upon his knees.*] Behold Sir Harcourt Courtly!

[*Meddle jumps up in the chair.*]

Lady Gay [*aside*]. Ha! ha! Yoicks! Puss has broken cover.

Sir Harcourt. Speak, adored, dearest Lady Gay!—speak—will you fly from the tyranny, the wretched misery of such a monster's roof, and accept the soul which lives but in your presence!

Lady Gay. Do not press me. Oh, spare a weak, yielding woman,—be contented to know that you are, alas! too dear to me. But the world—the world would say—

Sir Harcourt. Let us be a precedent, to open a more extended and liberal view of matrimonial advantages to society.

Lady Gay. How irresistible is your argument! Oh! pause!

Sir Harcourt. I have ascertained for a fact, every tradesman of mine lives with his wife, and thus you see it has become a vulgar and plebeian custom.

Lady Gay. Leave me; I feel I cannot withstand your powers of persuasion. Swear that you will never forsake me.

Sir Harcourt. Dictate the oath. May I grow wrinkled,—may two inches be added to the circumference of my waist,—may I lose the fall in my back,—may I be old and ugly the instant I forego one tithe of adoration!

Lady Gay. I must believe you.

Sir Harcourt. Shall we leave this detestable spot—this horrible vicinity?

Lady Gay. The sooner the better; tomorrow evening let it be. Now let me return; my absence will be remarked. [*He kisses her hand.*] Do I appear confused? Has my agitation rendered me unfit to enter the room?

Sir Harcourt. More angelic by a lovely tinge of heightened color.

Lady Gay. To-morrow, in this room, which opens on the lawn.

Sir Harcourt. At eleven o'clock.

Lady Gay. Have your carriage in waiting, and four horses. Remember please, be particular to have four; don't let the affair come off shabbily. Adieu, dear Sir Harcourt! [*Exit.*]

Sir Harcourt. Veni, vidi, vici! Hannibal, Caesar, Napoleon, Alexander never completed so fair a conquest in so short a time. She dropped fascinated. This is an unprecedented example of the irresistible force of personal appearance combined with polished address. Poor creature! how she loves me! I pity so prostrating a passion, and ought to return it. I will; it is a duty I owe to society and fashion. [*Exit.*]

Meddle [*turns the chair round*]. "There is a tide in the affairs of men, which, taken at the flood, leads on to fortune." This is my tide—I am the only witness. "Virtue is sure to find its own reward." But I've no time to contemplate what I shall be—something huge. Let me see—Spanker versus Courtly—Crim. Con.—Damages placed at 150,000*l.*, at least, for injuries always decimate your hopes.

[*Enter Mr. Spanker.*]

Spanker. I cannot find Gay anywhere.

Meddle. The plaintiff himself—I must commence the action. Mr. Spanker, as I have information of deep, vital importance to impart, will you take a seat? [*They sit solemnly. (Meddle) takes out a note-book and pencil.*] Ahem! you have a wife?

[*Re-enter Lady Gay, behind.*]

Spanker. Yes, I believe I—

Meddle. Will you be kind enough, without any prevarication, to answer my questions?

Spanker. You alarm—I—

Meddle. Compose yourself and reserve your feelings; take time to consider. You have a wife?

Spanker. Yes—

Meddle. He has a wife—good—a *bona-fide* wife—bound morally and legally to be your wife, and nobody else's in effect, except on your written permission—

Spanker. But what has this—

Meddle. Hush! allow me, my dear sir, to congratulate you. [*Shakes his hand.*]

Spanker. What for?

Meddle. Lady Gay Spanker is about to dishonor the bond of wedlock by eloping from you.

Spanker [*starting*]. What!

Meddle. Be patient—I thought you would be overjoyed. Will you place the affair in my hands, and I will venture to promise the largest damages on record.

Spanker. Damn the damages! I want my wife. Oh, I'll go and ask her not to run away. She may run away with me—she may hunt—she may ride—anything she likes. Oh, sir, let us put a stop to this affair.

Meddle. Put a stop to it! do not alarm me, sir. Sir, you will spoil the most exquisite brief that was ever penned. It must proceed—it shall proceed. It is illegal to prevent it, and I will bring an action against you for wilful intent to injure the profession.

Spanker. Oh, what an ass I am! Oh, I have driven her to this. It was all that damned brandy punch on the top of Burgundy. What a fool I was!

Meddle. It was the happiest moment of your life.

Spanker. So I thought at the time; but we live to grow wiser. Tell me, who is the vile seducer?

Meddle. Sir Harcourt Courtly.

Spanker. Ha! he is my best friend.

Meddle. I should think he is. If you will accompany me—here is a verbatim copy of the whole transaction in short-hand—sworn to by me.

Spanker. Only let me have Gay back again.

Meddle. Even that may be arranged—this way.

Spanker. That ever I should live to see my wife run away. Oh, I will do anything—keep two packs of hounds—buy up every horse and ass in England—myself included—oh! [*Exit with Meddle.*]

Lady Gay. Ha! ha! ha! Poor Dolly, I'm sorry I must continue to deceive him. If he would kindle up a little—so that fellow overheard all—well, so much the better.

[*Enter Young Courtly.*]

Young Courtly. My dear madam, how fares the plot? does my Governor nibble?

Lady Gay. Nibble! he is caught, and in the basket. I have just left him with a hook in his gills, panting for very lack of element. But how goes on your encounter?

Young Courtly. Bravely. By a simple ruse, I have discovered that she loves me. I see but one chance against the best termination I could hope.

Lady Gay. What is that?

Young Courtly. My father has told me that I return to town again to-morrow afternoon.

Lady Gay. Well, I insist you stop and dine—keep out of the way.

Young Courtly. Oh, but what excuse can I offer for disobedience? What can I say when he sees me before dinner?

Lady Gay. Say—say Grace.

[*Enter Grace, who gets behind the window curtains.*]

Young Courtly. Ha! ha!

Lady Gay. I have arranged to elope with Sir Harcourt myself to-morrow night.

Young Courtly. The deuce you have!

Lady Gay. Now if you could persuade Grace to follow that example—his carriage will be waiting at the Park—be there a little before eleven—and it will just prevent our escape. Can you make her agree to that?

Young Courtly. Oh, without the slightest difficulty, if Mr.
    Augustus Hamilton supplicates.
Lady Gay. Success attend you. [*Going.*]
Young Courtly. I will bend the haughty Grace. [*Going.*]
Lady Gay. Do. [*Exeunt severally.*]
Grace. Will you?

SCENE ONE

A drawing-room in Oak Hall.

[*Enter Cool.*]

Cool. This is the most serious affair Sir Harcourt has ever been engaged in. I took the liberty of considering him a fool when he told me he was going to marry: but voluntarily to incur another man's incumbrance is very little short of madness. If he continues to conduct himself in this absurd manner, I shall be compelled to dismiss him.

[*Enter Sir Harcourt, equipped for travelling.*]

Sir Harcourt. Cool!

Cool. Sir Harcourt.

Sir Harcourt. Is my chariot in waiting?

Cool. For the last half hour at the park wicket. But, pardon the insinuation, sir; would it not be more advisable to hesitate a little for a short reflection before you undertake the heavy responsibility of a woman?

Sir Harcourt. No: hesitation destroys the romance of [a] *faux pas*, and reduces it to the level of a mere mercantile calculation.

Cool. What is to be done with Mr. Charles?

Sir Harcourt. Ay, much against my will, Lady Gay prevailed on me to permit him to remain. You, Cool, must return him to college. Pass through London, and deliver these papers: here is a small notice of the coming elopement for the *Morning Post;* this, by an eye-witness, for the *Herald;* this, with all the particulars, for the *Chronicle;* and the full and circumstantial account for the evening journal—after which, meet us at Boulogne.

Cool. Very good, Sir Harcourt. [*Going.*]

Sir Harcourt. Lose no time. Remember—Hotel Anglais,

Boulogne-sur-Mer. And, Cool, bring a few copies with
you, and don't forget to distribute some amongst very
particular friends.

Cool. It shall be done. [*Exit Cool.*]

Sir Harcourt. With what indifference does a man of the
world view the approach of the most perilous catastrophe! My position, hazardous as it is, entails none
of that nervous excitement which a neophyte in the
school of fashion would feel. I am as cool and steady
as possible. Habit, habit. Oh! how many roses will
fade upon the cheek of beauty, when the defalcation
of Sir Harcourt Courtly is whispered—then hinted—
at last, confirmed and bruited. I think I see them.
Then, on my return, they will not dare to eject me—I
am their sovereign! Whoever attempts to think of
treason, I'll banish him from the West End—I'll cut
him—I'll put him out of fashion!

[*Enter Lady Gay.*]

Lady Gay. Sir Harcourt!

Sir Harcourt. At your feet.

Lady Gay. I had hoped you would have repented.

Sir Harcourt. Repented!

Lady Gay. Have you not come to say it was a jest?—say
you have!

Sir Harcourt. Love is too sacred a subject to be trifled
with. Come, let us fly! See, I have procured disguises—

Lady Gay. My courage begins to fail me. Let me return.

Sir Harcourt. Impossible!

Lady Gay. Where do you intend to take me?

Sir Harcourt. You shall be my guide. The carriage waits.

Lady Gay. You will never desert me?

Sir Harcourt. Desert! Oh, heavens! Nay, do not hesitate—
flight, now, alone is left to your desperate situation!
Come, every moment is laden with danger. [*They are
going.*]

Lady Gay. Oh! gracious!

Sir Harcourt. Hush! what is it?

Lady Gay. I have forgotten—I must return.

Sir Harcourt. Impossible!

Lady Gay. I must! I must! I have left Max—a pet stag-
hound, in his basket—without whom, life would be
unendurable—I could not exist!

Sir Harcourt. No, no. Let him be sent after us in a hamper.

Lady Gay. In a hamper! Remorseless man! Go—you love me not. How would you like to be sent after me— in a hamper? Let me fetch him. Hark! I hear him squeal! Oh! Max—Max!

Sir Harcourt. Hush! for heaven's sake. They'll imagine you're calling the Squire. I hear footsteps; where can I retire?

[*Enter Meddle, Spanker, Dazzle, and Max. Lady Gay screams.*]

Meddle. Spanker versus Courtly!—I subpoena every one of you as witnesses!—I have 'em ready—here they are—shilling a-piece. [*Giving them round.*]

Lady Gay. Where is Sir Harcourt?

Meddle. There!—bear witness!—calling on the vile delinquent for protection!

Spanker. Oh! his protection!

Lady Gay. What? ha!

Meddle. I'll swear I overheard the whole elopement planned—before any jury!—where's the book?

Spanker. Do you hear, you profligate?

Lady Gay. Ha! ha! ha! ha!

Dazzle. But where is this wretched Lothario?

Meddle. Aye, where is the defendant?

Spanker. Where lies the hoary villain?

Lady Gay. What villain?

Spanker. That will not serve you!—I'll not be blinded that way!

Meddle. We won't be blinded any way!

Max. I must seek Sir Harcourt, and demand an explanation!—Such a thing never occurred in Oak Hall before!—It must be cleared up! [*Exit.*]

Meddle [*aside to Spanker*]. Now, take my advice, remember your gender. Mind the notes I have given you.

Spanker [*aside*]. All right! Here they are! Now, madam, I have procured the highest legal opinion on this point.

Meddle. Hear! hear!

Spanker. And the question resolves itself into a—into— What's this? [*Looks at notes.*]

Meddle. A nutshell!

Spanker. Yes, we are in a nutshell. Will you, in every respect, subscribe to my requests—desires—commands

—[*looks at notes*]—orders—imperative—indicative—injunctive—or otherwise?

Lady Gay [*aside*]. 'Pon my life, he's actually going to assume the ribbons, and take the box-seat. I must put a stop to this. I will! It will all end in smoke. I know Sir Harcourt would rather run than fight!

Dazzle Oh! I smell powder!—command my services. My dear madam, can I be of any use?

Spanker. Oh! [a] challenge!—I must consult my legal adviser.

Meddle. No!—impossible!

Dazzle. Pooh! the easiest thing in life!—Leave it to me—what has an attorney to do with affairs of honor?—they are out of his element!

Meddle. Compromise the question!—pull his nose!—we have no objection to that!

Dazzle [*turning to Lady Gay*]. Well, we have no objection either—have we?

Lady Gay. No!—pull his nose—that will be something.

Meddle. And, moreover, it is not exactly actionable!

Dazzle. Isn't it!—thank you—I'll note down that piece of information—it may be useful.

Meddle. How! cheated out of my legal knowledge.

Lady Gay. Mr. Spanker, I am determined!—I insist upon a challenge being sent to Sir Harcourt Courtly!—and—mark me—if you refuse to fight him—I will.

Meddle. Don't. Take my advice—you'll incapacit—

Lady Gay. Look you, Mr. Meddle, unless you wish me to horsewhip you, hold your tongue.

Meddle. What a she-tiger—I shall retire and collect my costs. [*Exit*.]

Lady Gay. Mr. Spanker, oblige me, by writing as I dictate.

Spanker. He's gone—and now I am defenceless! Is this the fate of husbands?—A duel!—Is this the result of becoming master of my own family?

Lady Gay. "Sir, the situation in which you were discovered with my wife, admits neither of explanation nor apology."

Spanker. Oh, yes! but it does—I don't believe you really intended to run quite away.

Lady Gay. You do not; but I know better, I say I did; and if it had not been for your unfortunate interruption, I do not know where I might have been by this time.—Go on.

Spanker. "Nor apology." I'm writing my own death-warrant, committing suicide on compulsion.

Lady Gay. "The bearer will arrange all preliminary matters, for another day must see this sacrilege expiated by your life, or that of

"Yours very sincerely,

"DOLLY SPANKER."

Now, Mr. Dazzle. [*Gives it over his head.*]

Dazzle. The document is as sacred as if it were a hundred-pound bill.

Lady Gay. We trust to your discretion.

Spanker. His discretion! Oh, put your head in a tiger's mouth, and trust to his discretion!

Dazzle [*sealing letter, etc., with Spanker's seal*]. My dear Lady Gay, matters of this kind are indigenous to my nature, independently of their pervading fascination to all humanity; but this is more especially delightful, as you may perceive I shall be the intimate and bosom friend of both parties.

Lady Gay. Is it not the only alternative in such a case?

Dazzle. It is a beautiful panacea in any, in every case. [*Going—returns.*] By the way, where would you like this party of pleasure to come off? Open-air shooting is pleasant enough, but if I might venture to advise, we could order half a dozen of that Madeira and a box of cigars into the billiard-room, so make a night of it; take up the irons every now and then, string for first shot, and blaze away at one another in an amicable and gentlemanlike way; so conclude the matter before the potency of the liquor could disturb the individuality of the object, or the smoke of the cigars render its outline dubious. Does such an arrangement coincide with your views?

Lady Gay. Perfectly.

Dazzle. I trust shortly to be the harbinger of happy tidings. [*Exit.*]

Spanker [*coming forward*]. Lady Gay Spanker, are you ambitious of becoming a widow?

Lady Gay. Why, Dolly, woman is at best but weak, and weeds become me.

Spanker. Female! am I to be immolated on the altar of
     your vanity?

Lady Gay. If you become pathetic, I shall laugh.

Spanker. Farewell—base, heartless, unfeeling woman!
     [*Exit*.]

Lady Gay. Ha! well, so I am. I am heartless, for he is a
     dear, good little fellow, and I ought not to play upon
     his feelings; but 'pon my life he sounds so well up at
     concert pitch, that I feel disinclined to untune him.
     Poor Dolly, I didn't think he cared so much about me.
     I will put him out of pain. [*Exit. Sir Harcourt comes
     down*.]

Sir Harcourt. I have been a fool! a dupe of my own vanity.
     I shall be pointed at as a ridiculous old coxcomb—
     and so I am. The hour of conviction is *arrived*. Have
     I deceived myself?—Have I turned all my senses in-
     wards—looking towards self—always self?—and has
     the world been ever laughing at me? Well, if they
     have, I will revert the joke;—they may say I am an
     old ass; but I will prove that I am neither too old to
     repent my folly, nor such an ass as to flinch from
     confessing it. A blow half met is but half felt.

[*Enter Dazzle*.]

Dazzle. Sir Harcourt, may I be permitted the honor of a
     few minutes' conversation with you?

Sir Harcourt. With pleasure.

Dazzle. Have the kindness to throw your eye over that.
     [*Gives the letter*.]

Sir Harcourt [*reads*]. "Situation—my wife—apology—ex-
     piate—my life." Why, this is intended for a challenge.

Dazzle. Why, indeed, I am perfectly aware that it is not
     quite *en règle* in the couching, for with that I had
     nothing to do; but I trust that the irregularity of the
     composition will be confounded in the beauty of the
     subject.

Sir Harcourt. Mr. Dazzle, are you in earnest?

Dazzle. Sir Harcourt Courtly, upon my honor I am, and
     I hope that no previous engagement will interfere
     with an immediate reply *in propria persona*. We have
     fixed upon the billiard-room as the scene of action,
     which I have just seen properly illuminated in honor
     of the occasion; and, by-the-bye, if your implements

are not handy, I can oblige you with a pair of the sweetest things you ever handled—hair-triggered—saw grip; heirlooms in my family. I regard them almost in the light of relations.

Sir Harcourt. Sir, I shall avail myself of one of your relatives. [*Aside.*] One of the hereditaments of my folly—I must accept it. [*Aloud.*] Sir, I shall be happy to meet Mr. Spanker at any time or place he may appoint.

Dazzle. The sooner the better, sir. Allow me to offer you my arm. I see you understand these matters;—my friend Spanker is woefully ignorant—miserably uneducated. [*Exeunt. Re-enter Max, with Grace.*]

Max. Give ye joy, girl, give ye joy. Sir Harcourt Courtly must consent to waive all titles to your hand in favor of his son Charles.

Grace. Oh, indeed! Is that the pith of your congratulation—humph! the exchange of an old fool for a young one? Pardon me if I am not able to distinguish the advantage.

Max. Advantage!

Grace. Moreover, by what right am I a transferable cipher in the family of Courtly? So, then, my fate is reduced to this, to sacrifice my fortune, or unite myself with a worm-eaten edition of the Classics!

Max. Why, he certainly is not such a fellow as I could have chosen for my little Grace; but consider, to retain fifteen thousand a-year! Now, tell me honestly—but why should I say *honestly?* Speak, girl, would you rather not have the lad?

Grace. Why do you ask me?

Max. Why, look ye, I'm an old fellow, another hunting season or two, and I shall be in at my own death—I can't leave you this house and land, because they are entailed, nor can I say I'm sorry for it, for it is a good law; but I have a little box with my Grace's name upon it, where, since your father's death and miserly will, I have yearly placed a certain sum to be yours, should you refuse to fulfil the conditions prescribed.

Grace. My own dear uncle! [*Clasping him round the neck.*]

Max. Pooh! pooh! what's to do now? Why, it was only a trifle—why, you little rogue, what are you crying about?

Grace. Nothing, but—

Max. But what? Come, out with it, will you have young Courtly?

[*Re-enter Lady Gay.*]

Lady Gay. Oh! Max, Max!

Max. Why, what's amiss with you?

Lady Gay. I'm a wicked woman!

Max. What have you done?

Lady Gay. Everything—oh, I thought Sir Harcourt was a coward, but now I find a man may be a coxcomb without being a poltroon. Just to show my husband how inconvenient it is to hold the ribands sometimes, I made him send a challenge to the old fellow, and he, to my surprise, accepted it, and is going to blow my Dolly's brains out in the billiard-room.

Max. The devil!

Lady Gay. Just when I imagined I had got my whip hand of him again, out comes my linch-pin—and over I go —oh!

Max. I will soon put a stop to that—a duel under my roof! Murder in Oak Hall! I'll shoot them both! [*Exit.*]

Grace. Are you really in earnest?

Lady Gay. Do you think it [looks] like a joke? Oh! Dolly, if you allow yourself to be shot, I will never forgive you—never! Ah, he is a great fool, Grace; but I can't tell why, but I would sooner lose my bridle hand than he should be hurt on my account. [*Enter Sir Harcourt Courtly.*] Tell me—tell me—have you shot him—is he dead—my dear Sir Harcourt—you horrid old brute—have you killed him? I shall never forgive myself. [*Exit.*]

Grace. Oh! Sir Harcourt, what has happened?

Sir Harcourt. Don't be alarmed, I beg—your uncle interrupted us—discharged the weapons—locked the challenger up in the billiard-room to cool his rage.

Grace. Thank heaven!

Sir Harcourt. Miss Grace, to apologize for my conduct were useless, more especially as I am confident that no feelings of indignation or sorrow for my late acts are cherished by you; but still, reparation is in my

power, and I not only waive all title, right, or claim
to your person or your fortune, but freely admit your
power to bestow them on a more worthy object.

Grace. This generosity, Sir Harcourt, is most unexpected.

Sir Harcourt. No, not generosity, but simply justice, justice!

Grace. May I still beg a favor?

Sir Harcourt. Claim anything that is mine to grant.

Grace. You have been duped by Lady Gay Spanker, I have
also been cheated and played upon by her and Mr.
Hamilton—may I beg that the contract between us
may, to all appearances, be still held good?

Sir Harcourt. Certainly, although I confess I cannot see
the point of your purpose.

[*Enter Max, with Young Courtly.*]

Max. Now, Grace, I have brought the lad.

Grace. Thank you, uncle, but the trouble was quite unnecessary—Sir Harcourt holds to his original contract.

Max. The deuce he does!

Grace. And I am willing—nay, eager, to become Lady
Courtly.

Young Courtly [*aside*]. The deuce you are!

Max. But, Sir Harcourt—

Sir Harcourt. One word, Max, for an instant. [*They retire.*]

Young Courtly [*aside*]. What can this mean? Can it be
possible that I have been mistaken—that she is not
in love with Augustus Hamilton?

Grace. Now we shall find how he intends to bend the
haughty Grace.

Young Courtly. Madam—Miss, I mean,—are you really
in earnest—are you in love with my father?

Grace. No, indeed I am not.

Young Courtly. Are you in love with anyone else?

Grace. No, or I should not marry him.

Young Courtly. Then you actually accept him as your real
husband?

Grace. In the common acceptation of the word.

Young Courtly [*aside*]. Hang me if I have not been a pretty
fool! [*Aloud.*] Why do you marry him, if you don't
care about him?

Grace. To save my fortune.

Young Courtly [*aside*]. Mercenary, cold-hearted girl!
[*Aloud.*] But if there be any one you love in the
least—marry him;—were you never in love?

Grace. Never!

Young Courtly [*aside*]. Oh! what an ass I've been! [*Aloud.*] I heard Lady Gay mention something about a Mr. Hamilton.

Grace. Ah, yes, a person who, after an acquaintanceship of two days, had the assurance to make love to me, and I—

Young Courtly. Yes,—you—Well?

Grace. I pretended to receive his attentions.

Young Courtly [*aside*]. It was the best pretence I ever saw.

Grace. An absurd, vain, conceited coxcomb, who appeared to imagine that I was so struck with his fulsome speech, that he could turn me round his finger.

Young Courtly [*aside*]. My very thoughts!

Grace. But he was mistaken.

Young Courtly [*aside*]. Confoundedly! [*Aloud.*] Yet you seemed rather concerned about the news of his death?

Grace. His accident! No, but—

Young Courtly. But what?

Grace [*aside*]. What can I say? [*Aloud.*] Ah! but my maid Pert's brother is a post-boy, and I thought he might have sustained an injury, poor boy.

Young Courtly [*aside*]. Damn the post-boy! [*Aloud.*] Madam, if the retention of your fortune be the plea on which you are about to bestow your hand on one you do not love, and whose very actions speak his carelessness for that inestimable jewel he is incapable of appreciating—Know that I am devotedly, madly attached to you.

Grace. You, sir? Impossible!

Young Courtly. Not at all,—but inevitable,—I have been so for a long time.

Grace. Why, you never saw me until last night.

Young Courtly. I have seen you in imagination—you are the ideal I have worshipped.

Grace. Since you press me into a confession,—which nothing but this could bring me to speak,—know, I did love poor Augustus Hamilton—[*Re-enter Max and Sir Harcourt.*] but he—he is—no—more! Pray, spare me, sir.

Young Courtly [*aside*]. She loves me! And, oh! what a situation I am in!—if I own I am the man, my Governor will overhear, and ruin me—if I do not, she'll marry him.—What is to be done?

[*Enter Lady Gay.*]

Lady Gay. Where have you put my Dolly? I have been racing all round the house—tell me, is he quite dead!

Max. I'll have him brought in. [*Exit.*]

Sir Harcourt. My dear madam, you must perceive this unfortunate occurrence was no fault of mine. I was compelled to act as I have done—I was willing to offer any apology, but that resource was excluded, as unacceptable.

Lady Gay. I know—I know—'twas I made him write that letter—there was no apology required—'twas I that apparently seduced you from the paths of propriety,— 'twas all a joke, and here is the end of it. [*Enter Max, Mr. Spanker, and Dazzle.*] Oh! if he had but lived to say, "I forgive you, Gay!"

Spanker. So I do!

Lady Gay [*seeing Spanker*]. Ah! he is alive!

Spanker. Of course I am!

Lady Gay. Ha! ha! ha! [*Embraces him.*] I will never hunt again—unless you wish it. Sell your stable—

Spanker. No, no—do what you like—say what you like, for the future! I find the head of a family has less ease and more responsibility than I, as a member, could have anticipated. I abdicate!

[*Enter Cool.*]

Sir Harcourt. Ah! Cool, here! [*Aside.*] You may destroy those papers—I have altered my mind,—and I do not intend to elope at present. Where are they?

Cool. As you seemed particular, Sir Harcourt, I sent them off by mail to London.

Sir Harcourt. Why, then, a full description of the whole affair will be published to-morrow.

Cool. Most irretrievably!

Sir Harcourt. You must post to town immediately, and stop the press.

Cool. Beg pardon—they would see me hanged first, Sir Harcourt; they don't frequently meet with such a profitable lie.

Servant [*without*]. No, sir! no, sir!

[*Enter Simpson.*]

Simpson. Sir, there is a gentleman, who calls himself Mr. Solomon Isaacs, insists upon following me up.

[*Enter Mr. Solomon Isaacs.*]

Isaacs. Mr. Courtly, you will excuse my performance of a most disagreeable duty at any time, but more especially in such a manner. I must beg the honor of your company to town.

Sir Harcourt. What!—how!—what for?

Isaacs. For debt, Sir Harcourt.

Sir Harcourt. Arrested?—impossible! Here must be some mistake.

Isaacs. Not the slightest, sir. Judgment has been given in five cases, for the last three months; but Mr. Courtly is an eel, rather too nimble for my men.—We have been on his track, and traced him down to this village, with Mr. Dazzle.

Dazzle. Ah! Isaacs! how are you?

Isaacs. Thank you, sir. [*Speaks to Sir Harcourt.*]

Max. Do you know him?

Dazzle. Oh, intimately—distantly related to his family— same arms on our escutcheon—empty purse falling through a hole in a—pocket: motto, "Requiescat in pace"—which means, "Let virtue be its own reward."

Sir Harcourt [*to Isaacs*]. Oh, I thought there was a mistake! Know, to your misfortune, that Mr. Hamilton was the person you dogged to Oak Hall, between whom and my son a most remarkable likeness exists.

Isaacs. Ha! ha! Know, to your misfortune, Sir Harcourt, that Mr. Hamilton and Mr. Courtly are one and the same person!

Sir Harcourt. Charles!

Young Courtly. Concealment is in vain—I am Augustus Hamilton.

Sir Harcourt. Hang me, if I didn't think it all along! Oh, you infernal, cozening dog!

Isaacs. Now, then, Mr. Hamilton—

Grace. Stay, sir—Mr. Charles Courtly is under age—ask his father.

Sir Harcourt. Ahem!—I won't—I won't pay a shilling of the rascal's debts—not a sixpence!

Grace. Then, I will—you may retire.

[*Exit Isaacs.*]

Young Courtly. I can now perceive the generous point of

your conduct towards me; and, believe me, I appreciate, and will endeavor to deserve it.

Max. Ha! ha! Come, Sir Harcourt, you have been fairly beaten—you must forgive him—say you will.

Sir Harcourt. So, sir, it appears you have been leading, covertly, an infernal town life.

Young Courtly. Yes, please, father. [*Imitating Master Charles.*]

Sir Harcourt. None of your humbug sir! [*Aside.*] He is my own son—how could I expect him to keep out of the fire? [*Aloud.*] And you, Mr. Cool!—have you been deceiving me?

Cool. Oh! Sir Harcourt, if your perception was played upon, how could I be expected to see?

Sir Harcourt. Well, it would be useless to withhold my hand. There, boy! [*He gives his hand to Young Courtly. Grace comes down on the other side, and offers her hand; he takes it.*] What is all this? What do you want?

Young Courtly. Your blessing, father.

Grace. If you please, father.

Sir Harcourt. Oho! the mystery is being solved. So, so, you young scoundrel, you have been making love—under the rose.

Lady Gay. He learnt that from you, Sir Harcourt.

Sir Harcourt. Ahem! What would you do now, if I were to withhold my consent?

Grace. Do without it.

Max. The will says, if Grace marries any one but you,—her property reverts to your heir-apparent—and there he stands.

Lady Gay. Make a virtue of necessity.

Spanker. I married from inclination; and see how happy I am. And if ever I have a son—

Lady Gay. Hush! Dolly, dear!

Sir Harcourt. Well! take her, boy! Although you are too young to marry. [*They retire with Max.*]

Lady Gay. Am I forgiven, Sir Harcourt?

Sir Harcourt. Ahem! Why—a—[*Aside.*] Have you really deceived me?

Lady Gay. Can you not see through this?

Sir Harcourt. And you still love me?

Lady Gay. As much as I ever did.

Sir Harcourt [*is about to kiss her hand, when Spanker interposes between*]. A very handsome ring, indeed.

Spanker. Very. [*Puts her arm in his, and they go up.*]

Sir Harcourt. Poor little Spanker!

Max [*coming down, aside to Sir Harcourt*]. One point I wish to have settled. Who is Mr. Dazzle?

Sir Harcourt. A relative of the Spankers, he told me.

Max. Oh, no,—a near connection of yours.

Sir Harcourt. Never saw him before I came down here, in all my life. [*To Young Courtly.*] Charles, who is Mr. Dazzle?

Young Courtly. Dazzle, Dazzle,—will you excuse an impertinent question?—but who the deuce are you?

Dazzle. Certainly. I have not the remotest idea!

All. How, sir?

Dazzle. Simple question as you may think it, it would puzzle half the world to answer. One thing I can vouch—Nature made me a gentleman—that is, I live on the best that can be procured for credit. I never spend my own money when I can oblige a friend. I'm always thick on the winning horse. I'm an epidemic on the trade of a tailor. For further particulars, inquire of any sitting magistrate.

Sir Harcourt. And these are the deeds which attest your title to the name of gentleman? I perceive that you have caught the infection of the present age. Charles, permit me, as your father, and you, sir, as his friend, to correct you on one point. Bare-faced assurance is the vulgar substitute for gentlemanly ease; and there are many who, by aping the *vices* of the great, imagine that they elevate themselves to the rank of those whose faults alone they copy. No, sir! The title of gentleman is the only one *out* of any monarch's gift, yet within the reach of every peasant. It should be engrossed by *Truth*—stamped with *Honor*—sealed with *good-feeling*—signed *Man*—and enrolled in every true young English heart.

Leopold Lewis (1828–1890) **The Bells**

A DRAMA IN THREE ACTS

Irving's Masterpiece—"The Bells"

BY GORDON CRAIG

And now we come to that night on which London was given his masterpiece—*The Bells*.

I was not present at the first performance, in 1871, for I was not born, but I think I have seen Irving in it more than thirty times between the years 1889 and 1900, although I never played in the piece. The pieces I never played in under his management, I never watched at rehearsal—to watch a play being rehearsed is in the nature of an intrusion—a kind of eavesdropping—unless you are taking part in the work. I had ample opportunity of seeing many rehearsals of *The Bells* while I was a minor actor in Irving's company, but I never saw one. My old friend, Martin Harvey, the best actor that the company ever produced, could write an interesting essay upon these rehearsals, which I for one would read with delight; for he played in *The Bells*, though he was not in the first production of 1871, being then only four years old.

Gentle reader, you who have seen Irving in this play, you will know that I do not write about him for you; for you saw—you heard—what then do you need more? But some of the others did not see Irving. How shall we together explain him to them?

We who never saw Edmund Kean have a few pictures that speak vividly to us of him, and a few fragments in writing, notably those by Heine and Lord Byron, and we are not skeptical; but today, it is as likely as not that when we speak of Irving we are merely tolerated, for interest in the dramatic craft is not as vivid as it was. You may find a young man or a young woman of today keen to know what it actually was that Irving did, or how he did it, but you will not find many. In fact, like one of those Two Black Crows, they'd "rather hear no more about it."

And here I am, continuing to bore them to death about this event which astonished you and me until 1905—the year of Irving's death.

How shall I explain this event? There are actors living today, held as great actors by this generation: Irving was not exactly anything like these. We know that—but there is a great singer whom presumably you, the younger generation, do appreciate, and place even higher than the fine actors I have referred to but not mentioned —Chaliapine by name.

When you saw Chaliapine, what did you feel? What do you recall about him? He was pretty good, was he not? I think that you will say that he was really something worth while. There was nothing you could possibly call *charming* about Chaliapine—he was better than that. Speaking of him, you'd never find yourselves saying he was "interesting" or "able" or "intelligent." You would go much further than that. I think you would call him "immense," "magnetic." Well, Irving was all this about twice told. He was twofold what Chaliapine is, because there was greater depth—even as Shakespeare is greater than Marlowe for all his mighty line, because of a deep and human beauty which he lets you see.

Have you then caught some faint notion of the idea "Irving" at last?

And upon Saturday, the 25th of November, 1871 (Bram Stoker, his biographer, dates this first run as in 1872–73), the curtain rose at a quarter to eight, and disclosed an interior scene of a brownish tone . . . a parlour in Alsace.

It is evening. It is snowing outside, and the Burgomaster is expected back at any minute—Irving is expected to appear at any minute. Meantime, the actors who fill in the preliminary fifteen minutes are filling them in in a mighty able manner.

These first minutes never failed to charm me. I think that never was our company seen to better advantage than during this brief quarter of an hour; and although they played the whole piece admirably, it was before Irving's coming onto the stage that they were best.

On his appearance, they one and all fell back into their places, since to obtrude would have been out of the question. *Ensemble* was achieved, but there was something to achieve it for, something to which it could lend sup-

port; *ensemble* supporting itself, is it not rather a ridiculous spectacle? That's democratic acting if you like—
"for we are jolly good fellows . . . which none of us will deny."

I am not going to attempt to describe Irving's performance in *The Bells*, or *The Polish Jew*, as it is sometimes called. Stanislavsky, the great Russian theatre director, has in his memoirs devoted eight pages to a description of a performance which he seems to say he imagined, or a performance given by the Society of Art and Literature, of which he was a member. I cannot make out from his book which it was—imagined or actually done—and as he omits to date the performance (or the imaginings), though I believe it was in 1891—twenty years after Irving's—we are unable to know whether these imaginings are original, or are arrived at through suggestions, awakened by hearing someone describe what Irving was like in 1871. He does actually mention Irving by name at the end of the story, but he does it in this way: *"I thought I must have played well, and that I was a tragedian, for the rôle was in the repertoire of such great tragedians as Irving, Barnay, Paul Mounet, and others . . ."* which simply will not do. Stanislavsky has professed all his life *to hate the theatrical in the theatre*. I have heard him say how much he hated it. Well, I believe that an example of the worst part of the "theatrical" is to be found in those six words: *"Irving, Barnay, Paul Mounet, and others."* For even as *La Tosca* will always belong to Bernhardt, *Othello* to Salvini, and *The Miracle* to Reinhardt, so there was only one great actor who interpreted *The Bells*, and to whom it certainly belongs, and that was Irving. If a second actor of the rôle needs to be mentioned . . . it can only be Coquelin; but to refer to Mounet and Barnay is obviously to be caught in the act of drawing a herring rather theatrically across the trail. Yes, it is one of the worst examples of the theatrical (in that word's worst sense) that I know.

Since I have referred to this book by Stanislavsky, I may add that it is full of such examples of this particular form of "theatricalism." For professionals I need not explain further, but to others it is perhaps helpful, if I say that it is a state of mind not utterly separate from the Jesuitical state of mind . . . able to give a subtle representation of anything, it can sometimes give an even more subtle misrepresentation.

That theatrical side, I am sure, Stanislavsky despises in himself—for everyone who knows the man is aware of the nobility in his nature and that he is capable of much generosity, except when bitten by that asp, "the theatrical." Amateurs when bitten often suffer—a professional seems to be inoculated from birth. I have stopped to refer to this, for some day the historian will be puzzled that Stanislavsky should seem so innocent of the immensity of our English actor. Let the historian cease from puzzlement, and know that Stanislavsky was a very good actor, and here he was acting.

I HAVE said that I cannot describe Irving's performance in *The Bells:* but though I cannot describe it (and the whole play was merely a series of variations on one theme— Irving), I will try and put down a few notes of little moments remembered.

At his entrance, the applause was so instantaneous that it became part and parcel of the play—without it, or had it been at all lacking in warmth, one could have grown hypercritical, and delivered oneself of some wise words regarding the evil tendency of applause in a playhouse.

In the Moscow Art Theatre in 1909, applause was nearly always prevented. It was held by Stanislavsky to be something offensive—inartistic—and in no way necessary to theatrical performance. I am entirely in accord with this opinion—it is a good rule, "no applause." Irving is the exception here. In *The Bells,* the hurricane of applause at Irving's entrance was no interruption. It was no boisterous greeting by an excitable race, for a blustering actor—it was something which can only be described as part and parcel of the whole, as right as rain. It was a torrent while it lasted. Power responded to power. This applause was no false note, whereas silence would have been utterly false . . . for though Irving endured and did not accept the applause, he deliberately called it out of the spectators. It was necessary *to them*—not to him: it was something they had to experience, or to be rid of, or rather, released from, before they could exactly take in what he was going to give them.

So then, the applause came down like thunder, as Irving appeared in the door-way with the ordinary cry: "It is I." Now no one has ever been known to hear these words distinctly—they resolved themselves into a single exclamation—the door flung open—the figure is in the room, God knows how—with arms extended, face alight, and this single ejaculation: " 't'sI."

In those days—as in the noble days of the Greek Drama—as in those of the Nō Drama of Japan—an important entrance was to be preceded by suspense, and then to come as a surprise, or like a chapter-heading of some grand old romance: it thrilled, and was intended to thrill.

Do you remember these chapter-headings: *The Shoulder of Athos, The Baldric of Porthos,* and *The Handkerchief of Aramis; A Mousetrap in the Seventeenth Century; On the Utility of Stove Pipes:* they come from a book I need not name—and, *How to get rid of Dormice; The Cemetery of the Château d'If:* do you remember the excitement? Well then—we had reached this state of excitement, of expectancy, of watching, by the time the storm of applause greeted a spectacular entrance on to the stage in these older days.

I can only speak of Irving's entrances, but I believe that with Edmund Kean an entrance was also something to experience.

The *manner of coming on* made it extraordinary with great actors—it was this manner of timing the appearance—measuring its speed and direction—which created a rhythm that was irresistible.

An exit was important too—very important: but the going off of an actor was nothing comparable with the prime importance of his coming on.

To prepare for this entrance in *The Bells,* the entire first fifteen minutes of the play conspired.

The talk all hovered around the thought of the man who was coming, and about other things somehow connected with him.

The storm raging outside the house, the sudden blowing open of a window in the next room, which smashed a whole trayful of crockery and glass as it swung open—the looking at the clock which told of the overdue traveller—the slow, quiet talk which mumbled on—and above all, the queer "hurry music," as it is called, which was astonishingly dramatic: all these things led up to the first point to be made, and made with decision: "Here is the man!" And now watch what he will do—better still, how he will do it—best of all, watch his face and figure, and follow what it is these are hinting at.

Irving once on, the shout of applause going up, he lowers his arms, he lowers his head, he relaxes his force all over, seems to turn it off to an almost dead calm, while the applause rolls on and up. Twice, maybe three times, he, as it were, shifts one foot (his right, I think it was), and by this slight and meaningless gesture a limit is being reckoned to the applause which goes on and on—no other motion except that the foot, in shifting, sends a slight vibration, also without significance, through the whole person before us—and then as the applause dies away, at the first sign of it dying, the actor clips it off by a sudden gesture of awakening from his long and patiently-endured ordeal—flings cap and whip to right and left, and begins to shed his coat, his muffler, as his wife and daughter run to help him off with them.

The story of *The Bells* is this: A man, not by habit or by instinct a murderer, murders a Polish Jew for his money. He needs money—his child is crying in its cradle for food, and by chance this Jew stops at his hut in a storm, and the man sees him undo a belt which, as it clanks on the table, emits the sound of untold riches. This tempts him, he resolves on the deed, and when the Jew, refreshed by his punch and comforted by the warmth, goes on his way through the snow-storm, the man, taking a short cut across the fields, arrives at a cross-road and, hacking him down with an axe, takes the belt full of gold, drags the body to a limekiln, burns it and, now become rich, relieves the want of his household and thereafter lives a blameless life—finally becoming Burgomaster of his village.

But wherever he goes—whoever speaks to him— whatever he sees or hears, even as he stands speaking to someone about ordinary things, there comes to his ears the far-off sound of the sledge-bells of the Polish Jew. Haunted by this, he lives his life in sorrow which increases and increases until one night, dreaming that he is in the dock and being convicted and sentenced to death, he wakes only to die, believing that he is being hanged.

The thing Irving set out to do was to show us the sorrow which slowly and remorselessly beat him down. As, no matter who the human being may be, and what his crime, the sorrow which he suffers must appeal to our hearts, so Irving set out to wring our hearts, not to give us a clever exhibition of antics such as a murderer would be likely to go through. He does not appeal to any silly sentimentality in you—he merely states the case by showing you that quite obviously here is a strong human being who, through a moment of weakness, falls into error and becomes for two hours a criminal—does what he knows he is doing—acts deliberately—but (and here is Irving) acts automatically, as though impelled by an immense force, against which no resistance is possible.

To return to the moment after the first entrance—the process of getting rid of his coat and brushing off the snow as he stands on the mat by the door being over, he works his way down to a chair in the centre (Irving was always in the centre—he had no inferiority complex) and there, taking off his boots, he begins to put on and buckle his shoes.

Now you might think that the act of taking off some boots could be done in one way only—but the way Irving did it had never been thought of till he did it, and has never been done since.

It was, in every gesture, every half move, in the play of his shoulders, legs, head and arms, mesmeric in the highest degree—slowly we were drawn to watch every inch of his work as we are drawn to read and linger on every syllable of a strangely fine writer.

It was the perfection of craftsmanship.

While he is taking off the boots and pulling on the shoes, the men at the table, who are smoking and drinking lazily, are telling in drawling tones that just before he came in, they were saying that they did not remember a night like this since what was called the Polish Jew's winter.

By the time the speaker had got this slowly out—and it was dragged purposely—Irving was buckling his second shoe, seated, and leaning over it, with his two long hands stretched down over the buckles. We suddenly saw these fingers stop their work; the crown of the head suddenly seemed to glitter and become frozen—and then, at the pace of the slowest and most terrified snail, the two hands, still motionless and dead, were seen to be coming up the side of the leg . . . the whole torso of the man, also seeming frozen, was gradually, and by an almost imperceptible movement, seen to be drawing up and back, as it would straighten a little, and to lean a little against the back of the chair on which he was seated.

Once in that position—motionless—eyes fixed ahead of him and fixed on us all—there he sat for the space of ten to twelve seconds, which, I can assure you, seemed to us all like a lifetime, and then said—and said in a voice deep and overwhelmingly beautiful: "Oh, you were talking of that—were you?" And as the last syllable was uttered, there came, afar off, the regular throbbing sound of sledge-bells.

There he sat looking at us, and there sat the others, smoking and musing and comfortably motionless, except for the smoke from their pipes—and on and on went the sound of these bells—on and on and on—nothing else. Again, I assure you that time seemed out of joint, and moved as it moves to us who suffer, when we wish it would move on and it does not stir.

And the next step of his dance began.

He moves his head slowly from us—the eyes still somehow with us—and moves it to the right—taking as long as a long journey to discover a truth takes. He looks to the faces on the right—nothing: slowly the head revolves back again, down, and along the tunnels of thought and sorrow, and at the end the face and eyes are bent upon those to the left of him . . . utter stillness . . . nothing there either—everyone is concerned with his or her little doings—smoking or knitting or unravelling wool or scraping a plate slowly and silently—a long pause, endless, breaking our hearts, comes down over everything, and on and on go these bells. Puzzled, motionless . . . he glides up to a standing position: never has anyone seen another rising figure which slid slowly up like that: with one arm slightly raised, with sensitive hand speaking of far-off apprehended sounds, he asks, in the voice of some woman who is frightened, yet does not wish to frighten those with her: "Don't you . . . don't you hear the sound of sledge-bells on the road?" "Sledge-bells?" grumbles the smoking man; "Sledge-bells?" pipes his companion; "Sledge-bells?" says the wife—all of them seemingly too sleepy and comfortable to apprehend anything . . . see anything . . . or understand . . . and, as they grumble a negative, suddenly he staggers, and shivers from his toes to his neck; his jaws begin to chatter; the hair on his forehead, falling over a little, writhes as though it were a nest of little snakes. Everyone is on his feet at once, to help: "Caught a chill" . . . "Let's get him to bed" . . . and *one* of the moments of the immense and touching dance closes—only one—and the next one begins, and the next after—figure after figure of exquisite pattern and purpose is unfolded, and then closed, and ever a new one unfolded in its wake.

I can write no more; you may perhaps have felt something . . . I don't know—but, if you did, I know it was one thousandth part of what we felt. As we watched this figure, we felt as silent and as still as when we hear of things too sad to realize; and when it was over and we might move, we knew that this was the finest point that the craft of acting could reach.*

*You will say, perhaps, that Irving seems to have explained so much to us that the other characters in the play were daft not to notice too; that a hundred times, by eavesdropping, they might have caught him giving us a full explanation that he was the culprit.

You are quite right. Irving followed the most ancient and unshakable tradition, which says that the Dramatist is to take his audience into his confidence. The actor who fails to observe this fails as an actor. I have seen such actors recently in London. The villain of the play comes on the stage smiling: he is quite alone; and though he remains alone for five minutes, he does not dare to tell us that he is "the villain"—has not dared to let any tell-tale look escape him, and he fails to explain anything to us. It is called realism—it is no such thing: it is merely incompetence—an incapacity to understand that *everything* has to be clearly explained to the spectators, and little or no thought paid to whether the other characters on the stage overhear or see. If they overhear, if they see, they too have failed in the simplest rudiments of their craft.

First performed at the Lyceum Theatre, November 25, 1871

CHARACTERS

Mathias, the burgomaster
Catherine, his wife
Annette, his daughter
Walter
Hans } friends of Mathias
Christian, a gendarme
Sozel, a servant
Dr Zimmer
Notary
Tony
Karl } guests
Fritz
Judge of the court
Clerk of the court
Mesmerist

Villagers, Officers of the Court, Crowd

SCENE ONE

*Interior of a Village Inn in Alsace. Table and chairs, R.; L.
an old-fashioned sideboard, with curious china upon it, and
glasses; door, R.; door, L.; large window at back cut in
scene, R.; large door at back cut in scene, L. A candle or
lamp burns upon the table; a stove at back, R., with kettle
on it; the pipe of stove going off through the wing at R.
The country covered with snow is seen through the window;
snow is falling; a large clock in L. corner, at back—hands
to work. The Inn is the residence of the Burgomaster. It is
Christmas Eve.*

[*Catherine, the Burgomaster's wife, discovered seated at
a spinning wheel, L. Music upon rising of curtain.
Hans passes window; enters through door at back; he
is covered with snow; he carries a gun, and a large
game bag is slung across his shoulders.*]

Hans [*taking off his hat and shaking away the snow*]. More
snow, Madame Mathias, more snow! [*He places his
gun by the stove.*]
Catherine. Still in the village, Hans?
Hans. Yes, on Christmas Eve one may be forgiven some
small indulgence.
Catherine. You know your sack of flour is ready for you at
the mill?
Hans. Oh, yes; but I am not in a hurry. Father Walter
will take charge of it for me in his cart. Now one
glass of wine, madame, and then I'm off. [*He sits at
table, laughing.*]
Catherine. Father Walter still here? I thought he had left
long ago.
Hans. No, no. He is still at the Golden Fleece emptying
his bottle. As I came along, I saw his cart standing

outside the grocer's, with the coffee, the cinnamon, and the sugar, all covered with snow, he, he, he! He is a jolly old fellow. Fond of good wine, and I don't blame him, you may be sure. We shall leave together.

Catherine. And you have no fear of being upset?

Hans. What does it matter? As I said before, on Christmas Eve one may be forgiven some small indulgence.

Catherine. I will lend you a lanthorn when you go. Sozel!

Sozel [*from within*]. Madame!

Catherine. Some wine for Hans!

Sozel. Yes, madame.

Hans. That's the sort. Considering the festive character of weather like this, one really must take something.

Catherine. Yes, but take care, our white wine is very strong.

Hans. Oh, never fear, madame! But, where is our Burgomaster? How is it he is not to be seen? Is he ill?

Catherine. He went to Ribeauville five days ago. [*Enter Sozel, carrying a decanter of white wine and glass; she places it on table.*] Here is the wine, Master Hans. [*Exit Sozel.*]

Hans. Good, good! [*He pours out a glass, and drinks with gusto.*] I wager, now, that the Burgomaster has gone to buy the wine for the wedding.

Catherine [*laughing*]. Not at all improbable.

Hans. Only just now, when I was at the Golden Fleece, it was talked about publicly that the pretty Annette, the daughter of the Burgomaster, and Christian, the Quarter-master of Gendarmes, were going to be married! I could scarcely believe my ears. Christian is certainly a brave man, and an honest man, and a handsome man! I do not wish to maintain anything to the contrary. Our village is rather distinguished in that respect. But he has nothing but his pay to live upon, whilst Annette is the richest match in the village.

Catherine. Do you believe then, Hans, that money ought always to be the one consideration?

Hans. No, no, certainly not—on the contrary. Only, I thought that the Burgomaster—

Catherine. Well, you have been mistaken; Mathias did not even ask, "What have you?" He said at once, "Let Annette give her free consent and I give mine."

Hans. And did she give her free consent?

Catherine. Yes; she loves Christian, and as we have no other thought but the happiness of our child, we do not look for wealth.

Hans. Oh, if the Burgomaster consents and you consent and Annette consents, why, I suppose I cannot refuse my consent either. Only, I may make this observation: I think Christian a very lucky dog, and I wish I was in his place!

[*Music. Enter Annette.*]

Annette. Good evening, Hans! [*Music ceases.*]

Hans. Ah, it is you. Good evening! Good evening! We were just talking about you!

Annette. About me!

Hans. Yes! Oh, oh! How smiling you look, and how prettily dressed; one would almost think that you were going to a wedding.

Annette. Ah, you are always joking.

Hans. No, no, I am not joking! I say what I think, that's all! That pretty cap, and that pretty dress, and those pretty shoes were not put on for the pleasure of a tough middle-aged forest-keeper like myself. It has been all arranged for another—for another I say, and I know who that particular "another" happens to be—he, he, he!

Annette [*blushing*]. How can you talk such nonsense!

Hans. Oh, yes, it is nonsense to say that you are fascinating, merry, good and pretty, no doubt; and it is nonsense to say that the particular another I refer to— you know the one I mean—the tall one with the handsome moustaches, is a fellow to be envied. Yes, it is nonsense to say it, for I for one do not envy him at all—no, not at all!

[*Father Walter has passed the window, now opens door at back and puts his head in. Annette turns to look at him.*]

Father Walter [*laughing and coming in—he is covered with snow*]. Ah, she turned her head! It's not he you expect!

Annette. Who, Father Walter?

Walter. Ha, ha, ha! That's right. Up to the last minute she will pretend that she knows nothing.

Annette. I do not understand what you mean.

[*Walter and Hans both laugh.*]

Catherine. You are a couple of old fools!

Walter [*still laughing*]. You're not such an old fool as you look, are you, Hans?

Hans. No; and you don't look such an old fool as you are, do you, Walter?

[*Enter Sozel with a lighted lanthorn, which she places upon the sideboard; then exits.*]

Walter. No. What is the meaning of that lanthorn?

Hans. Why, to act as a light for the cart.

Annette. You can go by moonlight!

Walter. Yes, yes; certainly we will go by the light of the moon! Let us empty a glass in honour of the young couple. [*They fill glasses.*] Here's to the health of Christian and Annette! [*They drink—Hans taking a long time in drinking the contents of his glass, and then heaving a deep sigh, and music commences.*]

Walter. And now listen, Annette; as I entered I saw Christian returning with two gendarmes, and I am sure that in a quarter of an hour—

Annette. Listen! [*Wind off.*]

Catherine. The wind is rising. I hope that Mathias is not now on the road!

Annette. No, no, it is Christian!

[*Music, forte. Christian passes the window, enters the door at back, covered with snow.*]

All. Christian! [*Music ceases.*]

Christian. Good evening, all. [*Annette runs to him.*] Good evening, Annette.

Annette. Where have you come from, Christian?

Christian. From the Hôvald! From the Hôvald! What a snow-storm! I have seen many in Auvergne or the Pyrenees, but never anything like this. [*He sits by the stove, and warms his hands. After hanging up his hat, Annette goes out and returns with a jug of wine, which she places upon the stove.*]

Walter. There, look at that! What care she takes of him! It would not be for us that she would fetch the sugar and the cinnamon and warm the wine.

Christian [*laughing*]. Do not allow me, Annette, to be crushed by the satire of Father Walter, who knows how to defy the wind and the snow by the side of a good fire. I should like to see the figure he would present if he had been five hours on duty as I have been in the snow on the Hôvald.

Catherine. You have been five hours in the snow, Christian! Your duties must be terribly severe.

Christian. How can it be helped? At two o'clock we received information that smugglers had passed the river the previous night with tobacco and gunpowder; so we were bound to be off at once. [*Music.*]

Annette. Drink this, Christian; it will warm you.

Christian. Thank you, Annette. Ah! that's good!

Walter. The Quarter-master is not difficult to please. [*Music ceases.*]

Catherine. Never mind. Christian, you are fortunate to have arrived this early. [*Wind heard off.*] Listen to the wind! I hope that Mathias will have the prudence to stop for shelter somewhere on the road. [*To Hans and Walter.*] I was right, you see, in advising you to go; you would now have been safely at home.

Hans [*laughing*]. Annette was the cause of our stopping. Why did she blow out the lanthorn?

Annette. Oh, you were glad enough to stop!

Christian. Your winters are very severe here.

Walter. Oh, not every year, Quarter-master! For fifteen years we have not had a winter so severe as this.

Hans. No—I do not remember to have seen so much snow since what is called "The Polish Jew's Winter." In that year the Schnieberg was covered in the first days of November, and the frost lasted till the end of March.

Christian. And for that reason it is called "The Polish Jew's Winter"?

Walter. No—it is for another and terrible reason, which none of us will ever forget. Madame Mathias remembers it well, I am sure.

Catherine [*solemnly*]. You are right, Walter, you are right.

Hans. Had you been here at that time, Quarter-master, you might have won your cross.

Christian. How?

Walter. I can tell you all about this affair from the beginning to the end, since I saw it nearly all myself. Curiously enough, it was this very day, just fifteen years ago, that I was seated at this very table. There was Mathias, who sat there, and who had only

bought his mill just six months before; there was old
John Roebec, who sat there—they used to call him
"the Little Shoemaker"—and several others, who are
now sleeping under the turf—we shall all go there
some day! Happy are those who have nothing upon
their conscience! We were just beginning a game of
cards, when, just as the old clock struck ten, the
sound of horse bells was heard; a sledge stopped
before the door, and almost immediately afterwards
a Polish Jew entered. He was a well-made, vigorous
man, between forty and fifty years of age. I fancy
I can see him even now entering at that door with his
green cloak and his fur cap, his large black beard
and his great boots covered with hare skin. He was a
seed merchant. He said as he came in, "Peace be with
you!" Everybody turned to look at him, and thought,
"Where has he come from? What does he want?"
Because you must know that the Polish Jews who
come to dispose of seed do not arrive in this province
till the month of February. Mathias said to him,
"What can I do for you?" But the Jew, without re-
plying, first opened his cloak, and then unbuckled a
girdle which he wore round his waist. This he threw
upon the table, and we all heard the ringing sound
of the gold it contained. Then he said, "The snow
is deep; the road difficult; put my horse in the stable.
In one hour I shall continue my journey." After that
he drank his wine without speaking to anyone, and
sat like a man depressed, and who is anxious about
his affairs. At eleven o'clock the Night Watchman
came in. Everyone went his way, and the Jew was
left alone!

[*Chord of Music—loud gust of wind—crash of glass off
—hurry. All start to their feet. Music continued.*]

Catherine. What has happened? I must go and see.

Annette. Oh! no, you must not go!

Catherine. I will return immediately. Don't be alarmed.
[*Exit Catherine.*]

Christian. But I do not yet see how I could have gained
the cross in this affair—

Walter. Stop a minute. The next morning they found the
Jew's horse dead under the Bridge of Vechem, and a
hundred yards further on, the green cloak and the

fur cap, deeply stained with blood. As to what became of the Jew himself has never to this day been discovered. [*Music ceases.*]

Hans. Everything that Walter has stated is strictly true. The gendarmes came here the next morning, notwithstanding the snow; and, in fact, it is since that dreadful time that the brigade has been established here.

Christian. But was no inquiry instituted?

Hans. Inquiry! I should think there was. It was the former Quarter-master, Kelz, who undertook the case. How he travelled about! What witnesses he badgered! What clues he discovered! What information and reports were written! and how the coat and the cap were analysed, and examined by magistrates and doctors!— but it all came to nothing!

Christian. But, surely, suspicion fell on someone.

Hans. Oh, of course, the gendarmes are never at a loss for suspicions in such cases. But proofs are required. About that time, you see, there were two brothers living in the village who had an old bear, with his ears all torn, two big dogs, and a donkey, that they took about with them to the fairs, and made the dogs bait the bear. This brought them a great deal of money; and they lived a rollicking, dissipated life. When the Jew disappeared, they happened to be at Vechem; suspicions fastened upon them, and the report was that they had caused the Jew to be eaten by the dogs and the bear, and that they only refrained from swallowing the cloak and cap because they had had enough. They were arrested, and it would have gone hard with the poor devils, but Mathias interested himself in their case, and they were discharged, after being in prison fifteen months. That was the specimen of suspicion of the case.

Christian. What you have told me greatly astonishes me. I never heard a word of this before.

[*Re-enter Catherine.*]

Catherine. I was sure that Sozel had left the windows in the kitchen open. Now every pane of glass in them is broken. [*To Christian.*] Fritz is outside. He wishes to speak with you.

Christian. Fritz, the gendarme!

Catherine. Yes, I asked him to come in, but he would not.
It is upon some matter of duty.

Christian. Ah! good, I know what it is!

Annette. You will return, Christian?

Christian. In a few minutes. [*Music to take him off. Exit.*]

Walter. Ah! there goes a brave young fellow—gentle in
character, I will admit, but not a man to trifle with
rogues.

Hans. Yes, Mathias is fortunate in finding so good a son-
in-law; but everything has succeeded with Mathias
for the last fifteen years. [*Music commences.*] He was
comparatively poor then, and now he is one of the
richest men in the village, and the Burgomaster. He
was born under a lucky star.

Walter. Well, and he deserves all the success he has
achieved.

Catherine. Hark!

Annette. It is, perhaps, Christian returning as he promised.

[*Hurry. Mathias passes the window, then enters; he wears
a long cloak covered with snow, large cap made of
otter's skin, gaiters and spurs, and carries a large
riding whip in his hand—chord—tableau.*]

Mathias. It is I—It is I! [*Music ceases.*]

Catherine [*rising*]. Mathias!

Hans }
Walter }   [*starting up*]. The Burgomaster!

Annette [*running and embracing him*]. At last you have
come.

Mathias. Yes, yes! Heaven be praised! What a snow-storm.
I was obliged to leave the carriage at Vechem. It will
be brought over tomorrow.

Catherine [*embracing him and taking off his coat*]. Let me
take this off for you. It was very kind of you not to
stop away. We were becoming so anxious about
you.

Mathias. So I thought, Catherine; and that was the reason
I determined to reach home tonight. [*Looking round.*]
Ha, ha! Father Walter and Hans, you will have nice
weather in which to go home. [*He takes off his hat,
etc., and gives them to his wife and daughter.*] There!
You will have to get all those things dried.

Catherine. Sozel, get ready your master's supper at once,
and tell Nickel to take the horse to the stable!

Sozel [*within*]. Yes, madame.

Annette. We thought perhaps that your cousin Bôth would have detained you.

Mathias [*unbuttoning his gaiters*]. Oh, I had finished all my business yesterday morning, and I wished to come away; but Bôth made me stop to see a performance in the town.

Annette. A performance! Is Punchinello at Ribeauville?

Mathias. No, it was not Punchinello. It was a Parisian who did extraordinary tricks. He sent people to sleep.

Annette. Sent people to sleep!

Mathias. Yes.

Catherine. He gave them something to drink, no doubt.

Mathias. No; he simply looked at them and made signs, and they went fast asleep.—It certainly was an astonishing performance. If I had not myself seen it I should never have believed it.

Hans. Ah! the Brigadier Stenger was telling me about it the other day. He had seen the same thing at Saverne. This Parisian sends people to sleep, and when they are asleep he makes them tell him everything that weighs upon their consciences.

Mathias. Exactly. Annette?

Annette. What, father?

Mathias. Look in the big pocket of my cloak. [*Enter Sozel.*] Sozel! take these gaiters and spurs; hang them in the stable with the harness.

Sozel. Yes, Burgomaster. [*Exit.*]

[*Annette, who has taken a small box out of the pocket of the cloak, approaches her father. Music.*]

Annette. What is it, father?

Mathias. Open the box.

[*She opens the box, and takes out a handsome Alsatian hat, with gold and silver stars upon it—the others approach to look at it.*]

Annette. Oh, how pretty! Is it for me?

Mathias. For whom else could it be? Not for Sozel, I fancy.

[*Annette puts on the hat after taking off her ribbon, and looks at herself in glass on sideboard—all express admiration.*]

Annette. Oh! What will Christian say?

Mathias. He will say you are the prettiest girl in the province.

Annette [*kissing her father*]. Thank you, dear father. How good you are!

Mathias. It is my wedding present, Annette. The day of your marriage I wish you to wear it, and to preserve it for ever. In fifteen or twenty years hence, will you remember your father gave it you?

Annette [*with emotion*]. Yes, dear father!

Mathias. All that I wish is to see you happy with Christian. [*Music ceases.*] And now for supper and some wine. [*To Walter and Hans.*] You will stop and take a glass of wine with me?

Walter. With pleasure, Burgomaster.

Hans. For you, Burgomaster, we will try and make that little effort.

[*Sozel has entered with tray of supper and wine which she has placed upon table. Mathias now sits at table, helps wine, and then commences to eat with a good appetite. Sozel draws the curtains across window at back, and exits.*]

Mathias. There is one advantage about the cold. It gives you a good appetite. Here's to your health! [*He drinks.*]

Walter. ⎫ Here's yours, Burgomaster! ⎧[*They touch glasses*
Hans.   ⎭   ⎩*and drink.*]

Mathias. Christian has not been here this evening?

Annette. Yes; they came to fetch him, but he will return presently.

Mathias. Ah! Good! good!

Catherine. He came late today, in consequence of some duty he had to perform in the Hôvald, in the capture of smugglers.

Mathias. Nice weather for such a business. By the side of the river, I found the snow five feet deep.

Walter. Yes; we were talking about that. We were telling the Quarter-master that since the "Polish Jew's Winter" we had never seen weather like this.

[*Mathias, who was raising the glass to his lips, places it on the table again without drinking.*]

Mathias. Ah! you were talking of that? [*Distant sound of Bells heard. To himself—"Bells! Bells!" His whole aspect changes, and he leaves off eating, and sits listening. The Bells continue louder.*]

Hans. That winter, you remember, Burgomaster, the whole valley was covered several feet deep with snow, and it was a long time before the horse of the Polish Jew could be dug out.

Mathias [*with indifference*]. Very possibly; but that tale is too old! It is like an old woman's story now, and is thought about no more. [*Watching them and starting up.*] Do you not hear the sound of Bells upon the road? [*The Bells still go on.*]

Hans }
Walter } [*listening*]. Bells? No!

Catherine. What is the matter, Mathias? You appear ill. You are cold; some warm wine will restore you. The fire in the stove is low; come, Annette, we will warm your father his wine in the kitchen. [*Exeunt Catherine and Annette.*]

Mathias. Thank you; it is nothing.

Walter. Come, Hans, let us go and see to the horse. At the same time, it is very strange that it was never discovered who did the deed.

Mathias. The rogues have escaped, more's the pity. Here's your health! [*Music.*]

Walter. }
Hans. } Thank you!

Hans. It is just upon the stroke of ten! [*They drink, and go out together.*]

Mathias [*alone—comes forward and listens with terror. Music with frequent chords*]. Bells! Bells! [*He runs to the window and, slightly drawing the curtains, looks out.*] No one on the road. What is this jangling in my ears? What is tonight? Ah, it is the very night—the very hour! [*Clock strikes ten.*] I feel a darkness coming over me. [*Stage darkens.*] A sensation of giddiness seizes me. [*He staggers to chair.*] Shall I call for help? No, no, Mathias. Have courage! The Jew is dead!

[*Sinks on chair; the Bells come closer; then the back of the Scene rises and sinks, disclosing the Bridge of Vechem, with the snow-covered country and frozen rivulet; lime-kiln burning in the distance. The Jew is discovered seated in sledge dressed as described in speech in Act I; the horse carrying Bells; the Jew's face is turned away. The snow is falling fast; the scene is seen through a gauze; limelight. Vision of a man dressed in a brown blouse and hood over his head, carrying an axe; stands in an attitude of following the sledge. When the picture is fully disclosed the Bells cease.]*

Mathias [his back to scene]. Oh, it is nothing. It is the wine and cold that have overcome me! *[He rises and turns; goes up stage; starts violently upon seeing the vision before him. At the same time the Jew in the sledge suddenly turns his face, which is ashy pale, and fixes his eyes sternly upon him. Mathias utters a prolonged cry of terror, and falls senseless. Hurried Music.]*

SCENE ONE

Best Room in the Burgomaster's House. Door, L.; door, R.; three large windows at back, looking out upon a street of the village, the church and the buildings covered with snow. Large stove in the centre of room, practicable door to stove, tongs in grate; armchair near the stove; at L. (1st grooves) an old escritoire; near L., a table and arm-chair; chairs about room. It is morning; the room and street bright with sunlight.

[*As the Curtain rises to Music, Mathias is discovered seated in armchair at table; Catherine and Doctor Zimmer standing at back of stove contemplating him. They advance.*]

Doctor. You feel better, Burgomaster?
Mathias. Yes, I am quite well.
Doctor. No more pains in the head?
Mathias. No.
Doctor. No more strange noises in the ears?
Mathias. When I tell you that I am quite well—that I never was better—that is surely enough.
Catherine. For a long time he has had bad dreams. He talks in his sleep, and his thirst at night is constant, and feverish.
Mathias. Is there anything extraordinary in being thirsty during the night?
Doctor. Certainly not: but you must take more care of yourself. You drink too much white wine, Burgomaster. Your attack of the night before last arose from this cause. You had taken too much wine at your cousin's, and then the severe cold having seized you, the blood had flown to the head.

Mathias. I *was* cold, but that stupid gossip about the Polish Jew was the cause of all.

Doctor. How was that?

Mathias. Well, you must know, when the Jew disappeared, they brought me the cloak and cap that had belonged to the poor devil, and the sight of them quite upset me, remembering he had, the night before, stopped at our house. Since that time I had thought no more of the matter until the night before last, when some gossip brought the affair again to my mind. It was as if I had seen the ghost of the Jew. We all know that there are no such things, but—[*suddenly to his wife*] Have you sent for the Notary?

Catherine. Yes; but you must be calm.

Mathias. I am calm. But Annette's marriage must take place at once. When a man in robust health and strength is liable to such an attack as I have had, nothing should be postponed till the morrow. What occurred to me the night before last might again occur tonight. I might not survive the second blow, and then I should not have seen my dear children happy. And now leave me. Whether it was the wine, or the cold, or the gossip about the Polish Jew, it comes to the same thing. It is all past and over now.

Doctor. But, perhaps, Burgomaster, it would be better to adjourn the signing of the marriage contract for a few days. It is an affair of so much interest and importance that the agitation might—

Mathias [*angrily*]. Good heavens, why will not people attend to their own business! I was ill; you bled me—am well again—so much the better. Let the Notary be sent for at once. Let Father Walter and Hans be summoned as witnesses, and let the whole affair be finished without further delay.

Doctor [*to Catherine, aside*]. His nerves are still very much shaken. Perhaps it will be better to let him have his own way. [*To Mathias.*] Well, well, we'll say no more about it. Only don't forget what I have said—be careful of the white wine.

Mathias [*angrily striking the table, turning his back*]. Good! Good! Ah!

[*The doctor looks with pity towards him, bows to Cath-*

erine, and exits. The church bell commences to ring.
Music.]

Catherine. Annette! Annette!

Annette [*off*]. I am coming.

Catherine [*impatiently*]. Be quick. Be quick.

Annette. Directly—directly!

Mathias. Don't hurry the poor child. You know that she is dressing.

Catherine. But I don't take two hours to dress.

Mathias. You; oh! that is different. She expects Christian. He was to have been here this morning. Something has detained him.

[*Enter Annette; she is in gala dress, and wears the golden heart upon her breast, and the hat given her by Mathias in Act I.*]

Catherine. At last, you are ready!

Annette. Yes, I am ready.

Mathias [*with affection*]. How beautiful you look, Annette.

Annette. You see, dear father, I have put on the hat.

Mathias. You did right—you did right.

Catherine [*impatiently*]. Are you not coming, Annette? The service will have commenced. Come, come.

Annette. Christian has not yet been here.

Mathias. No, you may be sure some business detains him.

Catherine. Do come, Annette; you will see Christian by and by. [*Exit, Annette is following.*]

Mathias. Annette, Annette! Have you nothing to say to me?

[*Annette runs to him, and kisses him—he embraces her with affection.*]

Annette. You know, dear father, how much I love you.

Mathias. Yes, yes. There, go now, dear child; your mother is impatient.

[*Exit Annette. The villagers, men and women in Sunday clothes, pass the window in couples. Mathias goes up and looks through the window, Annette and Catherine pass and kiss hands to him—a woman in the group says, "Good morning, Burgomaster." Church bells cease. Music ceases.*]

Mathias. All goes well! Luckily all is over. But what a lesson, Mathias—what a lesson! Would anyone believe that the mere talk about the Jew could bring on such a fit? Fortunately the people about here are such idiots they suspect nothing. But it was that Parisian fellow at the fair who was the real cause of all. The rascal had really made me nervous. When he wanted to send me to sleep as well as the others, I said to myself, "Stop, stop, Mathias—this sending you to sleep may be an invention of the devil, you might relate certain incidents in your past life! You must be cleverer than that, Mathias; you mustn't run your neck into a halter; you must be cleverer than that— ah! you must be cleverer than that." You will die an old man yet, Mathias, and the most respected in the Province—only this, since you dream and are apt to talk in your dreams, for the future you will sleep alone in the room above, the door locked, and the key safe in your pocket. They say walls have ears— let them hear me as much as they please. [*Music. Takes bunch of keys out of his pocket.*] And now to count the dowry of Annette, to be given to our dear son-in-law, in order that our dear son-in-law may love us. [*He crosses, unlocks the escritoire, takes out a large leather bag, unties it and empties the contents, consisting of gold pieces and rouleaux, upon the table.*] Thirty thousand francs. [*He sits at table and commences to count the money.*] Thirty thousand francs—a fine dowry for Annette. Ah! it is pleasant to hear the sound of gold! A fine dowry for the husband of Annette. He's a clever fellow, is Christian. He's not a Kelz—half deaf and half blind; no, no—he's a clever fellow, is Christian, and quite capable of getting on a right track. [*A pause.*] The first time I saw him I said to myself, "You shall be my son-in-law, and if anything should be discovered, you will defend me." [*Continues to count, weighing piece upon his finger—takes up a piece and examines it.*] A piece of old gold! [*Looks at it more closely—starts.*] Ah! that came from the girdle; not for them—no, no, not for them, for me. [*Places the piece of gold in his waistcoat pocket—he goes to the escritoire, opens a drawer, takes out another piece of gold and throws it upon the table in substitution.*] That girdle did us a good turn—without it—without it we were ruined. If Catherine only knew—poor, poor Catherine. [*He sobs—*his head sinks on his breast. Music ceases— the Bells heard off; he starts.*] The Bells! the Bells again! They must come from the mill. [*Rushes across to door, calling.*] Sozel! Sozel, I say, Sozel! [*Enter Sozel holding an open book; she is in her Sunday dress.*] Is there anyone at the mill?

Sozel. No, Burgomaster. They have all gone to church and the wheel is stopped.

Mathias. Don't you hear the sound of Bells?

Sozel. No Burgomaster, I hear nothing. [*The Bells cease.*]

Mathias [*aside*]. Strange—strange. [*Rudely.*] What were you doing?

Sozel. I was reading, Burgomaster.

Mathias. Reading—what? Ghost stories, no doubt.

Sozel. Oh, no, Burgomaster! I was reading such a curious story, about a band of robbers being discovered after twenty-three years had passed, and all through the blade of an old knife having been found in a black-smith's shop, hidden under some rusty iron. They captured the whole of them, consisting of the mother, two sons, and the grandfather, and they hanged them all in a row. Look, Burgomaster, there's the picture. [*Shows book—he strikes it violently out of her hand.*]

Mathias. Enough, enough! It's pity you have nothing better to do. There, go—go! [*Exit Sozel. Seats himself at the table and puts remaining money into the bag.*] The fools!—not to destroy all evidence against them. To be hanged through the blade of an old knife. Not like that—not like that am *I* to be caught!

[*Music—sprightly military air. Christian passes at back, stops at centre window and taps upon it. Mathias looks round with a start, is reassured upon seeing who it is, and says, "Ah, it is Christian!"—he ties up the bag and places it in the escritoire. Christian enters. Mathias meets him half way—they shake hands. Music ceases. Christian is in full dress of a Quarter-master of Gendarmes.*]

Christian. Good morning, Burgomaster; I hope you are better.

Mathias. Oh, yes, I am well, Christian. I have just been counting Annette's dowry, in good sounding gold. It was a pleasure to me to do so, as it recalled to me the days gone by, when by industry and good fortune I had been enabled to gain it; and I thought that in the future my children would enjoy and profit by all that I had so acquired.

Christian. You are right, Burgomaster. Money gained by honest labour is the only profitable wealth. It is the good seed which in time is sure to bring a rich harvest.

Mathias. Yes, yes; especially when the good seed is sown in good ground. The contract must be signed today.

Christian. Today?

Mathias. Yes, the sooner the better. I hate postponements. Once decided, why adjourn the business? It shows a great want of character.

Christian. Well, Burgomaster, nothing to me could be more agreeable.

Mathias. Annette loves you.

Christian. Ah, she does.

Mathias. And the dowry is ready—then why should not the affair be settled at once? I hope, my boy, you will be satisfied.

Christian. You know, Burgomaster, I do not bring much.

Mathias. You bring courage and good conduct—I will take care of the rest; and now let us talk of other matters. You are late today. I suppose you were busy. Annette waited for you, and was obliged to go without you. [*He goes up and sits by stove in armchair, opens stove door, takes up tongs and arranges fire.*]

Christian [*unbuckling his sword and sitting in chair*]. Ah, it was a very curious business that detained me. Would you believe it, Burgomaster, I was reading old depositions from five o'clock till ten? The hours flew by, but the more I read the more I wished to read.

Mathias. And what was the subject of the depositions?

Christian. They were about the case of the Polish Jew who was murdered on the Bridge of Vechem fifteen years ago.

Mathias [*dropping the tongs*]. Ah!

Christian. Father Walter told me the story the night before last. It seems to me very remarkable that nothing was ever discovered.

Mathias. No doubt—no doubt.

Christian. The man who commited that murder must have been a clever fellow.

Mathias. Yes, he was not a fool.

Christian. A fool! He would have made one of the cleverest gendarmes in the department.

Mathias [*with a smile*]. Do you really think so?

Christian. I am sure of it. There as so many ways of detecting criminals, and so few escape, that to have committed a crime like this, and yet to remain undiscovered, showed the possession of extraordinary address.

Mathis. I quite agree with you, Christian; and what you say shows your good sense. When a man has committed a crime, and by it gained money, he becomes like a gambler, and tries his second and his third throw. I should think it requires a great amount of courage to resist the first success in crime.

Christian. You are right, but what is most remarkable to me in the case is this, that no trace of the murdered man was ever found. Now do you know what my idea is?

Mathias [*rising*]. No, no! What is your idea?

Christian. Well, I find at that time there were a great many lime-kilns in the neighbourhood of Vechem. Now it is my idea that the murderer, to destroy all traces of his crime, threw the body of the Jew into one of these kilns. Old Kelz, my predecessor, evidently never thought of that.

Mathias. Very likely—very likely. Do you know that idea never occurred to me? You are the first who ever suggested it.

Christian. And this idea leads to many others. Now suppose—suppose inquiry had been instituted as to those persons who were burning lime at that time.

Mathias. Take care, Christian—take care. Why, I myself had a lime-kiln burning at the time the crime was committed.

Christian [*laughing*]. Oh, you, Burgomaster!

[*Mathias laughs heartily. Annette and Catherine pass the window.*]

Annette [*as she passes the window before entering*]. He is there!

[*Enter Annette and Catherine.*]

Mathias. Is the Notary here?

Catherine. Yes, he is in the next room with Father Walter
    and Hans, and the others. He is reading the contract
    to them now.

Mathias. Good—good!

Christian. Oh, Annette, how that pretty hat becomes you!

Annette. Yes; it was dear father who gave it to me.
    [*Music.*]

Christian. It is today, Annette.

Annette. Yes, Christian, it is today.

Mathias. Well; you know what is customary when father,
    mother, and all consent.

Christian. What, Burgomaster?

Mathias [*smiling*]. You embrace your intended wife.

Christian. Is that so, Annette?

Annette. I don't know, Christian. [*He kisses her forehead,
    and leads her up to stove, talking.*]

Mathias. Look at our children, Catherine; how happy they
    are! When I think that we were once as happy! It's
    true; yes, it's true, we were once as happy as they
    are now! Why are you crying, Catherine? Are you
    sorry to see our children happy?

Catherine. No, no, Mathias; these are tears of joy, and I
    can't help them. [*Throws herself upon Mathias' shoul-
    der. Music ceases.*]

Mathias. And now to sign the contract! [*Crosses to door
    and throws it open.*] Walter, Hans, come in! Let
    everyone present come in! The most important acts in
    life should always take place in the presence of all.
    It is an old and honest custom of Alsace. [*Music—
    "The Lauterbach," played forte.*]

[*Enter Hans with two girls on his arm—Father Walter
    with two girls—men and women villagers arm-in-arm
    —they wear ribbons in their button-holes—the notary
    with papers—Sozel. The men wear their hats through
    the whole scene. Mathias advances and shakes hands
    with the Notary and conducts him to table on which is
    spread out the contract—pen and ink on table. The
    company fill the stage in groups.*

Notary. Gentlemen and witnesses—You have just heard
    read the marriage contract between Christian Bême,
    Quarter-master of Gendarmes, and Annette Mathias.

Has anyone any observations to make?

Several voices. No, no.

Notary. Then we can at once proceed to take the signatures.

Mathias [*goes to the escitoire and takes out the bag of gold which he places on the table before the notary*]. There is the dowry. It is not in promises made on paper, but in gold. Thirty thousand francs in good French gold.

All. Thirty thousand francs!

Christian. It is too much, Burgomaster.

Mathias. Not at all, not at all. When Catherine and myself are gone there will be more. And now, Christian —[*music commences*]—I wish you to make me one promise.

Christian. What promise?

Mathias. Young men are ambitious. It is natural they should be. You must promise me that you will remain in this village while both of us live. [*Takes Catherine's hand.*] You know Annette is our only child; we love her dearly, and to lose her altogether would break our hearts. Do you promise?

Christian [*looks to Annette; she returns a glance of approval*]. I do promise.

Mathias. Your word of honour, given before all?

Christian. My word of honour, given before all. [*They shake hands. Music ceases.*]

Mathias [*aside*]. It was necessary. And now to sign the contract. [*He goes to table; the notary hands him the pen, and points to the place where he is to sign his name. Mathias is about to write. The Bells heard off. Mathias stops, listens with terror—his face to the audience, and away from the persons upon the stage—aside.*] Bells! Courage, Mathias! [*After an effort he signs rapidly—the Bells cease—he throws the pen down.*] Come, Christian, sign! [*Christian approaches the table to sign —as he is about to do so Walter taps him on the shoulder. Mathias starts at the interruption.*]

Walter. It is not every day you sign a contract like that.

[*All laugh. Mathias heaves a sigh and is reassured. Christian signs—the notary hands the pen to Catherine, who makes her cross—she then takes Annette to table, who signs her name. Catherine kisses her affectionate-*

    ly and gives her to Christian.]

Mathias [*aside*]. And now should the Jew return to this
    world, Christian must drive him back again. [*Aloud.*]
    Come, come, just one waltz and then dinner.

Walter. Stop! stop! Before we go we must have the song
    of the betrothal.

All. Yes, yes, Annette! Annette! the song of the betrothal.

       Song, Annette. Air—"The Lauterbach"

        Suitors of wealth and high degree,
          In style superbly grand,
        Tendered their love on bended knee
          And sought to win my hand.

[*Tyrolienne by all, and waltz.*]

        But a soldier brave came to woo.
          No maid such love could spurn—
        Proving his heart was fond and true,
          Won my love in return.

[*Tyrolienne as before by all, and waltz. Mathias is seated—
    in the midst of the waltz Bells are heard off. Mathias
    starts up and rushes into the midst of the waltzers.*]

Mathias. The Bells! The Bells!

Catherine. Are you mad?

[*Mathias seizes her by the waist and waltzes wildly with
    her.*]

Mathias. Ring on! Ring on! Houp! Houp!

[*Music, forte—while the waltz is at its height the drop
    falls.*]

SCENE ONE

Bedroom in the Burgomaster's House. The whole back of Scene painted on a gauze; alcove on left; door, R.; two windows at back; small table by bed; chair, L. Night.

[*Music—Enter Mathias, Father Walter, Hans, Christian, Annette, and Catherine; Sozel carrying a lighted candle, bottle of water and glass, which she places on table. They enter suddenly; the men appear to be slightly excited by wine.*]

Hans [*laughing*]. Ha, ha! Everything has gone off admirably. We only wanted something to wind up with, and I may say that we are all as capitally wound up as the great clock at Strasbourg.

Walter. Yes, and what wine we have consumed! For many a day we shall remember the signing of Annette's marriage contract. I should like to witness such a contract every second day.

Hans. There I object to your argument. Every day, I say!

Christian. And so you are determined, Mathias, to sleep here tonight?

Mathias. Yes, I am decided. I wish for air. I know what is necessary for my condition. The heat was the cause of my accident. This room is cooler, and will prevent its recurrence.

[*Laughter heard outside.*]

Hans. Listen, how they are still revelling! Come, Father Walter, let us rejoin the revels!

Walter. But Mathias already deserts us, just at the moment when we were beginning to thoroughly enjoy ourselves.

Mathias. What more do you wish me to do? From noon till midnight is surely enough!

Walter. Enough, it may be, but not too much; never too much of such wine.

Hans. There again, I object to your argument—never enough, I say.

Catherine. Mathias is right. You remember that Doctor Zimmer told him to be careful of the wine he took, or it would one day play him false. He has already taken too much since this morning.

Mathias. One glass of water before I go to rest is all I require. It will calm me—it will calm me.

[*Karl, Fritz and Tony, three of the guests of the previous Act, enter suddenly, slightly merry, pushing each other.*]

Guests. Goodnight, Burgomaster, Goodnight.

Tony. I say, Hans! don't you know that the Night Watchman is below?

Hans. The Night Watchman! What in the name of all that is political does he want?

Karl. He requires us all to leave, and the house to be closed. It is past hours.

Mathias. Give him a bumper of wine, and then goodnight all!

Walter. Past hours! For a Burgomaster no regulations ought to exist.

Hans. } Certainly not.
Others. }

Mathias [*with fierceness*]. Regulations made for all must be obeyed by all.

Walter [*timidly*]. Well, then, shall we go?

Mathias. Yes, yes, go! Leave me to myself.

Catherine. Don't thwart his wish. Follow his directions.

Walter [*shaking hands with Mathias*]. Goodnight, Mathias. I wish you calm repose, and no unpleasant dreams.

Mathias [*fiercely*]. I never dream. [*Mildly.*] Goodnight, all. Go, friends, go. [*Music. Exeunt Walter, Hans, and the three guests, saying, "Goodnight, Burgomaster." Catherine, Annette and Christian remain.*] Goodnight, Catherine. [*Embracing her.*] I shall be better here. The wine, the riot, those songs have quite dazed my brain. I shall sleep better here; I shall sleep better.

Christian. Yes, this room is fresh and cool. Goodnight.

Mathias. The same to you, Christian; the same to you. [*They shake hands.*]

Annette [*running to her father and kissing him*]. Good-
night, dear father; may you sleep well!
Mathias [*kissing her with affection*]. Goodnight, dear child;
do not fear for me—do not fear. [*Music Exeunt all but
Mathias. Music ceases. He goes up cautiously, locks
the door, and puts the key in his pocket.*] At last I
am alone! Everything goes well. Christian the gendarme is caught! Tonight I shall sleep without a fear
haunting me! If any new danger should threaten the
father-in-law of the Quarter-master, it would soon be
averted. Ah! What a power it is to know how to guide
your destiny in life. You must hold good cards in
your hands. Good cards! as I have done, and if you
play them well you may defy ill fortune.
Chorus of Revellers outside [*without accompaniment*].

Now, since we must part, let's drain a last glass;
    Let's drink!
Let us first drink to this gentle young lass:
    Let's drink!
From drinking this toast, we'll none of us shrink;
Others shall follow, when we've time to think.
    Our burden shall be, let us drink!
    The burden to bear is good drink.

[*Loud laughter heard outside.*]
Mathias [*taking off his coat*]. Ha, ha, ha! Those jolly topers
have got all they want. What holes in the snow they
will make before they reach their homes! Drink!
Drink! Is it not strange? To drink and drown every
remorse! Yes, everything goes well! [*He drinks a glass
of water.*] Mathias, you can at least boast of having
well managed your affairs—the contract signed—rich
—prosperous—respected—happy! [*Takes off waistcoat.*] No one now will hear you, if you dream. No
one! No more folly!—no more Bells! Tonight I
triumph; for conscience is at rest!
[*He enters the alcove. The Chorus of Revellers heard again
in the distance. A hand is extended from alcove and
extinguishes the candle—stage dark. Curtain at back
of gauze rises, disclosing an extensive set of a Court of
Justice, arched, brilliantly lighted—at back, three
judges on the bench, dressed in black caps and red*

robes—at R. *and* L., *the public, in Alsatian costumes— in front of the judges, but beneath them, a table, on which lies the Jew's cloak and cap—on* R., *the public prosecutor and barristers—on* L., *the clerk or registrar of the court, and barristers—a gendarme at each corner of the Court. Mathias is discovered seated on a stool in* C. *of Court—he is dressed in the brown blouse and hood worn by the man in the vision in Act I—he has his back to the audience, face to judges.*]

The Clerk. Therefore, the prisoner, Mathias, is accused of having, on the night of the 24th December, 1818, between midnight and one o'clock, assassinated the Jew Koveski upon the Bridge of Vechem, to rob him of his gold.

President. Prisoner, you have heard the Act of Accusation read; you have already heard the depositions of the witnesses. What have you to say in answer?

Mathias [*violently—throws back hood, and starting up*]. Witnesses! People who saw nothing; people who live miles from the place where the crime was committed; at night, and in the winter time! You call such people witnesses!

President. Answer with calmness; these gestures—this violence will avail you nothing. You are a man full of cunning.

Mathias [*with humility*]. No, I am a man of simplicity.

President. You knew well the time to select; you knew well how to evade all suspicion; you knew well how to destroy all direct evidence. You are a dangerous man!

Mathias [*derisively*]. Because nothing can be proved against me I am dangerous! Every honest man then is dangerous when nothing can be proved against him! A rare encouragement for honesty!

President. The public voice accuses you. Answer me this; how is it that you hear the noise of Bells?

Mathias [*passionately*]. I do not hear the noise of Bells!

[*Music. Bells heard off as before. Mathias trembles.*]

President. Prisoner, you speak falsely. At this moment you hear that noise. Tell us why is this?

Mathias. It is nothing. It is simply a jangling in my ears.

President. Unless you acknowledge the true cause of this noise you hear, we shall summon the Mesmerist to explain the matter to us.

Mathias [*with defiance*]. It is true then that I hear this noise. [*Bells cease.*]

President [*to the Clerk of the Court*]. It is well; write that down.

Mathias. Yes; but I hear it in a dream.

President. Write that he hears it in a dream.

Mathias [*furiously*]. Is it a crime to dream?

The Crowd [*murmur very softly among themselves, and move simultaneously, each person performing exactly the same movement of negation*]. N-N-N-o!

Mathias [*with confidence*]. Listen, friends! Don't fear for me! All this is but a dream—I am in a dream. If it were not a dream should I be clothed in these rags? Should I have before me such judges as these? Judges who, simply acting upon their own empty ideas, would hang a fellow creature. Ha, ha, ha! It is a dream— a dream! [*He bursts into a loud derisive laugh.*]

President. Silence, prisoner—silence! [*Turning to his companion Judges.*] Gentlemen—this noise of Bells arises in the prisoner's mind from the remembrance of what is past. The prisoner hears this noise because there rankles in his heart the memory of that he would conceal from us. The Jew's horse carried Bells.

Mathias. It is false; I have no memories.

President. Be silent!

Mathias [*with rage*]. A man cannot be condemned upon such suppositions. You must have proofs. I do not hear the noise of Bells.

President. You see, gentlemen, the prisoner contradicts himself. He has already made the avowal—now he retracts it.

Mathias. No! I hear nothing. [*The Bells heard.*] It is the blood rushing to my brain—this jangling in my ears. [*The Bells increase in sound.*] I ask for Christian. Why is not Christian here?

President. Prisoner! do you persist in your denial?

Mathias [*with force*]. Yes. There is nothing proved against me. It is a gross injustice to keep an honest man in prison. I suffer in the cause of justice. [*The Bells cease.*]

President. You persist. Well! Considering that since this affair took place fifteen years have passed, and that it is impossible to throw light upon the circumstances

by ordinary means—first, through the cunning and
audacity of the prisoner, and second, through the
deaths of witnesses who could have given evidence—
for these reasons we decree that the Court hear the
Mesmerist. Officer, summon the Mesmerist.

Mathias [*in a terrible voice*]. I oppose it! I oppose it!
Dreams prove nothing.

President. Summon the Mesmerist! [*Exit Gendarme.*]

Mathias [*striking the table*]. It is abominable! It is in defiance of all justice!

President. If you are innocent, why should you fear the
Mesmerist; because he can read the inmost secrets of
your heart? Be calm, or, believe me, your own indiscretion will prove that you are guilty.

Mathias. I demand an advocate. I wish to instruct the advocate Linder of Saverne. In a case like this, I do
not care for cost. I am calm—as calm as any man who
has no reproach against himself. I fear nothing, but
dreams are dreams. [*Loudly.*] Why is Christian not
here? My honour is his honour! Let him be sent for.
He is an honest man. [*With exultation.*] Christian, I
have made you rich. Come, and defend me!

[*Music. The Gendarme who has gone out returns with
the Mesmerist.*

Mesmerist [*bending to the Court respectfully*]. Your hon-
ours, the President and Judges of the Court, it is your
decree that has brought me before your tribunal;
without such direction, terror alone would have kept
me far from here.

Mathias. Who can believe in the follies of the Mesmerists?
They deceive the public for the purpose of gaining
money! They merely perform the tricks of conjurers!
I have seen this fellow already at my cousin Bôth's, at
Ribeauville.

President. Can you send this man to sleep?

Mesmerist [*looking full at Mathias, who sinks upon chair,
unable to endure the Mesmerist's gaze*]. I can!

Mathias [*starting up*]. I will not be made the subject of this
conjurer's experiments.

President. I command it!

Mathias. Christian—where is Christian? He will prove
that I am an honest man.

President. Your resistance betrays you.

Mathias [*with defiance*]. I have no fear. [*Sits.*]

[*The Mesmerist goes up stage to back of Mathias, makes some passes. Music.*]

Mathias [*to himself*]. Mathias, if you sleep you are lost. [*His eyes are fixed as if struck with horror—in a hollow voice.*] No—no—I will not sleep—I will— [*in a hesitating voice*] I will—not—no—[*Falls asleep. Music ceases.*]

Mesmerist. He sleeps. What shall I ask him?

President. Ask him what he did on the night of the 24th of December, fifteen years ago.

Mesmerist [*to Mathias, in a firm voice*]. You are at the night of the 24th December, 1818?

Mathias [*in a low voice*]. Yes.

Mesmerist. What time is it?

Mathias. Half-past eleven.

Mesmerist. Speak on. I command you!

Mathias [*still in the same attitude, speaking as if he were describing a vision presented to his sight*]. The people are leaving the inn—Catherine and little Annette have gone to rest. Our man Kasper comes in. He tells me the lime-kiln is lighted. I answer him, it is well; go to bed, I will see to the kiln. He leaves me; I am alone with the Jew, who warms himself at the stove. Outside, everything sleeps. Nothing is heard, except from time to time the Jew's horse under the shed, when he shakes his bells.

Mesmerist. Of what are you thinking?

Mathias. I am thinking that I must have money—that if I have not three thousand francs by the 31st, the inn will be taken from me. I am thinking that no one is stirring; that it is night; that there are two feet of snow upon the ground, and that the Jew will follow the high road quite alone!

Mesmerist. Have you already decided to attack him?

Maithias [*after a short silence*]. That man is strong. He has broad shoulders. I am thinking that he would defend himself well, should anyone attack him. [*He makes a movement.*]

Mesmerist. What ails you?

Mathias [*in a low voice*]. He looks at me. He has grey eyes. [*As if speaking to himself.*] I must strike the blow!

Mesmerist. You are decided?

Mathias. Yes—yes; I will strike the blow! I will risk it!

Mesmerist. Go on!

Mathias. I must, however, look round. I go out; all is dark! It still snows; no one will trace my footsteps in the snow. [*He raises his hands as if feeling for something.*]

Mesmerist. What are you doing?

Mathias. I am feeling in the sledge—should he carry pistols! There is nothing—I will strike the blow! [*He listens.*] All is silent in the village! Little Annette is crying; a goat bleats in the stable; the Jew is walking in his room!

Mesmerist. You re-enter?

Mathias. Yes. The Jew has placed six francs upon the table; I return his money; he fixes his eyes steadily upon me!

Mesmerist. He speaks to you.

Mathias. He asks me how far it is to Mutzig? Four leagues. I wish him well on his journey! He answers—"God bless you!" He goes out—he is gone! [*Mathias, with body bent, takes several steps forward as if following and watching his victim; he extends his hands.*] The axe! Where is the axe? Ah, here, behind the door! How cold it is! [*He trembles.*] The snow falls—not a star! Courage, Mathias, you shall possess the girdle—courage!

Mesmerist. You follow him?

Mathias. Yes, yes. I have crossed the fields! [*Pointing.*] Here is the old bridge, and there below, the frozen rivulet! How the dogs howl at Daniel's farm—how they howl! And old Finck's forge, how brightly it glows upon the hillock. [*Low, as if speaking to himself.*] Kill a man!—kill a man! You will not do that, Mathias—you will not do that! Heaven forbids it. [*Proceeding to walk with measured steps and bent body.*] You are a fool! Listen, you will be rich; your wife and child will no longer want for anything! The Jew came; so much the worse—so much the worse. He ought not to have come! You will pay all you owe; you will no more be in debt. [*Loud, in a broken tone.*] It must be, Mathias, that you kill him! [*He listens.*] No one on the road—no one! [*With an expression of terror.*] What dreadful silence! [*He wipes his forehead with his hand.*] One o'clock strikes, and the moon shines. Ah! The Jew has already passed!

Thank God! Thank God! [*He kneels—a pause—he listens—the Bells heard without as before.*] No! The Bells! The Bells! He comes! [*He bends down in a watching attitude, and remains still—a pause—in a low voice.*] You will be rich—you will be rich—you will be rich! [*The noise of the Bells increases—the Crowd express alarm simultaneously—all at once Mathias springs forward, and with a species of savage roar, strikes a terrible blow with his right hand.*] Ah! ah! I have you now, Jew! [*He strikes again—the crowd simultaneously express horror. Mathias leans forward and gazes anxiously on the ground—he extends his hand as if to touch something, but draws it back in horror.*] He does not move! [*He raises himself, utters a deep sigh of relief and looks round.*] The horse has fled with the sledge! [*The Bells cease— kneeling down.*] Quick, quick! The girdle! I have it. Ha! [*He performs the action in saying this of taking it from the Jew's body and buckling it round his own.*] It is full of gold, quite full. Be quick, Mathias, be quick! Carry him away. [*He bends low down and appears to lift the body upon his back; then he walks across stage, his body bent, his steps slow, as a man who carries a heavy load.*]

Mesmerist. Where are you going?

Mathias [*stopping*]. To the lime-kiln. I am there. [*He appears to throw the body upon the kiln.*] How heavy he was! [*He breathes with force; then he again bends down to take up a pole—in a hoarse voice.*] Go into the fire, Jew, go into the fire! [*He appears to push the body with the pole, using his whole force; suddenly he utters a cry of horror and staggers away, his face covered with his hands.*] Those eyes, oh, those eyes! How he glares at me. [*He sinks on to stool, and takes the same attitude as when first thrown into sleep.*]

President [*with a sign to the Mesmerist*]. It is well. [*To the Clerk of the Court.*] You have written all?

Clerk. All!

President. It is well—awake him now, and let him read himself.

Mesmerist. Awake! I command you!

Mathias [*awakes gradually—he appears bewildered*]. Where am I? [*He looks round.*] Ah! Yes; what is going on?

Clerk [*handing him paper*]. Here is your deposition—read it.

Mathias [*takes it and, before reading it, aside*]. Wretched, wretched fool! I have told all; I am lost! [*With rage, after reading the paper.*] It is false! [*Tears the paper into pieces.*] You are a set of rogues! Christian—where is Christian? It is a crime against justice! They will not let my only witness speak. Christian! They would kill the father of your wife! Help me—help me!

President. You force me to speak of an event of which I had wished to remain silent. Your son-in-law Christian, upon hearing of the crimes with which you are charged, by his own hand sought his death. He is no more.

Mathias. Ah! [*He appears stupefied with dismay.*]

President [*after consulting the other judges, rises, speaks in a solemn tone of voice*]. Considering that on the night of the 24th December, 1818, between midnight and one o'clock, Mathias committed the crime of assassination upon the person of one Koveski, and considering that this crime was committed under circumstances which aggravate its enormity—such as premeditation, and for the purpose of highway robbery, the Court condemns the said Mathias to be hanged by the neck until he is dead!

[*Mathias staggers and falls on his knees. The crowd makes a movement of terror—the death-bell tolls—lights lowered gradually—then curtain at back of gauze descends, disclosing the Scene as at commencement—lights up. Music—a peal of joy bells heard ringing.*]

Crowd [*without*]. Annette! Annette! The bride!

[*Hurried steps are heard upon the stairs outside, and then a loud knocking at the door of the room.*]

Catherine [*without*]. Mathias! Mathias! get up at once. It is late in the morning, and all our guests are below. [*More knocking.*]

Christian [*without*]. Mathias! Mathias! [*Silence.*] How soundly he sleeps!

Walter [*without*]. Ho! Mathias, the wedding has commenced—Houp, houp! [*More knocking.*]

The Crowd [*outside*]. Burgomaster! Burgomaster! [*Loud knocking.*]

Catherine [*in an anxious voice*]. He does not answer. It is strange. Mathias! [*A discussion among many voices is heard without.*]

Christian. No—it is useless. Leave it to me! [*At the same moment several violent blows are struck upon the door, which falls into the room from its hinges. Enter Christian hurriedly—he runs to the alcove. Music, hurry.*] Mathias! [*Looks into alcove and staggers back into room.*] Ah!

[*Enter Catherine and Annette, followed by Walter, Hans, and the crowd, all dressed for the wedding.*]

Catherine. What has happened, Christian; what has happened? [*She is rushing to alcove.*]

Christian [*stopping her*]. Don't come near—don't come near.

Catherine [*endeavouring to pass*]. I will see what it is. Let me pass; do not fear for me.

[*Mathias appears from the alcove—he is dressed in the same clothes as when he retired into the alcove at the commencement of the Scene, but his face is haggard, and ghastly pale—he comes out, his eyes fixed, his arms extended—as he rushes forward with uncertain steps, the crowd fall back with horror, and form groups of consternation, with a general exclamation of terror.*]

Mathias [*in a voice of strangulation*]. The rope! the rope! Cut the rope!

[*He falls suddenly, and is caught in the arms of Hans and Walter, who carry him to the chair. The Bells heard off. Music, the melody played in the Second Act when promise given. His hands clutch at his throat as if to remove something that strangles him— he looks pitifully round as if trying to recognise those about him, and then his head falls on his breast. Catherine, kneeling, places her hand on Mathias' heart.*]

Catherine. Dead! [*The Bells cease. Annette bursts into tears. The women in the crowd kneeling; men remove their hats and bend their heads upon their breasts— tableau.*

Curtain.

W. S. Gilbert (1836–1911)

Patience

OR BUNTHORNE'S BRIDE

A Stage Play

BY W. S. GILBERT

Most men, whatever their occupation may be, are accustomed to study mankind exclusively from their own points of view. A man who passes his life behind a tavern-bar is apt to divide the human race into those who habitually refresh themselves in public-houses, and those who do not. A policeman classifies society under two great heads—prosecutors and prisoners. In a footman's eyes, his fellow-men are either visitors or servants; in an author's, they are publishers or reviewers. Now, it is conceivable that a man may be at once a prosecutor, a visitor, and a publisher; but a policeman will take no heed of him in the two latter capacities; a footman will care nothing that he is a prosecutor and a publisher; and an author will be in no way concerned that he is a prosecutor (unless, indeed, he is prosecuting the author), or that he is a visitor, unless the visit be paid in his capacity as a publisher. Each man allows his immediate surroundings to interfere between himself and the world at large. He sees mankind, not through a distorting medium, but through a medium so circumscribed that it permits only one feature of the object looked at to be seen at one time. In short, he examines mankind, not through a field-glass, but through a microscope.

A theatre, examined through the powerful medium employed by a person whose occupation is intimately associated with theatres, is as unlike a theatre, as it appears in the eyes of the outside public, as a drop of magnified Thames water is unlike the apparently inorganic liquid that enters into the composition of almost everything we drink. Not one person in a thousand who sits in the auditorium of a theatre has any definite idea of the complicated process by which the untidy, badly-scrawled, interleaved, and interlineated manuscript of the author is trans-

muted into the close, crisp, bright, interesting entertainment that, in the eyes of the spectator, represents the
value of the shilling he has paid for admittance. Still less
does he know of the complicated mental process by which
the manuscript (supposing it to have a genuine claim to
the title "original") has been put together. Let us trace
the progress of a modern three-act comedy from the blank-
paper state to completion, and from completion to production.

We will assume that the author, Mr. Horace Facile, has
such a recognized position in his profession as to justify a
manager in saying to him, "Facile, I want a three-act
comedy-drama from you, with parts for Jones and Brown
and Robinson. Name your own terms, and get it ready, if
you can, by this day two months."

Facile's engagements allow of his accepting the commission, and he sets to work on it as soon as may be.

In the first place, a "general idea" must be fixed upon,
and in selecting it, Facile is guided, to a certain extent, by
the resources of the company he is to write for. Jones is an
excellent light comedian, with a recognized talent for eccentric parts; Brown is the leading "old man" of the
establishment; Robinson is the handsome lover or *jeune
premier;* and Miss Smith plays the interesting young ladies
whose fortunes or misfortunes constitute the sentimental
interest of every piece in which she plays. Probably one or
more of these talented artists must be "exploited," and
the nature of the "general idea" will depend on the powers
or peculiarities of the actor or actress who is principally
entitled to consideration. The motif of the comedy having
been determined upon (we will suppose that it is to arise
from the unnecessary and unchristian antagonism existing
between the Theatre and the Church), Facile casts about
for a story in which this motif can be effectively displayed.
In selecting a story, Facile will probably be guided by the
peculiarities of the company he is writing for. Brown (the
"old man") has never played an Archbishop of Canterbury,
and Facile believes such a part woud afford that excellent
comedian a chance of distinguishing himself in a new line
of character; so the story must be put together in such a
manner as to admit of an Archbishop of Canterbury taking
a prominent part in it. It has often occurred to Facile that
Robinson, the *jeune premier,* could make a great deal of

the part of a professional Harlequin, who, under the influence of love or some equally potent agency, has "taken orders," notwithstanding that, at the time of his doing so, he is under engagement to play Harlequin in a forthcoming pantomime. So the story must admit, not only of an Archbishop, but also of a serious Harlequin; and, moreover, the interests of the Archbishop and the Harlequin must be interwoven in an interesting and yet sufficiently probable manner. However, the fact that there is a clerical side to Harlequin's character renders this exceedingly easy. The Harlequin loves the Archbishop's daughter; but the Archbishop (a very haughty ecclesiastic of the Thomas à Becket type) objects to Harlequins on principle, and determines that his daughter shall marry into the Church. Here is at once the necessary association of the interests of the Archbishop and the Harlequin, and here, moreover, is an excellent reason for the Harlequin's taking holy orders. The Archbishop admits him, in ignorance of his other professions, and places no obstacles in the way of his courting his daughter. But a great deal of the interest of the lover's part should obviously depend on the contrast between his duties as a clergyman and his duties as a Harlequin (for an obdurate manager declines to release him from his engagement in the latter capacity), and Facile sets to work to see how the two professions can be contrasted to the best advantage. This requires some consideration, but he sees his way to it at last. The Archbishop (a bitter enemy to the stage, which he denounces whenever an opportunity for doing so presents itself) happens to be the freeholder of the very theatre in which the Harlequin is engaged; and happening to call on the manager one evening, with the double object of collecting his quarter's rent and endeavouring to wean the manager from a godless profession, he meets his daughter's lover in Harlequin costume. Here is an opportunity for a scene of haughty recrimination—the Archbishop reproaching the curate for combining the pulpit with the stage (by-the-bye, here is the title for the piece—*The Pulpit and the Stage*), and the curate reproaching the Archbishop with his hypocritical denunciation of an institution from which he derives, in the shape of rent, an income of, say, four thousand a year. At this juncture the Archbishop's daughter must be introduced. It will be difficult to account, with

anything like probability, for her presence behind the
scenes during the performance of a pantomime; but with
a little ingenuity even this may be accomplished. For instance, she may have come with a view to proselytizing
the ballet; and a scene of the stage, in which she is seen
proselytizing the ballet, who can't get away from her because they are all hanging on irons, ready for the trans-
formation scene, might precede the arrival of the Archbishop. The act (the second) must end with the struggle
(on the daughter's part) between filial respect for her
venerable father and her love for Harlequin, resulting, of
course, in her declaring for the Harlequin, and the
Archbishop's renunciation of her "for ever."

This will fill two acts. The third act must show the Harlequin (now a curate) married to the Archbishop's daughter,
and living in the humblest circumstances somewhere in
Lambeth. They are happy, although they are extremely
poor. They have many friends—some clerical, some theatrical—but all on the best of terms with each other,
through the benevolent agency of the ex-Harlequin. Deans
drop in from Convocation at Westminster—actors and actresses from rehearsal at Astley's; and it is shown, beyond
the possibility of doubt, that the two professions have many
points in common (here is an opportunity for introducing
hits at High Church mummeries, with imitations of popular
preachers by Wilkinson, the low comedian). Now to introduce the Archbishop. Since his renunciation of his daughter, he has become a changed man. Too haughty to admit
his error frankly and take her and her husband to his
Heart and Palace, he is nevertheless painfully conscious
that he has acted harshly; and, in a spirit of secret self-
humiliation, he disguises himself as one of the undignified
clergy, and in that capacity goes through a course of house-
to-house visitation. The natural course of this duty brings
him to the humble abode of his daughter and son-in-law.
He enters unperceived (of course in ignorance of the fact
that it *is* their abode) during Wilkinson's imitations and
overhears a touching scene, in which his daughter indignantly rebukes Wilkinson for giving an imitation of her
Right Reverend father's pulpit peculiarities. The old man,
utterly softened by this unexpected touch of filial affection,
comes forward, and, in broken accents, admits both
the correctness of the imitation and the filial respect that

induced his daughter to check it, folds her and her husband to his heart, and gives him the next presentation to a valuable living—the present incumbent (who is present) being an aged man who cannot, in the course of nature, expect to survive many months. On this touching scene the curtain descends.

Here is an outline of a plot which Facile believes will answer every purpose. The Archbishop, the daughter, and the Harlequin will afford three excellent parts. The manager will be a bit of "character" for Jones, the eccentric comedian; the actor who gives imitations of popular preachers will fit Wilkinson's powers of mimicry to a T; the tottering old incumbent, to whose living the ex-Harlequin is to succeed, will afford Tompkins an opportunity of introducing one of his celebrated "cabinet pictures" of pathetic old men; and for the other members of the company small effective parts, arising naturally from the exigencies of the story, will readily be found.

The next thing Facile does is to arrange striking situations for the end of each act. The first act must end with announcement from the Harlequin that he has just taken holy orders, the happiness of the bishop's daughter at the information, and the entrance of the manager, who tells Harlequin that he shall nevertheless hold him to his engagement for the forthcoming pantomime. The second act must end with the renunciation of his daughter by the Archbishop, and the last with the general reconciliation. Facile then sets to work to write the dialogue. As a rule, this is not written straight off. He first tries his hand upon bits of dialogue that arise from suggestive situations—perhaps the first interview between the Archbishop's daughter and himself in Lambeth Palace. Then perhaps he will write the proselytizing scene in the second act; then the dialogue that leads to the situation at the end of Act I; and so on. After he has "settled" half-a-dozen little scenes of this description, he feels that it is time to arrange how the piece is to begin. The first act takes place in the Archbishop's library in Lambeth Palace. Shall the Archbishop and his daughter be "discovered" at breakfast? No; both the Archbishop and his daughter (that is to say, the actor and actress who are to play those parts) object to be "discovered." They want an "entrance," that they may receive special and individual "receptions," and they don't like to begin a piece, as in that case they are liable to constant interruption from the arrival of such of the audience as are not in their places when the curtain rises. Perhaps Jones (the manager) won't mind beginning, as his part is likely to be a particularly good one; he might call on the Archbishop about the rent of the theatre. But in this case there must be a servant to receive him. Well, Facile tries this: Servant discovered (dusting, of course); soliloquy (this gives the manager an entrance); knock; servant don't answer it on principle until several times repeated; eventually admits manager; treats manager contemptuously (or better still, as he is an Archbishop's servant, with a grave and pitying air), as who would say, "Poor worldly sheep (we—that is to say, the Archbishop and I—despise you, but we don't hate you)"; servant leaves to inform Archbishop; sarcastic soliloquy by manager; enter Archbishop; thunders of applause at Archbishop's "make-up"; and so on. Probably Facile writes and rewrites this scene half-a-dozen times—it gives him more trouble than all the rest of the act put together; for there are so many ways of beginning a piece, and it is so difficult to find sufficient reason for selecting one and rejecting all the rest. However, Facile is eventually satisfied; the scenes that he has already written are tacked together with dialogue of a more commonplace order, and Act I is completed.

At this point Facile is apt to pause and to take breath. Perhaps he will run over to Paris, or go to the sea-side for a month, "to collect his thoughts." His thoughts collected, he will make a tremendous effort to begin the second act; but here all the difficulty that he experienced in beginning Act I crops up again tenfold. We protest, from practical experience, that there is nothing in the dramatist's profession that presents so many distasteful difficulties as the commencing the second act of a three-act comedy. His first act is short, sharp, crisp, and to the point—*totus teres atque rotundis*—perfectly satisfactory in itself—artistically put together, and telling the audience all they require to know in order to understand what follows, but nothing more. The thread of interest is broken at an exacting point, and it has now to be taken up again and in such a way as not to anticipate secrets and "situations" that require time to develop. If, in commencing the first act, Facile was bothered with the choice of five hundred "openings," he is ten times as much bothered now from the fact that he has only two or three, and none of them likely to be effective when reduced to dialogue. However, a letter from the management probably wakes him up at this point. With a desperate effort he sets to work, writing detached scenes as before, and tacking them together as before, and writing the opening dialogue last as before; and, in process of time, Act II is completed. His work is now practically at an end. Act III is a simple matter enough. He has laid the train in Acts I and II, and all that remains is to bring about the catastrophe in the quickest possible manner consistent with the story he has to tell. By the time that he has finished Act II, he has cleared away all his difficulties. The different peculiarities of his principal characters have not only been irrevocably determined upon, but he has, by this time, become thoroughly saturated with their spirit; and he has no difficulty whatever in bringing the last act shortly and sharply to an effective conclusion. Facile, who knows his work pretty well, has a theory that no piece has ever yet been written which deserves to arrest the attention of an audience for more than two hours at a time, and he has not the vanity to believe that any piece of his is likely to prove an exception to the rule.

The piece, duly completed, is sent to the manager who is to produce it. That gentleman has sufficient faith in Facile to justify him in handing it over at once to his prompter, who proceeds to make a fair copy for his own use, and another for the Lord Chamberlain's inspection. He also copies the "parts" from which the actors and actresses are to study, and which contain simply the words that the actor for whom it is intended has to speak, the stage-directions that concern him, and the last three or four words of every speech that immediately precede his own. As soon as the parts are fairly copied, a "reading" is called—that is to say, the members of the company are summoned to hear the piece read by the author in the green-room. This is an ordeal that Facile particularly dreads. He reads abominably—all authors do—and he knows it. He begins well; he reads slowly and emphatically, with all the proper pauses duly marked; and he indicates the stage-directions with just the right modulation of voice. All is quite satisfactory until— say, on page 9—he comes to a "point" on which he relies for a hearty laugh. He makes his point, and dwells for a moment upon it. Nobody notices it except the stage manager, who thinks he has paused because he is hoarse and kindly pours him out a glass of water. Much abashed by this, Facile pounds through the rest of the manuscript at an astounding pace—hurrying intentionally over all the "good things" as if he were ashamed of them—which, for the moment, he is—and slurring over stirring passages as if they were merely incidental to the general purpose of the scene—as though, in fact, the scene had not been originally constructed in order to introduce them. As he approaches the end of the second act, he becomes quite unconscious of the fact that he is reading at all until recalled by an enforced pause occasioned by the accident of a misplaced leaf, or the opening or shutting of the green-room door. As he commences the third act, he finds himself wandering into falsetto every now and then; he becomes husky and out of tune; he takes a copious drink of water, and the words immediately begin to babble into each other in a manner altogether incomprehensible. He falls into his old habit of slurring over important passages, but endeavours to compensate for this by laying such exceptional stress upon sentences of no ultimate importance that his audience begin to wish that they had paid more attention to the earlier passages of the play, that they might understand more clearly the force of the old clergyman's remark about the weather, or the subtlety of the ex-Harlequin's invitation to the low comedian to sit down and make himself comfortable. Facile finds the "imitations" in the third act seem to make no impression, which is not to be wondered at, considering he reads them "off the reel" without any modification of voice at all. At length, very much to his surprise, he finds himself at the last page—which is always a tremendously long page to read; you never seem to get to the bottom of it—and, with his heart thumping away in his mouth, he pronounces the word "curtain," and closes the manuscript with—"There, that's over!" and proceeds at once to talk, with great volubility, about the sort of day that it is—the bad business they've been doing at the Folly —or the horrible report that Mrs. Miggleton, the wife of Miggleton, the first surgeon of the day, never "shows" in society, because her husband has, at different times, and in the interests of science, cut away so much of her, by way of experiment, that only the vital portions are left—about anything, in short, except the piece he has just been reading. The stage manager distributes the "parts," and the author hurries away—in order to avoid *that row* with Miss Smith —after appointing a day and hour for "comparing parts."

In the course of this process—a very dismal one indeed— the members of the company who are engaged in the piece endeavour to decipher the parts and to ascertain the context. The copyist's errors are corrected, and every one begins to have some idea of his or her position with reference to the other persons engaged. It is usually a long and tedious process, and eminently calculated to reduce Facile's self-esteem to vanishing-point. After this preliminary canter is over Facile thinks he may as well look up Mr. Flatting, the scene painter, who has been at work for the last fortnight on the Archbishop's library, and who is about to begin the "behind the scenes" scene in the second act. Facile climbs into the tall, narrow, dingy shed called by courtesy a painting-room, and finds Flatting describing the "model" to the carpenter and machinist, who will have a good deal to do with it, as it is a "set" of rather complicated description. Facile settles matters with Flatting and goes home to dine, sleep, wake at eleven o'clock, and set to work till three in the morning, altering this scene, polishing up that dialogue, making it crisper here, and filling it out with business there, as the experience of the morning may have suggested. The next day is the first rehearsal proper. A table and three chairs are set in the middle of the stage against the footlights. One of these is for the stage-manager, one for the prompter, and one for the author. Very often the stage-manager and prompter are one and the same individual, but the three chairs (one on the "prompt side" of the table and two on the "opposite prompt") are always there. Facile knows something of stage-management, and invariably stage-manages his own pieces—an exceptional thing in England, but the common custom in France. He is nothing of an actor, and when he endeavours to show what he wants his actors to do, he makes himself rather ridiculous, and there is a good deal of tittering at the wings; but he contrives, nevertheless, to make himself understood, and takes particularly good care that whatever his wishes are, they shall be carried out to the letter, unless good cause is shown to the contrary. He has his own way; and if the piece is a success, he feels that he has contributed something more than the mere words that are spoken. At the same time, if Facile is not a self-sufficient donkey he is only too glad to avail himself of valuable suggestions offered by persons who have ten times his experience in the details of stage management. And so the piece flounders through rehearsal—the dingy theatre lighted by a T-piece in front of the stage, which has no perceptible effect at the back; the performers usually (at all events during the first two or three rehearsals) standing in a row with their backs to the auditorium, that the light may fall on crabbed manuscripts they are reading from; the author endeavouring, but in vain, to arrange effective exits and entrances, because nobody can leave the T-piece; the stage-manager or prompter (who follows the performers) calling a halt from time to time that he may correct an overlooked error in his manuscript or insert a stage-direction. The actors themselves pause from time to time for the same reason. Every one has (or should have) a pencil in hand; all errors are corrected and insertions made on the spot; every important change of position is carefully marked; every "cross" indicated as the piece proceeds; and as alterations in dialogue and business are made up to the last moment—all of which have to be hurriedly recorded at the time—it will be understood that the "parts" are in rather a dilapidated condition before the rehearsals are concluded.

Eventually the piece is ready for representation—three weeks' preparation is supposed to be a liberal allowance—and with one imperfect scene rehearsal, and no dress rehearsal at all, the piece is presented to the public. It probably passes muster on the first night, whatever its merits may be; in a week or ten days actors begin to "do something" with their parts; and in a fortnight the piece is probably at its best.

There is much, very much, fault to be found (so Facile says) with the system—or rather the want of the system—that prevails at rehearsals in this country. In the first place, every actor and every person engaged in the piece should have a perfect copy of the piece, and that copy should be *printed*, not written. It costs from five to six pounds to print a three-act comedy, and in return for this trifling outlay much valuable time and an infinity of trouble would be saved, not only to the prompter, but to the actors and the author.* It is absolutely necessary that every actor should have the context of his scenes before his eyes as he studies them. He also says (does Facile) that it is a monstrous shame and an unheard-of injustice to place three-act pieces on the stage with fewer than thirty rehearsals, in ten of which the scenes should be as they will be set at night, and in five of which every soul engaged should be dressed and made up as they will be dressed and made up at night. As it is now, Jones, who is always fearfully nervous on "first nights," is embarrassed to find himself called upon to repeat his scarcely-learnt words in a spacious and handsomely furnished apartment, blazing with gas and gold-foil, instead of the cold, dark, empty stage on which he has been rehearsing them. This is of itself enough to drive the words out of the head of Jones. Then Jones, who has practised several scenes with Brown (on the stage an "old man," but in private life an airy, dressy gentleman of thirty summers), finds himself called upon to speak his words, not to the dressy Brown, but to a white-headed and generally venerable ecclesiastic, in gold spectacles and knee-breeches —that is to say, Brown the Archbishop. These surprises (for to a nervous man they *are* surprises) are enough to unhinge Jones altogether. He makes a mess of his part for a night or two, picks up again after that, and in a fortnight is the talk of the town. Now, if Jones had had an opportunity of rehearsing with Brown the Archbishop, instead of Brown the Swell, and if he had rehearsed his scenes in the Archbishop's library, and not on the empty stage, Jones might have become the talk of the town from the first. In first-class French theatres this system is adopted. Parts are distributed, learnt perfectly, and then rehearsed for six weeks or two months, sometimes for three or four months. Scene-rehearsals and dress-rehearsals occupy the last week of preparations. Actors and actresses act at rehearsal; they

*By-the-bye, here is an invaluable hint to Messieurs the Unacted. Never send a manuscript to a manager. Always print your play before you send it in. *It will be read;* and if rejected, it will be for a good and sufficient reason. There are thumping prizes in dramatic literature; and the five-pound outlay will be returned to you a thousand-fold, if your piece happens to turn up trumps.

have been taught and required to do so from the first; and the consequence is that a bad actor becomes a reasonably good actor, and a reasonably good actor becomes an admirable actor, by sheer dint of the microscopic investigation that his acting receives from the stage-manager and from the author. And until this system is in force in England; until the necessity for longer periods of preparation, for rehearsals that are rehearsals in fact, and not merely in name—rehearsals with scenery, dresses, and "make-up," as they are to be at night; earnest rehearsals, with every gesture given as it is to be given at night, every expression marked as it is to be marked at night; until the necessity for such preparation as this is recognized in England, the English stage will never take the position to which the intelligence of its actors and actresses, the enterprise of its managers, and the talent of its authors would otherwise entitle it. At least, so says Facile.

CHARACTERS

Colonel Calverley ⎫ (Officers of
Major Murgatroyd ⎬ Dragoon
Lieut. the Duke of Dunstable ⎭ Guards)
Reginald Bunthorne (a Fleshly Poet)
Archibald Grosvenor (an Idyllic Poet)
Mr. Bunthorne's Solicitor
The Lady Angela ⎫
The Lady Saphir ⎬ (Rapturous Maidens)
The Lady Ella ⎭
The Lady Jane ⎭
Patience (a Dairy Maid)
Chorus of Rapturous Maidens and Officers of
Dragoon Guards.

Act 1.—Exterior of Castle Bunthorne.

Act 2.—A Glade.

First produced at the Opéra Comique on April 23, 1881.

Scene
Exterior of Castle Bunthorne. Entrance to Castle by draw-
bridge over moat. Young ladies dressed in aesthetic draper-
ies are grouped about the stage. They play on lutes, man-
dolins, etc., as they sing, and all are in the last stage of
despair. Angela, Ella, and Saphir lead them.

CHORUS.

Twenty love-sick maidens we,
　　Love-sick all against our will.
Twenty years hence we shall be
　　Twenty love-sick maidens still.
Twenty love-sick maidens we,
And we die for love of thee.

SOLO—*Angela.*

Love feeds on hope, they say, or love will die—
All. 　　　　　　　　　　Ah, miserie!
Yet my love lives, although no hope have I!
All. 　　　　　　　　　　Ah, miserie!
Alas, poor heart, go hide thyself away—
To weeping concords tune thy roundelay!
　　　　　　　　　　Ah, miserie!

CHORUS.

All our love is all for one,
　　Yet that love he heedeth not,
He is coy and cares for none,
　　Sad and sorry is our lot!
　　　　　　　　Ah, miserie!

SOLO—*Ella.*

> Go, breaking heart,
>> Go, dream of love requited;
> Go, foolish heart,
>> Go, dream of lovers plighted;
> Go, madcap heart,
>> Go, dream of never waking;
> And in thy dream
>> Forget that thou art breaking!

Chorus.   Ah, miserie!

Ella.   Forget that thou art breaking!

Chorus.   Twenty love-sick maidens, etc.

Angela. There is a strange magic in this love of ours! Rivals as we all are in the affections of our Reginald, the very hopelessness of our love is a bond that binds us to one another!

Saphir. Jealousy is merged in misery. While he, the very cynosure of our eyes and hearts, remains icy insensible—what have we to strive for?

Ella. The love of maidens is, to him, as interesting as the taxes!

Saphir. Would that it were! He pays his taxes.

Angela. And cherishes the receipts!

[*Enter Lady Jane.*]

Saphir. Happy receipts!

Jane [*suddenly*]. Fools!

Angela. I beg your pardon?

Jane. Fools and blind! The man loves—wildly loves!

Angela. But whom? None of us!

Jane. No, none of us. His weird fancy has lighted, for the nonce, on Patience, the village milkmaid!

Saphir. On Patience? Oh, it cannot be!

Jane. Bah! But yesterday I caught him in her dairy, eating fresh butter with a tablespoon. To-day he is not well!

Saphir. But Patience boasts that she has never loved—that love is, to her, a sealed book! Oh, he cannot be serious!

Jane. 'Tis but a fleeting fancy—'twill quickly pass away. [*Aside.*] Oh, Reginald, if you but knew what a wealth of golden love is waiting for you, stored up in this rugged old bosom of mine, the milkmaid's triumph would be short indeed!

[*Patience appears on an eminence. She looks down with
   pity on the despondent Ladies.*]

RECIT.—*Patience.*

>   Still brooding on their mad infatuation!
>   I thank thee, Love, thou comest not to me!
>   Far happier I, free from thy ministration,
>   Than dukes or duchesses who love can be!

Saphir [*looking up*]. 'Tis Patience—happy girl! Loved by
   a Poet!
Patience.   Your pardon, ladies. I intrude upon you. [*Go-
   ing.*]
Angela.   Nay, pretty child, come hither. Is it true
             That you have never loved?
Patience.   Most true indeed.
Sopranos.   Most marvelous!
Contraltos.   And most deplorable!

SONG—*Patience.*

>   I cannot tell what this love may be
>   That cometh to all, but not to me.
>   It cannot be kind as they'd imply,
>   Or why do these ladies sigh?
>   It cannot be joy and rapture deep,
>   Or why do these gentle ladies weep?
>   It cannot be blissful as 'tis said,
>   Or why are their eyes so wondrous red?
>   Though everywhere true love I see
>   A-coming to all, but not to me,
>   I cannot tell what this love may be!
>   For I am blithe and I am gay,
>   While they sit sighing night and day.
>   Think of the gulf 'twixt them and me,
>   "Fal la la la!"—and "Miserie!"
Chorus.   Yes, she is blithe, etc.

Patience. If love is a thorn, they show no wit
            Who foolishly hug and foster it.
            If love is a weed, how simple they
            Who gather it, day by day!

> If love is a nettle that makes you smart,
> Then why do you wear it next your heart?
> And if it be none of these, say I,
> Ah, why do you sit and sob and sigh?
> Though everywhere, etc.

Chorus. For she is blithe, etc.

Angela. Ah, Patience, if you have never loved, you have never known true happiness! [*All sigh.*]

Patience. But the truly happy always seem to have so much on their minds. The truly happy never seem quite well.

Jane. There is a transcendentality of delirium—an acute accentuation of supremest ecstasy—which the earthy might easily mistake for indigestion. But it is *not* indigestion—it is aesthetic transfiguration! [*To the others.*] Enough of babble. Come!

Patience. But stay, I have some news for you. The 35th Dragoon Guards have halted in the village, and are even now on their way to this very spot.

Angela. The 35th Dragoon Guards!

Saphir. They are fleshy men, of full habit!

Ella. We care nothing for Dragoon Guards!

Patience. But, bless me, you were all engaged to them a year ago!

Saphir. A year ago!

Angela. My poor child, you don't understand these things. A year ago they were very well in our eyes, but since then our tastes have been etherealized, our perceptions exalted. [*To others.*] Come, it is time to lift up our voices in morning carol to our Reginald. Let us to his door.

[*The Ladies go off, two and two, into the Castle, singing refrain of "Twenty love-sick maidens we," and accompanying themselves on harps and mandolins. Patience watches them in surprise, as she climbs the rock by which she entered. March. Enter Officers of Dragoon Guards, led by Major.*]

CHORUS OF DRAGOONS.

> The soldiers of our Queen
> Are linked in friendly tether;
> Upon the battle scene
> They fight the foe together.

There every mother's son
Prepared to fight and fall is;
The enemy of one
     The enemy of all is!

[*Enter Colonel.*]

SONG—*Colonel.*

If you want a receipt for that popular mystery,
     Known to the world as a Heavy Dragoon,
Take all the remarkable people in history,
     Rattle them off to a popular tune.
The pluck of Lord Nelson on board of the *Victory*—
Genius of Bismark devising a plan—
The humour of Fielding (which sounds contradictory)—
     Coolness of Paget about to trepan—
The science of Jullien, the eminent musico—
     Wit of Macaulay, who wrote of Queen Anne—
The pathos of Paddy, as rendered by Boucicault—
     Style of the Bishop of Sodor and Man—
The dash of a D'Orsay, divested of quackery—
Narrative powers of Dickens and Thackeray—
Victor Emmanuel—peak-haunting Peveril—
Thomas Aquinas, and Doctor Sacheverell—
     Tupper and Tennyson—Daniel Defoe—
     Anthony Trollope and Mr. Guizot!
          Take of these elements all that is fusible,
          Melt them all down in a pipkin or crucible,
          Set them to simmer and take off the scum,
          And a Heavy Dragoon is the residuum!

Chorus.   Yes! yes! yes! yes!
               A Heavy Dragoon is the residuum!

Colonel. If you want a receipt for this soldier-like paragon,
     Get at the wealth of the Czar (if you can)—
The family pride of a Spaniard from Arragon—
     Force of Mephisto pronouncing a ban—
A smack of Lord Waterford, reckless and rollicky—
     Swagger of Roderick, heading his clan—
The keen penetration of Paddington Pollaky—
     Grace of an Odalisque on a divan—
The genius strategic of Caesar or Hannibal—
Skill of Sir Garnet in thrashing a cannibal—

Flavour of Hamlet—the Stranger, a touch of him—
Little of Manfred (but not very much of him)—
  Beadle of Burlington—Richardson's show—
  Mr. Micawber and Madame Tussaud!
    Take of these elements all that is fusible,
    Melt them all down in a pipkin or crucible,
    Set them to simmer and take off the scum,
    And a Heavy Dragoon is the residuum!

All.   Yes! yes! yes! yes!
        A Heavy Dragoon is the residuum!

Colonel. Well, here we are once more on the scene of our
    former triumphs. But where's the Duke?
[*Enter Duke, listlessly, and in low spirits.*]
Duke. Here I am! [*Sighs.*]
Colonel. Come, cheer up, don't give way!
Duke. Oh, for that, I'm as cheerful as a poor devil can be
    expected to be who has the misfortune to be a duke,
    with a thousand a day!
Major. Humph! Most men would envy you!
Duke. Envy *me?* Tell me, Major, are you fond of toffee?
Major. Very!
Colonel. We are all fond of toffee.
All. We are!
Duke. Yes, and toffee in moderation is a capital thing. But
    to *live* on toffee—toffee for breakfast, toffee for din-
    ner, toffee for tea—to have it supposed that you care
    for nothing *but* toffee, and that you would consider
    yourself insulted if anything but toffee were offered to
    you—how would you like *that?*
Colonel. I can quite believe that, under those circum-
    stances, even toffee would become monotonous.
Duke. For "toffee" read flattery, adulation, and abject
    deference, carried to such a pitch that I began, at last,
    to think that man was born bent at an angle of forty-
    five degrees! Great Heavens, what is there to adulate
    in me! Am I particularly intelligent, or remarkably
    studious, or excruciatingly witty, or unusually ac-
    complished, or exceptionally virtuous?
Colonel. You're about as commonplace a young man as
    ever I saw.
All. You are!

Duke. Exactly! That's it exactly! That describes me to a T!
Thank you all very much! Well, I couldn't stand it any
longer, so I joined this second-class cavalry regiment.
In the Army, thought I, I shall be occasionally
snubbed, perhaps even bullied, who knows? The
thought was rapture, and here I am.

Colonel [*looking off*]. Yes, and here are the ladies!

Duke. But who is the gentleman with the long hair?

Colonel. I don't know.

Duke. He seems popular!

Colonel. He *does* seem popular!

[*Bunthorne enters, followed by Ladies, two and two, singing and playing on harps as before. He is composing
a poem, and quite absorbed. He sees no one, but walks
across the stage, followed by Ladies. They take no
notice of Dragoons—to the surprise and indignation
of those Officers.*

CHORUS OF LADIES
In a doleful train
    Two and two we walk all day—
For we love in vain!
    None so sorrowful as they
        Who can only sigh and say,
        Woe is me, alackaday!

CHORUS OF DRAGOONS
Now is not this ridiculous—and is not this preposterous?
    A thorough-paced absurdity—explain it if you can.
Instead of rushing eagerly to cherish us and foster us,
    They all prefer this melancholy literary man.
        Instead of slyly peering at us,
        Casting looks endearing at us,
    Blushing at us, flushing at us—flirting with a fan;
    They're actually sneering at us, fleering at us, jeering
        at us!
        Pretty sort of treatment for a military man!
        Pretty sort of treatment for a military man!

Angela.   Mystic poet, hear our prayer,
                    Twenty love-sick maidens we—
                Young and wealthy, dark and fair—
                    All of country family.

And we die for love of thee—
Twenty love-sick maidens we!

Chorus of Ladies.   Yes, we die for love of thee—
Twenty love-sick maidens we!

Bunthorne [*aside—slyly*]. Though my book I seem to scan
In a rapt ecstatic way,
Like a literary man
Who despises female clay,
I hear plainly all they say,
Twenty love-sick maidens they!

Officers [*to each other*].   He hears plainly, etc.

Saphir.   Though so excellently wise,
For a moment mortal be,
Deign to raise thy purple eyes
From thy heart-drawn poesy.
Twenty love-sick maidens see—
Each is kneeling on her knee!   [*All kneel.*]

Chorus of Ladies.   Twenty love-sick, etc.

Bunthorne [*aside*]. Though, as I remarked before,
Any one convinced would be
That some transcendental lore
Is monopolizing me,
Round the corner I can see
Each is kneeling on her knee!

Officers [*to each other*].   Round the corner, etc.

ENSEMBLE

Officers.	*Ladies.*
Now is not this ridiculous, etc.	Mystic poet, hear our prayer, etc.

Colonel. Angela! what is the meaning of this?
Angela. Oh, sir, leave us; our minds are but ill-tuned to
light love-talk.

Major. But what in the world has come over you all?

Jane. Bunthorne! *He* has come over us. He has come among us, and he has idealized us.

Duke. Has he succeeded in idealizing *you?*

Jane. He has!

Duke. Good old Bunthorne!

Jane. My eyes are open; I droop despairingly; I am soul-fully intense; I am limp and I cling!

[*During this Bunthorne is seen in all the agonies of composition. The Ladies are watching him intently as he writhes. At last he hits on the word he wants and writes it down. A general sense of relief.*]

Bunthorne. Finished! At last! Finished! [*He staggers, overcome with the mental strain, into arms of Colonel.*]

Colonel. Are you better now?

Bunthorne. Yes—oh, it's you—I am better now. The poem is finished, and my soul had gone out into it. That was all. It was nothing worth mentioning, it occurs three times a day. [*Sees Patience, who has entered during this scene.*] Ah, Patience! Dear Patience! [*Holds her hand; she seems frightened.*]

Angela. Will it please you read it to us, sir?

Saphir. This we supplicate. [*All kneel.*]

Bunthorne. Shall I?

All the Dragoons. No!

Bunthorne [*annoyed—to Patience*]. I will read it if *you* bid me!

Patience [*much frightened*]. You can if you like!

Bunthorne. It is a wild, weird, fleshy thing; yet very tender, very yearning, very precious. It is called, "Oh, Hollow! Hollow! Hollow!"

Patience. It is a hunting song?

Bunthorne. A hunting song? No, it is *not* a hunting song. It is the wail of the poet's heart on discovering that everything is commonplace. To understand it, cling passionately to one another and think of faint lilies. [*They do so as he recites.*]—

"OH, HOLLOW! HOLLOW! HOLLOW!"

What time the poet hath hymned
    The writhing maid, lithe-limbed,
       Quivering on amaranthine asphodel,

How can he paint her woes,
Knowing, as well he knows,
   That all can be set right with calomel?

When from the poet's plinth
The amorous colocynth
   Yearns for the aloe, faint with rapturous thrills,
How can he hymn their throes
Knowing, as well he knows,
   That they are only uncompounded pills?

Is it, and can it be,
Nature hath this decree,
   Nothing poetic in the world shall dwell?
Or that in all her works
Something poetic lurks,
   Even in colocynth and calomel?

                        I cannot tell. [*Exit Bunthorne.*]

Angela. How purely fragrant!

Saphir. How earnestly precious!

Patience. Well, it seems to me to be nonsense.

Saphir. Nonsense, yes, perhaps—but oh, what precious nonsense!

Colonel. This is all very well, but you seem to forget that you are engaged to us.

Saphir. It can never be. You are not Empyrean. You are not Della Cruscan. You are not even Early English. Oh, be Early English ere it is too late! [*Officers look at each other in astonishment.*]

Jane [*looking at uniform*]. Red and Yellow! Primary colours! Oh, South Kensington!

Duke. We didn't design our uniforms, but we don't see how they could be improved.

Jane. No, you wouldn't. Still, there *is* a cobwebby grey velvet, with a tender bloom like cold gravy, which, made Florentine fourteenth-century, trimmed with Venetian leather and Spanish altar lace, and surmounted with something Japanese—it matters not what—would at least be Early English! Come, maidens.

[*Exeunt Maidens, two and two, singing refrain of "Twenty love-sick maidens we." The Officers watch them off in astonishment.*]

Duke. Gentlemen, this is an insult to the British uniform—
Colonel. A uniform that has been as successful in the
courts of Venus as on the field of Mars!

SONG—*Colonel.*

> When I first put this uniform on,
>   I said, as I looked in the glass,
>   "It's one to a million
>   That any civilian
>   My figure and form will surpass.
>   Gold lace has a charm for the fair,
>   And I've plenty of that, and to spare,
>   While a lover's professions,
>   When uttered in Hessians,
>   Are eloquent everywhere!"
>   A fact that I counted upon,
>   When I first put this uniform on!

>   CHORUS OF DRAGOONS.
>   By a simple coincidence, few
>   Could have counted upon,
>   The same thing occurred to me, too,
>   When I first put this uniform on!

Colonel.   I said, when I first put it on,
>   "It is plain to the veriest dunce
>   That every beauty
>   Will feel it her duty
>   To yield to its glamour at once.
>   They will see that I'm freely gold-laced
>   In a uniform handsome and chaste"—
>   But the peripatetics
>   Of long-haired aesthetics
>   Are very much more to their taste—
>   Which I never counted upon,
>   When I first put this uniform on!

Chorus.   By a simple coincidence, few
>   Could ever have reckoned upon,
>   I didn't anticipate that,
>   When I first put this uniform on!

[*The Dragoons go off angrily. Enter Bunthorne, who
    changes his manner and becomes intensely melo-
    dramatic.*]

RECIT. AND SONG—*Bunthorne.*

> Am I alone,
>> And unobserved? I am!
> Then let me own
>> I'm an aesthetic sham!
> This âir severe
>> Is but a mere
>>> Veneer!
> This cynic smile
>> Is but a wile
>>> Of guile!
> This costume chaste
>> Is but good taste
>>> Misplaced!
>> Let me confess!
> A languid love for lilies does *not* blight me!
> Lank limbs and haggard cheeks do *not* delight me!
>> I do *not* care for dirty greens
>>> By any means.

>> I do *not* long for all one sees
>>> That's Japanese.
> I am *not* fond of uttering platitudes
>> In stained-glass attitudes.
> In short, my mediaevalism's affectation,
> Born of a morbid love of admiration!

SONG.

If you're anxious for to shine in the high aesthetic line as a man of culture rare,
You must get up all the germs of the transcendental terms, and plant them everywhere.
You must lie upon the daisies and discourse in novel phrases of your complicated state of mind,
The meaning doesn't matter if it's only idle chatter of a transcendental kind.
>> And every one will say,
>> As you walk your mystic way,
"If this young man expresses himself in terms too deep for *me*,
Why, what a very singularly deep young man this deep young man must be!"

Be eloquent in praise of the very dull old days which have
    long since passed away,
And convince 'em, if you can, that the reign of good Queen
    Anne was Culture's palmiest day.
Of course you will pooh-pooh whatever's fresh and new,
    and declare it's crude and mean,
For Art stopped short in the cultivated court of the
    Empress Josephine.
                And every one will say,
                As you walk your mystic way,
"If that's not good enough for him which is good enough
    for *me,*
Why, what a very cultivated kind of youth this kind of
    youth must be!"

Then a sentimental passion of a vegetable fashion must ex-
    cite your languid spleen,
An attachment *à la* Plato for a bashful young potato, or a
    not-too-French French bean!
Though the Philistines may jostle, you will rank as an
    apostle in the high aesthetic band,
If you walk down Piccadilly with a poppy or a lily in your
    mediaeval hand.
                And every one will say,
                As you walk your flowery way,
"If he's content with a vegetable love which would cer-
    tainly not suit *me,*
Why, what a most particularly pure young man this pure
    young man must be!"

[*At the end of his song Patience enters. He sees her.*]
Bunthorne. Ah! Patience, come hither. I am pleased with
    thee. The bitter-hearted one, who finds all else hollow,
    is pleased with thee. For you are not hollow. *Are*
    you?
Patience. No, thanks, I have dined; but—I beg your pardon
    —I interrupt you.
Bunthorne. Life is made up of interruptions. The tortured
    soul, yearning for solitude, writhes under them. Oh,
    but my heart is a-weary! Oh, I am a cursed thing!
    Don't go.
Patience. Really, I'm very sorry—
Bunthorne. Tell me, girl, do you ever yearn?

Patience [*misunderstanding him*]. I earn my living.

Bunthorne [*impatiently*]. No, no! Do you know what it is to be heart-hungry? Do you know what it is to yearn for the Indefinable, and yet to be brought face to face, daily, with the Multiplication Table? Do you know what it is to seek oceans and to find puddles? —to long for whirlwinds and yet to have to do the best you can with the bellows? That's my case. Oh, I am a cursed thing! Don't go.

Patience. If you please, I don't understand you—you frighten me!

Bunthorne. Don't be frightened—it's only poetry.

Patience. Well, if that's poetry, I don't like poetry.

Bunthorne [*eagerly*]. Don't you? [*Aside.*] Can I trust her? [*Aloud.*] Patience, you don't like poetry—well, between you and me, *I* don't like poetry. It's hollow, unsubstantial—unsatisfactory. What's the use of yearning for Elysian Fields when you know you can't get 'em, and would only let 'em out on building leases if you had 'em?

Patience. Sir, I—

Bunthorne. Patience, I have long loved you. Let me tell you a secret. I am not as bilious as I look. If you like, I will cut my hair. There is more innocent fun within me than a casual spectator would imagine. You have never seen me frolicsome. Be a good girl—a very good girl—and one day you shall. If you are fond of touch-and-go jocularity—this is the shop for it.

Patience. Sir, I will speak plainly. In the matter of love I am untaught. I have never loved but my great-aunt. But I am quite certain that, under any circumstances, I couldn't possibly love *you.*

Bunthorne. Oh, you think not?

Patience. I'm quite sure of it. Quite sure. Quite.

Bunthorne. Very good. Life is henceforth a blank. I don't care what becomes of me. I have only to ask that you will not abuse my confidence; though *you* despise me, I am extremely popular with the other young ladies.

Patience. I only ask that you will leave me and never renew the subject.

Bunthorne. Certainly. Broken-hearted and desolate, I go. [*Recites.*]

"Oh, to be wafted away
    From this black Aceldama of sorrow,
Where the dust of an earthy to-day
    Is the earth of a dusty to-morrow!"

It is a little thing of my own. I call it "Heart Foam."
I shall not publish it. Farewell! Patience, Patience,
farewell! [*Exit Bunthorne.*]

Patience. What on earth does it all mean? Why does he
    love me? Why does he expect me to love him? He's
    not a relation! It frightens me!

[*Enter Angela.*]

Angela. Why, Patience, what is the matter?

Patience. Lady Angela, tell me two things. Firstly, what
    on earth is this love that upsets everybody; and,
    secondly, how is it to be distinguished from insanity?

Angela. Poor blind child! Oh, forgive her, Eros! Why, love
    is of all passions the most essential! It is the embodi-
    ment of purity, the abstraction of refinement! It is
    the one unselfish emotion in this whirlpool of grasping
    greed!

Patience. Oh, dear, oh! [*Beginning to cry.*]

Angela. Why are you crying?

Patience. To think that I have lived all these years without
    having experienced this ennobling and unselfish pas-
    sion! Why, what a wicked girl I must be! For it *is*
    unselfish, isn't it?

Angela. Absolutely! Love that is tainted with selfishness is
    no love. Oh, try, try, try to love! It really isn't difficult
    if you give your whole mind to it.

Patience. I'll set about it at once. I won't go to bed until
    I'm head over ears in love with somebody.

Angela. Noble girl! But it is possible that you have never
    loved anybody?

Patience. Yes, one.

Angela. Ah! Whom?

Patience. My great-aunt——

Angela. Great-aunts don't count.

Patience. Then there's nobody. At least—no, nobody. Not
    since I was a baby. But *that* doesn't count, I suppose.

Angela. I don't know. Tell me all about it.

DUET—*Patience* and *Angela*.

> Long years ago—fourteen, maybe—
> When but a tiny babe of four,
> Another baby played with me,
> My elder by a year or more;
> A little child of beauty rare,
> With marvellous eyes and wondrous hair,
> Who, in my child-eyes, seemed to me
> All that a little child should be!
> Ah, how we loved, that child and I!
> How pure our baby joy!
> How true our love—and, by the by,
> *He* was a little boy!

Angela.   Ah, old, old tale of Cupid's touch!
> I thought as much—I thought as much!
> He *was* a little boy!

Patience [*shocked*].   Pray don't misconstrue what I say—
> Remember, pray—remember, pray,
> He was a *little* boy!

Angela.   No doubt! Yet, spite of all your pains,
> The interesting fact remains—
> He was a little *boy!*

Ensemble.   { Ah, yes, in } {spite of all{ my   }pains, etc.
              { No doubt! Yet, }   { your }

[*Exit Angela.*]

Patience. It's perfectly dreadful to think of the appalling state I must be in! I had no idea that love was a duty. No wonder they all look so unhappy! Upon my word, I hardly like to associate with myself. I don't think I'm respectable. I'll go at once and fall in love with— [*Enter Grosvenor.*] A stranger!

DUET—*Patience* and *Grosvenor*.

Grosvenor. Prithee, pretty maiden—prithee, tell me true,
> (Hey, but I'm doleful, willow willow waly!)

Have you e'er a lover a-dangling after you?
>Hey willow waly O!
>>I would fain discover
>>If you have a lover?
>Hey willow waly O!

Patience. Gentle sir, my heart is frolicsome and free—
>(Hey, but he's doleful, willow willow waly!)
Nobody I care for comes a-courting me—
>Hey willow waly O!
>>Nobody I care for
>>Comes a-courting—therefore,
>Hey willow waly O!

Grosvenor. Prithee, pretty maiden, will you marry me?
>(Hey, but I'm hopeful, willow willow waly!)
I may say, at once, I'm a man of propertee—
>Hey willow waly O!
>>Money, I despise it;
>>Many people prize it,
>Hey willow waly O!

Patience. Gentle sir, although to marry I design—
>(Hey, but he's hopeful, willow willow waly!)
As yet I do not know you, and so I must decline.
>Hey willow waly O!
>>To other maidens go you—
>>As yet I do not know you,
>Hey willow waly O!

Grosvenor. Patience! Can it be that you don't recognise me?
Patience. Recognise you? No, indeed I don't!
Grosvenor. Have fifteen years so greatly changed me?
Patience. Fifteen years? What do you mean?
Grosvenor. Have you forgotten the friend of your youth, your Archibald?—your little playfellow? Oh, Chronos, Chronos, this is too bad of you!
Patience. Archibald! Is it possible? Why, let me look! It is! It is! It must be! Oh, how happy I am! I thought we should never meet again! And how you've grown!
Grosvenor. Yes, Patience, I am much taller and much stouter than I was.

Patience. And how you've improved!

Grosvenor. Yes, Patience, I am very beautiful! [*Sighs*.]

Patience. But surely *that* doesn't make you unhappy?

Grosvenor. Yes, Patience. Gifted as I am with a beauty which probably has not its rival on earth, I am, nevertheless, utterly and completely miserable.

Patience. Oh—but why?

Grosvenor. My child-love for you has never faded. Conceive, then, the horror of my situation when I tell you that it is my hideous destiny to be madly loved at first sight by every woman I come across!

Patience. But why do you make yourself so picturesque? Why not disguise yourself, disfigure yourself, anything to escape this persecution?

Grosvenor. No, Patience, that may not be. These gifts—irksome as they are—were given to me for the enjoyment and delectation of my fellow-creatures. I am a trustee for Beauty, and it is my duty to see that the conditions of my trust are faithfully discharged.

Patience. And you, too, are a Poet?

Grosvenor. Yes, I am the Apostle of Simplicity. I am called "Archibald the All-Right"—for I am infallible!

Patience. And is it possible that you condescend to love such a girl as I?

Grosvenor. Yes, Patience, is it not strange? I have loved you with a Florentine fourteenth-century frenzy for full fifteen years!

Patience. Oh, marvellous! I have hitherto been deaf to the voice of love. I seem now to know what love is! It has been revealed to me—it is Archibald Grosvenor!

Grosvenor. Yes, Patience, it is!

Patience [*as in a trance*]. We will never, never part!

Grosvenor. We will live and die together!

Patience. I swear it!

Grosvenor. We both swear it!

Patience [*recoiling from him*]. But—oh, horror!

Grosvenor. What's the matter?

Patience. Why, you are perfection! A source of endless ecstasy to all who know you!

Grosvenor. I know I am. Well?

Patience. Then, bless my heart, there can be nothing unselfish in loving *you!*

Grosvenor. Merciful powers! I never thought of that!

Patience. To monopolize those features on which all
    women love to linger! It would be unpardonable!
Grosvenor. Why, so it would! Oh, fatal perfection, again
    you interpose between me and my happiness!
Patience. Oh, if you were but a thought less beautiful than
    you are!
Grosvenor. Would that I were; but candour compels me
    to admit that I'm not!
Patience. Our duty is clear; we must part, and for ever!
Grosvenor. Oh, misery! And yet I cannot question the
    propriety of your decision. Farewell, Patience!
Patience. Farewell, Archibald! But stay!
Grosvenor. Yes, Patience?
Patience. Although I may not love *you*—for you are per-
    fection—there is nothing to prevent your loving *me*.
    I am plain, homely, unattractive!
Grosvenor. Why, that's true!
Patience. The love of such a man as you for such a girl as
    I must be unselfish!
Grosvenor. Unselfishness itself!

DUET—*Patience and Grosvenor.*

Patience. Though to marry you would very selfish be—
Grosvenor. Hey, but I'm doleful—willow willow waly!
Patience. You may, all the same, continue loving me—
Grosvenor. Hey willow waly O!
Both.   All the world ignoring,
                  You'll ⎫
                        ⎬ go on adoring—
                  I'll   ⎭
                  Hey willow waly O!

[*At the end, exeunt despairingly, in opposite directions.*]

FINALE—ACT I.

[*Enter Bunthorne, crowned with roses and hung about with
    garlands, and looking very miserable. He is led by
    Angela and Saphir (each of whom holds an end of
    the rose-garland by which he is bound), and accom-
    panied by procession of Maidens. They are dancing
    classically, and playing on cymbals, double pipes,
    and other archaic instruments.*]

CHORUS.

Let the merry cymbals sound,
    Gaily pipe Pandaean pleasure,
With a Daphnephoric bound
    Tread a gay but classic measure.
Every heart with hope is beating,
For at this exciting meeting
    Fickle Fortune will decide
    Who shall be our Bunthorne's bride!

[*Enter Dragoons, led by Colonel, Major, and Duke. They are surprised at proceedings.*]

CHORUS OF DRAGOONS.

Now tell us, we pray you,
Why thus they array you—
Oh, poet, how say you—
    What is it you've done?

Duke.   Of rite sacrificial,
By sentence judicial,
This seems the initial,
    Then why don't you run?

Colonel.   They cannot have led you
To hang or behead you,
Nor may they *all* wed you,
    Unfortunate one!

CHORUS OF DRAGOONS.

Then tell us, we pray you,
Why thus they array you—
Oh, poet, how say you—
    What is it you've done?

RECIT.—*Bunthorne.*

Heart-broken at my Patience's barbarity,
    By the advice of my solicitor [*introducing his Solicitor*],
In aid—in aid of a deserving charity,
    I've put myself up to be raffled for!

Maidens.   By the advice of his solicitor
    He's put himself up to be raffled for!

Dragoons. Oh, horror! urged by his solicitor
      He's put himself up to be raffled for!
Maidens. Oh, heaven's blessing on his solicitor!
Dragoons. A hideous curse on his solicitor!
[*The Solicitor, horrified at the Dragoons' curse, rushes off.*]
Colonel. Stay, we implore you,
      Before our hopes are blighted;
   You see before you
      The men to whom you're plighted!

      CHORUS OF DRAGOONS.
      Stay, we implore you,
      For we adore you;
      To us you're plighted
      To be united—
         Stay, we implore you!

SOLO—*Duke.*

     Your maiden hearts, ah, do not steel
     To pity's eloquent appeal,
     Such conduct British soldiers feel.
[*Aside to Dragoons.*] Sigh, sigh, all sigh! [*They all sigh.*]

     To foeman's steel we rarely see
     A British soldier bend the knee,
     Yet, one and all, they kneel to ye—
[*Aside to Dragoons.*] Kneel, kneel, all kneel!
                  [*They all kneel.*]

     Our soldiers very seldom cry,
     And yet—I need not tell you why—
     A tear-drop dews each martial eye!
[*Aside to Dragoons.*] Weep, weep, all weep!
                  [*They all weep.*]

ENSEMBLE.

     Our soldiers very seldom cry,
     And yet—I need not tell you why—
     A tear-drop dews each manly eye!
       Weep, weep, all weep!

Bunthorne [who has been impatient during this appeal].
Come, walk up, and purchase with avidity,
Overcome your diffidence and natural timidity,
Tickets for the raffle should be purchased with avidity,
   Put in half a guinea and a husband you may gain—
Such a judge of blue-and-white and other kinds of pottery—
From early Oriental down to modern terra-cotta-ry—
Put in half a guinea—you may draw him in a lottery—
   Such an opportunity may not occur again.

Chorus.   Such a judge of blue-and-white, etc.

*[Maidens crowd up to purchase tickets; during this
    Dragoons dance in single file round stage, to express
    their indifference.]*

Dragoons. We've been thrown over, we're aware,
           But we don't care—but we don't care!
           There's fish in the sea, no doubt of it,
           As good as ever came out of it,
           And some day we shall get our share,
           So we don't care—so we don't care!

*[During this the Maidens have been buying tickets. At
    last Jane presents herself. Bunthorne looks at her
    with aversion.]*

RECIT.

Bunthorne.   And are *you* going a ticket for to buy?
Jane [surprised].   Most certainly I am; why shouldn't I?
Bunthorne [aside]. Oh, Fortune, this is hard! *[Aloud.]*
               Blindfold your eyes;
               Two minutes will decide who wins the
                 prize!
[Maidens blindfold themselves.]

CHORUS OF MAIDENS.

O, Fortune, to my aching heart be kind!
Like us, thou art blindfolded, but not blind! *[Each un-
    covers one eye.]*
Just raise your bandage, thus, that you may see,
And give the prize, and give the prize to me! *[They cover
    their eyes again.]*
Bunthorne. Come, Lady Jane, I pray you draw the first!
Jane [joyfully]. He loves me best!

Bunthorne [*aside*].   I want to know the worst!

[*Jane puts hand in bag to draw ticket. Patience enters and
    prevents her doing so.*]

Patience. Hold! Stay your hand!
All [*uncovering their eyes*]. What means this interference?
        Of this bold girl I pray you make a clearance!
Jane. Away with you, and to your milk-pails go!
Bunthorne [*suddenly*]. She wants a ticket! Take a dozen!
Patience.   No!

SOLO—*Patience* [*kneeling to Bunthorne*].

        If there be pardon in your breast
            For this poor penitent,
        Who, with remorseful thought opprest,
            Sincerely doth repent;
        If you, with one so lowly, still
            Desire to be allied,
        Then you may take me, if you will,
            For I will be your bride!

All.   Oh, shameless one!
                            Oh, bold-faced thing!
                        Away you run,
                            Go, take you wing,
                        You shameless one!
                            You bold-faced thing!

Bunthorne.
        How strong is love! For many and many a week
        She's loved me fondly and has feared to speak,
        But Nature, for restraint too mighty far,
        Has burst the bonds of Art—and here we are!

Patience. No, Mr. Bunthorne, no—you're wrong again;
            Permit me—I'll endeavour to explain!

SONG—*Patience.*

Patience. True love must single-hearted be—
Bunthorne.   Exactly so!

Patience. From every selfish fancy free—
Bunthorne.   Exactly so!
Patience. No idle thought of gain or joy
           A maiden's fancy should employ—
           True love must be without alloy.
All.   Exactly so!
Patience. Imposture to contempt must lead—
Colonel.   Exactly so!
Patience. Blind vanity's dissension's seed—
Major.   Exactly so!
Patience. It follows, then, a maiden who
           Devotes herself to loving you [*indicating
              Bunthorne*]
           Is prompted by no selfish view—
All.   Exactly so!
Saphir. Are you resolved to wed this shameless one?
Angela. Is there no chance for any other?
Bunthorne [*decisively*]. None! [*Embraces Patience. Exeunt
    Patience and Bunthorne. Angela, Saphir, and Ella take
    Colonel, Duke, and Major down, while Girls gaze
    fondly at other Officers.*]

SESTETTE.

        I hear the soft note of the echoing voice
            Of an old, old love, long dead—
        It whispers my sorrowing heart "rejoice"—
            For the last sad tear is shed—
        The pain that is all but a pleasure will change
            For the pleasure that's all but pain,
        And never, oh never, this heart will range
            From that old, old love again!
[*Girls embrace Officers.*]

Chorus. Yes, the pain that is all, etc. [*Embrace.*]

[*Enter Patience and Bunthorne. As the Dragoons and Girls
    are embracing, enter Grosvenor, reading. He takes
    no notice of them, but comes slowly down, still
    reading. The Girls are all strangely fascinated by him,
    and gradually withdraw from Dragoons.*]
Angela. But who is this, whose god-like grace
           Proclaims he comes of noble race?

And who is this, whose manly face
Bears sorrow's interesting trace?

ENSEMBLE—*Tutti.*

Yes, who is this, etc.

Grosvenor. I am a broken-hearted troubadour,
   Whose mind's aesthetic and whose tastes are pure!
Angela. Aesthetic! He is aesthetic!
Grosvenor. Yes, yes—I am aesthetic
                  And poetic!
All the Ladies. Then, we love you!
[*The girls leave Dragoons and group, kneeling, around
      Grosvenor. Fury of Bunthorne, who recognizes a
      rival.*]
Dragoons. They love him! Horror!
Bunthorne and Patience. They love him! Horror!
Grosvenor. They love me! Horror! Horror! Horror!

ENSEMBLE—*Tutti.*

GIRLS.	GROSVENOR.
Oh, list while we a love confess	Again my cursed comeliness
That words imperfectly express.	Spreads hopeless anguish and distress!
Those shell-like ears, ah, do not close	Thine ears, oh Fortune, do not close
To blighted love's distracting woes!	To my intolerable woes.

PATIENCE.	BUNTHORNE.
List, Reginald, while I confess	My jealousy I can't express,
A love that's all unselfishness;	Their love they openly confess;
That it's unselfish, goodness knows,	His shell-like ears he does not close
You won't dispute it, I suppose?	To their recital of their woes.

Dragoons.   Now is not this ridiculous, etc.

END OF ACT 1

act 2

Scene.
A glade. Jane is discovered leaning on a violoncello, upon which she presently accompanies herself. Chorus of Maidens are heard singing in the distance.

Jane. The fickle crew have deserted Reginald and sworn allegiance to his rival, and all, forsooth, because he has glanced with passing favour on a puling milkmaid! Fools! of that fancy he will soon weary—and then I, who alone am faithful to him, shall reap my reward. But do not dally too long, Reginald, for my charms are ripe, Reginald, and already they are decaying. Better secure me ere I have gone too far!

RECIT.—*Jane.*

Sad is that woman's lot who, year by year,
Sees, one by one, her beauties disappear,
When Time, grown weary of her heart-drawn sighs,
Impatiently begins to "dim her eyes"!
Compelled, at last, in life's uncertain gloamings,
To wreathe her wrinkled brow with well-saved "combings,"
Reduced, with rouge, lip-salve, and pearly grey,
To "make up" for lost time as best she may!

SONG—*Jane.*

Silvered is the raven hair,
Spreading is the parting straight,
Mottled the complexion fair,
Halting is the youthful gait,
Hollow is the laughter free,
Spectacled the limpid eye—

Little will be left of me
   In the coming by and by!

Fading is the taper waist,
   Shapeless grows the shapely limb,
And although severely laced,
   Spreading is the figure trim!
Stouter than I used to be,
   Still more corpulent grow I—
There will be too much of me
   In the coming by and by! [*Exit Jane.*]

[*Enter Grosvenor, followed by Maidens, two and two, each
   playing on an archaic instrument, as in Act I. He is
   reading abstractedly, as Bunthorne did in Act I., and
   pays no attention to them.*]

CHORUS OF MAIDENS.

Turn, oh, turn in this direction,
   Shed, oh, shed a gentle smile,
With a glance of sad perfection
   Our poor fainting hearts beguile!
On such eyes as maidens cherish
   Let thy fond adorers gaze,
Or incontinently perish
   In their all-consuming rays!

[*He sits—they group around him.*]

Grosvenor [*aside*]. The old, old tale. How rapturously these
   maidens love me, and how hopelessly! Oh, Patience,
   Patience, with the love of thee in my heart, what have
   I for these poor mad maidens but an unvalued pity?
   Alas, they will die of hopeless love for me, as I shall
   die of hopeless love for thee!

Angela. Sir, will it please you read to us?

Grosvenor [*sighing*]. Yes, child, if you will. What shall I
   read?

Angela. One of your own poems.

Grosvenor. One of my own poems? Better not, my child.
   They will not cure thee of thy love.

Ella. Mr. Bunthorne used to read us a poem of his own
   every day.

Saphir. And, to do him justice, he read them extremely
   well.

Grosvenor. Oh, did he so? Well, who am I that I should

take upon myself to withhold my gifts from you?
What am I but a trustee? Here is a decalet—a pure
and simple thing, a very daisy—a babe might understand it. To appreciate it, it is not necessary to think
of anything at all.

Angela. Let us think of nothing at all!

GROSVENOR *recites.*

Gentle Jane was as good as gold,
She always did as she was told;
She never spoke when her mouth was full,
Or spilt plum jam on her nice new frock,
Or put white mice in the eight-day clock,
Or vivisected her last new doll,
Or fostered a passion for alcohol.
And when she grew up she was given in marriage
To a first-class earl who keeps his carriage!

Grosvenor. I believe I am right in saying that there is not
one word in that decalet which is calculated to bring
the blush of shame to the cheek of modesty.

Angela. Not one; it is purity itself.

Grosvenor. Here's another.

Teasing Tom was a very bad boy,
A great big squirt was his favourite toy;
He put live shrimps in his father's boots,
And sewed up the sleeves of his Sunday suits;
He punched his poor little sisters' heads,
And cayenne-peppered their four-post beds,
He plastered their hair with cobbler's wax,
And dropped hot halfpennies down their backs.
The consequence was he was lost totally,
And married a girl in the *corps de bally*!

Angela. Marked you how grandly—how relentlessly—the
damning catalogue of crime strode on, till Retribution,
like a poisèd hawk, came swooping down upon the
Wrong-Doer? Oh, it was terrible!

Ella. Oh, sir, you are indeed a true poet, for you touch our
hearts, and they go out to you!

Grosvenor [*aside*]. This is simply cloying. [*Aloud.*] Ladies,
I am sorry to appear ungallant, but this is Saturday,

and you have been following me about ever since
Monday. I should like the usual half-holiday. I shall
take it as a personal favour if you will kindly allow
me to close early to-day.

Saphir. Oh, sir, do not send us from you!

Grosvenor. Poor, poor girls! It is best to speak plainly. I
know that I am loved by you, but I never can love
you in return, for my heart is fixed elsewhere! Remember the fable of the Magnet and the Churn.

Angela [*wildly*]. But we don't know the fable of the Magnet
and the Churn!

Grosvenor. Don't you? Then I will sing it to you.

SONG—*Grosvenor.*

> A magnet hung in a hardware shop,
> And all around was a loving crop
> Of scissors and needles, nails and knives,
> Offering love for all their lives;
> But for iron the magnet felt no whim,
> Though he charmed iron, it charmed not him;
> From needles and nails and knives he'd turn,
> For he'd set his love on a Silver Churn!

All.	A Silver Churn?
Grosvenor.	A Silver Churn!

> His most aesthetic,
> Very magnetic
> Fancy took this turn—
> "If I can wheedle
> A knife or a needle,
> Why not a Silver Churn?"

Chorus.   His most aesthetic, etc.

Grosvenor.

> And Iron and Steel expressed surprise,
> The needles opened their well-drilled eyes,
> The penknives felt "shut up," no doubt,
> The scissors declared themselves "cut out,"
> The kettles they boiled with rage, 'tis said,
> While every nail went off its head,

And hither and thither began to roam,
Till a hammer came up—and drove them home.
All. It drove them home?
Grosvenor. It drove them home!

> While this magnetic,
> Peripatetic
> Lover he lived to learn,
> By no endeavour
> Can magnet ever
> Attract a Silver Churn!

All.   While this magnetic, etc.

[They go off in low spirits, gazing back at him from time to time.]

Grosvenor. At last they are gone! What is this mysterious fascination that I seem to exercise over all I come across? A curse on my fatal beauty, for I am sick of conquests!

[Patience appears.]

Patience. Archibald!

Grosvenor [turns and sees her]. Patience!

Patience. I have escaped with difficulty from my Reginald. I wanted to see you so much that I might ask you if you still love me as fondly as ever?

Grosvenor. Love you? If the devotion of a lifetime— *[Seizes her hand.]*

Patience [indignantly]. Hold! Unhand me, or I scream! *[He releases her.]* If you are a gentleman, pray remember that I am another's! *[Very tenderly.]* But you *do* love me, don't you?

Grosvenor. Madly, hopelessly, despairingly!

Patience. That's right! I never can be yours; but that's right!

Grosvenor. And you love this Bunthorne?

Patience. With a heart-whole ecstasy that withers, and scorches, and burns, and stings! *[Sadly.]* It is my duty.

Grosvenor. Admirable girl! But you are not happy with him?

Patience. Happy? I am miserable beyond description!

Grosvenor. That's right! I never can be yours; but that's right!

Patience. But go now. I see dear Reginald approaching. Farewell, dear Archibald; I cannot tell you how happy it has made me to know that you still love me.

Grosvenor. Ah, if I only dared—[*Advances towards her.*]

Patience. Sir! this language to one who is promised to another! [*Tenderly.*] Oh, Archibald, think of me sometimes, for my heart is breaking! He is so unkind to me, and you would be so loving!

Grosvenor. Loving! [*Advances towards her.*]

Patience. Advance one step, and as I am a good and pure woman, I scream! [*Tenderly.*] Farewell, Archibald! [*Sternly.*] Stop there! [*Tenderly.*] Think of me sometimes! [*Angrily.*] Advance at your peril! Once more, adieu!

[*Grosvenor sighs, gazes sorrowfully at her, sighs deeply, and exit. She bursts into tears. Enter Bunthorne, followed by Jane. He is moody and preoccupied.*]

JANE *sings.*

In a doleful train,
    One and one I walk all day;
For I love in vain—
    None so sorrowful as they
        Who can only sigh and say,
        Woe is me, alackaday!

Bunthorne [*seeing Patience*]. Crying, eh? What are you crying about?

Patience. I've only been thinking how dearly I love you!

Bunthorne. Love me! Bah!

Jane. Love him! Bah!

Bunthorne [*to Jane*]. Don't you interfere.

Jane. He always crushes me!

Patience [*going to him*]. What is the matter, dear Reginald? If you have any sorrow, tell it to me, that I may share it with you. [*Sighing.*] It is my duty!

Bunthorne [*snappishly*]. Whom were you talking with just now?

Patience. With dear Archibald.

Bunthorne [*furiously*]. With dear Archibald! Upon my honour, this is too much!

Jane. A great deal too much!

Bunthorne [*angrily to Jane*]. Do be quiet!

Jane. Crushed again!

Patience. I think he is the noblest, purest, and most perfect
being I have ever met. But I don't love him. It is true
that he is devotedly attached to me, but indeed I
don't love *him*. Whenever he grows affectionate, I
scream. It is my duty! [*Sighing.*]

Bunthorne. I dare say!

Jane. So do I! *I* dare say!

Patience. Why, how could I love him and love you too?
You can't love two people at once!

Bunthorne. Oh, can't you, though!

Patience. No, you can't; I only wish you could.

Bunthorne. I don't believe you know what love is!

Patience [*sighing*]. Yes, I do. There was a happy time when
I didn't, but a bitter experience has taught me.

[*Exeunt Bunthorne and Jane.*]

BALLAD—*Patience.*

> Love is a plaintive song,
>   Sung by a suffering maid,
> Telling a tale of wrong,
>   Telling of hope betrayed;
> Tuned to each changing note,
>   Sorry when *he* is sad,
> Blind to his every mote,
>   Merry when he is glad!
>   Love that no wrong can cure,
>   Love that is always new,
>   That is the love that's pure,
>   That is the love that's true!
>
> Rendering good for ill,
>   Smiling at every frown,
> Yielding your own self-will,
>   Laughing your tear-drops down;
> Never a selfish whim,
>   Trouble, or pain to stir;
> Everything for him,
>   Nothing at all for her!
>   Love that will aye endure,

Though the rewards be few,
That is the love that's pure,
That is the love that's true!

[*At the end of ballad exit Patience, weeping. Enter Bunthorne and Jane.*]

Bunthorne. Everything has gone wrong with me since that
smug-faced idiot came here. Before that I was admired—I may say, loved.

Jane. Too mild—adored!

Bunthorne. Do let a poet soliloquize! The damozels used to
follow me wherever I went; now they all follow him!

Jane. Not all! *I* am still faithful to you.

Bunthorne. Yes, and a pretty damozel *you* are!

Jane. No, not pretty. Massive. Cheer up! I will never leave
you, I swear it!

Bunthorne. Oh, thank you! I know what it is; it's his confounded mildness. They find me too highly spiced, if
you please! And no doubt I *am* highly spiced.

Jane. Not for my taste!

Bunthorne [*savagely*]. No, but I am for theirs. But I will
show the world I can be as mild as he. If they want
insipidity, they shall have it. I'll meet this fellow on
his own ground and beat him on it.

Jane. You shall. And I will help you.

Bunthorne. You will? Jane, there's a good deal of good in
you, after all!

DUET—*Bunthorne and Jane.*

Jane.

So go to him and say to him, with compliment
ironical—

Bunthorne.   Sing "Hey to you—
Good day to you"—
And that's what I shall say!

Jane.

"Your style is much too sanctified—your cut is too
canonical"—

Bunthorne.   Sing "Bah to you—
Ha! ha! to you"—
And that's what I shall say!

Jane.

"I was the beau ideal of the morbid young
aesthetical—
To doubt my inspiration was regarded as
heretical—
Until you cut me out with your placidity
emetical."—

Bunthorne.   Sing "Booh to you—
Pooh, pooh to you"—
And that's what I shall say!

Both.   Sing "Hey to you—good day to you"—
Sing "Bah to you—ha! ha! to you"—
Sing "Booh to you—pooh, pooh to you"—

And that's what $\begin{Bmatrix} you \\ I \end{Bmatrix}$ shall say!

Bunthorne.

I'll tell him that unless he will consent to be more
jocular—

Jane.   Sing "Booh to you—
Pooh, pooh to you"—
And that's what you should say!

Bunthorne.

To cut his curly hair, and stick an eyeglass in his
ocular—

Jane.   Sing "Bah to you—
Ha! ha! to you"—
And that's what you should say!

Bunthorne.

To stuff his conversation full of quibble and of
quiddity—
To dine on chops and roly-poly pudding with
avidity—
He'd better clear away with all convenient
rapidity.

Jane.   Sing "Hey to you—
Good day to you"—
And that's what you should say!

Both. Sing "Booh to you—pooh, pooh to you"—
        Sing "Bah to you—ha! ha! to you"—
        Sing "Hey to you—good day to you"—
        And that's what $\begin{cases} I \\ you \end{cases}$ shall say!

[*Exeunt Jane and Bunthorne together. Enter Duke, Colonel, and Major. They have abandoned their uniforms, and are dressed and made up in imitation of Aesthetics. They have long hair, and other outward signs of attachment to the brotherhood. As they sing they walk in stiff, constrained, and angular attitudes—a grotesque exaggeration of the attitudes adopted by Bunthorne and the young Ladies in Act I.*]

TRIO—*Duke, Colonel,* and *Major.*

It's clear that mediaeval art alone retains its zest,
To charm and please its devotees we've done our little best.
We're not quite sure if all we do has the Early English
    ring;
But, as far as we can judge, it's something like this sort of
    thing:
            You hold yourself like this [*attitude*],
            You hold yourself like that [*attitude*],
By hook and crook you try to look both angular and flat
    [*attitude*].
            We venture to expect
            That what we recollect,
Though but a part of true High Art, will have its due effect.

If this is not exactly right, we hope you won't upbraid;
You can't get high Aesthetic tastes, like trousers, ready
    made.
True views on Mediaevalism Time alone will bring,
But, as far as we can judge, it's something like this sort of
    thing:
            You hold yourself like this [*attitude*],
            You hold yourself like that [*attitude*],
By hook and crook you try to look both angular and flat
    [*attitude*].
            To cultivate the trim

Rigidity of limb,
You ought to get a Marionette, and form your style on him [*attitude*].

Colonel [*attitude*]. Yes, it's quite clear that our only chance of making a lasting impression on these young ladies is to become as aesthetic as they are.

Major [*attitude*]. No doubt. The only question is how far we've succeeded in doing so. I don't know why, but I've an idea that this is not quite right.

Duke [*attitude*]. *I* don't like it. I never did. I don't see what it means. I do it, but I don't like it.

Colonel. My good friend, the question is not whether we like it, but whether they do. They understand these things—we don't. Now I shouldn't be surprised if this is effective enough—at a distance.

Major. I can't help thinking we're a little stiff at it. It would be extremely awkward if we were to be "struck" so!

Colonel. I don't think we shall be struck so. Perhaps we're a little awkward at first—but everything must have a beginning. Oh, here they come! 'Tention!

[*They strike fresh attitudes, as Angela and Saphir enter.*]

Angela [*seeing them*]. Oh, Saphir—see—see! The immortal fire has descended on them, and they are of the Inner Brotherhood—perceptively intense and consummately utter. [*The Officers have some difficulty in maintaining their constrained attitudes.*]

Saphir [*in admiration*]. How Botticellian! How Fra Angelican! Oh, Art, we thank thee for this boon!

Colonel [*apologetically*]. I'm afraid we're not quite right.

Angela. Not supremely, perhaps, but oh, so all-but! [*To Saphir.*] Oh, Saphir, are they not quite too all-but?

Saphir. They are indeed jolly utter!

Major [*in agony*]. I wonder what the Inner Brotherhood usually recommend for cramp?

Colonel. Ladies, we will not deceive you. We are doing this at some personal inconvenience with a view of expressing the extremity of our devotion to you. We trust that it is not without its effect.

Angela. We will not deny that we are much moved by this proof of your attachment.

Saphir. Yes, your conversion to the principles of Aesthetic Art in its highest development has touched us deeply.

Angela. And if Mr. Grosvenor should remain obdurate—

Saphir. Which we have every reason to believe he will—

Major [*aside, in agony*]. I wish they'd make haste.

Angela. We are not prepared to say that our yearning hearts will not go out to you.

Colonel [*as giving a word of command*]. By sections of threes—Rapture! [*All strike a fresh attitude, expressive of aesthetic rapture.*]

Saphir. Oh, it's extremely good—for beginners it's admirable.

Major. The only question is, who will take who?

Colonel. Oh, the Duke chooses first, as a matter of course.

Duke. Oh, I couldn't think of it—you are really too good!

Colonel. Nothing of the kind. You are a great matrimonial fish, and it's only fair that each of these ladies should have a chance of hooking you. It's perfectly simple. Observe, suppose you choose Angela, I take Saphir, Major takes nobody. Suppose you choose Saphir, Major takes Angela, I take nobody. Suppose you choose neither, I take Angela, Major takes Saphir. Clear as day!

QUINTET.

> *Duke, Colonel, Major, Angela,* and *Saphir.*

> DUKE [*taking Saphir*].
> If Saphir I choose to marry,
>   I shall be fixed up for life;
> Then the Colonel need not tarry,
>   Angela can be his wife.

[*Duke dances with Saphir, Colonel with Angela, Major dances alone.*]

> MAJOR [*dancing alone*].
> In that case unprecedented,
>   Single I shall live and die—
> I shall have to be contented
>   With their heartfelt sympathy!

ALL [*dancing as before*].
He will have to be contented
   With our heartfelt sympathy!

DUKE [*taking Angela*].
If on Angy I determine,
   At my wedding she'll appear
Decked in diamonds and in ermine,
   Major then can take Saphir.

[*Duke dances with Angela, Major with Saphir, Colonel dances alone.*]

COLONEL [*dancing*].
In that case unprecedented,
   Single I shall live and die—
I shall have to be contented
   With their heartfelt sympathy!

ALL [*dancing as before*].
He will have to be contented
   With our heartfelt sympathy!

DUKE [*taking both Angela and Saphir*].
After some debate internal,
   If on neither I decide,
Saphir then can take the Colonel,
         [*Handing Saphir to Colonel.*]
   Angy be the Major's bride!
         [*Handing Angela to Major.*]

[*Colonel dances with Saphir, Major with Angela, Duke dances alone.*]

DUKE [*dancing*].
In that case unprecedented,
   Single I must live and die—
I shall have to be contented
   With their heartfelt sympathy!

ALL [*dancing as before*].
He will have to be contented
   With our heartfelt sympathy.

[*At the end, Duke, Colonel, and Major, and two girls dance off arm-in-arm. Enter Grosvenor.*]

Grosvenor. It is very pleasant to be alone. It is pleasant to be able to gaze at leisure upon those features which all others may gaze upon at their good will! [*Looking at his reflection in hand-mirror.*] Ah, I am a very Narcissus!

[*Enter Bunthorne, moodily.*]

Bunthorne. It's no use; I can't live without admiration. Since Grosvenor came here, insipidity has been at a premium. Ah, he is there!

Grosvenor. Ah, Bunthorne! come here—look! Very graceful, isn't it!

Bunthorne [*taking hand-mirror*]. Allow me; I haven't seen it. Yes, it is graceful.

Grosvenor [*re-taking hand-mirror*]. Oh, good gracious! not that—this—

Bunthorne. You don't mean that! Bah! I am in no mood for trifling.

Grosvenor. And what is amiss?

Bunthorne. Ever since you came here, you have entirely monopolized the attentions of the young ladies. I don't like it, sir!

Grosvenor. My dear sir, how can I help it? They are the plague of my life. My dear Mr. Bunthorne, with your personal disadvantages, you can have no idea of the inconvenience of being madly loved, at first sight, by every woman you meet.

Bunthorne. Sir, until you came here I was adored!

Grosvenor. Exactly—until I came here. That's my grievance. I cut everybody out! I assure you, if you could only suggest some means whereby, consistently with my duty to society, I could escape these inconvenient attentions, you would earn my everlasting gratitude.

Bunthorne. I will do so at once. However popular it may be with the world at large, your personal appearance is highly objectionable to *me*.

Grosvenor. It is? [*Shaking his hand.*] Oh, thank you! thank you! How can I express my gratitude?

Bunthorne. By making a complete change at once. Your conversation must henceforth be perfectly matter-of-fact. You must cut your hair, and have a back parting.

In appearance and costume you must be absolutely commonplace.

Grosvenor [*decidedly*]. No. Pardon me, that's impossible.

Bunthorne. Take care! When I am thwarted I am very terrible.

Grosvenor. I can't help that. I am a man with a mission. And that mission must be fulfilled.

Bunthorne. I don't think you quite appreciate the consequences of thwarting me.

Grosvenor. I don't care what they are.

Bunthorne. Suppose—I won't go so far as to say that I will do it—but suppose for one moment I were to curse you? [*Grosvenor quails.*] Ah! Very well. Take care.

Grosvenor. But surely you would never do that? [*In great alarm.*]

Bunthorne. I don't know. It would be an extreme measure, no doubt. Still—

Grosvenor [*wildly*]. But you would not do it—I am sure you would not. [*Throwing himself at Bunthorne's knees, and clinging to him.*] Oh, reflect, reflect! You had a mother once.

Bunthorne. Never!

Grosvenor. Then you had an aunt! [*Bunthorne affected.*] Ah! I see you had! By the memory of that aunt, I implore you to pause ere you resort to this last fearful expedient. Oh, Mr. Bunthorne, reflect, reflect! [*Weeping.*]

Bunthorne [*aside, after a struggle with himself*]. I must not allow myself to be unmanned! [*Aloud.*] It is useless. Consent at once, or may a nephew's curse—

Grosvenor. Hold! Are you absolutely resolved?

Bunthorne. Absolutely.

Grosvenor. Will nothing shake you?

Bunthorne. Nothing. I am adamant.

Grosvenor. Very good. [*Rising.*] Then I yield.

Bunthorne. Ha! You swear it?

Grosvenor. I do, cheerfully. I have long wished for a reasonable pretext for such a change as you suggest. It has come at last. I do it on compulsion!

Bunthorne. Victory! I triumph!

DUET—*Bunthorne* and *Grosvenor*.

Bunthorne. When I go out of door,
      Of damozels a score
        (All sighing and burning,
        And clinging and yearning)
      Will follow me as before.
      I shall, with cultured taste,
      Distinguish gems from paste,
        And "High diddle diddle"
        Will rank as an idyll,
      If I pronounce it chaste!

Both.   A most intense young man,
      A soulful-eyed young man,
    An ultra-poetical, super-aesthetical,
      Out-of-the-way young man!

Grosvenor. Conceive me, if you can,
      An every-day young man:
        A commonplace type,
        With a stick and a pipe,
      And a half-bred black-and-tan;
        Who thinks suburban "hops"
        More fun than "Monday Pops,"
      Who's fond of his dinner,
      And doesn't get thinner
        On bottled beer and chops.

Both.   A commonplace young man,
      A matter-of-fact young man,
    A steady and stolid-y, jolly Bank-holiday
      Every-day young man!

Bunthorne. A Japanese young man,
      A blue-and-white young man,
    Francesca di Rimini, miminy, piminy,
      Je-ne-sais-quoi young man!

Grosvenor. A Chancery Lane young man,
      A Somerset House young man,
    A very delectable, highly respectable,
      Threepenny-bus young man!

Bunthorne. A pallid and thin young man,

> A haggard and lank young man,
> A greenery-yallery, Grosvenor Gallery,
> Foot-in-the-grave young man!

Grosvenor. A Sewell & Cross young man,
> A Howell & James young man,
> A pushing young particle—"What's the next
>   article?"—
> Waterloo House young man!

ENSEMBLE

BUNTHORNE	GROSVENOR
Conceive me, if you can,	Conceive me, if you can,
A crotchety, cracked young man,	A matter-of-fact young man,
An ultra-poetical, super-aesthetical,	An alphabetical, arithmetical,
Out-of-the-way young man!	Every-day young man!

[*At the end, Grosvenor dances off. Bunthorne remains.*]

Bunthorne. It is all right! I have committed my last act of
    ill-nature, and henceforth I'm a changed character.
    [*Dances about stage, humming refrain of last air.*]

[*Enter Patience. She gazes in astonishment at him.*]

Patience. Reginald! Dancing! And—what in the world is
    the matter with you?

Bunthorne. Patience, I'm a changed man. Hitherto I've
    been gloomy, moody, fitful—uncertain in temper
    and selfish in disposition—

Patience. You have, indeed! [*Sighing.*]

Bunthorne. All that is changed. I have reformed. I have
    modelled myself upon Mr. Grosvenor. Henceforth I
    am mildly cheerful. My conversation will blend
    amusement with instruction. I shall still be aesthetic;
    but my aestheticism will be of the most pastoral
    kind.

Patience. Oh, Reginald! Is all this true?

Bunthorne. Quite true. Observe how amiable I am. [*Assuming a fixed smile.*]

Patience. But, Reginald, how long will this last?

Bunthorne. With occasional intervals for rest and refreshment, as long as I do.

Patience. Oh, Reginald, I'm so happy! [*In his arms.*] Oh,
   dear, dear Reginald, I cannot express the joy I feel
   at this change. It will no longer be a duty to love you,
   but a pleasure—a rapture—an ecstasy!
Bunthorne. My darling!
Patience. But—oh, horror! [*Recoiling from him.*]
Bunthorne. What's the matter?
Patience. Is it quite certain that you have absolutely re-
   formed—that you are henceforth a perfect being—
   utterly free from defect of any kind?
Bunthorne. It is quite certain. I have sworn it.
Patience. Then I never can be yours!
Bunthorne. Why not?
Patience. Love, to be pure, must be absolutely unselfish,
   and there can be nothing unselfish in loving so perfect
   a being as you have now become!
Bunthorne. But, stop a bit! I don't want to change—I'll
   relapse—I'll be as I was—interrupted!
[*Enter Grosvenor, followed by all the young Ladies, who
   are followed by Chorus of Dragoons. He has had his
   hair cut, and is dressed in an ordinary suit of dittoes
   and a pot hat. They all dance cheerfully round the
   stage in marked contrast to their former languor.*]

CHORUS—*Grosvenor* and *Girls*.

GROSVENOR	GIRLS
I'm a Waterloo House young man,	We're Swears & Wells young girls,
A Sewell & Cross young man,	We're Madame Louise young girls,
A steady and stolid-y, jolly Bank-holiday,	We're prettily pattering, cheerily chattering,
Every-day young man!	Every-day young girls!

Bunthorne. Angela—Ella—Saphir—what—what does this
   mean?
Angela. It means that Archibald the All-Right cannot be
   all-wrong; and if the All-Right chooses to discard
   aestheticism, it proves that aestheticism ought to be
   discarded.
Patience. Oh, Archibald! Archibald! I'm shocked—surprised—horrified!
Grosvenor. I can't help it. I'm not a free agent. I do it on
   compulsion.

Patience. This is terrible. Go! I shall never set eyes on you
again. But—oh, joy!

Grosvenor. What is the matter?

Patience. Is it quite, quite certain that you will always be a
commonplace young man?

Grosvenor. Always—I've sworn it.

Patience. Why, then, there's nothing to prevent my loving
you with all the fervour at my command!

Grosvenor. Why, that's true.

Patience. My Archibald!

Grosvenor. My Patience! [*They embrace.*]

Bunthorne. Crushed again!

[*Enter Jane.*]

Jane [*who is still aesthetic*]. Cheer up! I am still here. I
have never left you, and I never will!

Bunthorne. Thank you, Jane. After all, there is no denying
it, you're a fine figure of a woman!

Jane. My Reginald!

Bunthorne. My Jane!

[*Flourish. Enter Colonel, Duke, and Major.*]

Colonel. Ladies, the Duke has at length determined to
select a bride! [*General excitement.*]

Duke. I have a great gift to bestow. Approach, such of
you as are truly lovely. [*All come forward, bashfully,
except Jane and Patience.*] In personal appearance
you have all that is necessary to make a woman happy. In common fairness, I think I ought to choose the
only one among you who has the misfortune to be
distinctly plain. [*Girls retire disappointed.*] Jane!

Jane [*leaving Bunthorne's arms*]. Duke! [*Jane and Duke
embrace. Bunthorne is utterly disgusted.*]

Bunthorne. Crushed again!

FINALE.

Duke.   After much debate internal,
                    I on Lady Jane decide,
                Saphir now may take the Colonel,
                    Angy be the Major's bride!

[*Saphir pairs off with Colonel, Angela with Major, Ella
with Solicitor.*]

Bunthorne. In that case unprecedented,

Single I must live and die—
I shall have to be contented
  With a tulip or li*ly*!

[*Takes a lily from button-hole and gazes affectionately
    at it.*]

All.   He will have to be contented
  With a tulip or li*ly*!

Greatly pleased with one another,
  To get married we decide.
Each of us will wed the other,
  Nobody be Bunthorne's Bride!

DANCE.

CURTAIN

Arthur W. Pinero (1855–1935)

The Second Mrs. Tanqueray

A PLAY IN FOUR ACTS

An Old New Play and a New Old One

BY GEORGE BERNARD SHAW

It is somewhat surprising to find Mr. Oscar Wilde, who does not usually model himself on Mr. Henry Arthur Jones, giving his latest play a five-chambered title like *The Case of Rebellious Susan*. So I suggest with some confidence that *The Importance of Being Earnest* dates from a period long anterior to Susan. However it may have been retouched immediately before its production, it must certainly have been written before *Lady Windermere's Fan*. I do not suppose it to be Mr. Wilde's first play: he is too susceptible to fine art to have begun otherwise than with a strenuous imitation of a great dramatic poem, Greek or Shakespearian; but it was perhaps the first which he designed for practical commercial use at the West End theatres. The evidence of this is abundant. The play has a plot —a gross anachronism; there is a scene between the two girls in the second act quite in the literary style of Mr. Gilbert, and almost inhuman enough to have been conceived by him; the humor is adulterated by stock mechanical fun to an extent that absolutely scandalizes one in a play with such an author's name to it; and the punning title and several of the more farcical passages recall the epoch of the late H. J. Byron. The whole has been varnished, and here and there veneered, by the author of *A Woman of no Im-*

portance; but the general effect is that of a farcical comedy dating from the seventies, unplayed during that period because it was too clever and too decent, and brought up to date as far as possible by Mr. Wilde in his now completely formed style. Such is the impression left by the play on me. But I find other critics, equally entitled to respect, declaring that *The Importance of Being Earnest* is a strained effort of Mr. Wilde's at ultra-modernity, and that it could never have been written but for the opening up of entirely new paths in drama last year by *Arms and the Man.* At which I confess to a chuckle.

I cannot say that I greatly cared for *The Importance of Being Earnest.* It amused me, of course; but unless comedy touches me as well as amuses me, it leaves me with a sense of having wasted my evening. I go to the theatre to be moved to laughter, not to be tickled or bustled into it; and that is why, though I laugh as much as anybody at a farcical comedy, I am out of spirits before the end of the second act, and out of temper before the end of the third, my miserable mechanical laughter intensifying these symptoms at every outburst. If the public ever becomes intelligent enough to know when it is really enjoying itself and when it is not, there will be an end of farcical comedy. Now in *The Importance of Being Earnest* there is a good deal of this rib-tickling: for instance, the lies, the deceptions, the cross-purposes, the sham mourning, the christening of the two grown-up men, the muffin eating, and so forth. These could only have been raised from the farcical plane by making them occur to characters who had, like Don Quixote, convinced us of their reality and obtained some hold on our sympathy. But that unfortunate moment of Gilbertism breaks our belief in the humanity of the play. Thus we are thrown back on the force of daintiness of its wit, brought home by an exquisitely grave, natural, and unconscious execution on the part of the actors. Alas! the latter is not forthcoming. Mr. Kinsey Peile as a man-servant, and Miss Irene Vanburgh as Gwendolen Fairfax, alone escaped from a devastating consciousness of Mr. Wilde's reputation, which more or less preoccupied all the rest, except perhaps Miss Millard, with whom all comedy is a preoccupation, since she is essentially a sentimental actress. In such passages as the Gilbertian quarrel with Gwendolen, her charm rebuked the scene instead of enhancing it. The older ladies were, if they will excuse my saying so, quite maddening. The violence of their affectation, the insufferable low comedy soars and swoops of the voice, the rigid shivers of elbow, shoulder, and neck, which are supposed on the stage to characterize the behavior of ladies after the age of forty, played havoc with the piece. In Miss Rose Leclercq a good deal of this sort of thing is only the mannerism of a genuine if somewhat impossible style; but Miss Leclercq was absent through indisposition on the night of my visit, so that I had not her style to console me. Mr. Aynesworth's easy-going *Our Boys* style of play suited his part rather happily; and Mr. Alexander's graver and more refined manner made the right contrast with it. But Mr. Alexander, after playing with very nearly if not quite perfect conviction in the first two acts, suddenly lost confidence in the third, and began to spur up for a rattling finish. From the moment that began, the play was done with. The speech in which Worthing forgives his supposed mother, and the business of searching the army lists, which should have been conducted with subdued earnestness, was bustled through to the destruction of all verisimilitude and consequently all interest. That is the worst of having anyone who is not an inveterate and hardened comedian in a leading comedy part. His faith, patience, and relish begin to give out after a time; and he finally commits the unpardonable sin against the author of giving the signal that the play is over ten minutes before the fall of the curtain, instead of speaking the last line as if the whole evening were still before the audience. Mr. Alexander does not throw himself genuinely into comedy: he condescends to amuse himself with it; and in the end he finds that he cannot condescend enough. On the whole I must decline to accept *The Importance of Being Earnest* as a day less than ten years old; and I am altogether unable to perceive any uncommon excellence in its presentation.

I am in a somewhat foolish position concerning a play at the Opera Comique, whither I was bidden this day week. For some reason I was not supplied with a programme; so that I never learnt the name of the play. I believe I recognized some of the members of the company—generally a very difficult thing to do in a country where, with a few talented exceptions, every actor is just

like every other actor—but they have now faded from my
memory. At the end of the second act the play had advanced about as far as an ordinàry dramatist would have
brought it five minutes after the first rising of the curtain;
or, say, as far as Ibsen would have brought it ten years
before that event. Taking advantage of the second interval
to stroll out into the Strand for a little exercise, I unfortunately forgot all about my business, and actually reached
home before it occurred to me that I had not seen the end
of the play. Under these circumstances it would ill become
me to dogmatize on the merits of the work or its performance. I can only offer the management my apologies.

I am indebted to Mr. Heinemann for a copy of *The
Second Mrs. Tanqueray,* which he has just published in a
five-shilling volume, with an excellent photographic portrait of the author by Mr. Hollyer. Those who did not see
the play at the St. James's Theatre can now examine the
literary basis of the work that so immoderately fascinated
playgoing London in 1893. But they must not expect the
play to be as imposing in the library as it was on the stage.
Its merit there was relative to the culture of the playgoing
public. Paula Tanqueray is an astonishingly well-drawn
figure as stage figures go nowadays, even allowing for the
fact that there is no cheaper subject for the character
draughtsman than the ill-tempered sensual woman seen
from the point of view of the conventional man. But off
the stage her distinction vanishes. The novels of Anthony
Trollope, Charles Lever, Bulwer Lytton, Charles Reade,
and many other novelists, whom nobody praised thirty
years ago in the terms in which Mr. Pinero is praised now,
are full of feats of character drawing in no way inferior—
to say the least—to Mr. Pinero's. The theatre was not
ready for that class of work then: it is now; and accordingly
Mr. Pinero, who in literature is a humble and somewhat
belated follower of the novelists of the middle of the nineteenth century, and who has never written a line from
which it could be guessed that he is a contemporary of
Ibsen, Tolstoi, Meredith, or Sarah Grand, finds himself
at the dawn of the twentieth hailed as a man of new ideas,
of daring originality, of supreme literary distinction, and
even—which is perhaps oddest—of consummate stage
craft. Stage craft, after all, is very narrowly limited by the
physical conditions of stage representation; but when one

turns over the pages of *The Second Mrs. Tanqueray*, and notes the naïve machinery of the exposition in the first act, in which two whole actors are wasted on sham parts, and the hero, at his own dinner party, is compelled to get up and go ignominiously into the next room "to write some letters" when something has to be said behind his back; when one follows Cayley Drummle, the confidant to whom both Paula and her husband explain themselves for the benefit of the audience; when one counts the number of doors which Mr. Pinero needs to get his characters on and off the stage, and how they have finally to be supplemented by the inevitable "French windows" (two of them); and when the activity of the postman is taken into consideration, it is impossible to avoid the conclusion that what most of our critics mean by mastery of stage craft is recklessness in the substitution of dead machinery and lay figures for vital action and real characters. I do not deny that an author may be driven by his own limitations to ingenuities which Shakespeare had no occasion to cultivate, just as a painter without hands or feet learns to surpass Michael Angelo in the art of drawing with the brush held in the mouth; but I regard such ingenuity as an extremity to be deplored, not as an art to be admired. In *The Second Mrs. Tanqueray* I find little except a scaffold for the situation of a step-daughter and a step-mother finding themselves in the positions respectively of affianced wife and discarded mistress to the same man. Obviously, the only necessary conditions of this situation are that the persons concerned shall be respectable enough to be shocked by it, and that the step-mother shall be an improper person. Mr. Pinero has not got above this minimum. He is, of course, sufficiently skilled in fiction to give Ellean, Mrs. Cortelyon, Ardale, Tanqueray, and Cayley Drummle a passable air of being human beings. He has even touched up Cayley into a Thackerayan flaneur in order to secure toleration of his intrusiveness. But who will pretend that any of these figures are more than the barest accessories to the main situation? To compare them with the characters in Robertson's *Caste* would be almost as ridiculous as to compare *Caste* with *A Doll's House*. The two vulgar characters produce the requisite jar—a pitilessly disagreeable jar—and that is all. Still, all the seven seem good as far as they go; and that very little way may suggest that Mr. Pinero might have done good creative work if he had carried them further. Unfortunately for this surmise, he has carried Paula further; and with what result? The moment the point is reached at which the comparatively common gift of "an eye for character" has to be supplemented by the higher dramatic gift of sympathy with character—of the power of seeing the world from the point of view of others instead of merely describing or judging them from one's own point of view in terms of the conventional systems of morals, Mr. Pinero breaks down. I remember that when I saw the play acted I sat up very attentively when Tanqueray said to Paula, "I know what you were at Ellean's age. You hadn't a thought that wasn't a wholesome one; you hadn't an impulse that didn't tend towards good; you never harbored a notion you couldn't have gossiped about to a parcel of children. And this was a very few years back, etc., etc." On the reply to that fatuous but not unnatural speech depended the whole question of Mr. Pinero's rank as a dramatist. One can imagine how, in a play by a master-hand, Paula's reply would have opened Tanqueray's foolish eyes to the fact that a woman of that sort is already the same at three as she is at thirty-three, and that however she may have found by experience that her nature is in conflict with the ideals of differently constituted people, she remains perfectly valid to herself, and despises herself, if she sincerely does so at all, for the hypocrisy that the world forces on her instead of for being what she is. What reply does Mr. Pinero put into her mouth? Here it is, with the stage directions: "A few —years ago! [*She walks slowly towards the door, then suddenly drops upon the ottoman in a paroxysm of weeping.*] O God! A few years ago!" That is to say, she makes her reply from the Tanqueray-Ellean-Pinero point of view, and thus betrays the fact that she is a work of prejudiced observation instead of comprehension, and that the other characters only owe their faint humanity to the fact that they are projections of Mr. Pinero's own personal amiabilities and beliefs and conventions. Mr. Pinero, then, is no interpreter of character, but simply an adroit describer of people as the ordinary man sees and judges them. Add to this a clear head, a love of the stage, and a fair talent for fiction, all highly cultivated by hard and honorable work as a writer of effective stage plays for the modern commercial theatre; and you have him on his real level. On that level he is entitled to all the praise *The Second Mrs. Tanqueray* has won him; and I very heartily regret that the glamor which Mrs. Patrick Campbell cast round the play has forced me to examine pretensions which Mr. Pinero himself never put forward rather than to acknowledge the merits with which his work is so concisely packed.

First produced at the St. James' Theatre, May 27, 1893.

CHARACTERS

    Aubrey Tanqueray
    Paula
    Ellean
    Cayley Drummle
    Mrs. Cortelyon
    Captain Hugh Ardale
    Gordon Jayne, M.D.
    Frank Misquith, Q.C., M.P.
    Sir George Orreyed, Bart.
    Lady Orreyed
    Morse

The Present Day.

The Scene of Act 1 is laid at Mr. Tanqueray's rooms, No. 2 x, The Albany, in the month of November; the occurrences of the succeeding Acts take place at his house, "Highercoombe," near Willowmere, Surrey, during the early part of the following year.

act 1

Aubrey Tanqueray's Chambers in the Albany—a richly and tastefully-decorated room, elegantly and luxuriously furnished: on the right a large pair of doors opening into another room, on the left at the further end of the room a small door leading to a bed-chamber. A circular table is laid for a dinner for four persons, which has now reached the stage of dessert and coffee. Everything in the apartment suggests wealth and refinement. The fire is burning brightly.

Aubrey Tanqueray, Misquith, and Jayne are seated at the dinner-table. Aubrey is forty-two, handsome, winning in manner, his speech and bearing retaining some of the qualities of young-manhood. Misquith is about forty-seven, genial and portly. Jayne is a year or two Misquith's senior; soft-speaking and precise—in appearance a type of the prosperous town physician. Morse, Aubrey's servant, places a little cabinet of cigars and the spirit-lamp on the table beside Aubrey and goes out.

Misquith. Aubrey, it is a pleasant yet dreadful fact to contemplate, but it's nearly fifteen years since I first dined with you. You lodged in Piccadilly in those days, over a hat-shop. Jayne, I met you at that dinner, and Cayley Drummle.

Jayne. Yes, yes. What a pity it is that Cayley isn't here to-night.

Aubrey. Confound the old gossip! His empty chair has been staring us in the face all through dinner. I ought to have told Morse to take it away.

Misquith. Odd, his sending no excuse.

Aubrey. I'll walk round to his lodgings later on and ask after him.

Misquith. I'll go with you.

Jayne. So will I.

Aubrey [*opening the cigar-cabinet*]. Doctor, it's useless to

tempt you, I know. Frank—[*Misquith and Aubrey
smoke.*] I particularly wished Cayley Drummle to be
one of us to-night. You two fellows and Cayley are my
closest, my best friends—

Misquith. My dear Aubrey!

Jayne. I rejoice to hear you say so.

Aubrey. And I wanted to see the three of you round this
table. You can't guess the reason.

Misquith. You desired to give us a most excellent dinner.

Jayne. Obviously.

Aubrey [*hesitatingly*]. Well—I—[*glancing at the clock*]—
Cayley won't turn up now.

Jayne. H'm, hardly.

Aubrey. Then you two shall hear it. Doctor, Frank, this
is the last time we are to meet in these rooms.

Jayne. The last time?

Misquith. You're going to leave the Albany?

Aubrey. Yes. You've heard me speak of a house I built
in the country years ago, haven't you?

Misquith. In Surrey.

Aubrey. Well, when my wife died I cleared out of that
house and let it. I think of trying the place again.

Misquith. But you'll go raving mad if ever you find yourself down there alone.

Aubrey. Ah, but I sha'n't be alone, and that's what I wanted
to tell you. I'm going to be married.

Jayne. Going to be married?

Misquith. Married?

Aubrey. Yes—to-morrow.

Jayne. To-morrow?

Misquith. You take my breath away! My dear fellow, I—
I—of course, I congratulate you.

Jayne. And—and—so do I—heartily.

Aubrey. Thanks—thanks.

[*There is a moment or two of embarrassment.*]

Misquith. Er—ah—this is an excellent cigar.

Jayne. Ah—um—your coffee is remarkable.

Aubrey. Look here; I dare say you two old friends think
this treatment very strange, very unkind. So I want
you to understand me. You know a marriage often
cools friendships. What's the usual course of things?
A man's engagement is given out, he is congratulated,
complimented upon his choice; the church is filled

with troops of friends, and he goes away happily to a chorus of good wishes. He comes back, sets up house in town or country, and thinks to resume the old associations, the old companionships. My dear Frank, my dear good doctor, it's very seldom that it can be done. Generally, a worm has begun to eat its way into those hearty, unreserved, pre-nuptial friendships; a damnable constraint sets in and acts like a wasting disease; and so, believe me, in nine cases out of ten a man's marriage severs for him more close ties than it forms.

Misquith. Well, my dear Aubrey, I earnestly hope—

Aubrey. I know what you're going to say, Frank. I hope so, too. In the meantime let's face dangers. I've reminded you of the *usual* course of things, but my marriage isn't even the conventional sort of marriage likely to satisfy society. Now, Cayley's a bachelor, but you two men have wives. By-the-bye, my love to Mrs. Misquith and to Mrs. Jayne when you get home— don't forget that. Well, your wives may not—like— the lady I'm going to marry.

Jayne. Aubrey, forgive me for suggesting that the lady you are going to marry may not like our wives—mine at least; I beg your pardon, Frank.

Aubrey. Quite so; then I must go the way my wife goes.

Misquith. Come, come, pray don't let us anticipate that either side will be called upon to make such a sacrifice.

Aubrey. Yes, yes, let us anticipate it. And let us make up our minds to have no slow bleeding-to-death of our friendship. We'll end a pleasant chapter here to-night, and after to-night start afresh. When my wife and I settle down at Willowmere it's possible that we shall all come together. But if this isn't to be, for Heaven's sake let us recognise that it is simply because it *can't* be, and not wear hypocritical faces and suffer and be wretched. Doctor, Frank—[*holding out his hands, one to Misquith, the other to Jayne*]—good luck to all of us!

Misquith. But—but—do I understand we are to ask nothing? Not even the lady's name, Aubrey?

Aubrey. The lady, my dear Frank, belongs to the next chapter, and in that her name is Mrs. Aubrey Tanqueray.

Jayne [*raising his coffee-cup*]. Then, in an old-fashioned way, I propose a toast. Aubrey, Frank, I give you "The Next Chapter!"

[*They drink the toast, saying,* "The Next Chapter!"

Aubrey. Doctor, find a comfortable chair; Frank, you too. As we're going to turn out by-and-bye, let me scribble a couple of notes now while I think of them.

Misquith and *Jayne.* Certainly—yes, yes.

Aubrey. It might slip my memory when I get back.

[*Aubrey sits at a writing-table at the other end of the room, and writes.*]

Jayne [*to Misquith in a whisper*]. Frank—[*Misquith quietly leaves his chair, and sits nearer to Jayne.*] What is all this? Simply a morbid crank of Aubrey's with regard to ante-nuptial acquaintances.

Misquith. H'm! Did you notice *one* expression he used?

Jayne. Let me think—

Misquith. "My marriage is not even the conventional sort of marriage likely to satisfy society."

Jayne. Bless me, yes! What does that suggest?

Misquith. That he has a particular rather than a general reason for anticipating estrangement from his friends, I'm afraid.

Jayne. A horrible *mésalliance!* A dairymaid who has given him a glass of milk during a day's hunting, or a little anaemic shopgirl! Frank, I'm utterly wretched!

Misquith. My dear Jayne, speaking in absolute confidence, I have never been more profoundly depressed in my life.

[*Morse enters.*]

Morse [*announcing*]. Mr. Drummle.

[*Cayley Drummle enters briskly. He is a neat little man of about five-and-forty, in manner bright, airy, debonair, but with an undercurrent of seriousness. Morse retires.*]

Drummle. I'm in disgrace; nobody realises that more thoroughly than I do. Where's my host?

Aubrey [*who has risen*]. Cayley.

Drummle [*shaking hands with him*]. Don't speak to me till I have tendered my explanation. A harsh word from anybody would unman me.

[*Misquith and Jayne shake hands with Drummle.*]

Aubrey. Have you dined?

Drummle. No—unless you call a bit of fish, a cutlet, and a pancake dining.

Aubrey. Cayley, this is disgraceful.

Jayne. Fish, a cutlet, and a pancake will require a great deal of explanation.

Misquith. Especially the pancake. My dear friend, your case looks miserably weak.

Drummle. Hear me! hear me!

Jayne. Now then!

Misquith. Come!

Aubrey. Well!

Drummle. It so happens that to-night I was exceptionally early in dressing for dinner.

Misquith. For which dinner—the fish and cutlet?

Drummle. For *this* dinner, of course—really, Frank! At a quarter to eight, in fact, I found myself trimming my nails, with ten minutes to spare. Just then enter my man with a note—would I hasten, as fast as cab could carry me, to old Lady Orreyed in Bruton Street?—"sad trouble." Now, recollect, please, I had ten minutes on my hands, old Lady Orreyed was a very dear friend of my mother's, and was in some distress.

Aubrey. Cayley, come to the fish and cutlet!

Misquith and Jayne. Yes, yes, and the pancake!

Drummle. Upon my word! Well, the scene in Bruton Street beggars description; the women servants looked scared, the men drunk; and there was poor old Lady Orreyed on the floor of her boudoir like Queen Bess among her pillows.

Aubrey. What's the matter?

Drummle [*to everybody*]. You know George Orreyed?

Misquith. Yes.

Jayne. I've met him.

Drummle. Well, he's a thing of the past.

Aubrey. Not dead!

Drummle. Certainly, in the worst sense. He's married Mabel Hervey.

Misquith. What!

Drummle. It's true—this morning. The poor mother showed me his letter—a dozen curt words, and some of those ill-spelt.

Misquith [*walking up to the fireplace*]. I'm very sorry.

Jayne. Pardon my ignorance—who *was* Mabel Hervey?

Drummle. You don't—? Oh, of course not. Miss Hervey
—Lady Orreyed, as she now is—was a lady who
would have been, perhaps has been, described in the
reports of the Police or the Divorce Court as an
actress. Had she belonged to a lower stratum of our
advanced civilisation she would, in the event of
judicial inquiry, have defined her calling with equal
justification as that of a dressmaker. To do her justice,
she is a type of a class which is immortal. Physically,
by the strange caprice of creation, curiously beautiful;
mentally, she lacks even the strength of deliberate
viciousness. Paint her portrait, it would symbolize a
creature perfectly patrician; lance a vein of her
superbly-modelled arm, you would get the poorest
vin ordinaire! Her affections, emotions, impulses, her
very existence—a burlesque! Flaxen, five-and-twenty,
and feebly frolicsome; anybody's, in less gentle society
I should say everybody's property! That, doctor, was
Miss Hervey who is the new Lady Orreyed. Dost thou
like the picture?

Misquith. Very good, Cayley! Bravo!

Aubrey [*laying his hand on Drummle's shoulder*]. You'd
scarcely believe it, Jayne, but none of us really know
anything about this lady, our gay young friend here,
I suspect, least of all.

Drummle. Aubrey, I applaud your chivalry.

Aubrey. And perhaps you'll let me finish a couple of letters which Frank and Jayne have given me leave
to write. [*Returning to the writing-table.*] Ring for
what you want, like a good fellow! [*Aubrey resumes
his writing.*]

Misquith [*to Drummle*]. Still, the fish and cutlet remain
unexplained.

Drummle. Oh, the poor old woman was so weak that I insisted upon her taking some food, and felt there was
nothing for it but to sit down opposite her. The fool!
the blackguard!

Misquith. Poor Orreyed! Well, he's gone under for a time.

Drummle. For a time! My dear Frank, I tell you he has
absolutely ceased to be. [*Aubrey, who has been writing
busily, turns his head towards the speakers and listens.
His lips are set, and there is a frown upon his face.*]

For all practical purposes you may regard him as the late George Orreyed. To-morrow the very characteristics of his speech, as we remember them, will have become obsolete.

Jayne. But surely, in the course of years, he and his wife will outlive—

Drummle. No, no, doctor, don't try to upset one of my settled beliefs. You may dive into many waters, but there is *one* social Dead Sea—!

Jayne. Perhaps you're right.

Drummle. Right! Good God! I wish you could prove me otherwise! Why, for years I've been sitting, and watching and waiting.

Misquith. You're in form to-night, Cayley. May we ask where you've been in the habit of squandering your useful leisure?

Drummle. Where? On the shore of that same sea.

Misquith. And, pray, what have you been waiting for?

Drummle. For some of my best friends *to come up.* [*Aubrey utters a half-stifled exclamation of impatience; then he hurriedly gathers up his papers from the writing-table. The three men turn to him.*] Eh?

Aubrey. Oh, I—I'll finish my letters in the other room if you'll excuse me for five minutes. Tell Cayley the news. [*He goes out.*]

Drummle [*hurrying to the door*]. My dear fellow, my jabbering has disturbed you! I'll never talk again as long as I live!

Misquith. Close the door, Cayley.

[*Drummle shuts the door.*]

Jayne. Cayley—

Drummle [*advancing to the dinner table*]. A smoke, a smoke, or I perish! [*Selects a cigar from the little cabinet.*]

Jayne. Cayley, marriages are in the air.

Drummle. Are they? Discover the bacillus, doctor, and destroy it.

Jayne. I mean, among our friends.

Drummle. Oh, Nugent Warrinder's engagement to Lady Alice Tring. I've heard of that. They're not to be married till the spring.

Jayne. Another marriage that concerns us a little takes place to-morrow.

Drummle. Whose marriage?

Jayne. Aubrey's.

Drummle. Aub—! [*Looking towards Misquith.*] Is it a joke?

Misquith. No.

Drummle [*looking from Misquith to Jayne*]. To whom?

Misquith. He doesn't tell us.

Jayne. We three were asked here to-night to receive the announcement. Aubrey has some theory that marriage is likely to alienate a man from his friends, and it seems to me he has taken the precaution to wish us good-bye.

Misquith. No, no.

Jayne. Practically, surely.

Drummle [*thoughtfully*]. Marriage in general, does he mean, or *this* marriage?

Jayne. That's the point. Frank says—

Misquith. No, no, no; I feared it suggested—

Jayne. Well, well. [*To Drummle.*] What do you think of it?

Drummle [*after a slight pause*]. Is there a light there? [*Lighting his cigar.*] He—wraps the lady—in mystery —you say?

Misquith. Most modestly.

Drummle. Aubrey's—not—a very—young man.

Jayne. Forty-three.

Drummle. Ah! *L'age critique!*

Misquith. A dangerous age—yes, yes.

Drummle. When you two fellows go home, do you mind leaving me behind here?

Misquith. Not at all.

Jayne. By all means.

Drummle. All right. [*Anxiously.*] Deuce take it, the man's second marriage mustn't be another mistake! [*With his head bent he walks up to the fireplace.*]

Jayne. You knew him in his short married life, Cayley. Terribly unsatisfactory, wasn't it?

Drummle. Well—[*Looking at the door.*] I quite closed that door?

Misquith. Yes. [*Settles himself on the sofa; Jayne is seated in an arm-chair.*]

Drummle [*smoking with his back to the fire*]. He married a Miss Herriott; that was in the year eighteen—confound dates—twenty years ago. She was a lovely creature—by Jove, she was; by religion a Roman Catholic. She was one of your cold sort, you know —all marble arms and black velvet. I remember her with painful distinctness as the only woman who ever made me nervous.

Misquith. Ha, ha!

Drummle. He loved her—to distraction, as they say. Jupiter, how fervently that poor devil courted her! But I don't believe she allowed him even to squeeze her fingers. She *was* an iceberg! As for kissing, the mere contact would have given him chapped lips. However, he married her and took her away, the latter greatly to my relief.

Jayne. Abroad, you mean?

Drummle. Eh? Yes. I imagine he gratified her by renting a villa in Lapland, but I don't know. After a while they returned, and then I saw how wofully Aubrey had miscalculated results.

Jayne. Miscalculated—?

Drummle. He had reckoned, poor wretch, that in the early days of marriage she would thaw. But she didn't. I used to picture him closing his doors and making up the fire in the hope of seeing her features relax. Bless her, the thaw never set in! I believe she kept a thermometer in her stays and always registered ten degrees below zero. However, in time a child came— a daughter.

Jayne. Didn't that—?

Drummle. Not a bit of it; it made matters worse. Frightened at her failure to stir up in him some sympathetic religious belief, she determined upon strong measures with regard to the child. He opposed her for a miserable year or so, but she wore him down, and the insensible little brat was placed in a convent, first in France, then in Ireland. Not long afterwards the mother died, strangely enough, of fever, the only warmth, I believe, that ever came to that woman's body.

Misquith. Don't, Cayley!

Jayne. The child is living, we know.

Drummle. Yes, if you choose to call it living. Miss Tanqueray—a young woman of nineteen now—is in the Loretto convent at Armagh. She professes to have found her true vocation in a religious life, and within a month or two will take final vows.

Misquith. He ought to have removed his daughter from the convent when the mother died.

Drummle. Yes, yes, but absolutely at the end there was reconciliation between husband and wife, and she won his promise that the child should complete her conventual education. He reaped his reward. When he attempted to gain his girl's confidence and affection he was too late; he found he was dealing with the spirit of the mother. You remember his visit to Ireland last month?

Jayne. Yes.

Drummle. That was to wish his girl good-bye.

Misquith. Poor fellow!

Drummle. He sent for me when he came back. I think he must have had a lingering hope that the girl would relent—would come to life, as it were—at the last moment, for, for an hour or so, in this room, he was terribly shaken. I'm sure he'd clung to that hope from the persistent way in which he kept breaking off in his talk to repeat one dismal word, as if he couldn't realise his position without dinning this damned word into his head.

Jayne. What word was that?

Drummle. Alone—alone.

[*Aubrey enters.*]

Aubrey. A thousand apologies!

Drummle [*gaily*]. We are talking about you, my dear Aubrey.

[*During the telling of the story, Misquith has risen and gone to the fire, and Drummle has thrown himself full-length on the sofa. Aubrey now joins Misquith and Jayne.*]

Aubrey. Well, Cayley, are you surprised?

Drummle. Surp—! I haven't been surprised for twenty years.

Aubrey. And you're not angry with me?

Drummle. Angry! [*Rising.*] Because you considerately withhold the name of a lady with whom it is now the object of my life to become acquainted? My dear fellow, you pique my curiosity, you give zest to my existence! And as for a wedding, who on earth wants to attend that familiar and probably draughty function? Ugh! My cigar's out.

Aubrey. Let's talk about something else.

Misquith [*looking at his watch*]. Not to-night, Aubrey.

Aubrey. My dear Frank!

Misquith. I go up to Scotland to-morrow, and there are some little matters—

Jayne. I am off too.

Aubrey. No, no.

Jayne. I must: I have to give a look to a case in Clifford Street on my way home.

Aubrey [*going to the door*]. Well! [*Misquith and Jayne exchange looks with Drummle. Opening the door and calling.*] Morse, hats and coats! I shall write to you all next week from Genoa or Florence. Now, doctor, Frank, remember, my love to Mrs. Misquith and to Mrs. Jayne!

[*Morse enters with hats and coats.*]

Misquith and Jayne. Yes, yes—yes, yes.

Aubrey. And your young people!

[*As Misquith and Jayne put on their coats there is the clatter of careless talk.*]

Jayne. Cayley, I meet you at dinner on Sunday.

Drummle. At the Stratfields'. That's very pleasant.

Misquith [*putting on his coat with Aubrey's aid*]. Ah-h!

Aubrey. What's wrong?

Misquith. A twinge. Why didn't I go to Aix in August?

Jayne [*shaking hands with Drummle*]. Good-night, Cayley.

Drummle. Good-night, my dear doctor!

Misquith [*shaking hands with Drummle*]. Cayley, are you in town for long?

Drummle. Dear friend, I'm nowhere for long. Good-night.

Misquith. Good-night.

[*Aubrey, Jayne, and Misquith go out, followed by Morse; the hum of talk is continued outside.*]

Aubrey. A cigar, Frank?

Misquith. No, thank you.

Aubrey. Going to walk, doctor?

Jayne. If Frank will.

Misquith. By all means.

Aubrey. It's a cold night.

[*The door is closed. Drummle remains standing with his coat on his arm and his hat in his hand.*]

Drummle [*to himself, thoughtfully*]. Now then! What the
    devil!—

[*Aubrey returns.*]

Aubrey [*eyeing Drummle a little awkwardly*]. Well, Cay-
    ley?

Drummle. Well, Aubrey?

[*Aubrey walks up to the fire and stands looking into it.*]

Aubrey. You're not going, old chap?

Drummle [*sitting*]. No.

Aubrey [*after a slight pause, with a forced laugh*]. Hah!
    Cayley, I never thought I should feel—shy—with you.

Drummle. Why do you?

Aubrey. Never mind.

Drummle. Now, I can quite understand a man wishing to
    be married in the dark, as it were.

Aubrey. You can?

Drummle. In your place I should very likely adopt the
    same course.

Aubrey. You think so?

Drummle. And if I intended marrying a lady not promi-
    nently in society, as I presume you do—as I pre-
    sume you do—

Aubrey. Well?

Drummle. As I presume you do, I'm not sure that *I* should
    tender her for preliminary dissection at afternoon
    tea-tables.

Aubrey. No?

Drummle. In fact, there is probably only one person—
    were I in your position to-night—with whom I should
    care to chat the matter over.

Aubrey. Who's that?

Drummle. Yourself, of course. [*Going to Aubrey and
    standing beside him.*] Of course, yourself, old friend.

Aubrey [*after a pause*]. I must seem a brute to you, Cay-
    ley. But there are some acts which are hard to explain,
    hard to defend—

Drummle. To defend—

Aubrey. Some acts which one must trust to time to put
    right.

[*Drummle watches him for a moment, then takes up his
hat and coat.*]

Drummle. Well, I'll be moving.

Aubrey. Cayley! Confound you and your old friendship!

Do you think I forget it? Put your coat down! Why did you stay behind here? Cayley, the lady I am going to marry is the lady—who is known as—Mrs. Jarman.

[*There is a pause.*]

Drummle [*in a low voice*]. Mrs. Jarman! are you serious? [*He walks up to the fireplace, where he leans upon the mantelpiece uttering something like a groan.*]

Aubrey. As you've got this out of me I give you leave to say all you care to say. Come, we'll be plain with each other. You know Mrs. Jarman?

Drummle. I first met her at—what does it matter?

Aubrey. Yes, yes, everything! Come!

Drummle. I met her at Homburg, two—three seasons ago.

Aubrey. Not as Mrs. Jarman?

Drummle. No.

Aubrey. She was then—?

Drummle. Mrs. Dartry.

Aubrey. Yes. She has also seen you in London, she says.

Drummle. Certainly.

Aubrey. In Alford Street. Go on.

Drummle. Please!

Aubrey. I insist.

Drummle [*with a slight shrug of the shoulders*]. Some time last year I was asked by a man to sup at his house, one night after the theatre.

Aubrey. Mr. Selwyn Ethurst—a bachelor.

Drummle. Yes.

Aubrey. You were surprised therefore to find Mr. Ethurst aided in his cursed hospitality by a lady.

Drummle. I was unprepared.

Aubrey. The lady you had known as Mrs. Dartry? [*Drummle inclines his head silently.*] There is something of a yachting cruise in the Mediterranean too, is there not?

Drummle. I joined Peter Jarman's yacht at Marseilles, in the Spring, a month before he died.

Aubrey. Mrs. Jarman was on board?

Drummle. She was a kind hostess.

Aubrey. And an old acquaintance?

Drummle. Yes.

Aubrey. You have told your story.

Drummle. With your assistance.

Aubrey. I have put you to the pain of telling it to show
you that this is not the case of a blind man entrapped
by an artful woman. Let me add that Mrs. Jarman has
no legal right to that name; that she is simply Miss
Ray—Miss Paula Ray.

Drummle [*after a pause*]. I should like to express my regret, Aubrey, for the way in which I spoke of George
Orreyed's marriage.

Aubrey. You mean you compare Lady Orreyed with Miss
Ray? [*Drummle is silent.*] Oh, of course! To you,
Cayley, all women who have been roughly treated,
and who dare to survive by borrowing a little of our
philosophy, are alike. You see in the crowd of the
ill-used only one pattern; you can't detect the shades
of goodness, intelligence, even nobility there. Well,
how should you? The crowd is dimly lighted! And,
besides, yours is the way of the world.

Drummle. My dear Aubrey, I *live* in the world.

Aubrey. The name we give our little parish of St. James's.

Drummle [*laying a hand on Aubrey's shoulder*]. And you
are quite prepared, my friend, to forfeit the esteem
of your little parish?

Aubrey. I avoid mortification by shifting from one parish
to another. I give up Pall Mall for the Surrey hills;
leave off varnishing my boots, and double the thickness of the soles.

Drummle. And your skin—do you double the thickness of
that also?

Aubrey. I know you think me a fool, Cayley—you needn't
infer that I'm a coward into the bargain. No! I know
what I'm doing, and I do it deliberately, defiantly. I'm
alone: I injure no living soul by the step I'm going
to take; and so you can't urge the one argument
which might restrain me. Of course, I don't expect you
to think compassionately, fairly even, of the woman
whom I—whom I am drawn to—

Drummle. My dear Aubrey, I assure you I consider Mrs.
—Miss Jarman—Mrs. Ray—Miss Ray—delightful.
But I confess there is a form of chivalry which I
gravely distrust, especially in a man of—our age.

Aubrey. Thanks. I've heard you say that from forty till
fifty a man is at heart either a stoic or a satyr.

Drummle [*protestingly*]. Ah! now—

Aubrey. I am neither. I have a temperate, honourable affection for Mrs. Jarman. She has never met a man who has treated her well—I intend to treat her well. That's all. And in a few years, Cayley, if you've not quite forsaken me, I'll prove to you that it's possible to rear a life of happiness, of good repute, on a— miserable foundation.

Drummle [*offering his hand*]. Do prove it!

Aubrey [*taking his hand*]. We have spoken too freely of —of Mrs. Jarman. I was excited—angry. Please forget it!

Drummle. My dear Aubrey, when we next meet I shall remember nothing but my respect for the lady who bears your name.

[*Morse enters, closing the door behind him carefully.*]

Aubrey. What is it?

Morse [*hesitatingly*]. May I speak to you, sir? [*In an undertone.*] Mrs. Jarman, sir.

Aubrey [*softly to Morse*]. Mrs. Jarman! Do you mean she is at the lodge in her carriage?

Morse. No, sir—here. [*Aubrey looks towards Drummle, perplexed.*] There's a nice fire in your—in that room, sir. [*Glancing in the direction of the door leading to the bedroom.*]

Aubrey [*between his teeth, angrily*]. Very well.

[*Morse retires.*]

Drummle [*looking at his watch*]. A quarter to eleven— horrible! [*Taking up his hat and coat.*] Must get to bed—up late every night this week. [*Aubrey assists Drummle with his coat.*] Thank you. Well, good-night, Aubrey. I feel I've been dooced serious, quite out of keeping with myself; pray overlook it.

Aubrey [*kindly*]. Ah, Cayley!

Drummle [*putting on a neck-handkerchief*]. And remember that, after all, I'm merely a spectator in life; nothing more than a man at a play, in fact; only, like the old-fashioned playgoer, I love to see certain characters happy and comfortable at the finish. You understand?

Aubrey. I think I do.

Drummle. Then, for as long as you can, old friend, will you—keep a stall for me?

Aubrey. Yes, Cayley.

Drummle [*gaily*]. Ah, ha! Good-night! [*Bustling to the door.*] Don't bother! I'll let myself out! Good-night! God bless yer! [*He goes out; Aubrey follows him. Morse enters by the other door, carrying some unopened letters, which after a little consideration he places on the mantelpiece against the clock. Aubrey returns.*]

Aubrey. Yes?

Morse. You hadn't seen your letters that came by the nine o'clock post, sir; I've put 'em where they'll catch your eye by-and-bye.

Aubrey. Thank you.

Morse [*hesitatingly*]. Gunter's cook and waiter have gone, sir. Would you prefer me to go to bed?

Aubrey [*frowning*]. Certainly not.

Morse. Very well, sir. [*He goes out.*]

Aubrey [*opening the upper door*]. Paula! Paula!

[*Paula enters and throws her arms round his neck. She is a young woman of about twenty-seven: beautiful, fresh, innocent-looking. She is in superb evening dress.*]

Paula. Dearest!

Aubrey. Why have you come here?

Paula. Angry?

Aubrey. Yes—no. But it's eleven o'clock.

Paula [*laughing*]. I know.

Aubrey. What on earth will Morse think?

Paula. Do you trouble yourself about what servants *think*?

Aubrey. Of course.

Paula. Goose! They're only machines made to wait upon people—and to give evidence in the Divorce Court. [*Looking round.*] Oh, indeed! A snug little dinner!

Aubrey. Three men.

Paula [*suspiciously*]. Men?

Aubrey. Men.

Paula [*penitently*]. Ah! [*Sitting at the table.*] I'm so hungry.

Aubrey. Let me get you some game pie, or some—

Paula. No, no, hungry for this. What beautiful fruit! I love fruit when it's expensive. [*He clears a space on the table, places a plate before her, and helps her to fruit.*] I haven't dined, Aubrey dear.

Aubrey. My poor girl! Why?

Paula. In the first place, I forgot to order any dinner, and my cook, who has always loathed me, thought he'd pay me out before he departed.

Aubrey. The beast!

Paula. That's precisely what I—

Aubrey. No, Paula!

Paula. What I told my maid to call him. What next will you think of me?

Aubrey. Forgive me. You must be starved.

Paula [*eating fruit*]. *I* didn't care. As there was nothing to eat, I sat in my best frock, with my toes on the dining-room fender, and dreamt, oh, such a lovely dinner party.

Aubrey. Dear lonely little woman!

Paula. It was perfect. I saw you at the end of a very long table, opposite me, and we exchanged sly glances now and again over the flowers. We were host and hostess, Aubrey, and had been married about five years.

Aubrey [*kissing her hand*]. Five years.

Paula. And on each side of us was the nicest set imaginable—you know, dearest, the sort of men and women that can't be imitated.

Aubrey. Yes, yes. Eat some more fruit.

Paula. But I haven't told you the best part of my dream.

Aubrey. Tell me.

Paula. Well, although we had been married only such a few years, I seemed to know by the look on their faces that none of our guests had ever heard anything—anything—anything peculiar about the fascinating hostess.

Aubrey. That's just how it will be, Paula. The world moves so quickly. That's just how it will be.

Paula [*with a little grimace*]. I wonder! [*Glancing at the fire.*] Ugh! Do throw another log on.

Aubrey [*mending the fire*]. There. But you mustn't be here long.

Paula. Hospitable wretch! I've something important to tell you. No, stay where you are. [*Turning from him, her face averted.*] Look here, that was my dream, Aubrey; but the fire went out while I was dozing, and I woke

up with a regular fit of the shivers. And the result
of it all was that I ran upstairs and scribbled you a
letter.

Aubrey. Dear baby!

Paula. Remain where you are. [*Taking a letter from her
pocket.*] This is it. I've given you an account of myself,
furnished you with a list of my adventures since I—
you know. [*Weighing the letter in her hand.*] I wonder if it would go for a penny. Most of it you're
acquainted with; *I've* told you a good deal, haven't I?

Aubrey. Oh, Paula!

Paula. What I haven't told you I dare say you've heard
from others. But in case they've omitted anything—
the dears—it's all here.

Aubrey. In Heaven's name, why must you talk like this
to-night?

Paula. It may save discussion by-and-bye, don't you think?
[*Holding out the letter.*] There you are.

Aubrey. No, dear, no.

Paula. Take it. [*He takes the letter.*] Read it through after
I've gone, and then—read it again, and turn the
matter over in your mind finally. And if, even at the
very last moment, you feel you—oughtn't to go to
church with me, send a messenger to Pont Street, any
time before eleven to-morrow, telling me that you're
afraid, and I—I'll take the blow.

Aubrey. Why, what—what do you think I am?

Paula. That's it. It's because I know you're such a dear
good fellow that I want to save you the chance of
ever feeling sorry you married me. I really love you
so much, Aubrey, that to save you that, I'd rather
you treated me as—as the others have done.

Aubrey [*turning from her with a cry*]. Oh!

Paula [*after a slight pause*]. I suppose I've shocked you.
I can't help it if I have. [*She sits, with assumed
languor and indifference. He turns to her, advances,
and kneels by her.*]

Aubrey. My dearest, you don't understand me. I—I can't
bear to hear you always talking about—what's done
with. I tell you I'll never remember it; Paula, can't you
dismiss it? Try. Darling, if we promise each other to
forget, to forget, we're bound to be happy. After all,
it's a mechanical matter; the moment a wretched

thought enters your head, you quickly think of something bright—it depends on one's will. Shall I burn this, dear? [*Referring to the letter he holds in his hand.*] Let me, let me!

Paula [*with a shrug of the shoulders*]. I don't suppose there's much that's new to you in it,—just as you like. [*He goes to the fire and burns the letter.*]

Aubrey. There's an end of it. [*Returning to her.*] What's the matter?

Paula [*rising, coldly*]. Oh, nothing! I'll go and put my cloak on.

Aubrey [*detaining her*]. What *is* the matter?

Paula. Well, I think you might have said, "You're very generous, Paula," or at least, "Thank you, dear," when I offered to set you free.

Aubrey [*catching her in his arms*]. Ah!

Paula. Ah! ah! Ha! ha! It's all very well, but you don't know what it cost me to make such an offer. I do so want to be married.

Aubrey. But you never imagined—?

Paula. Perhaps not. And yet I *did* think of what I'd do at the end of our acquaintance if you had preferred to behave like the rest. [*Taking a flower from her bodice.*]

Aubrey. Hush!

Paula. Oh, I forgot!

Aubrey. What would you have done when we parted?

Paula. Why, killed myself.

Aubrey. Paula, dear!

Paula. It's true. [*Putting the flower in his buttonhole.*] Do you know, I feel certain I should make away with myself if anything serious happened to me.

Aubrey. Anything serious! What, has nothing ever been serious to you, Paula?

Paula. Not lately; not since a long while ago. I made up my mind then to have done with taking things seriously. If I hadn't, I— However, we won't talk about that.

Aubrey. But now, now, life will be different to you, won't it—quite different? Eh, dear?

Paula. Oh, yes, now. Only, Aubrey, mind you keep me always happy.

Aubrey. I will try to.

Paula. I know I couldn't swallow a second big dose of
misery. I know that if ever I felt wretched again—
truly wretched—I should take a leaf out of Connie
Tirlemont's book. You remember? They found her—
[*With a look of horror.*]

Audrey. For God's sake, don't let your thoughts run on
such things!

Paula [*laughing*]. Ha, ha, how scared you look! There, think
of the time! Dearest, what will my coachman say?
My cloak! [*She runs off, gaily, by the upper door.
Aubrey looks after her for a moment, then he walks
up to the fire and stands warming his feet at the bars.
As he does so he raises his head and observes the
letters upon the mantelpiece. He takes one down
quickly.*]

Aubrey. Ah! Ellean! [*Opening the letter and reading.*] "My
dear father,—A great change has come over me. I
believe my mother in Heaven has spoken to me, and
counselled me to turn to you in your loneliness. At
any rate, your words have reached my heart, and I no
longer feel fitted for this solemn life. I am ready to
take my place by you. Dear father, will you receive
me?—Ellean."

[*Paula re-enters, dressed in a handsome cloak. He stares
at her as if he hardly realised her presence.*]

Paula. What are you staring at? Don't you admire my
cloak?

Aubrey. Yes.

Paula. Couldn't you wait till I'd gone before reading your
letters?

Aubrey [*putting the letter away*]. I beg your pardon.

Paula. Take me down-stairs to the carriage. [*Slipping her
arm through his.*] How I tease you! To-morrow! I'm
so happy! [*They go out.*]

A morning-room in Aubrey Tanqueray's house, "Higher-coombe," near Willowmere, Surrey—a bright and prettily furnished apartment of irregular shape, with double doors opening into a small hall at the back, another door on the left, and a large recessed window through which is obtained a view of extensive grounds. Everything about the room is charming and graceful. The fire is burning in the grate, and a small table is tastefully laid for breakfast. It is a morning in early spring, and the sun is streaming in through the window.

Aubrey and Paula are seated at breakfast, and Aubrey is silently reading his letters. Two servants, a man and a woman, hand dishes and then retire. After a little while Aubrey puts his letters aside and looks across to the window.

Aubrey. Sunshine! Spring!

Paula [glancing at the clock]. Exactly six minutes.

Aubrey. Six minutes?

Paula. Six minutes, Aubrey dear, since you made your last remark.

Aubrey. I beg your pardon: I was reading my letters. Have you seen Ellean this morning?

Paula [coldly]. Your last observation but one was about Ellean.

Aubrey. Dearest, what shall I talk about?

Paula. Ellean breakfasted two hours ago, Morgan tells me, and then went out walking with her dog.

Aubrey. She wraps up warmly, I hope; this sunshine is deceptive.

Paula. I ran about the lawn last night, after dinner, in satin shoes. Were you anxious about me?

Aubrey. Certainly.

Paula [*melting*]. Really?

Aubrey. You make me wretchedly anxious; you delight in doing incautious things. You are incurable.

Paula. Ah, what a beast I am! [*Going to him and kissing him, then glancing at the letters by his side.*] A letter from Cayley?

Aubrey. He is staying very near here, with Mrs.—Very near here.

Paula. With the lady whose chimneys we have the honour of contemplating from our windows?

Aubrey. With Mrs. Cortelyon—yes.

Paula. Mrs. Cortelyon! The woman who might have set the example of calling on me when we first threw out roots in this deadly-lively soil! Deuce take Mrs. Cortelyon!

Aubrey. Hush! my dear girl!

Paula [*returning to her seat*]. Oh, I know she's an old acquaintance of yours—and of the first Mrs. Tanqueray. And she joins the rest of 'em in slapping the second Mrs. Tanqueray in the face. However, I have my revenge—she's six-and-forty, and I wish nothing worse to happen to any woman.

Aubrey. Well, she's going to town, Cayley says here, and his visit's at an end. He's coming over this morning to call on you. Shall we ask him to transfer himself to us? Do say yes.

Paula. Yes.

Aubrey [*gladly*]. Ah, ha! old Cayley.

Paula [*coldly*]. He'll amuse *you*.

Aubrey. And you too.

Paula. Because you find a companion, shall I be boisterously hilarious?

Aubrey. Come, come! He talks London, and you know you like that.

Paula. London! London or Heaven! which is farther from me!

Aubrey. Paula!

Paula. Oh! Oh, I am so bored, Aubrey!

Aubrey [*gathering up his letters and going to her, leaning over her shoulder*]. Baby, what can I do for you?

Paula. I suppose, nothing. You have done all you can for me.

Aubrey. What do you mean?

Paula. You have married me.

[*He walks away from her thoughtfully, to the writing table. As he places his letters on the table he sees an addressed letter, stamped for the post, lying on the blotting-book; he picks it up.*]

Aubrey [*in an altered tone*]. You've been writing this morning before breakfast?

Paula [*looking at him quickly, then away again*]. Er—that letter.

Aubrey [*with the letter in his hand*]. To Lady Orreyed. Why?

Paula. Why not? Mabel's an old friend of mine.

Aubrey. Are you—corresponding?

Paula. I heard from her yesterday. They've just returned from the Riviera. She seems happy.

Aubrey [*sarcastically*]. That's good news.

Paula. Why are you always so cutting about Mabel? She's a kind-hearted girl. Everything's altered; she even thinks of letting her hair go back to brown. She's Lady Orreyed. She's married to George. What's the matter with her?

Aubrey [*turning away*]. Oh!

Paula. You drive me mad sometimes with the tone you take about things! Great goodness, if you come to that, George Orreyed's wife isn't a bit worse than yours! [*He faces her suddenly.*] I suppose I needn't have made that observation.

Aubrey. No, there was scarcely a necessity. [*He throws the letter on to the table, and takes up the newspaper.*]

Paula. I am very sorry.

Aubrey. All right, dear.

Paula [*trifling with the letter*]. I—I'd better tell you what I've written. I meant to do so, of course. I—I've asked the Orreyeds to come and stay with us. [*He looks at her, and lets the paper fall to the ground in a helpless way.*] George was a great friend of Cayley's; I'm sure *he* would be delighted to meet them here.

Aubrey [*laughing mirthlessly*]. Ha, ha, ha! They say Orreyed has taken to tippling at dinner. Heavens above!

Paula. Oh! I've no patience with you! You'll kill me with this life! [*She selects some flowers from a vase on the table, cuts and arranges them, and fastens them in her bodice.*] What is my existence, Sunday to Saturday? In the morning, a drive down to the village, with the groom, to give my orders to the tradespeople. At lunch, you and Ellean. In the afternoon, a novel, the newspapers: if fine, another drive—*if* fine! Tea—you and Ellean. Then two hours of dusk; then dinner—you and Ellean. Then a game of Bésique, you and I, while Ellean reads a religious book in a dull corner. Then a yawn from me, another from you, a sigh from Ellean; three figures suddenly rise—"Good-night, good-night, good-night!" [*Imitating a kiss.*] "God bless you!" Ah!

Aubrey. Yes, yes, Paula—yes, dearest—that's what it is *now.* But, by-and-bye, if people begin to come round us—

Paula. Hah! That's where we've made the mistake, my friend Aubrey! [*Pointing to the window.*] Do you believe these people will *ever* come round us? Your former crony, Mrs. Cortelyon? Or the grim old vicar, or that wife of his whose huge nose is positively indecent? Or the Ullathornes, or the Gollans, or Lady William Petres? I know better! And when the young ones gradually take the place of the old, there will still remain the sacred tradition that the dreadful person who lives at the top of the hill is never, under any circumstances, to be called upon! And so we shall go on here, year in and year out, until the sap is run out of our lives, and we're stale and dry and withered from sheer, solitary respectability. Upon my word, I wonder we didn't see that we should have been far happier if we'd gone in for the devil-may-care, *café*-living sort of life in town! After all, *I* have a set, and you might have joined it. It's true, I did want, dearly, dearly, to be a married woman, but where's the pride in being a married woman among married women who are—married! If—[*Seeing that Aubrey's head has sunk into his hands.*] Aubrey! My dear boy! You're not—crying?

[*He looks up, with a flushed face. Ellean enters, dressed very simply for walking. She is a low-voiced, grave girl of about nineteen, with a face somewhat resembling a Madonna. Towards Paula her manner is cold and distant.*]

Aubrey [*in an undertone*]. Ellean!

Ellean. Good-morning, papa. Good-morning, Paula.

[*Paula puts her arms round Ellean and kisses her. Ellean makes little response.*]

Paula. Good-morning. [*Brightly.*] We've been breakfasting this side of the house, to get the sun. [*She sits at the piano and rattles at a gay melody. Seeing that Paula's back is turned to them, Ellean goes to Aubrey and kisses him; he returns the kiss almost furtively. As they separate, the servants re-enter, and proceed to carry out the breakfast table.*]

Aubrey [*to Ellean*]. I guess where you've been: there's some gorse clinging to your frock.

Ellean [*removing a sprig of gorse from her skirt*]. Rover and I walked nearly as far as Black Moor. The poor fellow has a thorn in his pad; I am going up-stairs for my tweezers.

Aubrey. Ellean! [*She returns to him.*] Paula is a little depressed—out of sorts. She complains that she has no companion.

Ellean. I am with Paula nearly all the day, papa.

Aubrey. Ah, but you're such a little mouse. Paula likes cheerful people about her.

Ellean. I'm afraid I am naturally rather silent; and it's so difficult to seem to be what one is not.

Aubrey. I don't wish that, Ellean.

Ellean. I will offer to go down to the village with Paula this morning—shall I?

Aubrey [*touching her hand gently*]. Thank you—do.

Ellean. When I've looked after Rover, I'll come back to her. [*She goes out; Paula ceases playing, and turns on the music-stool, looking at Aubrey.*]

Paula. Well, have you and Ellean had your little confidence?

Aubrey. Confidence?

Paula. Do you think I couldn't feel it, like a pain between my shoulders?

Aubrey. Ellean is coming back in a few minutes to be with you. [*Bending over her.*] Paula, Paula dear, is this how you keep your promise?

Paula. Oh! [*Rising impatiently, and crossing swiftly to the settee, where she sits, moving restlessly.*] I *can't* keep my promise; I *am* jealous; it won't be smothered. I see you looking at her, watching her; your voice drops when you speak to her. I know how fond you are of that girl, Aubrey.

Aubrey. What would you have? I've no other home for her. She is my daughter.

Paula. She is your saint. Saint Ellean!

Aubrey. You have often told me how good and sweet you think her.

Paula. Good!—yes! Do you imagine *that* makes me less jealous? [*Going to him and clinging to his arm.*] Aubrey, there are two sorts of affection—the love for a woman you respect, and the love for the woman you—love. She gets the first from you: I never can.

Aubrey. Hush, hush! you don't realise what you say.

Paula. If Ellean cared for me only a little, it would be different. I shouldn't be jealous then. Why doesn't she care for me?

Aubrey. She—she—she will, in time.

Paula. You can't say that without stuttering.

Aubrey. Her disposition seems a little unresponsive; she resembles her mother in many ways; I can see it every day.

Paula. She's marble. It's a shame. There's not the slightest excuse; for all she knows, I'm as much a saint as she —only married. Dearest, help me to win her over!

Aubrey. Help you?

Paula. You can. Teach her that it is her duty to love me; she hangs on to every word you speak. I'm sure, Aubrey, that the love of a nice woman who believed me to be like herself would do me a world of good. You'd get the benefit of it as well as I. It would soothe me; it would make me less horribly restless; it would take this—this—mischievous feeling from me. [*Coaxingly.*] Aubrey!

Aubrey. Have patience; everything will come right.

Paula. Yes, if you help me.

Aubrey. In the meantime you will tear up your letter to Lady Orreyed, won't you?

Paula [*kissing his hand*]. Of course I will—anything!

Aubrey. Ah, thank you, dearest! [*Laughing.*] Why, good gracious!—ha, ha!—just imagine "Saint Ellean" and that woman side by side!

Paula [*going back with a cry*]. Ah!

Aubrey. What?

Paula [*passionately*]. It's Ellean you're considering, not me? It's all Ellean with you! Ellean! Ellean!

[*Ellean re-enters.*]

Ellean. Did you call me, Paula? [*Clenching his hands, Aubrey turns away and goes out.*] Is papa angry?

Paula. I drive him distracted sometimes. There, I confess it!

Ellean. Do you? Oh, why do you?

Paula. Because I—because I'm jealous.

Ellean. Jealous?

Paula. Yes—of you. [*Ellean is silent.*] Well, what do you think of that?

Ellean. I knew it; I've seen it. It hurts me dreadfully. What do you wish me to do? Go away?

Paula. Leave us! [*Beckoning her with a motion of the head.*] Look here! [*Ellean goes to Paula slowly and unresponsively.*] You could cure me of my jealousy very easily. Why don't you—like me?

Ellean. What do you mean by—like you? I don't understand.

Paula. Love me.

Ellean. Love is not a feeling that is under one's control. I shall alter as time goes on, perhaps. I didn't begin to love my father deeply till a few months ago, and then I obeyed my mother.

Paula. Ah, yes, you dream things, don't you—see them in your sleep? You fancy your mother speaks to you?

Ellean. When you have lost your mother it is a comfort to believe that she is dead only to this life, that she still watches over her child. I do believe that of my mother.

Paula. Well, and so you haven't been bidden to love *me*?

Ellean [*after a pause, almost inaudibly*]. No.

Paula. Dreams are only a hash-up of one's day-thoughts, I suppose you know. Think intently of anything, and it's bound to come back to you at night. I don't cultivate dreams myself.

Ellean. Ah, I knew you would only sneer!

Paula. I'm not sneering; I'm speaking the truth. I say that if you cared for me in the daytime I should soon make friends with those nightmares of yours. Ellean, why don't you try to look on me as your second mother?

Of course there are not many years between us, but
I'm ever so much older than you—in experience. I
shall have no children of my own, I know that; it
would be a real comfort to me if you would make me
feel we belonged to each other. Won't you? Perhaps
you think I'm odd—not nice. Well, the fact is I've two
sides to my nature, and I've let the one almost smother
the other. A few years ago I went through some
trouble, and since then I haven't shed a tear. I believe if you put your arms round me just once I
should run up-stairs and have a good cry. There,
I've talked to you as I've never talked to a woman
in my life. Ellean, you seem to fear me. Don't! Kiss
me!

[*With a cry, almost of despair, Ellean turns from Paula
and sinks on to the settee, covering her face with her
hands.*]

Paula [*indignantly*]. Oh! Why is it! How dare you treat
me like this? What do you mean by it? What do you
mean?

[*A Servant enters.*]

Servant. Mr. Drummle, ma'am.

[*Cayley Drummle, in riding-dress, enters briskly. The
Servant retires.*]

Paula [*recovering herself*]. Well, Cayley!

Drummle [*shaking hands with her cordially*]. How are
you? [*Shaking hands with Ellean, who rises.*] I saw
you in the distance an hour ago, in the gorse near
Stapleton's.

Ellean. I didn't see you, Mr. Drummle.

Drummle. My dear Ellean, it is my experience that no
charming young lady of nineteen ever does see a
man of forty-five. [*Laughing.*] Ha, Ha!

Ellean [*going to the door*]. Paula, papa wishes me to drive
down to the village with you this morning. Do you
care to take me?

Paula [*coldly*]. Oh, by all means. Pray tell Watts to balance
the cart for three.

[*Ellean goes out.*]

Drummle. How's Aubrey?

Paula. Very well—when Ellean's about the house.

Drummle. And you? I needn't ask.

Paula [*walking away to the window*]. Oh, a dog's life, my dear Cayley, mine.

Drummle. Eh?

Paula. Doesn't that define a happy marriage? I'm sleek, well-kept, well-fed, never without a bone to gnaw and fresh straw to lie upon. [*Gazing out of the window.*] Oh, dear me!

Drummle. H'm! Well, I heartily congratulate you on your kennel. The view from the terrace here is superb.

Paula. Yes; I can see London.

Drummle. London! Not quite so far, surely?

Paula. I can. Also the Mediterranean, on a fine day. I wonder what Algiers looks like this morning from the sea! [*Impulsively.*] Oh, Cayley, do you remember those jolly times on board Peter Jarman's yacht when we lay off—? [*Stopping suddenly, seeing Drummle staring at her.*] Good gracious! What are we talking about!

[*Aubrey enters.*]

Aubrey [*to Drummle*]. Dear old chap! Has Paula asked you?

Paula. Not yet.

Aubrey. We want you to come to us, now that you're leaving Mrs. Cortelyon—at once, to-day. Stay a month, as long as you please—eh, Paula?

Paula. As long as you can possibly endure it—do, Cayley.

Drummle [*looking at Aubrey*]. Delighted. [*To Paula.*] Charming of you to have me.

Paula. My dear man, you're a blessing. I must telegraph to London for more fish! A strange appetite to cater for! Something to do, to do, to do! [*She goes out in a mood of almost childish delight.*]

Drummle [*eyeing Aubrey*]. Well?

Aubrey [*with a wearied anxious look*]. Well, Cayley?

Drummle. How are you getting on?

Aubrey. My position doesn't grow less difficult. I told you, when I met you last week, of this feverish, jealous attachment of Paula's for Ellean?

Drummle. Yes. I hardly know why, but I came to the conclusion that you don't consider it an altogether fortunate attachment.

Aubrey. Ellean doesn't respond to it.

Drummle. These are early days. Ellean will warm towards
your wife by-and-bye.

Aubrey. Ah, but there's the question, Cayley!

Drummle. What question?

Aubrey. The question which positively distracts me. Ellean is so different from—most women; I don't
believe a purer creature exists out of heaven. And
I—I ask myself, am I doing right in exposing her
to the influence of poor Paula's light, careless nature?

Drummle. My dear Aubrey!

Aubrey. That shocks you! So it does me. I assure you I
long to urge my girl to break down the reserve which
keeps her apart from Paula, but somehow I can't
do it—well, I don't do it. How can I make you
understand? But when you come to us you'll understand quickly enough. Cayley, there's hardly a subject
you can broach on which poor Paula hasn't some
strange, out-of-the-way thought to give utterance to;
some curious, warped notion. They are not mere
worldly thoughts—unless, good God! they belong
to the little hellish world which our blackguardism has
created: no, her ideas have too little calculation in
them to be called worldly. But it makes it the more
dreadful that such thoughts should be ready, spon-
taneous; that expressing them has become a perfectly
natural process; that her words, acts even, have almost
lost their proper significance for her, and seem beyond her control. Ah, and the pain of listening to it
all from the woman one loves, the woman one hoped
to make happy and contented, who is really and truly
a good woman, as it were, maimed! Well, this is my
burden, and I shouldn't speak to you of it but for my
anxiety about Ellean. Ellean! What is to be her
future? It is in my hands; what am I to do? Cayley,
when I remember how Ellean comes to me, from
another world I always think,—when I realise the
charge that's laid on me, I find myself wishing, in a
sort of terror, that my child were safe under the
ground!

Drummle. My dear Aubrey, aren't you making a mistake?

Aubrey. Very likely. What is it?

Drummle. A mistake, not in regarding your Ellean as an
angel, but in believing that, under any circum-

stances, it would be possible for her to go through life without getting her white robe—shall we say, a little dusty at the hem? Don't take me for a cynic. I am sure there are many women upon earth who are almost divinely innocent; but being on earth, they must send their robes to the laundry occasionally. Ah, and it's right that they should have to do so, for what can they learn from the checking of their little washing-bills but lessons of charity? Now I see but two courses open to you for the disposal of your angel.

Aubrey. Yes?

Drummle. You must either restrict her to a paradise which is, like every earthly paradise, necessarily somewhat imperfect, or treat her as an ordinary flesh-and-blood young woman, and give her the advantages of that society to which she properly belongs.

Aubrey. Advantages?

Drummle. My dear Aubrey, of all forms of innocence mere ignorance is the least admirable. Take my advice, let her walk and talk and suffer and be healed with the great crowd. Do it, and hope that she'll some day meet a good, honest fellow who'll make her life complete, happy, secure. Now you see what I'm driving at.

Aubrey. A sanguine programme, my dear Cayley! Oh, I'm not pooh-poohing it. Putting sentiment aside, of course I know that a fortunate marriage for Ellean would be the best—perhaps the only—solution of my difficulty. But you forget the danger of the course you suggest.

Drummle. Danger?

Aubrey. If Ellean goes among men and women, how can she escape from learning, sooner or later, the history of—poor Paula's—old life?

Drummle. H'm! You remember the episode of the Jeweller's Son in the Arabian Nights? Of course you don't. Well, if your daughter lives, she *can't* escape—what you're afraid of. [*Aubrey gives a half-stifled exclamation of pain.*] And when she does hear the story, surely it would be better that she should have some knowledge of the world to help her to understand it.

Aubrey. To understand!

Drummle. To understand, to—philosophise.

Aubrey. To philosophise?

Drummle. Philosophy is toleration, and it is only one step from toleration to forgiveness.

Aubrey. You're right, Cayley; I believe you always are. Yes, yes. But, even if I had the courage to attempt to solve the problem of Ellean's future in this way, I—I'm helpless.

Drummle. How?

Aubrey. What means have I now of placing my daughter in the world I've left?

Drummle. Oh, some friend—some woman friend.

Aubrey. I have none; they're gone.

Drummle. You're wrong there; I know one—

Aubrey [*listening*]. That's Paula's cart. Let's discuss this again.

Drummle [*going up to the window and looking out*]. It isn't the dog-cart. [*Turning to Aubrey.*] I hope you'll forgive me, old chap.

Aubrey. What for?

Drummle. Whose wheels do you think have been cutting ruts in your immaculate drive?

[*A Servant enters.*]

Servant [*to Aubrey*]. Mrs. Cortelyon, sir.

Aubrey. Mrs. Cortelyon! [*After a short pause.*] Very well. [*The Servant withdraws.*] What on earth is the meaning of this?

Drummle. Ahem! While I've been our old friend's guest, Aubrey, we have very naturally talked a good deal about you and yours.

Aubrey. Indeed, have you?

Drummle. Yes; and Alice Cortelyon has arrived at the conclusion that it would have been far kinder had she called on Mrs. Tanqueray long ago. She's going abroad for Easter before settling down in London for the season, and I believe she has come over this morning to ask for Ellean's companionship.

Aubrey. Oh, I see! [*Frowning.*] Quite a friendly little conspiracy, my dear Cayley!

Drummle. Conspiracy! Not at all, I assure you. [*Laughing.*] Ha, ha!

[*Ellean enters from the hall with Mrs. Cortelyon, a hand-*

some, good-humoured, spirited woman of about forty-five.]

Ellean. Papa—

Mrs. Cortelyon [*to Aubrey, shaking hands with him heartily*]. Well, Aubrey, how are you? I've just been telling this great girl of yours that I knew her when she was a sad-faced, pale baby. How is Mrs. Tanqueray? I have been a bad neighbour, and I'm here to beg forgiveness. Is she indoors?

Aubrey. She's up-stairs putting on a hat, I believe.

Mrs. Cortelyon [*sitting comfortably*]. Ah! [*She looks round: Drummle and Ellean are talking together in the hall.*] We used to be very frank with each other, Aubrey. I suppose the old footing is no longer possible, eh?

Aubrey. If so, I'm not entirely to blame, Mrs. Cortelyon.

Mrs. Cortelyon. Mrs. Cortelyon? H'm! No, I admit it. But you must make some little allowance for me, *Mr. Tanqueray*. Your first wife and I, as girls, were like two cherries on one stalk, and then I was the confidential friend of your married life. That post, perhaps, wasn't altogether a sinecure. And now— well, when a woman gets to my age I suppose she's a stupid, prejudiced, conventional creature. However, I've got over it and—[*giving him her hand*]— I hope you'll be enormously happy and let me be a friend once more.

Aubrey. Thank you, Alice.

Mrs. Cortelyon. That's right. I feel more cheerful than I've done for weeks. But I suppose it would serve me right if the second Mrs. Tanqueray showed me the door. Do you think she will?

Aubrey [*listening*]. Here is my wife. [*Mrs. Cortelyon rises, and Paula enters, dressed for driving; she stops abruptly on seeing Mrs. Cortelyon.*] Paula, dear, Mrs. Cortelyon has called to see you.

[*Paula starts, looks at Mrs. Cortelyon irresolutely, then after a slight pause barely touches Mrs. Cortelyon's extended hand.*]

Paula [*whose manner now alternates between deliberate insolence and assumed sweetness*]. Mrs.—? What name, Aubrey?

Aubrey. Mrs. Cortelyon.

Paula. Cortelyon? Oh, yes. Cortelyon.

Mrs. Cortelyon [*carefully guarding herself throughout against any expression of resentment*]. Aubrey ought to have told you that Alice Cortelyon and he are very old friends.

Paula. Oh, very likely he has mentioned the circumstance. I have quite a wretched memory.

Mrs. Cortelyon. You know we are neighbours, Mrs. Tanqueray.

Paula. Neighbours? Are we really? Won't you sit down? [*They both sit.*] Neighbours! That's most interesting!

Mrs. Cortelyon. Very near neighbours. You can see my roof from your windows.

Paula. I fancy I *have* observed a roof. But you have been away from home; you have only just returned.

Mrs. Cortelyon. I? What makes you think that?

Paula. Why, because it is two months since we came to Highercoombe, and I don't remember your having called.

Mrs. Cortelyon. Your memory is now terribly accurate. No, I've not been away from home, and it is to explain my neglect that I am here, rather unceremoniously, this morning.

Paula. Oh, to explain—quite so. [*With mock solicitude.*] Ah, you've been very ill; I ought to have seen that before.

Mrs. Cortelyon. Ill!

Paula. You look dreadfully pulled down. We poor women show illness so plainly in our faces, don't we?

Aubrey [*anxiously*]. Paula dear, Mrs. Cortelyon is the picture of health.

Mrs. Cortelyon [*with some asperity*]. I have never *felt* better in my life.

Paula [*looking round innocently*]. Have I said anything awkward? Aubrey, tell Mrs. Cortelyon how stupid and thoughtless I always am!

Mrs. Cortelyon [*to Drummle, who is now standing close to her*]. Really, Cayley—! [*He soothes her with a nod and smile and a motion of his finger to his lip.*] Mrs. Tanqueray, I am afraid my explanation will not be quite so satisfactory as either of those you have just helped me to. You may have heard—but, if you have heard, you have doubtless forgotten—that twenty years ago, when your husband first lived here, I was a constant visitor at Highercoombe.

Paula. Twenty years ago—fancy! I was a naughty little child then.

Mrs. Cortelyon. Possibly. Well, at that time, and till the end of her life, my affections were centred upon the lady of this house.

Paula. Were they? That was very sweet of you.

[*Ellean approaches Mrs. Cortelyon, listening intently to her.*]

Mrs. Cortelyon. I will say no more on that score, but I must add this: when, two months ago, you came here, I realised, perhaps for the first time, that I was a middle-aged woman, and that it had become impossible for me to accept without some effort a breaking-in upon many tender associations. There, Mrs. Tanqueray, that is my confession. Will you try to understand it and pardon me?

Paula [*watching Ellean,—sneeringly*]. Ellean dear, you appear to be very interested in Mrs. Cortelyon's reminiscences; I don't think I can do better than make you my mouthpiece—there is such sympathy between us. What do you say—can we bring ourselves to forgive Mrs. Cortelyon for neglecting us for two weary months?

Mrs. Cortelyon [*to Ellean, pleasantly*]. Well, Ellean? [*With a little cry of tenderness Ellean impulsively sits beside Mrs. Cortelyon and takes her hand.*] My dear child!

Paula [*in an undertone to Aubrey*]. Ellean isn't so very slow in taking to Mrs. Cortelyon!

Mrs. Cortelyon [*to Paula and Aubrey*]. Come, this encourages me to broach my scheme. Mrs. Tanqueray, it strikes me that you two good people are just now excellent company for each other, while Ellean would perhaps be glad of a little peep into the world you are anxious to avoid. Now, I'm going to Paris tomorrow for a week or two before settling down in Chester Square, so—don't gasp, both of you!—if this girl is willing, and you have made no other arrangements for her, will you let her come with me to Paris, and afterwards remain with me in town during the season? [*Ellean utters an exclamation of surprise. Paula is silent.*] What do you say?

Aubrey. Paula—Paula dear. [*Hesitatingly.*] My dear Mrs.
    Cortelyon, this is wonderfully kind of you; I am really
    at a loss to—eh, Cayley?

Drummle [*watching Paula apprehensively*]. Kind! Now I
    must say I don't think so! I begged Alice to take
    me to Paris, and she declined. I am thrown over
    for Ellean! Ha! ha!

Mrs. Cortelyon [*laughing*]. What nonsense you talk,
    Cayley!

[*The laughter dies out. Paula remains quite still.*]

Aubrey. Paula dear.

Paula [*slowly collecting herself*]. One moment. I—I don't
    quite—[*To Mrs. Cortelyon.*] You propose that Ellean
    leaves Highercoombe almost at once, and remains
    with you some months?

Mrs. Cortelyon. It would be a mercy to me. You can afford
    to be generous to a desolate old widow. Come, Mrs.
    Tanqueray, won't you spare her?

Paula. Won't *I* spare her. [*Suspiciously.*] Have you men-
    tioned your plan to Aubrey—before I came in?

Mrs. Cortelyon. No; I had no opportunity.

Paula. Nor to Ellean?

Mrs. Cortelyon. Oh, no.

Paula [*looking about her in suppressed excitement*]. This
    hasn't been discussed at all, behind my back?

Mrs. Cortelyon. My dear Mrs. Tanqueray!

Paula. Ellean, let us hear your voice in the matter!

Ellean. I should like to go with Mrs. Cortelyon—

Paula. Ah!

Ellean. That is, if—if—

Paula. If—what?

Ellean [*looking towards Aubrey, appealingly*]. Papa!

Paula [*in a hard voice*]. Oh, of course—I forgot. [*To
    Aubrey.*] My dear Aubrey, it rests with you, naturally,
    whether I am—to lose—Ellean.

Aubrey. Lose Ellean! [*Advancing to Paula.*] There is no
    question of losing Ellean. You would see Ellean in
    town constantly when she returned from Paris; isn't
    that so, Mrs. Cortelyon?

Mrs. Cortelyon. Certainly.

Paula [*laughing softly*]. Oh, I didn't know I should be
    allowed that privilege.

Mrs. Cortelyon. Privilege, my dear Mrs. Tanqueray!

Paula. Ha, ha! that makes all the difference, doesn't it?

Aubrey [*with assumed gaiety*]. All the difference? I should think so! [*To Ellean, laying his hand upon her head tenderly.*] And you are quite certain you wish to see what the world is like on the other side of Black Moor!

Ellean. If you are willing, papa, I am quite certain.

Aubrey [*looking at Paula irresolutely, then speaking with an effort*]. Then I—I am willing.

Paula [*rising and striking the table lightly with her clenched hand*]. That decides it! [*There is a general movement. Excitedly to Mrs. Cortelyon, who advances towards her.*] When do you want her?

Mrs. Cortelyon. We go to town this afternoon at five o'clock, and sleep to-night at Bayliss's. There is barely time for her to make her preparations.

Paula. I will undertake that she is ready.

Mrs. Cortelyon. I've a great deal to scramble through at home too, as you may guess. Good-bye!

Paula [*turning away*]. Mrs. Cortelyon is going. [*Paula stands looking out of the window, with her back to those in the room.*]

Mrs. Cortelyon [*to Drummle*]. Cayley—

Drummle [*to her*]. Eh?

Mrs. Cortelyon. I've gone through it, for the sake of Aubrey and his child, but I—I feel a hundred. Is that a madwoman?

Drummle. Of course; all jealous women are mad. [*He goes out with Aubrey.*]

Mrs. Cortelyon [*hesitatingly, to Paula*]. Good-bye, Mrs. Tanqueray.

[*Paula inclines her head with the slightest possible movement, then resumes her former position. Ellean comes from the hall and takes Mrs. Cortelyon out of the room. After a brief silence, Paula turns with a fierce cry, and hurriedly takes off her coat and hat, and tosses them upon the settee.*]

Paula. Who's that? Oh! Oh! Oh! [*She drops into the chair as Aubrey returns; he stands looking at her.*]

Aubrey. I—you have altered your mind about going out?

Paula. Yes. Please to ring the bell.

Aubrey [*touching the bell*]. You are angry about Mrs. Cortelyon and Ellean. Let me try to explain my reasons—

Paula. Be careful what you say to me just now! I have never felt like this—except once—in my life. Be careful what you say to me!

[*A Servant enters.*]

Paula [*rising*]. Is Watts at the door with the cart?

Servant. Yes, ma'am.

Paula. Tell him to drive down to the post-office directly with this. [*Picking up the letter which has been lying upon the table.*]

Aubrey. With that?

Paula. Yes. My letter to Lady Orreyed. [*Giving the letter to the Servant, who goes out.*]

Aubrey. Surely you don't wish me to countermand any order of yours to a servant? Call the man back—take the letter from him!

Paula. I have not the slightest intention of doing so.

Aubrey. I must, then. [*Going to the door. She snatches up her hat and coat and follows him.*] What are you going to do?

Paula. If you stop that letter, I walk out of the house.

[*He hesitates, then leaves the door.*]

Aubrey. I am right in believing that to be the letter inviting George Orreyed and his wife to stay here, am I not?

Paula. Oh, yes—quite right.

Aubrey. Let it go; I'll write to him by-and-bye.

Paula [*facing him*]. You dare!

Aubrey. Hush, Paula!

Paula. Insult me again and, upon my word, I'll go straight out of the house!

Aubrey. Insult you?

Paula. Insult me! What else is it? My God! what else is it? What do you mean by taking Ellean from me?

Aubrey. Listen—!

Paula. Listen to *me!* And how do you take her? You pack her off in the care of a woman who has deliberately held aloof from me, who's thrown mud at me! Yet this Cortelyon creature has only to put foot here once to be entrusted with the charge of the girl you know I dearly want to keep near me!

Aubrey. Paula dear! hear me—!

Paula. Ah! of course, of course! I can't be so useful to your daughter as such people as this; and so I'm to be given the go-by for any town friend of yours who turns up and chooses to patronise us! Hah! Very well, at any rate, as you take Ellean from me you justify my looking for companions where I can most readily find 'em.

Aubrey. You wish me to fully appreciate your reason for sending that letter to Lady Orreyed?

Paula. Precisely—I do.

Aubrey. And could you, after all, go back to associates of that order? It's not possible!

Paula [*mockingly*]. What, not after the refining influence of these intensely respectable surroundings? [*Going to the door.*] We'll see!

Aubrey. Paula!

Paula [*violently*]. We'll see! [*She goes out. He stands still looking after her.*]

act 3

The drawing-room at "Highercoombe." Facing the spec-
tator are two large French windows, sheltered by a ver-
andah, leading into the garden; on the right is a door
opening into a small hall. The fireplace, with a large mirror
above it, is on the left-hand side of the room, and higher
up in the same wall are double doors recessed. The room is
richly furnished, and everything betokens taste and luxury.
The windows are open, and there is moonlight in the
garden.

Lady Orreyed, a pretty, affected doll of a woman, with a
mincing voice and flaxen hair, is sitting on the ottoman,
her head resting against the drum, and her eyes closed.
Paula, looking pale, worn, and thoroughly unhappy, is
sitting at a table. Both are in sumptuous dinner-gowns.

Lady Orreyed [*opening her eyes*]. Well, I never! I dropped
off! [*Feeling her hair.*] Just fancy! Where are the
men?
Paula [*icily*]. Outside, smoking.
[*A Servant enters with coffee, which he hands to Lady*
Orreyed. Sir George Orreyed comes in by the win-
dow. He is a man of about thirty-five, with a low
forehead, a receding chin, a vacuous expression, and
an ominous redness about the nose.]
Lady Orreyed [*taking coffee*]. Here's Dodo.
Sir George. I say, the flies under the verandah make you
swear. [*The Servant hands coffee to Paula, who declines*
it, then to Sir George, who takes a cup.] Hi! wait a bit!
[*He looks at the tray searchingly, then puts back his*
cup.] Never mind. [*Quietly to Lady Orreyed.*] I say,
they're dooced sparin' with their liqueur, ain't they?
[*The Servant goes out at window.*]
Paula [*to Sir George*]. Won't you take coffee, George?

Sir George. No, thanks. It's gettin' near time for a whiskey and potass. [*Approaching Paula, regarding Lady Orreyed admiringly.*] I say, Birdie looks rippin' to-night, don't she?

Paula. Your wife?

Sir George. Yaas—Birdie.

Paula. Rippin'?

Sir George. Yaas.

Paula. Quite—quite rippin'.

[*He moves round to the settee. Paula watches him with distaste, then rises and walks away. Sir George falls asleep on the settee.*]

Lady Orreyed. Paula love, I fancied you and Aubrey were a little more friendly at dinner. You haven't made it up, have you?

Paula. We? Oh, no. We speak before others, that's all.

Lady Orreyed. And how long do you intend to carry on this game, dear?

Paula [*turning away impatiently*]. I really can't tell you.

Lady Orreyed. Sit down, old girl; don't be so fidgety. [*Paula sits on the upper seat of the ottoman, with her back to Lady Orreyed.*] Of course, it's my duty, as an old friend, to give you a good talking to—[*Paula glares at her suddenly and fiercely.*]—but really I've found one gets so many smacks in the face through interfering in matrimonial squabbles that I've determined to drop it.

Paula. I think you're wise.

Lady Orreyed. However, I must say that I do wish you'd look at marriage in a more solemn light—just as I do, in fact. It is such a beautiful thing—marriage, and if people in our position don't respect it, and set a good example by living happily with their husbands, what can you expect from the middle classes? When did this sad state of affairs between you and Aubrey actually begin?

Paula. Actually, a fortnight and three days ago; I haven't calculated the minutes.

Lady Orreyed. A day or two before Dodo and I turned up—arrived.

Paula. Yes. One always remembers one thing by another; we left off speaking to each other the morning I wrote asking you to visit us.

Lady Orreyed. Lucky for you I was able to pop down, wasn't it, dear?

Paula [*glaring at her again*]. Most fortunate.

Lady Orreyed. A serious split with your husband without a pal on the premises—I should say, without a friend in the house—would be most unpleasant.

Paula [*turning to her abruptly*]. This place must be horribly doleful for you and George just now. At least you ought to consider him before me. Why didn't you leave me to my difficulties?

Lady Orreyed. Oh, we're quite comfortable, dear, thank you—both of us. George and me are so wrapped up in each other, it doesn't matter where we are. I don't want to crow over you, old girl, but I've got a perfect husband.

[*Sir George is now fast asleep, his head thrown back and his mouth open, looking hideous.*]

Paula [*glancing at Sir George*]. So you've given me to understand.

Lady Orreyed. Not that we don't have our little differences. Why, we fell out only this very morning. You remember the diamond and ruby tiara Charley Prestwick gave poor dear Connie Tirlemont years ago, don't you?

Paula. No, I do not.

Lady Orreyed. No? Well, it's in the market. Benjamin of Piccadilly has got it in his shop window, and I've set my heart on it.

Paula. You consider it quite necessary?

Lady Orreyed. Yes; because what I say to Dodo is this—a lady of my station must smother herself with hair ornaments. It's different with you, love—people don't look for so much blaze from you, but I've got rank to keep up; haven't I?

Paula. Yes.

Lady Orreyed. Well, that was the cause of the little set-to between I and Dodo this morning. He broke two chairs, he was in such a rage. I forgot they're your chairs; do you mind?

Paula. No.

Lady Orreyed. You know, poor Dodo can't lose his temper without smashing something; if it isn't a chair, it's a mirror; if it isn't that, it's china—a bit of Dresden

for choice. Dear old pet! he loves a bit of Dresden
when he's furious. He doesn't really throw things *at*
me, dear; he simply lifts them up and drops them, like
a gentleman. I expect our room upstairs will look
rather wrecky before I get that tiara.

Paula. Excuse the suggestion; perhaps your husband can't
afford it.

Lady Orreyed. Oh, how dreadfully changed you are, Paula!
Dodo can always mortgage something, or borrow of
his ma. What *is* coming to you!

Paula. Ah! [*She sits at the piano and touches the keys.*]

Lady Orreyed. Oh, yes, do play! That's the one thing I
envy you for.

Paula. What shall I play?

Lady Orreyed. What was that heavenly piece you gave us
last night, dear?

Paula. A bit of Schubert. Would you like to hear it again?

Lady Orreyed. You don't know any comic songs, do you?

Paula. I'm afraid not.

Lady Orreyed. I leave it to you.

[*Paula plays. Aubrey and Cayley Drummle appear outside
the window; they look into the room.*]

Aubrey [*to Drummle*]. You can see her face in that mirror.
Poor girl, how ill and wretched she looks.

Drummle. When are the Orreyeds going?

Aubrey. Heaven knows! [*Entering the room.*]

Drummle. But *you're* entertaining them; what's it to do
with heaven? [*Following Aubrey.*]

Aubrey. Do you know, Cayley, that even the Orreyeds
serve a useful purpose? My wife actually speaks
to me before our guests—think of that! I've come to
rejoice at the presence of the Orreyeds!

Drummle. I dare say; we're taught that beetles are sent for
a benign end.

Aubrey. Cayley, talk to Paula again to-night.

Drummle. Certainly, if I get the chance.

Aubrey. Let's contrive it. George is asleep; perhaps I
can get that doll out of the way. [*As they advance
into the room, Paula abruptly ceases playing and finds
interest in a volume of music. Sir George is now nodding and snoring apoplectically.*] Lady Orreyed, whenever you feel inclined for a game of billiards I'm at
your service.

Lady Orreyed [*jumping up*]. Charmed, I'm sure! I really thought you'd forgotten poor little me. Oh, look at Dodo!

Aubrey. No, no, don't wake him; he's tired.

Lady Orreyed. I must, he looks so plain. [*Rousing Sir George.*] Dodo! Dodo!

Sir George [*stupidly*]. 'Ullo!

Lady Orreyed. Dodo dear, you were snoring.

Sir George. Oh, I say, you could 'a told me that by-and-bye.

Aubrey. You want a cigar, George; come into the billiard-room. [*Giving his arm to Lady Orreyed.*] Cayley, bring Paula. [*Aubrey and Lady Orreyed go out.*]

Sir George [*rising*]. Hey, what! Billiard-room! [*Looking at his watch.*] How goes the——? Phew! 'Ullo, 'Ullo! Whiskey and potass! [*He goes rapidly after Aubrey and Lady Orreyed. Paula resumes playing.*]

Paula [*after a pause*]. Don't moon about after me, Cayley; follow the others.

Drummle. Thanks, by-and-bye. [*Sitting.*] That's pretty.

Paula [*after another pause, still playing*]. I wish you wouldn't stare so.

Drummle. Was I staring? I'm sorry. [*She plays a little longer, then stops suddenly, rises, and goes to the window, where she stands looking out. Drummle moves from the ottoman to the settee.*] A lovely night.

Paula [*startled*]. Oh! [*Without turning to him.*] Why do you hop about like a monkey?

Drummle. Hot rooms play the deuce with the nerves. Now, it would have done you good to have walked in the garden with us after dinner and made merry. Why didn't you?

Paula. You know why.

Drummle. Ah, you're thinking of the——difference between you and Aubrey?

Paula. Yes, I *am* thinking of it.

Drummle. Well, so am I. How long——?

Paula. Getting on for three weeks.

Drummle. Bless me, it must be! And this would have been such a night to have healed it! Moonlight, the stars, the scent of flowers; and yet enough darkness to enable a kind woman to rest her hand for an instant on the arm of a good fellow who loves her. Ah, ha!

It's a wonderful power, dear Mrs. Aubrey, the power of an offended woman! Only realise it! Just that one touch—the mere tips of her fingers—and, for herself and another, she changes the colour of the whole world.

Paula [*turning to him calmly*]. Cayley, my dear man, you talk exactly like a very romantic old lady. [*She leaves the window and sits playing with the knick-knacks on the table.*]

Drummle [*to himself*]. H'm, that hasn't done it! Well—ha, ha!—I accept the suggestion. An old woman, eh?

Paula. Oh, I didn't intend—

Drummle. But why not? I've every qualification—well, almost. And I confess it would have given this withered bosom a throb of grandmotherly satisfaction if I could have seen you and Aubrey at peace before I take my leave to-morrow.

Paula. To-morrow, Cayley!

Drummle. I must.

Paula. Oh, this house is becoming unendurable.

Drummle. You're very kind. But you've got the Orreyeds.

Paula [*fiercely*]. The Orreyeds! I—I hate the Orreyeds! I lie awake at night, hating them!

Drummle. Pardon me, I've understood that their visit is, in some degree, owing to—hem—your suggestion.

Paula. Heavens! that doesn't make me like them better. Somehow or another, I—I've outgrown these people. This woman—I used to think her "jolly!"—sickens me. I can't breathe when she's near me: the whiff of her handkerchief turns me faint! And she patronises me by the hour, until I—I feel my nails growing longer with every word she speaks!

Drummle. My dear lady, why on earth don't you say all this to Aubrey?

Paula. Oh, I've been such an utter fool, Cayley!

Drummle [*soothingly*]. Well, well, mention it to Aubrey!

Paula. No, no, you don't understand. What do you think I've done?

Drummle. Done! What, *since* you invited the Orreyeds?

Paula. Yes; I must tell you—

Drummle. Perhaps you'd better not.

Paula. Look here! I've intercepted some letters from Mrs. Cortelyon and Ellean to—him. [*Producing three*

unopened letters from the bodice of her dress.] There
are the accursed things! From Paris—two from the
Cortelyon woman, the other from Ellean!

Drummle. But why—why?

Paula. I don't know. Yes, I do! I saw letters coming from
Ellean to her father; not a line to me—not a line. And
one morning it happened I was downstairs before he
was, and I spied this one lying with his heap on the
breakfast-table, and I slipped it into my pocket—out
of malice, Cayley, pure deviltry! And a day or two
afterwards I met Elwes the postman at the Lodge, and
took the letters from him, and found these others
amongst 'em. I felt simply fiendish when I saw them
—fiendish! [*Returning the letters to her bodice.*] And
now I carry them about with me, and they're scorch-
ing me like a mustard plaster!

Drummle. Oh, this accounts for Aubrey not hearing from
Paris lately!

Paula. That's an ingenious conclusion to arrive at! Of
course it does! [*With an hysterical laugh.*] Ha, ha!

Drummle. Well, well! [*Laughing.*] Ha, ha, ha!

Paula [*turning upon him*]. I suppose it *is* amusing!

Drummle. I beg pardon.

Paula. Heavens knows I've little enough to brag about!
I'm a bad lot, but not in mean tricks of this sort.
In all my life this is the most caddish thing I've
done. How am I to get rid of these letters—that's
what I want to know? How am I to get rid of them?

Drummle. If I were you I should take Aubrey aside and
put them into his hands as soon as possible.

Paula. What! and tell him to his face that I—! No, thank
you. I suppose *you* wouldn't like to—

Drummle. No, no; I won't touch 'em!

Paula. And you call yourself my friend?

Drummle [*good-humouredly*]. No, I don't!

Paula. Perhaps I'll tie them together and give them to his
man in the morning.

Drummle. That won't avoid an explanation.

Paula [*recklessly*]. Oh, then he must miss them—

Drummle. And trace them.

Paula [*throwing herself upon the ottoman*]. I don't care!

Drummle. I know you don't; but let me send him to you
now, may I?

Paula. Now! What do you think a woman's made of? I couldn't stand it, Cayley. I haven't slept for nights; and last night there was thunder, too! I believe I've got the horrors.

Drummle [*taking the little hand-mirror from the table*]. You'll sleep well enough when you deliver those letters. Come, come, Mrs. Aubrey—a good night's rest! [*Holding the mirror before her face.*] It's quite time.

[*She looks at herself for a moment, then snatches the mirror from him.*]

Paula. You brute, Cayley, to show me that!

Drummle. Then—may I? Be guided by a fr—a poor old woman! May I?

Paula. You'll kill me, amongst you!

Drummle. What do you say?

Paula [*after a pause*]. Very well. [*He nods his head and goes out rapidly. She looks after him for a moment, and calls "Cayley! Cayley!" Then she again produces the letters, deliberately, one by one, fingering them with aversion. Suddenly she starts, turning her head towards the door.*] Ah!

[*Aubrey enters quickly.*]

Aubrey. Paula!

Paula [*handing him the letters, her face averted*]. There! [*He examines the letters, puzzled, and looks at her enquiringly.*] They are many days old. I stole them, I suppose to make you anxious and unhappy.

[*He looks at the letters again, then lays them aside on the table.*]

Aubrey [*gently*]. Paula, dear, it doesn't matter.

Paula [*after a short pause*]. Why—why do you take it like this?

Aubrey. What did you expect?

Paula. Oh, but I suppose silent reproaches are really the severest. And then, naturally, you are itching to open your letters. [*She crosses the room as if to go.*]

Aubrey. Paula! [*She pauses.*] Surely, surely, it's all over now?

Paula. All over! [*Mockingly.*] Has my step-daughter returned then? When did she arrive? I haven't heard of it!

Aubrey. You can be very cruel.

Paula. That word's always on a man's lips; he uses it if

his soup's cold. [*With another movement as if to go.*] Need we—

Aubrey. I know I've wounded you, Paula? But isn't there any way out of this?

Paula. When does Ellean return? To-morrow? Next week?

Aubrey [*wearily*]. Oh! Why should we grudge Ellean the little pleasure she is likely to find in Paris and in London.

Paula. I grudge her nothing, if that's a hit at me. But with that woman—?

Aubrey. It must be that woman or another. You know that at present we are unable to give Ellean the opportunity of—of—

Paula. Of mixing with respectable people.

Aubrey. The opportunity of gaining friends, experience, ordinary knowledge of the world. If you are interested in Ellean, can't you see how useful Mrs. Cortelyon's good offices are?

Paula. May I put one question? At the end of the London season, when Mrs. Cortelyon has done with Ellean, is it quite understood that the girl comes back to us? [*Aubrey is silent.*] Is it? Is it?

Aubrey. Let us wait till the end of the season—

Paula. Oh! I knew it. You're only fooling me; you put me off with any trash. I believe you've sent Ellean away, not for the reasons you give, but because you don't consider me a decent companion for her, because you're afraid she might get a little of her innocence rubbed off in my company? Come, isn't that the truth? Be honest! Isn't that it?

Aubrey. Yes. [*There is a moment's silence on both sides.*]

Paula [*with uplifted hands as if to strike him*]. Oh!

Aubrey [*taking her by the wrists*]. Sit down. Sit down. [*He puts her into a chair; she shakes herself free with a cry.*] Now listen to me. Fond as you are, Paula, of harking back to your past, there's one chapter of it you always let alone. I've never asked you to speak of it; you've never offered to speak of it. I mean the chapter that relates to the time when you were— like Ellean. [*She attempts to rise; he restrains her.*] No, no.

Paula. I don't choose to talk about that time. I won't satisfy your curiosity.

Aubrey. My dear Paula, I have no curiosity—I know what
you were at Ellean's age. I'll tell you. You hadn't a
thought that wasn't a wholesome one, you hadn't an
impulse that didn't tend towards good, you never
harboured a notion you couldn't have gossiped about
to a parcel of children. [*She makes another effort to
rise: he lays his hand lightly on her shoulder.*] And
this was a very few years back—there are days now
when you look like a schoolgirl—but think of the
difference between the two Paulas. You'll have to
think hard, because after a cruel life, one's perceptions grow a thick skin. But, for God's sake, do think
till you get these two images clearly in your mind,
and then ask yourself what sort of a friend such a
woman as you are to-day would have been for the
girl of seven or eight years ago.

Paula [*rising*]. How dare you? I could be almost as good
a friend to Ellean as her own mother would have been
had she lived. I know what you mean. How dare
you?

Aubrey. You say that; very likely you believe it. But you're
blind, Paula; you're blind. You! Every belief that a
young, pure-minded girl holds sacred—that you once
held sacred—you now make a target for a jest, a
sneer, a paltry cynicism. I tell you, you're not mistress
any longer of your thoughts or your tongue. Why,
how often, sitting between you and Ellean, have I seen
her cheeks turn scarlet as you've rattled off some tale
that belongs by right to the club or the smoking-room!
Have you noticed the blush? If you have, has the
cause of it ever struck you? And this is the girl you
say you love, I admit that you *do* love, whose love you
expect in return! Oh, Paula, I make the best, the only,
excuse for you when I tell you you're blind!

Paula. Ellean—Ellean blushes easily.

Aubrey. You blushed as easily a few years ago.

Paula [*after a short pause*]. Well! Have you finished your
sermon?

Aubrey [*with a gesture of despair*]. Oh, Paula! [*Going up
to the window, and standing with his back to the
room.*]

Paula [*to herself*]. A few—years ago! [*She walks slowly
towards the door, then suddenly drops upon the*

ottoman in a paroxysm of weeping.] O God! A few
years ago!

Aubrey [*going to her*]. Paula!

Paula [*sobbing*]. Oh, don't touch me!

Aubrey. Paula!

Paula. Oh, go away from me! [*He goes back a few steps,
and after a little while she becomes calmer and rises
unsteadily; then in an altered tone.*] Look here—! [*He
advances a step; she checks him with a quick gesture.*]
Look here! Get rid of these people—Mabel and her
husband—as soon as possible! I—I've done with
them!

Aubrey [*in a whisper*]. Paula!

Paula. And then—then—when the time comes for Ellean
to leave Mrs. Cortelyon, give me—give me another
chance! [*He advances again, but she shrinks away.*]
No, no! [*She goes out by the door on the right. He
sinks on to the settee, covering his eyes with his
hands. There is a brief silence, then a Servant enters.*]

Servant. Mrs. Cortelyon, sir, with Miss Ellean.

[*Aubrey rises to meet Mrs. Cortelyon, who enters, followed
by Ellean, both being in travelling dresses. The Servant
withdraws.*]

Mrs. Cortelyon [*shaking hands with Aubrey*]. Oh, my dear
Aubrey!

Aubrey. Mrs. Cortelyon! [*Kissing Ellean.*] Ellean dear!

Ellean. Papa, is all well at home?

Mrs. Cortelyon. We're shockingly anxious.

Aubrey. Yes, yes, all's well. This is quite unexpected. [*To
Mrs. Cortelyon.*] You've found Paris insufferably
hot?

Mrs. Cortelyon. Insufferably hot! Paris is pleasant enough.
We've had no letter from you!

Aubrey. I wrote to Ellean a week ago.

Mrs. Cortelyon. Without alluding to the subject I had
written to you upon.

Aubrey [*thinking*]. Ah, of course—

Mrs. Cortelyon. And since then we've both written, and
you've been absolutely silent. Oh, it's too bad!

Aubrey [*picking up the letters from the table*]. It isn't
altogether my fault. Here are the letters—

Ellean. Papa!

Mrs. Cortelyon. They're unopened.

Aubrey. An accident delayed their reaching me till this evening. I'm afraid this has upset you very much.

Mrs. Cortelyon. Upset me!

Ellean [*in an undertone to Mrs. Cortelyon*]. Never mind. Not now, dear—not to-night.

Aubrey. Eh?

Mrs. Cortelyon [*to Ellean, aloud*]. Child, run away and take your things off. She doesn't look as if she'd journeyed from Paris to-day.

Aubrey. I've never seen her with such a colour. [*Taking Ellean's hands.*]

Ellean [*to Aubrey, in a faint voice*]. Papa, Mrs. Cortelyon has been so very, very kind to me, but I—I have come home. [*She goes out.*]

Aubrey. Come home! [*To Mrs. Cortelyon.*] Ellean returns to us then?

Mrs. Cortelyon. That's the very point I put to you in my letters, and you oblige me to travel from Paris to Willowmere on a warm day to settle it. I think perhaps it's right that Ellean should be with you just now, although I— My dear friend, circumstances are a little altered.

Aubrey. Alice, you're in some trouble.

Mrs. Cortelyon. Well—yes, I *am* in trouble. You remember pretty little Mrs. Brereton who was once Caroline Ardale?

Aubrey. Quite well.

Mrs. Cortelyon. She's a widow now, poor thing. She has the *entresol* of the house where we've been lodging in the Avenue de Friedland. Caroline's a dear chum of mine; she formed a great liking for Ellean.

Aubrey. I'm very glad.

Mrs. Cortelyon. Yes, it's nice for her to meet her mother's friends. Er—that young Hugh Ardale the papers were full of some time ago—he's Caroline Brereton's brother, you know.

Aubrey. No, I didn't know. What did he do? I forget.

Mrs. Cortelyon. Checked one of those horrid mutinies at some far-away station in India. Marched down with a handful of his men and a few faithful natives, and held the place until he was relieved. They gave him his company and a V.C. for it.

Aubrey. And he's Mrs. Brereton's brother?

Mrs. Cortelyon. Yes. He's with his sister—*was*, rather—in Paris. He's home—invalided. Good gracious, Aubrey, why don't you help me out? Can't you guess what has occurred?

Aubrey. Alice!

Mrs. Cortelyon. Young Ardale—Ellean!

Aubrey. An attachment?

Mrs. Cortelyon. Yes, Aubrey. [*After a little pause.*] Well, I suppose I've got myself into sad disgrace. But really I didn't foresee anything of this kind. A serious, reserved child like Ellean, and a boyish, high-spirited soldier—it never struck me as being likely. [*Aubrey paces to and fro thoughtfully.*] I did all I could directly Captain Ardale spoke—wrote to you at once. Why on earth don't you receive your letters promptly, and when you do get them why can't you open them? I endured the anxiety till last night, and then made up my mind—home! Of course, it has worried me terribly. My head's bursting. Are there any salts about? [*Aubrey fetches a bottle from the cabinet and hands it to her.*] We've had one of those hateful smooth crossings that won't let you be properly indisposed.

Aubrey. My dear Alice, I assure you I've no thought of blaming you.

Mrs. Cortelyon. That statement always precedes a quarrel.

Aubrey. I don't know whether this is the worst or the best luck. How will my wife regard it? Is Captain Ardale a good fellow?

Mrs. Cortelyon. My dear Aubrey, you'd better read up the accounts of his wonderful heroism. Face to face with death for a whole week; always with a smile and a cheering word for the poor helpless souls depending on him! Of course it's that that has stirred the depths of your child's nature. I've watched her while we've been dragging the story out of him, and if angels look different from Ellean at that moment, I don't desire to meet any, that's all!

Aubrey. If you were in my position—? But you can't judge.

Mrs. Cortelyon. Why, if I had a marriageable daughter of my own, and Captain Ardale proposed for her, naturally I should cry my eyes out all night—but I should thank Heaven in the morning.

Aubrey. You believe so thoroughly in him?

Mrs. Cortelyon. Do you think I should have only a head-ache at this minute if I didn't! Look here, you've got to see me down the lane; that's the least you can do, my friend. Come into my house for a moment and shake hands with Hugh.

Aubrey. What, is he here?

Mrs. Cortelyon. He came through with us, to present him-self formally to-morrow. Where are my gloves? [*Aubrey fetches them from the ottoman.*] Make my apolo-gies to Mrs. Tanqueray, please. She's well, I hope? [*Going towards the door.*] I can't feel sorry she hasn't seen me in this condition.

[*Ellean enters.*]

Ellean [*to Mrs. Cortelyon*]. I've been waiting to wish you good-night. I was afraid I'd missed you.

Mrs. Cortelyon. Good night, Ellean.

Ellean [*in a low voice, embracing Mrs. Cortelyon*]. I can't thank you. Dear Mrs. Cortelyon!

Mrs. Cortelyon [*her arms round Ellean, in a whisper to Aubrey*]. Speak a word to her. [*Mrs. Cortelyon goes out.*]

Aubrey [*to Ellean*]. Ellean, I'm going to see Mrs. Cortelyon home. Tell Paula where I am; explain, dear. [*Going to the door.*]

Ellean [*her head drooping*]. Yes. [*Quickly.*] Father! You are angry with me—disappointed?

Aubrey. Angry? No.

Ellean. Disappointed?

Aubrey [*smiling and going to her and taking her hand*]. If so, it's only because you've shaken my belief in my discernment. I thought you took after your poor mother a little, Ellean; but there's a look on your face to-night, dear, that I never saw on hers—never, never.

Ellean [*leaning her head on his shoulder*]. Perhaps I ought not to have gone away.

Aubrey. Hush! You're quite happy?

Ellean. Yes.

Aubrey. That's right. Then, as you are quite happy, there is something I particularly want you to do for me, Ellean.

Ellean. What is that?

Aubrey. Be very gentle with Paula. Will you?

Ellean. You think I have been unkind.

Aubrey [*kissing her upon the forehead*]. Be very gentle
     with Paula. [*He goes out, and she stands looking after
     him; then, as she turns thoughtfully from the door, a
     rose is thrown through the window and falls at her
     feet. She picks up the flower wonderingly and goes
     to the window.*]

Ellean [*starting back*]. Hugh!

[*Hugh Ardale, a handsome young man of about seven-and-
     twenty, with a boyish face and manner, appears out-
     side the window.*]

Hugh. Nelly! Nelly dear!

Ellean. What's the matter?

Hugh. Hush! Nothing. It's only fun. [*Laughing.*] Ha, ha,
     ha! I've found out that Mrs. Cortelyon's meadow runs
     up to your father's plantation; I've come through a
     gap in the hedge.

Ellean. Why, Hugh?

Hugh. I'm miserable at The Warren: it's so different
     from the Avenue de Friedland. Don't look like that!
     Upon my word I meant just to peep at your home and
     go back, but I saw figures moving about here, and
     came nearer, hoping to get a glimpse of you. Was
     that your father? [*Entering the room.*]

Ellean. Yes.

Hugh. Isn't this fun! A rabbit ran across my foot while I
     was hiding behind that old yew.

Ellean. You must go away; it's not right for you to be here
     like this.

Hugh. But it's only fun, I tell you. You take everything
     so seriously. Do wish me good-night.

Ellean. We have said good-night.

Hugh. In the hall at The Warren, before Mrs. Cortelyon
     and a man-servant. Oh, it's so different from the
     Avenue de Friedland!

Ellean [*giving him her hand hastily*]. Good-night, Hugh.

Hugh. Is that all? We might be the merest acquaintances.
     [*He momentarily embraces her, but she releases her-
     self.*]

Ellean. It's when you're like this that you make me feel
     utterly miserable. [*Throwing the rose from her an-
     grily.*] Oh!

Hugh. I've offended you now, I suppose?

Ellean. Yes.

Hugh. Forgive me, Nelly. Come into the garden for five minutes; we'll stroll down to the plantation.

Ellean. No, no.

Hugh. For two minutes—to tell me you forgive me.

Ellean. I forgive you.

Hugh. Evidently. I sha'n't sleep a wink to-night after this. What a fool I am! Come down to the plantation. Make it up with me.

Ellean. There is somebody coming into this room. Do you wish to be seen here?

Hugh. I shall wait for you behind that yew-tree. You must speak to me. Nelly! [*He disappears. Paula enters.*]

Paula. Ellean!

Ellean. You—you are very surprised to see me, Paula, of course.

Paula. Why are you here? Why aren't you with—your friend?

Ellean. I've come home—if you'll have me. We left Paris this morning; Mrs. Cortelyon brought me back. She was here a minute or two ago; papa has just gone with her to The Warren. He asked me to tell you.

Paula. There are some people staying with us that I'd rather you didn't meet. It was hardly worth your while to return for a few hours.

Ellean. A few hours?

Paula. Well, when do you go to London?

Ellean. I don't think I go to London, after all.

Paula [*eagerly*]. You—you've quarrelled with her?

Ellean. No, no, no, not that; but—Paula! [*In an altered tone.*] Paula!

Paula [*startled*]. Eh? [*Ellean goes deliberately to Paula and kisses her.*] Ellean!

Ellean. Kiss me.

Paula. What—what's come to you?

Ellean. I want to behave differently to you in the future. Is it too late?

Paula. Too—late! [*Impulsively kissing Ellean and crying.*] No—no—no! No—no!

Ellean. Paula, don't cry.

Paula [*wiping her eyes*]. I'm a little shaky; I haven't been sleeping. It's all right,—talk to me.

Ellean. There is something I want to tell you—

Paula. Is there—is there?

[*They sit together on the ottoman, Paula taking Ellean's hand.*]

Ellean. Paula, in our house in the Avenue de Friedland, on the floor below us, there was a Mrs. Brereton. She used to be a friend of my mother's. Mrs. Cortelyon and I spent a great deal of our time with her.

Paula [*suspiciously*]. Oh! [*Letting Ellean's hand fall.*] Is this lady going to take you up in place of Mrs. Cortelyon?

Ellean. No, no. Her brother is staying with her—*was* staying with her. Her brother—[*Breaking off in confusion.*]

Paula. Well?

Ellean [*almost inaudibly*]. Paula—[*She rises and walks away, Paula following her.*]

Paula. Ellean! [*Taking hold of her.*] You're not in love! [*Ellean looks at Paula appealingly.*] Oh, *you* in love! You! Oh, this is why you've come home! Of course, you can make friends with me now! You'll leave us for good soon, I suppose; so it doesn't much matter being civil to me for a little while!

Ellean. Oh, Paula!

Paula. Why, how you have deceived us—all of us! We've taken you for a cold-blooded little saint. The fools you've made of us! Saint Ellean, Saint Ellean!

Ellean. Ah, I might have known you'd only mock me!

Paula [*her tone changing*]. Eh?

Ellean. I—I can't talk to you. [*Sitting on the settee.*] You do nothing else but mock and sneer, nothing else.

Paula. Ellean dear! Ellean! I didn't mean it. I'm so horribly jealous, it's a sort of curse on me. [*Kneeling beside Ellean and embracing her.*] My tongue runs away with me. I'm going to alter, I swear I am. I've made some good resolutions, and as God's above me, I'll keep them! If you are in love, if you do ever marry, that's no reason why we shouldn't be fond of each other. Come, you've kissed me of your own accord— you can't take it back. Now we're friends again, aren't we? Ellean dear! I want to know everything, everything. Ellean dear, Ellean!

Ellean. Paula, Hugh has done something that makes me

very angry. He came with us from Paris to-day, to
see papa. He is staying with Mrs. Cortelyon and—I
ought to tell you—

Paula. Yes, yes. What?

Ellean. He has found his way by The Warren meadow
through the plantation up to this house. He is waiting to bid me good-night. [*Glancing towards the garden.*] He is—out there.

Paula. Oh!

Ellean. What shall I do?

Paula. Bring him in to see me! Will you?

Ellean. No, no.

Paula. But I'm dying to know him. Oh, yes, you must.
I shall meet him before Aubrey does. [*Excitedly running her hands over her hair.*] I'm so glad. [*Ellean
goes out by the window.*] The mirror—mirror. What
a fright I must look! [*Not finding the hand-glass on
the table, she jumps on to the settee, and surveys herself in the mirror over the mantelpiece, then sits
quietly down and waits.*] Ellean! Just fancy! Ellean!

[*After a pause Ellean enters by the window with Hugh.*]

Ellean. Paula, this is Captain Ardale—Mrs. Tanqueray.

[*Paula rises and turns, and she and Hugh stand staring
blankly at each other for a moment or two; then
Paula advances and gives him her hand.*]

Paula [*in a strange voice, but calmly*]. How do you do?

Hugh. How do you do?

Paula [*to Ellean*]. Mr. Ardale and I have met in London,
Ellean. Er—Captain Ardale now?

Hugh. Yes.

Ellean. In London?

Paula. They say the world's very small, don't they?

Hugh. Yes.

Paula. Ellean, dear, I want to have a little talk about you
to Mr. Ardale—Captain Ardale—alone. [*Putting her
arms round Ellean, and leading her to the door.*] Come
back in a little while. [*Ellean nods to Paula with a
smile and goes out, while Paula stands watching her
at the open door.*] In a little while—in a little—
[*Closing the door and then taking a seat facing Hugh.*]
Be quick! Mr. Tanqueray has only gone down to The
Warren with Mrs. Cortelyon. What is to be done?

Hugh [*blankly*]. Done?

Paula. Done—done. Something must be done.

Hugh. I understood that Mr. Tanqueray had married a Mrs.—Mrs.—

Paula. Jarman?

Hugh. Yes.

Paula. I'd been going by that name. You didn't follow my doings after we separated.

Hugh. No.

Paula [*sneeringly*]. No.

Hugh. I went out to India.

Paula. What's to be done?

Hugh. Damn this chance!

Paula. Oh, my God!

Hugh. Your husband doesn't know, does he?

Paula. That you and I—?

Hugh. Yes.

Paula. No. He knows about others.

Hugh. Not about me. How long were we—?

Paula. I don't remember, exactly.

Hugh. Do you—do you think it matters?

Paula. His—his daughter. [*With a muttered exclamation he turns away, and sits with his head in his hands.*] What's to be done?

Hugh. I wish I could think.

Paula. Oh! Oh! What happened to that flat of ours in Ethelbert Street?

Hugh. I let it.

Paula. All that pretty furniture?

Hugh. Sold it.

Paula. I came across the key of the escritoire the other day in an old purse! [*Suddenly realising the horror and hopelessness of her position, and starting to her feet with an hysterical cry of rage.*] What am I maundering about?

Hugh. For God's sake, be quiet! Do let me think.

Paula. This will send me mad! [*Suddenly turning and standing over him.*] You—you beast, to crop up in my life again like this!

Hugh. I always treated you fairly.

Paula [*weakly*]. Oh! I beg your pardon—I know you did —I—[*She sinks on to the settee crying hysterically.*]

Hugh. Hush!

Paula. She kissed me to-night! I'd won her over! I've had

such a fight to make her love me! And now—just
as she's beginning to love me, to bring this on her!

Hugh. Hush, hush! Don't break down!

Paula [*sobbing*]. You don't know! I—I haven't been getting
on well in my marriage. It's been my fault. The life
I used to lead spoilt me completely. But I'd made up
my mind to turn over a new leaf from to-night. From
to-night!

Hugh. Paula—

Paula. Don't you call me that!

Hugh. Mrs. Tanqueray, there is no cause for you to
despair in this way. It's all right, I tell you—it *shall* be
all right.

Paula [*shivering*]. What are we to do?

Hugh. Hold our tongues.

Paula. Eh? [*Staring vacantly.*]

Hugh. The chances are a hundred to one against any one
ever turning up who knew us when we were together.
Besides, no one would be such a brute as to split on
us. If anybody did do such a thing we should have to
lie! What are we upsetting ourselves like this for,
when we've simply got to hold our tongues?

Paula. You're as mad as I am!

Hugh. Can you think of a better plan?

Paula. There's only one plan possible—let's come to our
senses!—Mr. Tanqueray must be told.

Hugh. Your husband! What, and I lose Ellean! I lose
Ellean!

Paula. You've got to lose her.

Hugh. I won't lose her; I can't lose her!

Paula. Didn't I read of your doing any number of brave
things in India? Why, you seem to be an awful
coward!

Hugh. That's another sort of pluck altogether; I haven't
this sort of pluck.

Paula. Oh, I don't ask *you* to tell Mr. Tanqueray. That's my
job.

Hugh [*standing over her*]. You—you—you'd better! You—

Paula [*rising*]. Don't bully me! I intend to.

Hugh [*taking hold of her; she wrenches herself free*].
Look here, Paula, I never treated you badly—you've
owned it. Why should you want to pay me out like
this? You don't know how I love Ellean!

Paula. Yes, that's just what I *do* know.

Hugh. I say you don't! She's as good as my own mother.
    I've been downright honest with her, too. I told her,
    in Paris, that I'd been a bit wild at one time, and, after
    a damned wretched day, she promised to forgive me
    because of what I'd done since in India. She's behaved
    like an angel to me! Surely I oughtn't to lose her,
    after all, just because I've been like other fellows!
    No; I haven't been half as rackety as a hundred men
    we could think of. Paula, don't pay me out for
    nothing; be fair to me, there's a good girl—be fair to
    me!

Paula. Oh, I'm not considering you at all! I advise you
    not to stay here any longer: Mr. Tanqueray is sure
    to be back soon.

Hugh [*taking up his hat*]. What's the understanding be-
    tween us, then? What have we arranged to do?

Paula. I don't know what you're going to do; I've got to
    tell Mr. Tanqueray.

Hugh. By God, you shall do nothing of the sort! [*Approach-
    ing her fiercely.*]

Paula. You shocking coward!

Hugh. If you dare! [*Going up to the window.*] Mind! If you
    dare!

Paula [*following him*]. Why, what would you do?

Hugh [*after a short pause, sullenly*]. Nothing. I'd shoot my-
    self—that's nothing. Good-night.

Paula. Good-night.

[*He disappears. She walks unsteadily to the ottoman, and
    sits; and as she does so her hand falls upon the little
    silver mirror, which she takes up, staring at her own
    reflection.*]

act 4

The Drawing-room at "Highercoombe," the same evening. Paula is still seated on the ottoman, looking vacantly before her, with the little mirror in her hand. Lady Orreyed enters.

Lady Orreyed. There you are! You never came into the billiard-room. Isn't it maddening—Cayley Drummle gives me sixty out of a hundred, and beats me. I must be out of form, because I know I play remarkably well for a lady. Only last month—[*Paula rises.*] Whatever is the matter with you, old girl?

Paula. Why?

Lady Orreyed [*staring*]. It's the light, I suppose. [*Paula replaces the mirror on the table.*] By Aubrey's bolting from the billiard-table in that fashion I thought perhaps—

Paula. Yes; it's all right.

Lady Orreyed. You've patched it up? [*Paula nods.*] Oh, I am jolly glad—! I mean—

Paula. Yes, I know what you mean. Thanks, Mabel.

Lady Orreyed [*kissing Paula*]. Now take my advice; for the future—

Paula. Mabel, if I've been disagreeable to you while you've been staying here, I—I beg your pardon. [*Walking away and sitting down.*]

Lady Orreyed. You disagreeable, my dear? I haven't noticed it. Dodo and me both consider you make a first-class hostess; but then you've had such practice, haven't you? [*Dropping on to the ottoman and gaping.*] Oh, talk about being sleepy—!

Paula. Why don't you—!

Lady Orreyed. Why, dear, I must hang about for Dodo. You may as well know it; he's in one of his moods.

Paula [*under her breath*]. Oh—!

Lady Orreyed. Now, it's not his fault; it was deadly dull
for him while we were playing billiards. Cayley Drummle did ask him to mark, but I stopped that; it's so
easy to make a gentleman look like a billiard-marker.
This is just how it always is; if poor old Dodo has
nothing to do, he loses count, as you may say.

Paula. Hark!

[*Sir George Orreyed enters, walking slowly and deliberately;
he looks pale and watery-eyed.*]

Sir George [*with mournful indistinctness*]. I'm 'fraid we've
lef' you a grea' deal to yourself to-night, Mrs. Tanqueray. Attra'tions of billiards. I apol'gise. I say,
where's ol' Aubrey?

Paula. My husband has been obliged to go out to a
neighbour's house.

Sir George. I want his advice on a rather pressing matter
connected with my family—my family. [*Sitting.*] To-
morrow will do just as well.

Lady Orreyed [*to Paula*]. This is the mood I hate so—
drivelling about his precious family.

Sir George. The fact is, Mrs. Tanqueray, I am not easy in
my min' 'bout the way I am treatin' my poor ol'
mother.

Lady Orreyed [*to Paula*]. Do you hear that? That's *his*
mother, but *my* mother he won't so much as look at!

Sir George. I shall write to Bruton Street firs' thing in the
morning.

Lady Orreyed [*to Paula*]. Mamma has stuck to me through
everything—well, you know!

Sir George. I'll get ol' Aubrey to figure out a letter. I'll drop
line to Uncle Fitz too—dooced shame of the ol'
feller to chuck me over in this manner. [*Wiping his
eyes.*] All my family have chucked me over.

Lady Orreyed [*rising*]. Dodo!

Sir George. Jus' because I've married beneath me, to be
chucked over! Aunt Lydia, the General, Hooky
Whitgrave, Lady Sugnall—my own dear sister!—all
turn their backs on me. It's more than I can stan'!

Lady Orreyed [*approaching him with dignity*]. Sir George,
wish Mrs. Tanqueray good-night at once, and come
upstairs. Do you hear me?

Sir George [*rising angrily*]. Wha—!

Lady Orreyed. Be quiet!

Sir George. You presoom to order me about!

Lady Orreyed. You're making an exhibition of yourself!

Sir George. Look 'ere—!

Lady Orreyed. Come along, I tell you!

[*He hesitates, utters a few inarticulate sounds, then snatches up a fragile ornament from the table, and is about to dash it on the ground. Lady Orreyed retreats, and Paula goes to him.*]

Paula. George!

[*He replaces the ornament.*]

Sir George [*shaking Paula's hand*]. Good ni', Mrs. Tanqueray.

Lady Orreyed [*to Paula*]. Good-night, darling. Wish Aubrey good-night for me. Now Dodo? [*She goes out.*]

Sir George [*to Paula*]. I say, are you goin' to sit up for ol' Aubrey?

Paula. Yes.

Sir George. Shall I keep you comp'ny?

Paula. No, thank you, George.

Sir George. Sure?

Paula. Yes, sure.

Sir George [*shaking hands*]. Good-night again.

Paula. Good-night. [*She turns away. He goes out, steadying himself carefully. Drummle appears outside the window, smoking.*]

Drummle [*looking into the room and seeing Paula*]. My last cigar. Where's Aubrey?

Paula. Gone down to The Warren, to see Mrs. Cortelyon home.

Drummle [*entering the room*]. Eh? Did you say Mrs. Cortelyon?

Paula. Yes. She has brought Ellean back.

Drummle. Bless my soul! Why?

Paula. I—I'm too tired to tell you, Cayley. If you stroll along the lane you'll meet Aubrey. Get the news from him.

Drummle [*going up to the window*]. Yes, yes. [*Returning to Paula.*] I don't want to bother you, only—the anxious old woman, you know. Are you and Aubrey—?

Paula. Good friends again?

Drummle [*nodding*]. Um.

Paula [*giving him her hand*]. Quite, Cayley, quite.

Drummle [*retaining her hand*]. That's capital. As I'm off so
early to-morrow morning, let me say now—thank you
for your hospitality. [*He bends over her hand gallant-
ly, then goes out by the window.*]

Paula [*to herself*]. "Are you and Aubrey—?" "Good
friends again?" "Yes." "Quite, Cayley, quite."

[*There is a brief pause, then Aubrey enters hurriedly,
wearing a light overcoat and carrying a cap.*]

Aubrey. Paula dear! Have you seen Ellean?

Paula. I found her here when I came down.

Aubrey. She—she's told you?

Paula. Yes, Aubrey.

Aubrey. It's extraordinary, isn't it! Not that somebody
should fall in love with Ellean, or that Ellean herself
should fall in love. All that's natural enough and
was bound to happen, I suppose, sooner or later. But
this young fellow! You know his history?

Paula. His history?

Aubrey. You remember the papers were full of his name a
few months ago?

Paula. Oh, yes.

Aubrey. The man's as brave as a lion, there's no doubt
about that; and, at the same time, he's like a big good-
natured school-boy, Mrs. Cortelyon says. Have you
ever pictured the kind of man Ellean would marry
some day?

Paula. I can't say that I have.

Aubrey. A grave, sedate fellow I've thought about—hah!
She has fallen in love with the way in which Ardale
practically laid down his life to save those poor people
shut up in the Residency. [*Taking off his coat.*] Well,
I suppose if a man can do that sort of thing, one ought
to be content. And yet—[*Throwing his coat on the
settee.*] I should have met him to-night, but he'd gone
out. Paula dear, tell me how you look upon this
business.

Paula. Yes, I will—I must. To begin with, I—I've seen Mr.
Ardale.

Aubrey. Captain Ardale?

Paula. Captain Ardale.

Aubrey. Seen him?

Paula. While you were away he came up here, through

our grounds, to try to get a word with Ellean. I
made her fetch him in and present him to me.

Aubrey [*frowning*]. Doesn't Captain Ardale know there's
a lodge and a front door to this place? Never mind!
What is your impression of him?

Paula. Aubrey, do you recollect my bringing you a letter
—a letter giving you an account of myself—to the
Albany late one night—the night before we got
married?

Aubrey. A letter?

Paula. You burnt it; don't you know?

Aubrey. Yes; I know.

Paula. His name was in that letter.

Aubrey. [*going back from her slowly, and staring at her*].
I don't understand.

Paula. Well—Ardale and I once kept house together. [*He
remains silent, not moving.*] Why don't you strike me?
Hit me in the face—I'd rather you did! Hurt me!
hurt me!

Aubrey [*after a pause*]. What did you—and this man—
say to each other—just now?

Paula. I—hardly—know.

Aubrey. Think!

Paula. The end of it all was that I—I told him I must
inform you of—what had happened . . . he didn't
want me to do that . . . I declared that I would . . .
he dared me to. [*Breaking down.*] Let me alone!—oh!

Aubrey. Where was my daughter while this went on?

Paula. I—I had sent her out of the room . . . that is all
right.

Aubrey. Yes, yes—yes, yes. [*He turns his head towards the
door.*]

Paula. Who's that?

[*A Servant enters with a letter.*]

Servant. The coachman has just run up with this from The
Warren, sir. [*Aubrey takes the letter.*] It's for Mrs.
Tanqueray, sir; there's no answer.

[*The Servant withdraws. Aubrey goes to Paula and drops
the letter into her lap: she opens it with uncertain
hands.*]

Paula [*reading it to herself*]. It's from—him. He's going
away—or gone—I think. [*Rising in a weak way.*]

What does it say? I never could make out his writing.
[*She gives the letter to Aubrey, and stands near him,
looking at the letter over his shoulder as he reads.*]

Aubrey [*reading*]. "I shall be in Paris by to-morrow evening. Shall wait there, at Meurice's, for a week, ready
to receive any communication you or your husband
may address to me. Please invent some explanation to
Ellean. Mrs. Tanqueray, for God's sake, do what
you can for me."

[*Paula and Aubrey speak in low voices, both still looking
at the letter.*]

Paula. Has he left The Warren, I wonder, already?

Aubrey. That doesn't matter.

Paula. No; but I can picture him going quietly off. Very
likely he's walking on to Bridgefort or Cottering to-
night, to get the first train in the morning. A pleasant
stroll for him.

Aubrey. We'll reckon he's gone, that's enough.

Paula. That isn't to be answered in any way?

Aubrey. Silence will answer that.

Paula. He'll soon recover his spirits, I know.

Aubrey. You know. [*Offering her the letter.*] You don't
want this, I suppose?

Paula. No.

Aubrey. It's done with—done with. [*He tears the letter into
small pieces. She has dropped the envelope; she
searches for it, finds it, and gives it to him.*]

Paula. Here!

Aubrey [*looking at the remnants of the letter*]. This is no
good; I must burn it.

Paula. Burn it in your room.

Aubrey. Yes.

Paula. Put it in your pocket for now.

Aubrey. Yes. [*He does so. Ellean enters, and they both
turn, guiltily, and stare at her.*]

Ellean [*after a short silence, wonderingly*]. Papa—

Aubrey. What do you want, Ellean?

Ellean. I heard from Willis that you had come in; I only
want to wish you good-night. [*Paula steals away, without looking back.*] What's the matter? Ah! Of course,
Paula has told you about Captain Ardale?

Aubrey. Well?

Ellean. Have you and he met?

Aubrey. No.

Ellean. You are angry with him; so was I. But to-morrow when he calls and expresses his regret—to-morrow—

Aubrey. Ellean—Ellean!

Ellean. Yes, papa?

Aubrey. I—I can't let you see this man again. [*He walks away from her in a paroxysm of distress, then, after a moment or two, he returns to her and takes her to his arms.*] Ellean! my child!

Ellean [*releasing herself*]. What has happened, papa? What is it?

Aubrey [*thinking out his words deliberately*]. Something has occurred, something has come to my knowledge, in relation to Captain Ardale, which puts any further acquaintanceship between you two out of the question.

Ellean. Any further acquaintanceship . . . out of the question?

Aubrey. Yes. [*Advancing to her quickly, but she shrinks from him.*]

Ellean. No, no—I am quite well. [*After a short pause.*] It's not an hour ago since Mrs. Cortelyon left you and me together here; you had nothing to urge against Captain Ardale then.

Aubrey. No.

Ellean. You don't know each other; you haven't even seen him this evening. Father!

Aubrey. I have told you he and I have not met.

Ellean. Mrs. Cortelyon couldn't have spoken against him to you just now. No, no, no; she's too good a friend to both of us. Aren't you going to give me some explanation? You can't take this position towards me —towards Captain Ardale—without affording me the fullest explanation.

Aubrey. Ellean, there are circumstances connected with Captain Ardale's career which you had better remain ignorant of. It must be sufficient for you that I consider these circumstances render him unfit to be your husband.

Ellean. Father!

Aubrey. You must trust me, Ellean; you must try to understand the depth of my love for you and the— the agony it gives me to hurt you. You must trust me.

Ellean. I will, father; but you must trust me a little too. Circumstances connected with Captain Ardale's career?

Aubrey. Yes.

Ellean. When he presents himself here to-morrow of course you will see him and let him defend himself?

Aubrey. Captain Ardale will not be here to-morrow.

Ellean. Not! You have stopped his coming here?

Aubrey. Indirectly—yes.

Ellean. But just now he was talking to me at that window! Nothing had taken place then! And since then nothing can have—! Oh! Why—you have heard something against him from Paula.

Aubrey From—Paula!

Ellean. She knows him.

Aubrey. She has told you so?

Ellean. When I introduced Captain Ardale to her she said she had met him in London. Of course! It is Paula who has done this!

Aubrey [*in a hard voice*]. I—I hope you—you'll refrain from rushing at conclusions. There's nothing to be gained by trying to avoid the main point, which is that you must drive Captain Ardale out of your thoughts. Understand that! You're able to obtain comfort from your religion, aren't you? I'm glad to think that's so. I talk to you in a harsh way, Ellean, but I feel your pain almost as acutely as you do. [*Going to the door*.] I—I can't say anything more to you to-night.

Ellean. Father! [*He pauses at the door*.] Father, I'm obliged to ask you this; there's no help for it—I've no mother to go to. Does what you have heard about Captain Ardale concern the time when he led a wild, a dissolute life in London?

Aubrey [*returning to her slowly and staring at her*]. Explain yourself!

Ellean. He has been quite honest with me. One day—in Paris—he confessed to me—what a man's life is—what his life had been.

Aubrey [*under his breath*]. Oh!

Ellean. He offered to go away, not to approach me again.

Aubrey. And you—you accepted his view of what a man's life is?

Ellean. As far as *I* could forgive him, I forgave him.

Aubrey [*with a groan*]. Why, when was it you left us? It hasn't taken you long to get your robe "just a little dusty at the hem!"

Ellean. What do you mean?

Aubrey. Hah! A few weeks ago my one great desire was to keep you ignorant of evil.

Ellean. Father, it is impossible to be ignorant of evil. Instinct, common instinct, teaches us what is good and bad. Surely I am none the worse for knowing what is wicked and detesting it!

Aubrey. Detesting it! Why, you love this fellow!

Ellean. Ah, you don't understand! I have simply judged Captain Ardale as we all pray to be judged. I have lived in imagination through that one week in India when he deliberately offered his life back to God to save those wretched, desperate people. In his whole career I see now nothing but that one week; those few hours bring him nearer the saints, I believe, than fifty uneventful years of mere blamelessness would have done! And so, father, if Paula has reported anything to Captain Ardale's discredit—

Aubrey. Paula—!

Ellean. It must be Paula; it can't be anybody else.

Aubrey. You—you'll please keep Paula out of the question. Finally, Ellean, understand me—I have made up my mind. [*Again going to the door.*]

Ellean. But wait—listen! I have made up my mind also.

Aubrey. Ah! I recognise your mother in you now!

Ellean. You need not speak against my mother because you are angry with me!

Aubrey. I—I hardly know what I'm saying to you. In the morning—in the morning—[*He goes out. She remains standing, and turns her head to listen. Then, after a moment's hesitation she goes softly to the window, and looks out under the verandah.*]

Ellean [*in a whisper*]. Paula! Paula!

[*Paula appears outside the window and steps into the room; her face is white and drawn, her hair is a little disordered.*]

Paula [*huskily*]. Well?

Ellean. Have you been under the verandah all the while —listening?

Paula. N—no.

Ellean. You *have* overheard us—I see you have. And it *is* you who have been speaking to my father against Captain Ardale. Isn't it? Paula, why don't you own it or deny it?

Paula. Oh, I—I don't mind owning it; why should I?

Ellean. Ah! You seem to have been very, very eager to tell your tale.

Paula. No, I wasn't eager, Ellean. I'd have given something not to have had to do it. I wasn't eager.

Ellean. Not! Oh, I think you might safely have spared us all for a little while.

Paula. But, Ellean, you forget I—I am your stepmother. It was my—my duty—to tell your father what I —what I knew—

Ellean. What you knew! Why, after all, what can you know? You can only speak from gossip, report, hearsay! How is it possible that you—! [*She stops abruptly. The two women stand staring at each other for a moment; then Ellean backs away from Paula slowly.*]
    Paula!

Paula. What—what's the matter?

Ellean. You—you knew Captain Ardale in London!

Paula. Why—what do you mean?

Ellean. Oh! [*She makes for the door, but Paula catches her by the wrist.*]

Paula. You shall tell me what you mean!

Ellean. Ah! [*Suddenly, looking fixedly into Paula's face.*] You know what I mean.

Paula. You accuse me!

Ellean. It's in your face!

Paula [*hoarsely*]. You—you think I'm—that sort of creature, do you?

Ellean. Let me go!

Paula. Answer me! You've always hated me! [*Shaking her.*] Out with it!

Ellean. You hurt me!

Paula. You've always hated me! You shall answer me!

Ellean. Well, then, I have always—always—

Paula. What?

Ellean. I have always known what you were!

Paula. Ah! Who—who told you?

Ellean. Nobody but yourself. From the first moment I
saw you I knew you were altogether unlike the good
women I'd left; directly I saw you I knew what my
father had done. You've wondered why I've turned
from you! There—that's the reason! Oh, but this is
a horrible way for the truth to come home to every
one! Oh!

Paula. It's a lie! It's all a lie! [*Forcing Ellean down upon
her knees.*] You shall beg my pardon for it. [*Ellean
utters a loud shriek of terror.*] Ellean, I'm a good
woman! I swear I am! I've always been a good
woman! You dare to say I've ever been anything else!
It's a lie! [*Throwing her off violently.*]

[*Aubrey re-enters.*]

Aubrey. Paula! [*Paula staggers back as Aubrey advances.
Raising Ellean.*] What's this? What's this?

Ellean [*faintly*]. Nothing. It—it's my fault. Father, I—I
don't wish to see Captain Ardale again. [*She goes out,
Aubrey slowly following her to the door.*]

Paula. Aubrey, she—she guesses.

Aubrey. Guesses?

Paula. About me—and Ardale.

Aubrey. About you—and Ardale?

Paula. She says she suspected my character from the
beginning . . . that's why she's always kept me at
a distance . . . and now she sees through—[*She falters;
he helps her to the ottoman, where she sits.*]

Aubrey [*bending over her*]. Paula, you must have said
something—admitted something—

Paula. I don't think so. It—it's in my face.

Aubrey. What?

Paula. She tells me so. She's right! I'm tainted through
and through; anybody can see it, anybody can find
it out. You said much the same to me to-night.

Aubrey. If she has got this idea into her head we must
drive it out, that's all. We must take steps to— What
shall we do? We had better—better— What—what?
[*Sitting and staring before him.*]

Paula. Ellean! So meek, so demure! You've often said she
reminded you of her mother. Yes, I know now what
your first marriage was like.

Aubrey. We must drive this idea out of her head. We'll
do something. What shall we do?

Paula. She's a regular woman too. She could forgive *him*
    easily enough—but *me!* That's just a woman!
Aubrey. What *can* we do?
Paula. Why, nothing! She'd have no difficulty in following
    up her suspicions. Suspicions! You should have seen
    how she looked at me! [*He buries his head in his
    hands. There is silence for a time, then she rises
    slowly, and goes and sits beside him.*] Aubrey.
Aubrey. Yes.
Paula. I'm very sorry.
[*Without meeting her eyes, he lays his hand on her arm for
a moment.*]
Aubrey. Well, we must look things straight in the face.
    [*Glancing around.*] At any rate, we've done with this.
Paula. I suppose so. [*After a brief pause.*] Of course, she
    and I can't live under the same roof any more. You
    know she kissed me to-night, of her own accord.
Aubrey. I asked her to alter towards you.
Paula. That was it, then.
Aubrey. I—I'm sorry I sent her away.
Paula. It was my fault; I made it necessary.
Aubrey. Perhaps now she'll propose to return to the con-
    vent,—well, she must.
Paula. Would you like to keep her with you and—and
    leave me?
Aubrey. Paula—!
Paula. You needn't be afraid I'd go back to—what I was.
    I couldn't.
Aubrey. S—sh, for God's sake! We—you and I—we'll get
    out of this place . . . what a fool I was to come here
    again!
Paula. You lived here with your first wife!
Aubrey. We'll get out of this place and go abroad again,
    and begin afresh.
Paula. Begin afresh?
Aubrey. There's no reason why the future shouldn't be
    happy for us—no reason that I can see—
Paula. Aubrey!
Aubrey. Yes?
Paula. You'll never forget this, you know.
Aubrey. This?
Paula. To-night, and everything that's led up to it. Our

coming here, Ellean, our quarrels—cat and dog!—
Mrs. Cortelyon, the Orreyeds, this man! What an
everlasting nightmare for you!

Aubrey. Oh, we can forget it, if we choose.

Paula. That was always your cry. How *can* one do it!

Aubrey. We'll make our calculations solely for the future,
talk about the future, think about the future.

Paula. I believe the future is only the past again, entered
through another gate.

Aubrey. That's an awful belief.

Paula. To-night proves it. You must see now that, do
what we will, go where we will, you'll be continually
reminded of—what I was. I see it.

Aubrey. You're frightened to-night; meeting this man has
frightened you. But that sort of thing isn't likely to
recur. The world isn't quite so small as all that.

Paula. Isn't it! The only great distances it contains are
those we carry within ourselves—the distances that
separate husbands and wives, for instance. And so
it'll be with us. You'll do your best—oh, I know
that—you're a good fellow. But circumstances will
be too strong for you in the end, mark my words.

Aubrey. Paula—!

Paula. Of course I'm pretty now—I'm pretty still—and a
pretty woman, whatever else she may be, is always
—well, endurable. But even now I notice that the lines
of my face are getting deeper; so are the hollows
about my eyes. Yes, my face is covered with little
shadows that usen't to be there. Oh, I know I'm
"going off." I hate paint and dye and those messes,
but, by-and-bye, I shall drift the way of the others; I
sha'n't be able to help myself. And then, some day—
perhaps very suddenly, under a queer, fantastic light
at night or in the glare of the morning—that horrid,
irresistible truth that physical repulsion forces on men
and women will come to you, and you'll sicken at me.

Aubrey. I—!

Paula. You'll see me then, at last, with other people's
eyes; you'll see me just as your daughter does now,
as all wholesome folks see women like me. And I
shall have no weapon to fight with—not one ser-
viceable little bit of prettiness left me to defend

myself with! A worn-out creature—broken up, very likely, some time before I ought to be—my hair bright, my eyes dull, my body too thin or too stout, my cheeks raddled and ruddled—a ghost, a wreck, a caricature, a candle that gutters, call such an end what you like! Oh, Aubrey, what shall I be able to say to you then? And this is the future you talk about! I know it—I know it! [*He is still sitting staring forward; she rocks herself to and fro as if in pain.*] Oh, Aubrey! Oh! Oh!

Aubrey. Paula—! [*Trying to comfort her.*]

Paula. Oh, and I wanted so much to sleep to-night! [*Laying her head upon his shoulder. From the distance, in the garden, there comes the sound of Drummle's voice; he is singing as he approaches the house.*] That's Cayley, coming back from The Warren. [*Starting up.*] He doesn't know, evidently. I—I won't see him! [*She goes out quickly. Drummle's voice comes nearer. Aubrey rouses himself and snatches up a book from the table, making a pretence of reading. After a moment or two, Drummle appears at the window and looks in.*]

Drummle. Aha! my dear chap!

Aubrey. Cayley?

Drummle [*coming into the room*]. I went down to The Warren after you?

Aubrey. Yes?

Drummle. Missed you. Well—I've been gossiping with Mrs. Cortelyon. Confound you, I've heard the news!

Aubrey. What have you heard?

Drummle. What have I heard! Why—Ellean and young Ardale! [*Looking at Aubrey keenly.*] My dear Aubrey! Alice is under the impression that you are inclined to look on the affair favourably.

Aubrey [*rising and advancing to Drummle*]. You've not —met—Captain Ardale?

Drummle. No. Why do you ask? By-the-bye, I don't know that I need tell you—but it's rather strange. He's not at The Warren to-night.

Aubrey. No?

Drummle. He left the house half an hour ago, to stroll about the lanes; just now a note came from him, a scribble in pencil, simply telling Alice that she would receive a letter from him to-morrow. What's the matter? There's nothing very wrong, is there? My dear chap, pray forgive me if I'm asking too much.

Aubrey. Cayley, you—you urged me to send her away!

Drummle. Ellean! Yes, yes. But—but—by all accounts this is quite an eligible young fellow. Alice has been giving me the history—

Aubrey. Curse him! [*Hurling his book to the floor.*] Curse him! Yes, I do curse him—him and his class! Perhaps I curse myself too in doing it. He has only led "a man's life"—just as I, how many of us, have done! The misery he has brought on me and mine it's likely enough we, in our time, have helped to bring on other's by this leading "a man's life!" But I do curse him for all that. My God, *I've* nothing more to fear— I've paid *my* fine! And so I can curse him in safety. Curse him! Curse him!

Drummle. In Heaven's name, tell me what's happened?

Aubrey [*gripping Drummle's arm*]. Paula! Paula!

Drummle. What?

Aubrey. They met to-night here. They—they—they're not strangers to each other.

Drummle. Aubrey.

Aubrey. Curse him! My poor, wretched wife! My poor, wretched wife!

[*The door opens and Ellean appears. The two men turn to her. There is a moment's silence.*]

Ellean. Father . . . father . . . !

Aubrey. Ellean?

Ellean. I—I want you. [*He goes to her.*] Father . . . go to Paula! [*He looks into her face, startled.*] Quickly— quickly! [*He passes her to go out; she seizes his arm, with a cry.*] No, no; don't go!

[*He shakes her off and goes. Ellean staggers back towards Drummle.*]

Drummle [*to Ellean*]. What do you mean? What do you mean?

Ellean. I—I went to her room—to tell her I was sorry for something I had said to her. And I *was* sorry —I *was* sorry. I heard the fall. I—I've seen her. It's horrible.

Drummle. She—she has—!

Ellean. Killed—herself? Yes—yes. So everybody will say. But I know—I helped to kill her. If I'd only been merciful! [*She faints upon the ottoman. He pauses for a moment irresolutely—then he goes to the door, opens it, and stands looking out.*]

The End.

George Bernard Shaw (1856–1950)

Arms and the Man

The Making of a Dramatist (1892–1903)

BY ERIC BENTLEY

It was clear from the start that Bernard Shaw was a man of ideas. Later it turned out that he was a fabulous entertainer. But few have granted that the two Shaws were one. The old tendency was to grant that he was a publicist, a critic, an essayist, even a philosopher, but to add: "not, of course, a dramatist." The later tendency was to concede that he was a great showman but to discount his thoughtful side. As Egon Friedell said, you could suck the theatrical sugar from the pill of propaganda, and put the pill itself back on the plate.

Neither in the old days, then, nor in the later ones was Shaw considered a dramatist, for even the later generations have only thought him a master of the theatrical occasion, a man with a theatrical line of talk and a theatrical bag of tricks, a highly histrionic jokester—a comedian, certainly, but hardly a writer of serious comedy. The fact is that the shock of that long career in the theater has still not been absorbed. Shaw has not yet been seen in perspective.

In these circumstances, it is interesting to go back and look at what happened in the eighteen nineties. In 1891, Bernard Shaw had still not written a play, though he was thirty-five years old. A dozen years later, though he could describe himself as "an unperformed playwright in London," he had written *Widowers' Houses* (1892), *The Philanderer* (1893), *Mrs. Warren's Profession* (1893–94), *Arms and the Man* (1894), *Candida* (1894–95), *The Man of Destiny* (1895), *You Never Can Tell* (1895–96), *The Devil's Disciple* (1896–97), *Caesar and Cleopatra* (1898), *Captain Brassbound's Conversion* (1899), *The Admirable Bashville* (1901), and *Man and Superman* (1901–03).

Let us take for granted that these plays are full of ideas and jokes, and ask if they do not also meet the demands of dramatic criticism as such. The drama, everyone agrees, presents character in action. Human actions become "an action" in the drama when they are arranged effectively—when, that is, they are given what we can recognize as a proper and praiseworthy structure. Of character dramatic critics have required many different things. One of them is emotional substance.

Let us ask, then, how Shaw, when he set about playwriting, tackled the problem of structure; and let us ask if he gave his characters' existence the requisite emotional substance.

STRUCTURE

How did Shaw put a play together? To think of questions about Shaw is to think also of the answers he invariably provided to them. In this case, he said: "I avoid plots like the plague. . . . My procedure is to imagine characters and let them rip. . . ." The quotation is from his *Table-talk* but (again, as usual) he said the same thing on many other occasions. One always has to ask not what he means (which may be clear) but what he is getting at. All Shaw's critical prose is polemical, as he freely admitted, and his writing on the theater is devoted to the destruction of some kinds of drama and their replacement by some others (or one other). Here the enemy is the kind of play which had been dominant throughout the latter half of the nineteenth century—"the well-made play," as perfected by Eugène Scribe. In this dramaturgy, the Aristotelian doctrine of the primacy of plot had been driven to an improper extreme. The plot was now not *primus inter pares,* but all that mattered. It lost its originally organic relation to character and theme. So it became anathema to the apostles of the New Drama at the century's close. As late as 1946, when Allardyce Nicoll declared that Shaw was himself influenced by the well-made play, the old playwright went into print to deny it.

If the well-made play is defined as having no serious content, if it is defined by the relation (or lack of relation) of its plot to character and theme, then obviously Shaw did not write well-made plays. Yet, Professor Nicoll had a point, and a strong one, which was that, for all the disclaimers, Shaw's plays did have plots and, furthermore, that these plots tended to be old acquaintances for those who knew their well-made play. Actually, the playright had no need to be scandalized, for no dramatist had been more influenced by the well-made play than his own idol of those days, Henrik Ibsen. The Norwegian had begun his theatrical career by directing a large number of these plays; he made an exact imitation of them in his own *Lady Inger of Östrât;* and he had continued to the end to use many of their characteristic devices. Hence, it would have been quite possible for a writer in 1890 to denounce Scribe and Sardou and simultaneously to steal their bag of tricks—from Ibsen. It is doubtful, though, if Bernard Shaw needed to deceive himself in this way. It seems more likely that he took the main situation in *Arms and the Man* from one of Scribe's most successful plays, *Bataille de Dames.*

A situation is not, of course, a plot, and the plot of *Arms and the Man* is not simply lifted from Scribe, even though parts of it may have been. Plagiarism is not the point. The point is that even when Shaw's story diverges from Scribe, it remains Scribean. The play *Arms and the Man* is hung, as it were, on the cunningly told tale of the lost coat with the photograph in its pocket. The reader need only go through the text and mark the hints, incidents, accidents, and contretemps of this tale and he will be finding the layout, the plan—yes, the plot—of this play. Or at any rate, the plot of what could have been a first draft of the play. Shaw, one gathers, did not write such first drafts but, supposing he had, what would be the difference between the first draft and the final one? In the answer to this question lies the secret of Shavian dramaturgy.

A corollary of the view that "plot is all" is this proposition: the cause of any incident is another incident. It is known that Scribe used to chart out a configuration of incidents and then write his play. This is to go far beyond Aristotle. It is to set no store at all by human initiative and assign to events themselves a kind of fatality: they are a network in which mankind is caught. Granted that the conception might in certain hands have its awesomeness; in Scribe's hands it had only triviality, because he manipulated the events till the issue was a pleasant one. It is curious how often that manipulation had to be arbitrary and drastic. Do events, when given their head, rush downward to disaster? To guarantee a happy ending, the well-making playwrights often needed their emergency weapon: sheer accident.

Hence the Shavian complaint that well-made plays were badly made, after all.

Hence also Bernard Shaw's first drama, which is an adaptation of an adaptation of a well-made play. The subject is one that Scribe and the younger Dumas brought to the nineteenth-century theater: marrying, or refusing to marry, money. The immediate source is an unfinished play of William Archer's, *Rhinegold*. Archer's source is *La Ceinture Dorée*, by Emile Augier. When a young man discovers that his young lady's inherited money was acquired by her father in an immoral way, what does he do? William Archer's answer was: he pitches it into the Rhine. One presumes that Archer's action would have been set on a convenient balcony beside that river. Augier's hero is not so privileged. To preserve his honor, he would simply have to forgo the pleasure of marrying the lady, if the author did not provide him and the play with a convenient accident (or money *ex machina*). The whole French economy has to meet with a crisis (war breaks out) so that our heroine's father may be reduced to poverty; it is now honorable for our hero to propose to our heroine. In the well-made play, one incident leads to another with a logic that is inescapable—except when the author decides to escape it. Perhaps Shaw's objection was less to the inescapability than to the egregious, last-minute escapes.

His first play, *Widowers' Houses*, may not be great art but it is a great reversal of custom. Shaw's key decision was to refuse to accept Augier's ending, to refuse to have accident (masquerading as fate or otherwise) intervene. Such a refusal leads a man—leads a born playwright, at least— back and back into the earlier stages of a story and he ends up writing an utterly different play—an utterly different *kind* of play.

Not one but two conceptions of Augier's were being rejected: not just the solution-by-sheer-accident (which condemns a play to meaninglessness) but also the autonomy-of-incidents—something, by the way, which was no part of Augier's conscious philosophy but was imposed on him by the Scribean design. Dramatists are committed to the doctrine of free will. They can say they don't believe in it, but they have to write their plays as if they did. (In this they resemble human beings in general, for your most ardent determinist acts on the assumption that determinism is false.) People in plays have got to be able to make decisions, and these decisions have got to be both real and influential: they have to affect events. I see no reason to object to Aristotle's declaration that plot is the soul of the drama, but Aristotle would have objected to Scribe's attempt to cut the soul off from the body—that is, from character.

What *does* a young man do when he finds that his bride's dowry comes from a tainted source? There are two ways for a writer to arrive at an answer. He can say: "I can think of several answers—on the basis of several different possibilities of 'theater.' Answer A will give you Big Scene X; Answer B will give you Ending Y; and so on." Or he can say: "I cannot give you any answer at all until the terms of the proposition are defined, including the term 'tainted.' Above all, I need to know who these people are: what bride? what young man?" The first way to arrive at an answer would commonly be thought the playwright's way: the reasoning is "craftsmanlike" and "of the theater," and would earn a man commendation on Broadway in 1960. The second way is only the human way. That makes it the way of the real dramatist and so of Bernard Shaw.

It could be said that we have this perfectly functioning machine of the well-made play and that a Bernard Shaw is throwing a monkey wrench into it—the monkey wrench of character. That is how it must seem from the Scribean viewpoint. From the viewpoint of dramatic art, however, one would say that this particular engine had been revolving all too fast and uselessly; only when a Shaw slips in the clutch can the gear engage and the vehicle prove itself a vehicle by moving.

"My procedure is to imagine characters and let them rip. . . ." The pertinence of this remark may by now be clearer: if the young man has been "imagined," the dramatist can find the decision he would make as to the young lady's money. But at this point, we realize that Shaw's words leave out of account the fact that the situation confronting the young man had been established in advance of the imagining of his character. It had been established by Augier and Archer and by Shaw's own decision to use their work. Hence, Shaw's own interpretation is both helpful and misleading—or, perhaps, is helpful only if those who are helped do a lot of work on their own.

Shaw put *Widowers' Houses* together—how? He took
from certain predecessors not only a situation but a story,
and not only a story but that clever, orderly, and theatrical
arrangement of a story which we call a plot. Then he
changed the plot—or as he would have said, let the characters change it for him. Now, had he retained Augier's
characters, they could only have caused him to break off
the action one scene earlier than Augier did: instead of the
happy ending created by a national emergency, we would
get the unhappy ending which the emergency reversed.

Characters in a well-made play are "conventional"—that
is, they behave, not according to laws of psychology but according to the expectations of an audience in a theater. A
type of drama in which the plot is given a free hand cannot
afford any less passive or more obtrusive *personae*. Con-
versely, if a playright abandons the plot-determined play,
he will have to be more inventive as to character. To assume the initiative, his characters will have to be capable of
it. So Shaw's first contribution to the drama was: more
active characters. They were more active, first of all, in the
most obvious fashion: they were violent. More important,
they made decisions which affected the course of events,
and they made them on the basis of their own nature, not of
the spectator's. And so these characters were surprising.
For a number of years, they were too surprising to be ac-
ceptable. Like all surprising art, Shaw's dramaturgy was
damned as non-art. The critics' formula was: Not a Play.

Augier's hero could not consider being the husband of a
woman with a tainted dowry. Shaw creates a hero who has
the effrontery to ask the heroine to throw up her dowry for
his sake. But the Shavian joke—the Shavian reversal—is already what it would characteristically be in the future: a
double one. To this demanding hero he adds an even more
demanding heroine: she simply refuses to be poor to preserve her innocence. That is the nub of the first Shaw
comedy. Then Shaw works his way out of the apparent
deadlock, not by having the heroine weaken (that is, "improve"), but by having the hero renew his strength (that is,
"deteriorate"). This the latter does by way of recovering
from a shock. The shock comes from without and might be
called an accident (like Augier's outbreak of war), except
that it belongs to the logic of the situation. It turns out
that the source of the hero's own unearned income is the

same as that of his girl's father. End of Act Two. In the third and last act, our hero comes around and gets the girl by accepting the nature of capitalism. Socialist propaganda? Precisely. Shaw boasted of it. But he boasted with equal reason that he was writing comedy in the most traditional sense.

"Take what would be done by Scribe, Sardou, Dumas *fils,* or Augier and do the opposite." Is that the Shavian formula? It is certain that Shavian comedy is parodistic in a way, or to an extent, that Plautus, Jonson, and Molière were not. These others, one would judge, took a convention they respected and brought it to the realization of its best possibilities. Shaw took conventions in which he saw no possibilities—except insofar as he would expose their bankruptcy. The injunction "Do the opposite" was not whimsical. Shaw decided to "do the opposite" of Scribe in much the way Marx decided to do the opposite of Hegel—not to stand everything on its head (Hegel, he held, had done this) but to set everything back on its feet again. That was revolutionary thinking, and Shaw's art, for all the polite and charming trappings, was revolutionary art. The usual relations were reversed.

Such reversals as we see in the ending of *Widowers' Houses* are relatively simple. Shaw's weakest plays are those in which he has done little more than turn the ending around: the price you pay for the brilliant ending of *The Devil's Disciple* is that of a rather dull, and decidedly conventional, first act. His best plays are those in which the principle of reversal has pervaded the whole. Such a play is *Arms and the Man.*

The idea of taking two couples and causing them to exchange partners is hardly novel and, as I have said, the little tale of the coat and the portrait is Scribean in pattern. But Shaw can justifiably plead that this is no well-made play because the artifices of the plot are not what ultimately achieve the result. Here is one of the decisive turns in the action:

> *Bluntschli.* When you get into that noble attitude and
>   speak in that thrilling voice, I admire you; but I
>   find it impossible to believe a single word you say.
> *Raina.* Captain Bluntschli!
> *Bluntschli.* Yes?

> *Raina.* Do you mean what you said just now? Do you
>   *know* what you said just now?
> *Bluntschli.* I do.
> *Raina.* I! I!!! How did you find me out?

With this last query, Raina passes over forever from
Sergius's world to Bluntschli's: as a result of nothing in
the Scribean arrangement of incidents, but of words, words,
words. It is here that, to many, the Shavian drama seems
vulnerable. In drama, actions are supposed to speak louder
than words. Writers on the subject invariably know their
etymology—"drama" derives from a Greek verb meaning
"to do"—and use it as a cudgel. Their error is a vulgar
one: action need not be external. It can often be carried by
words alone. Shaw used to remark that his plays were all
words just as Raphael's paintings were all paint.

There is a degree of legerdemain in that remark, for
Scribe, too, put down his plays in words. What was con-
fusing to Shaw's readers and spectators half a century ago
was that after indicating unmistakably that he was playing
Scribe's game, Shaw proceeded to break the rules. The fact
that Bluntschli conquers by words gains its peculiar force
from a context in which the opposite was to be expected. To
look over *Arms and the Man* with an eye to technique
would be to conclude that what we have here is Scribe
most subtly interwoven with Shaw. Yet this formulation is
inadequate, for who did the interweaving? There was a
Scribe in Shaw, and there was a counter-Scribe in Shaw;
what makes his works dramatic is the interaction of the
two.

The passion and preoccupation of Scribe was the idea of
climax: to the Big Scene at the end—or, rather, a little before the end—all his arts are dedicated. In Bernard Shaw
there was almost as great a predilection for anticlimax. It
is the Shavian "effect" par excellence; no other playwright
has come near finding so many possibilities in it. The bit I
have quoted from Bluntschli and Raina is an apt example.
Arms and the Man contains a corresponding scene between
Sergius and Louka. Where, in a well-made play, Bluntschli
and Louka would have to soar to the heights of Raina and
Sergius, in the Shaw play Raina and Sergius drop with a
bump to the level of Bluntschli and Louka. Such is resolution by anticlimax. It is dramaturgically effective, and it en-

forces the author's theme. But this is not all of Shaw: it is only the counter-Scribe.

The dual anticlimaxes do not round off *Arms and the Man*. What does? Not the disenchantment of Raina and Sergius but the discovery that Bluntschli the realist is actually an enchanted soul whom nothing will disenchant. He has destroyed their romanticism but is himself "incurably romantic." This is another point that is made in "mere words"—"mere words stuck on at the end," if you wish—and yet stuck on very well, for they are firmly attached to that little tale of the coat and the photograph which gives the work its continuity and shape:

> *Bluntschli.* Yes: that's the coat I mean. . . . Do you suppose I am the sort of fellow a young girl falls in love with? Why, look at our ages! I'm thirty-four: I don't suppose the young lady is much over seventeen. All that adventure which was life or death to me was only a schoolgirl's game to her . . . would a woman who took the affair seriously have sent me this and written on it: "Raina, to her chocolate cream soldier—a souvenir"?
>
> *Petkoff.* That's what I was looking for. How the deuce did it get there?
>
> Bluntschli. I have put everything right, I hope, gracious young lady.
>
> *Raina.* I quite agree with your account of yourself. You are a romantic idiot. Next time I hope you will know the difference between a schoolgirl of seventeen and a woman of twenty-three.

In this scene, plot and theme reach completion together, and the play of thesis and antithesis ends in synthesis.

The supreme triumph of Shaw's dramaturgical dialectics is to be found in *Man and Superman*, and, for all the blarney in the preface about the medieval *Everyman* and the eighteenth-century *Don Giovanni*, the method is the conversion of old materials into nineteenth-century terms, both thematic and technical. Shaw's claim to be returning to a pristine Don Juan is valid to the extent that the theme had originally been less of psychological than of philosophical, indeed theological, interest. It is also true that Don Juan had run away from his women. However, he had

run away from them only after possessing them. In Shaw's
play, he runs away to prevent *them* from possessing *him*. It
is a comic parody of the old motif, embodying Shaw's
standard new motif: the courting of the man by the woman.
And where the old dramatists and librettists had used the
old, "open" type of plot (or nonplot), Shaw substitutes an
utterly Scribean "closed" structure.

This very "modern" and "twentieth-century" play is
made up of narrative materials familiar to every Victorian
theatergoer. We have a hero who spends the entire evening
hotly pursued by his foes; a clandestine marriage celebrated
in defiance of a hostile father; a lovelorn hero who sacri-
fices himself so that the girl will go to his rival; a villain
whose function is to constitute for a while the barrier to
denouement and happy ending. The subplot about the
Malone family rests upon two separate uses of the "secret
skillfully withheld," then skillfully released. Traditional
farcical coincidence binds together Straker and Mendoza.
The play bears every sign of careful workmanship—all of
it School of Scribe.

But as with *Arms and the Man,* as soon as we examine
particulars, we find, interwoven with the Scribean elements,
those typically Shavian verbal exchanges which constitute
further action. Violet's marriage could have been made a
secret of in any Scribe play, and Scribe could have been
relied on to choose an effective moment for the release of
the secret. In Shaw, what creates both the fun and the point
of the news release is not the organization of the incidents
but their relation to theme:

> *Tanner.* I know, and the whole world really knows,
>   though it dare not say so, that you were right to
>   follow your instinct; that vitality and bravery are
>   the greatest qualities a woman can have, and
>   motherhood her solemn initiation into woman-
>   hood; and that the fact of your not being legally
>   married matters not one scrap either to your own
>   worth or to our real regard for you.
>
> *Violet.* Oh! You think me a wicked woman, like the
>   rest. . . . I won't bear such a horrible insult as to
>   be complimented by Jack on being one of the
>   wretches of whom he approves. I have kept my
>   marriage a secret for my husband's sake.

An incident which Tanner wishes to use to illustrate his "modern" philosophy thus comes to illustrate a contrasting thesis: that Violet lives by a nonmodern philosophy.

Simple? Yes, but closely linked to a point that is unsimple enough to have generally been missed: Tanner is a windbag. Indeed, the mere fact of the woman courting the man would probably not yield comedy at all were it not for a further and more dynamic reversal: the woman, who makes no great claims for herself, has all the shrewdness, the real *Lebensweisheit*, while the man, who knows everything and can discourse like Bernard Shaw, is—a fool. Tanner is, in fact, like Molière's Alceste, the traditional fool of comedy in highly sophisticated intellectual disguise. Ann Whitefield, into whose trap Tanner falls, is the knave —in skirts.

While Don Juan Tenorio is Superman—or is on the road to him—John Tanner, M.I.R.C., is merely Man, and as such belongs to The World As It Is. Of dramaturgical interest is that the kind of plot Shaw evidently considers capable of giving an image of The World as It Is should be the kind that is generally considered (by himself, for instance) artificial, unreal, arbitrary, inane. Shaw the critic championed the new Naturalism, and among French dramatists especially favored Brieux, who produced dully literal theatrical documentaries. Yet, when Shaw wrote an essay entitled "A Dramatic Realist to His Critics," the example of "realism" he gave from his own work was *Arms and the Man*—on the grounds that the characters respond naturally even if the situations aren't natural. We are entitled, then, to insist on his choice of "unnatural" situations. He must intuitively have understood something which, as a critic, he failed to grasp: that plot does not merely reproduce external reality. The violence and intrigue in Shakespeare, which Shaw the critic declared extraneous, provides the objective correlative of Shakespeare's feelings about life, and the "idiocies" of the plot of *Man and Superman* provide an objective correlative for Shaw's sense of modern life. The very fact that Shaw despised Scribe helps to explain the particular use he made of him.

The Don Juan episode in Act Three is neither a wellmade play nor a portion of a well-made play. It stands apart as something appropriately more austere and august.

It is not a traditional work of any kind, not even a Platonic dialogue, the relation between Socrates and his interlocutors being quite different. It is not even a debate, for two of the speakers, the Commander and Ana, hardly present arguments at all: they simply represent a point of view. Do even the Devil and Don Juan *discuss* anything? A devil is scarcely a being one can convert to a Cause, and if the Don is busy convincing anyone it is himself. Certainly it is the philosophy of Bernard Shaw that he is given to speak, but is persuasion exercised—even on the audience? Rather, the contributions of the four presences come together as a vision of life—and an intimation of superlife.

Man—and Superman. The comedy of John Tanner—and the vision of Don Juan Tenorio. Shaw—and counter-Shaw. Thesis and antithesis are, to be sure, of separate interest, and yet, as usual, the great Shavian achievement is to have related one to the other. Tanner seems a wise man and proves a fool. Don Juan passes for a philanderer but proves an explorer and a missionary of the truth. In our trivial, tawdry, clever, Scribean world, intellect is futile and ever at the mercy of instinct. Take away the episode in hell, and Shaw has written an anti-intellectual comedy. The episode assigns to intellect the highest role. No longer, therefore, is Ann the center and source of things—only a possible mother for Superman. Here Don Juan dominates. Here (or rather, in heaven) intellect is at home, and the Don is cured of that occupational disease of Shavian heroes—homelessness. He "comes to a good end"—only it is not an end, it is an episode, and from these celestial-infernal heights we must descend to earth with the shock of Shavian anticlimax, to earth and to Tanner, from Superman back to Man. One section of the play gets an electric charge from the other.

Of Shaw's "playmaking" one must conclude that he knew how to put together a Scribean plot; that he knew how to subordinate such a plot to his own purposes; and that, in *Man and Superman*, he knew how to take the resultant Shavian comedy and combine it dynamically with a disquisition on (and by) Don Juan.

EMOTIONAL SUBSTANCE

If Shaw's plays are, or begin by being, a parody of the more conventional drama of his time, that parody is by no means confined to the form. We have already seen that the themes, too, tend to get turned around: these compositions not only do the opposite, as it were, but say the opposite.

What of the emotions? Whatever the ultimate purpose of drama, its immediate impact is a strongly emotional one, and one cannot conceive of a story having an emotional effect upon an audience unless it is an emotional story and has a certain emotional structure. I may be forgiven for stating so rudimentary a principle because the Shavian drama presents us with a paradox: it has flooded a thousand theaters with emotion and yet has often been held to be emotionless.

Of course, this common opinion is absurd, bolstered though it can be with remarks of Shaw's own about being a mere "work machine" and the like. What we confront here is originality. Shaw may not have been an original thinker; he tried, rather, to make a synthesis of what certain others had thought. But he was an original person. What fitted him so well for the role of the enemy of convention was that his natural responses were not those of other people but all his own. His emotional constitution was a peculiar one, and that peculiarity is reflected in his plays.

Sex is, without doubt, the crucial issue. Comedy remains fertility worship, however sublimated, and it is fair enough to ask what Bernard Shaw made of the old sexual rigmarole —courtship and the barriers thereto. It is even fair to use any facts about Shaw himself that are a matter of public record.

On the other hand, one is not honor-bound to side with "modern" opinion against "Victorian" as to what is good and bad. The very "modern" Dr. Kinsey implied that human vitality could be measured in statistics on orgasms. Our subject Bernard Shaw will not pass into any Kinseyite paradise. Though he lived to be ninety-four, he seems to have experienced sexual intercourse only between the ages of twenty-nine and forty-three. "I lived a continent virgin . . . until I was 29. . . . During the fourteen years before my marriage at 43 there was always some lady in the case. . . . As man and wife we found a new relation in which sex had no part. It ended the old gallantries, flirtations, and philanderings for both of us." This quotation is from a letter to Frank Harris, who, as a Kinseyite before

Kinsey, wrote: "Compare his [Shaw's] private life with Shakespeare's. While Mary Fitton was banished from London Shakespeare could write nothing but tragedies. That went on for five years. When the Queen died and Shakespeare's Dark Lady returned, he wrote *Antony and Cleopatra,* his greatest love story. As nothing like that happened in Shaw's life we can only get a textbooky, sexless type of play." A remarkable blend of ignorance, invention, and arbitrary assumption! For, actually, Shaw concealed from Harris most of his private life; nothing whatever is known about Shakespeare's feelings for any woman; and no critic or psychologist of repute has even argued that a man's writing has to be "textbooky" and "sexless" unless he is carrying on an adulterous romance; a more familiar argument would be that precisely the abstinent man's imagination might well be crammed with sex. But there is no settling the question a priori.

William Archer declared that Shaw's plays reeked with sex. It is a more suggestive declaration than Harris's. It reminds us that Shaw was able to re-create the sexual charm of both men and women to a degree unequaled by any English dramatist except Shakespeare. To be sure, he doesn't need bedroom scenes to do this. Morell only has to talk and we understand "Prossy's complaint." Undershaft only has to talk and we understand why he is a problem to his daughter. To say nothing of the long line of sirens from Candida to Orinthia! Few of the "sexy" ladies of Restoration comedy, by contrast, have any sex appeal at all. One thing Archer is sure to have had in mind is that the women in Shaw pursue a sexual purpose in a way absolutely unknown to Victorian literature. Of all the reversals in Shavian drama, this is inevitably the most famous: the reversal in the roles of the sexes. Shaw once committed himself to the view that all superior women are masculine and all superior men are feminine. In his comedies, most often, the woman is active, the man passive. Perhaps by 1960 the theme has been restated *ad nauseam;* to Archer it was startling—as was Shaw's determination to rub the sore places of the sexual morality of his time. *Mrs. Warren's Profession* was for many years too "raw" a play for production in London, and it created a memorable scandal when it was produced in New Haven and New York in 1905. Like most of the major modern dramatists and novelists, Shaw mentioned the unmentionable. He even claimed to have "put the physical act of sexual intercourse on the stage" (in *Overruled*). Archer evidently felt that Shaw could not give the subject of sex a rest: he may not always have been at the center of it but he was forever touching its fringes.

Here Frank Harris would have interjected: "He was always *avoiding* the center of it." And the interjection is called for. The impression that a man is unemotional in general and sexless in particular does not come from nowhere. Nor are the kinds of sex I have been noting what the average spectator is looking for if he demands a "sexy" show. *Overruled* does not really "put the physical act of sexual intercourse on the stage," and, even if it did, it would do so comically—depriving the act of precisely that element which people miss in Shaw, which is not sex in general but the torridity of sexual romance. At that, if this element were simply absent, Shaw might very well have got away with the omission. But it is explicitly rejected. It is not that a Shavian couple cannot consider intercourse but that they are likely to consider it and decide not to. If the characteristic act of the French drama of the period was the plunge into bed, that of the Shavian drama is the precipitate retreat from the bedroom door.

Harris would be right in reminding us that such was Bernard Shaw's emotional constitution. What other writer has ever created all the normal expectations in a scene between a king and his mistress (*The Apple Cart*), only to reveal later that their relationship is purely platonic? *Captain Brassbound's Conversion* shows the Shavian pattern to perfection. Is there sexual feeling in the play? There is. The process by which Brassbound and Lady Cicely are brought closer and closer is positively titillating. After which, what happens? They are parted. The play has a superb final curtain. "How glorious!" says Lady Cicely, "how glorious!" Then with one of those quick changes of tone that mark the Shavian dialogue: "And what an escape!" Is this unemotional? No. But the emotion is not erotic—rather, it is relief at a release from the erotic. Such is the emotional content of this particular Shavian anticlimax.

As far as conscious intention goes, all Shaw's plays might bear the title he gave to three of them—Plays for Puritans —for that intention is to show romance transcended by a higher-than-erotic purpose. It is a classic intention—an application, really, of the traditional conflict of love and honor, with honor winning hands down, as it did in Corneille and even in one masterpiece of Racine's, *Bérénice*. We are concerned here not with philosophic intention but psychological substance. Where the philosopher insists that Shaw does not cross the threshold of the bedroom, the psychologist asks: why does he hover at the bedroom door?

We know from the correspondence with Mrs. Pat Campbell that Shaw liked to play with fire. Even the correspondence with Ellen Terry entailed a playfulness not quite devoid of "danger." The boy Shaw had been witness to an odd household arrangement whereby his mother's music teacher contrived to be (it would seem) almost but not quite her lover. A slightly older Shaw has recently been portrayed as the intruder into a friend's marriage, like his own Eugene Marchbanks: this is speculation. Let us look at the play *Candida*, which is a fact.

It has a notable Big Scene at the end, which is characterized by an equally notable improbability. A comfortable, sensible parson's wife doesn't let herself get jockeyed into "choosing" between her husband and an almost total stranger. People—such people at least—don't do such things. A respectable woman's choice was made before the banns were read.

Perhaps Candida is not really respectable? That is the line of interpretation taken by Beatrice Webb, who declared her a prostitute. Will the play, taken as a play, bear this interpretation out? A dramatist's license to have the truth turn out different from the impression given to the audience is very limited, for it is to a large extent by giving impressions that he creates characters. Shaw has given the impression that Candida is *not* a prostitute.

Against this it can be urged that Shaw himself took Beatrice Webb's side and attacked Candida—in remarks he made about her in letters to James Huneker, Richard Burton, and others. True, but was that legitimate? He himself admitted that he had no more right to say what his plays meant than any other critic. One might add that he may have had less, for when an author intervenes to correct our impressions of his work, he is often intervening to change or misinterpret that work.

Outside the play, Shaw is against Candida. Inside it, he is

both for and against her, but he is for her effectually, and against her ineffectually, because the direct impression is favorable, while it is only by throwing logic back into the story when it is over that you can reach an unfavorable judgment. This means, I should think, that though Shaw's intellect is against Candida, his emotions are for her.

What is it that this play has always projected in the theater, and can always be counted on to project again? The charm of Candida. This is a reality so immediate and all-pervasive that it is hard for any other element in the play to make headway against it. Leading actresses know this, and hearing their director speak of Candida's essential badness, can afford to smile a Candida smile, strong in the knowledge that there is nothing a director can do about this badness, once that smile has been displayed on stage as well as off.

I would say that it is a confused play but that the confusion goes unnoticed because of Candida's charm and may even be the cause of a degree of emotional tension unusual in a Shaw play. Candida is made out of a Shavian ambivalence: he would like to reject this kind of woman, but actually he dotes on her. One quickly senses that he *is* March-banks. One also finds he protests (too much) that he is *not* Marchbanks. "I had in mind De Quincey's account of his adolescence in his Confessions," he wrote. "I certainly never thought of myself as a model." From the empty pretense of being De Quincey, no doubt, comes the prodigious unreality of many of the lines. As a character, Marchbanks must be reckoned a failure. Shaw was hiding. What better image to hide behind than that of the kind of writer he himself was not—a romantic poet? Especially if De Quincey would do the job for him?

It didn't work, of course, except as pure histrionics. (Marchbanks, though a poorly drawn character, is always an effective stage role, and still seems to correspond to the actor's idea of a poet.) But if no one in the play can reject Candida, there is a noteworthy niche in it for the man whom she will reject. This niche Marchbanks can fill nobly, and has his dramatic moment as he marches into it: his final exit is a magnificent piece of action. Possibly everything before that (in this role) is just an improvisation. Shaw could not make us believe in the poet's poetry, but he does make us believe in his pain and his nobility, for at these points he could identify himself with Eugene completely without having to "think of himself as a model."

Dramatists usually speak of their characters individually, and that could be regarded as strange, because the drama, all through the centuries, has done much less with separate persons than with relationships. The traditional characters are, if you will, simplified to the point of crudity. What is not crude, as treated by the old dramatists, is the interaction of these characters: the dynamics of human relations are fully rendered. If what you do not get is detailed psychological biography, what you do get is the essence of such relations as parent and child, boy and girl, man and wife.

Now, modern playwrights, happily, have not departed from the classic patterns as much as they are supposed to have, and what rings true, emotionally, in *Candida* corresponds to Shaw's ability to find and re-create some of these elemental relationships. An inner obstacle, one would judge, hampered him when he tried to "do" the Marchbanks-Candida relationship, but the Morell-Candida relation is both clear and challenging. It is, as Shaw himself said, the relationship of Nora and Torvald Helmer turned around: in Shaw's play the man is the doll. But where Ibsen tells the story of a doll who finally comes to life, Shaw tells the story of a seemingly living person who turns out to have been a doll all along. (In other words, the relation of Shaw to Ibsen, instead of being as direct as it might seem, is an inverse one, exactly like the relation of Shaw to other nineteenth-century drama.) Into Morell Shaw can put that part of himself (a child) which finds Candida irresistible, just as into Candida he can put that part of Woman which he finds irresistible—the mother in her. One would have to be as naïve a psychologist as Frank Harris to consider the mother-and-child relation less emotional than that of lovers.

Or less dramatic. Relationships become dramatic not in the degree of their eroticism but to the extent that they contain conflict. Pure love would not be a dramatic subject at all. Love becomes dramatic when it is impure—when the loving element is submerged in a struggle for power. The axis about which *Candida* revolves is that of strength and weakness, not love and hate. And if one knows Shaw's views on the topic of the "weaker sex" in general, the conclusion of *Candida* follows naturally: instead of the little woman reaching up toward the arms of the strong man, we have the strong woman reaching down to pick up her child. It is remarkable how far Shaw's thought is from the standard "advanced thinking" of his generation, with its prattle of equality and comradeship. He is closer to Nietzsche.

Of the ending of *A Doll's House* it has been said: perhaps Nora has walked out in a mere tantrum and will be back in the morning. How much more savage is the ending of *Candida!* Only Strindberg could have written a sequel to it. The cruelty of the heroine—merely implicit in the present play—would have to come to the surface in any continuation of the story. Candida has chosen to let her husband discover his shame: she, as well as he, will have to take the consequences. Let the stage manager hold razors and straitjackets in readiness!

One reason why Shaw got so little credit for his treatment of the emotions is that the emotions he treats are not the ones people expect. The very fact that his favorite device is anticlimax should tell us that what he most insistently feels is "letdown." It may be retorted that on the contrary, Bernard Shaw was the most buoyant and vivacious of men. That is also true. The axis "strength-weakness" is not more important to Shaw's content than the axis "elation-depression" is to his form. The dialogue ripples gaily along; then comes the sudden letdown. The circus has familiarized us with the pattern: it is the light of heart who take the pratfall. Even as the fool pops up in Shavian comedy in the highly intellectualized shape of a Jack Tanner, so the pratfall is transmuted into an anticlimax that has a positively climactic force. It has been customary to take these anticlimaxes as expressions of an idea—the idea of disenchantment. It is *the* idea of modern literature, and it is inseparable from an emotion far commoner and far more influential than romantic excitement. There seems to be no name for this emotion—and that, too, is significant. Let us call it desolation.

You cannot be disenchanted without having been enchanted. One is sometimes tempted to believe that our human desolation might have been avoided if only we had not started out so undesolate. It is not the fact that we don't have things that worries us, but that we have lost them—

or rather, been deprived of them. Desolation is the feeling of having been driven from paradise.

A friend of Bernard Shaw's said that when he saw *The Wild Duck,* the bottom dropped out of the universe. One difference between Ibsen and Shaw is that the former produced this effect on the audience, whereas the latter produced it on the characters in a play. Just as a character in a melodrama loses a fortune, so a character in a Shaw play loses a universe. The experience may be given a playful treatment, as with Raina and Sergius. In the case of Morell, the treatment is only partly playful. It gets more serious as the play *Candida* proceeds. Morell finally loses his image of his wife and of himself. The curtain has to be rung down to save us from the Strindberg play that would have to follow.

What of *Mrs. Warren's Profession?* The starting point was a treatment by Maupassant of the theme of a girl finding out that her mother is a courtesan. In an early version of the tale, Maupassant had the girl kill herself. In the later and better-known text (*Yvette*), he saves her life to engineer for himself an ironic-poignant ending: she becomes a kept woman like her mother before her. Curtain! That is the kind of inversion of a suicidal ending which Shaw did *not* go in for. Or not any more. If Shaw had shown a "surrender to the system" (in comical fashion) in the ending to *Widowers' Houses,* he was now intent on showing a rejection of the system. In the first instance, Vivie Warren's revolt represents Shaw's rational rejection of capitalism, but the play culminates in a scene that has no necessary connection with economics—a scene of family crisis, a scene in which a daughter rejects her mother. Which, after all, is archetypal Shaw: instead of the emotions of lover and mistress, he renders the emotions of parents and children, and particularly the emotion of the child rejecting the parent. *Major Barbara* is perhaps the grandest example of this archetype. The great last act of *Pygmalion* is the same thing in disguise, for Henry Higgins is the progenitor of the new Eliza, and that is why she must break free of him. Shaw's Joan has a father, too— in heaven—and she comes at times almost to the point of breaking with Him. That she does not quite do so is the upshot of a play which, while it shows Joan's isolation from men, ends with a stretching of arms toward the heavenly

Father. Vivie Warren is already a Saint Joan in that the experience Shaw gives her is that of being desolated. It is the experience he felt most deeply—presumably because it was the experience he had most deeply experienced. In any event, the two long scenes between Vivie and Mrs. Warren are emotional playwriting such as England had not seen for a couple of centuries.

The background, however, is blurred. A Scribean climax is arranged to provide *élan* for the announcement that Vivie's romance is incestuous:

> *Crofts.* Allow me, Mister Frank, to introduce you to your half-sister, the eldest daughter of the Reverend Samuel Gardner. Miss Vivie: your half-brother. Good morning.
>
> *Frank* [. . . *raising the rifle*]. You'll testify before the coroner that it's an accident, Viv. [*He takes aim at the retreating figure of Crofts. Vivie seizes the muzzle and pulls it round against her breast.*]
>
> *Vivie.* Fire now. You may.

Direct climax (as against anticlimax) was not really in Shaw's line, and in failing to parody Scribe here, Shaw has himself tumbled into the ridiculous. Perhaps the following act was bound to be an anticlimax in a way not intended—a mere disappointment. Yet, it is hard to believe that the particular disappointments it brings are simply the result of a technical ineptitude. Rather, they involve hesitations about the subject. After so strongly creating the impression of incest, Shaw shuffles the notion off in the next act in a surprisingly ambiguous way. It would be easy enough, from a technical viewpoint, to make clear that no incest had been committed. Why did Shaw leave the situation doubtful? So that Vivie could dismiss the issue as irrelevant? In that case, what is relevant? Why is she giving Frank up? One can think of possible reasons, but what reason is one *supposed* to think of?

Unclarity in the work of so careful a craftsman, a writer, moreover, who has more than once been accused of excessive clarity, surely bears witness to inner uncertainty and conflict. To think of *Mrs. Warren's Profession* in this personal way is to realize what powerful aggressions it embodies. Shaw combined the themes of prostitution and incest in order to make quite a rational point: our mad society draws back in horror from incest, which is certainly not a pressing menace and perhaps not even a bad thing, while it encourages prostitution, which is a virulent social pestilence. But both themes have a resonance far beyond the bounds of intellect. It is as if they proved more than Shaw had bargained for. The incest theme is sounded—all too boldly. Then the young dramatist has no idea what to do with it. He takes it back. Only, it is too late. So he half takes it back. After all, what is troubling Vivie does go beyond the rationally established causes. Deep water! And Shaw flounders in it. Which has some interest for the student of the emotions. Even where Shaw's plays are faulty, they are not unemotional. On the contrary, it is because of a certain emotional involvement in the material, not because of incapacity for such involvement, that Shaw was not able to resolve certain problems and truly finish certain plays. *Candida* and *Mrs. Warren's Profession* could be cited in evidence. There is material in both which was not successfully "worked through."

Is there similar material in Shaw's collected plays which *was* worked through? To my mind, a good answer would be: yes, *Pygmalion*. This play might well have proved just as ambiguous as the others, for it might have seemed that Eliza must love Higgins, and therefore that her leaving him is but an overrational afterthought of the author's, like his afterthoughts on *Candida*. Some people, including the author of *My Fair Lady*, think that is just what the Shavian ending is. I, on the other hand, feel—and it is feeling that is in question—that Eliza's rebellion grows organically out of what preceded. She is Higgins' creation: she cannot *be* at all unless she becomes independent of her creator. If he has "sex appeal," that makes the break more difficult but not less necessary. A girl's father quite normally has sex appeal for her. That is not to justify incest. Here Shaw does cope with incest, and in the best way—by avoiding it.

The ending of *Pygmalion* is the classic Shavian situation: someone is clamorously refusing to enter the bedroom. The friends of Frank Harris are thereby disgusted. That is their right. But there is a point to be made about Shaw's rendering of emotion. Refusal is emotional. There is more turbulence in conflict between Eliza and Higgins as conceived by Shaw than in romance between them as in *My Fair Lady*.

Man and Superman, on the other hand, might seem to be without emotional substance. The attempt made at a straightforward emotional climax is certainly rather unsuccessful:

> *Tanner.* I love you. The Life Force enchants me. I have the whole world in my arms when I clasp you. But I am fighting for my freedom, for my honor, for my self, one and undivisible.
>
> *Ann.* Your happiness will be worth them all.
>
> *Tanner.* You would sell freedom and honor and self for happiness?
>
> *Ann.* It would not be all happiness for me. Perhaps death.
>
> *Tanner* [*groaning*]. Oh, that clutch holds and hurts. What have you grasped in me? Is there a father's heart as well as a mother's?

If there is capital here, it is the kind that yields no dramatic return, and indeed a criticism of this false climax would lead us to complain of the introduction of the "Life Force" in the first place. There seems no such organic relation between Tanner and Ann as there is between Vivie and her mother, Eliza and Higgins, Candida and Morell. The pair are sometimes compared to Benedick and Beatrice. The comparison is not apt. Shakespeare shows the erotically "dangerous" element in the hostility of his couple. But Tanner and Ann draw no sparks from each other. A cynic might say: here there can be no love since there is no hate. There is really no relationship at all, except that she insists on having him and he cannot evade her successfully because the author won't let him. In this case, we have either to conclude that Frank Harris's kind of criticism applies—or that this is "drama of ideas" and we must not ask it to be otherwise.

Emotional substance? The farce of Tanner and Ann, taken in isolation, has very little, but oddly enough, the episode in hell has a good deal, and this spreads itself over the work as a whole. Even here, though, there is a discrepancy between intention and achievement. The final effect of the Don Juan scene is not that we find the positive message inspiring. We find it at best important, at worst gallant—a brave effort to make sense of things that cannot be made sense of. It is all rather like a speech made in war-time, saying that our side is bound to win because we are right. Perhaps. Perhaps. But the words that burn with irre-futability are all words expressing not aspiration toward a better future, but recognition of a bad present. Don Juan himself is at his best when denouncing people. The speech that steals the show ("And is Man any the less destroying himself . . .") is made by the Devil. Which is because it is not only a very reasonable speech but a very emotional one, a speech that springs from that very desolation which Shaw's best people experience.

This note of personal poignancy is not heard very often after *Saint Joan* (1923). So much the worse, perhaps, for the later plays. They have considerable merit, yet they often lack urgency even when the author makes Urgent Statements in them. And it is interesting that they lack not only dynamic and turbulent personal relationships but also close structure. There had been a connection between the emotional and the dramaturgic construction of the earlier plays; and when one went, so did the other.

I am not proposing a complete theory of the Shavian drama. Nor am I asking my reader to assume that all drama is dominated by the emotional conflicts of its author, much less that it ought to be. For that matter, I have had to remark that unresolved conflict sometimes resulted in un-resolved art. What I am affirming is, first, that some Shaw plays communicate personal feeling of great intensity and, second, that even some Shaw plays which are less overtly emotional do embody powerful feelings, though not of the kind that is usually expected.

First produced April 21, 1894.

act 1

Night. A lady's bedchamber in Bulgaria, in a small town near the Dragoman Pass. It is late in November in the year 1885, and through an open window with a little balcony on the left can be seen a peak of the Balkans, wonderfully white and beautiful in the starlit snow. The interior of the room is not like anything to be seen in the east of Europe. It is half rich Bulgarian, half cheap Viennese. The counterpane and hangings of the bed, the window curtains, the little carpet, and all the ornamental textile fabrics in the room are oriental and gorgeous: the paper on the walls is occidental and paltry. Above the head of the bed, which stands against a little wall cutting off the right hand corner of the room diagonally, is a painted wooden shrine, blue and gold, with an ivory image of Christ, and a light hanging before it in a pierced metal ball suspended by three chains. On the left, further forward, is an ottoman. The washstand, against the wall on the left, consists of an enamelled iron basin with a pail beneath it in a painted metal frame, and a single towel on the rail at the side. A chair near it is Austrian bent wood, with cane seat. The dressing table, between the bed and the window, is an ordinary pine table, covered with a cloth of many colors, but with an expensive toilet mirror on it. The door is on the right; and there is a chest of drawers between the door and the bed. This chest of drawers is also covered by a variegated native cloth, and on it there is a pile of paper backed novels, a box of chocolate creams, and a miniature easel, on which is a large photograph of an extremely handsome officer, whose lofty bearing and magnetic glance can be felt even from the portrait. The room is lighted by a candle on the chest of drawers, and another on the dressing table, with a box of matches beside it.

The window is hinged doorwise and stands wide open,

folding back to the left. Outside a pair of wooden shutters, opening outwards, also stand open. On the balcony, a young lady, intensely conscious of the romantic beauty of the night, and of the fact that her own youth and beauty is a part of it, is on the balcony, gazing at the snowy Balkans. She is covered by a long mantle of furs, worth, on a moderate estimate, about three times the furniture of her room.

Her reverie is interrupted by her mother, Catherine Petkoff, a woman over forty, imperiously energetic, with magnificent black hair and eyes, who might be a very splendid specimen of the wife of a mountain farmer, but is determined to be a Viennese lady, and to that end wears a fashionable tea gown on all occasions.

Catherine [*entering hastily, full of good news*]. Raina— [*she pronounces it Rah-eena, with the stress on the ee*] Raina—[*She goes to the bed, expecting to find Raina there.*] Why, where—[*Raina looks into the room.*] Heavens! child, are you out in the night air instead of in your bed? You'll catch your death. Louka told me you were asleep.

Raina [*coming in*]. I sent her away. I wanted to be alone. The stars are so beautiful! What is the matter?

Catherine. Such news. There has been a battle!

Raina [*her eyes dilating*]. Ah! [*She throws the cloak on the ottoman, and comes eagerly to Catherine in her nightgown, a pretty garment, but evidently the only one she has on.*]

Catherine. A great battle at Slivnitza! A victory! And it was won by Sergius.

Raina [*with a cry of delight*]. Ah! [*Rapturously.*] Oh, mother! [*Then, with sudden anxiety.*] Is father safe?

Catherine. Of course: he sent me the news. Sergius is the hero of the hour, the idol of the regiment.

Raina. Tell me, tell me. How was it! [*Ecstatically.*] Oh, mother, mother, mother! [*Raina pulls her mother down on the ottoman; and they kiss one another frantically.*]

Catherine [*with surging enthusiasm*]. You can't guess how splendid it is. A cavalry charge—think of that! He defied our Russian commanders—acted without orders —led a charge on his own responsibility—headed it himself—was the first man to sweep through their

guns. Can't you see it, Raina; our gallant splendid
Bulgarians with their swords and eyes flashing, thundering down like an avalanche and scattering the
wretched Servian dandies like chaff. And you—you
kept Sergius waiting a year before you would be betrothed to him. Oh, if you have a drop of Bulgarian
blood in your veins, you will worship him when he
comes back.

Raina. What will he care for my poor little worship after
the acclamations of a whole army of heroes? But no
matter: I am so happy—so proud! [*She rises and
walks about excitedly.*] It proves that all our ideas were
real after all.

Catherine [*indignantly*]. Our ideas real! What do you
mean?

Raina. Our ideas of what Sergius would do—our patriotism—our heroic ideals. Oh, what faithless little crea-
tures girls are!—I sometimes used to doubt whether
they were anything but dreams. When I buckled on
Sergius's sword he looked so noble: it was treason to
think of disillusion or humiliation or failure. And
yet—and yet—[*Quickly.*] Promise me you'll never tell
him.

Catherine. Don't ask me for promises until I know what
I am promising.

Raina. Well, it came into my head just as he was holding
me in his arms and looking into my eyes, that perhaps
we only had our heroic ideas because we are so fond
of reading Byron and Pushkin, and because we were
so delighted with the opera that season at Bucharest.
Real life is so seldom like that—indeed never, as far
as I knew it then. [*Remorsefully.*] Only think, mother,
I doubted him: I wondered whether all his heroic
qualities and his soldiership might not prove mere
imagination when he went into a real battle. I had an
uneasy fear that he might cut a poor figure there beside all those clever Russian officers.

Catherine. A poor figure! Shame on you! The Servians
have Austrian officers who are just as clever as our
Russians; but we have beaten them in every battle for
all that.

Raina [*laughing and sitting down again*]. Yes, I was only a prosaic little coward. Oh, to think that it was all true—that Sergius is just as splendid and noble as he looks—that the world is really a glorious world for women who can see its glory and men who can act its romance! What happiness! what unspeakable fulfilment! Ah! [*She throws herself on her knees beside her mother and flings her arms passionately round her. They are interrupted by the entry of Louka, a handsome, proud girl in a pretty Bulgarian peasant's dress with double apron, so defiant that her servility to Raina is almost insolent. She is afraid of Catherine, but even with her goes as far as she dares. She is just now excited like the others; but she has no sympathy for Raina's raptures and looks contemptuously at the ecstasies of the two before she addresses them.*]

Louka. If you please, madam, all the windows are to be closed and the shutters made fast. They say there may be shooting in the streets. [*Raina and Catherine rise together, alarmed.*] The Servians are being chased right back through the pass; and they say they may run into the town. Our cavalry will be after them; and our people will be ready for them you may be sure, now that they are running away. [*She goes out on the balcony and pulls the outside shutters to; then steps back into the room.*]

Raina. I wish our people were not so cruel. What glory is there in killing wretched fugitives?

Catherine [*business-like, her housekeeping instincts aroused*]. I must see that everything is made safe downstairs.

Raina [*to Louka*]. Leave the shutters so that I can just close them if I hear any noise.

Catherine [*authoritatively, turning on her way to the door*]. Oh, no, dear, you must keep them fastened. You would be sure to drop off to sleep and leave them open. Make them fast, Louka.

Louka. Yes, madam. [*She fastens them.*]

Raina. Don't be anxious about me. The moment I hear a shot, I shall blow out the candles and roll myself up in bed with my ears well covered.

Catherine. Quite the wisest thing you can do, my love. Good-night.

Raina. Good-night. [*They kiss one another, and Raina's*

emotion comes back for a moment.] Wish me joy of the happiest night of my life—if only there are no fugitives.

Catherine. Go to bed, dear, and don't think of them. [*She goes out.*]

Louka [*secretly, to Raina*]. If you would like the shutters open, just give them a push like this. [*She pushes them: they open: she pulls them to again.*] One of them ought to be bolted at the bottom; but the bolt's gone.

Raina [*with dignity, reproving her*]. Thanks, Louka; but we must do what we are told. [*Louka makes a grimace.*] Good-night.

Louka [*carelessly*]. Good-night. [*She goes out, swaggering.*]

[*Raina, left alone, goes to the chest of drawers, and adores the portrait there with feelings that are beyond all expression. She does not kiss it or press it to her breast, or shew it any mark of bodily affection; but she takes it in her hands and elevates it like a priestess.*]

Raina [*looking up at the picture with worship*]. Oh, I shall never be unworthy of you any more, my hero—never, never, never. [*She replaces it reverently, and selects a novel from the little pile of books. She turns over the leaves dreamily; finds her page; turns the book inside out at it; and then, with a happy sigh, gets into bed and prepares to read herself to sleep. But before abandoning herself to fiction, she raises her eyes once more, thinking of the blessed reality and murmurs.*] My hero! my hero! [*A distant shot breaks the quiet of the night outside. She starts, listening; and two more shots, much nearer, follow, startling her so that she scrambles out of bed, and hastily blows out the candle on the chest of drawers. Then, putting her fingers in her ears, she runs to the dressing-table and blows out the light there, and hurries back to bed. The room is now in darkness: nothing is visible but the glimmer of the light in the pierced ball before the image, and the starlight seen through the slits at the top of the shutters. The firing breaks out again: there is a startling fusillade quite close at hand. Whilst it is still echoing, the shutters disappear, pulled open from without, and for an instant the rectangle of snowy starlight flashes out with the figure of a man in black upon it. The shutters close immediately and the room*]

*is dark again. But the silence is now broken by the
sound of panting. Then there is a scrape; and the
flame of a match is seen in the middle of the room.*]

Raina [*crouching on the bed*]. Who's there? [*The match
is out instantly.*] Who's there? Who is that?

A Man's Voice [*in the darkness, subduedly, but threateningly*]. Sh—sh! Don't call out or you'll be shot. Be
good; and no harm will happen to you. [*She is heard
leaving her bed, and making for the door.*] Take care,
there's no use in trying to run away. Remember, if you
raise your voice my pistol will go off. [*Commandingly.*]
Strike a light and let me see you. Do you hear? [*Another moment of silence and darkness. Then she is
heard retreating to the dressing-table. She lights a
candle, and the mystery is at an end. A man of about
35, in a deplorable plight, bespattered with mud and
blood and snow, his belt and the strap of his revolver
case keeping together the torn ruins of the blue coat
of a Servian artillery officer. As far as the candlelight
and his unwashed, unkempt condition make it possible
to judge, he is a man of middling stature and un-
distinguished appearance, with strong neck and shoulders, a roundish, obstinate looking head covered with
short crisp bronze curls, clear quick blue eyes and
good brows and mouth, a hopelessly prosaic nose like
that of a strong-minded baby, trim soldierlike carriage and energetic manner, and with all his wits
about him in spite of his desperate predicament—
even with a sense of humor of it, without, however,
the least intention of trifling with it or throwing away
a chance. He reckons up what he can guess about
Raina—her age, her social position, her character,
the extent to which she is frightened—at a glance,
and continues, more politely but still most determinedly.*] Excuse my disturbing you; but you recognise my
uniform—Servian. If I'm caught I shall be killed.
[*Determinedly.*] Do you understand that?

Raina. Yes.

Man. Well, I don't intend to get killed if I can help it.
[*Still more determinedly.*] Do you understand that?
[*He locks the door with a snap.*]

Raina [*disdainfully*]. I suppose not. [*She draws herself up
superbly, and looks him straight in the face, saying*

with emphasis] Some soldiers, I know, are afraid of
death.

Man [*with grim goodhumor*]. All of them, dear lady, all
of them, believe me. It is our duty to live as long as
we can, and kill as many of the enemy as we can.
Now if you raise an alarm—

Raina [*cutting him short*]. You will shoot me. How do you
know that I am afraid to die?

Man [*cunningly*]. Ah; but suppose I don't shoot you, what
will happen then? Why, a lot of your cavalry—the
greatest blackguards in your army—will burst into
this pretty room of yours and slaughter me here like
a pig; for I'll fight like a demon: they shan't get me
into the street to amuse themselves with: I know
what they are. Are you prepared to receive that sort
of company in your present undress? [*Raina, suddenly
conscious of her nightgown, instinctively shrinks and
gathers it more closely about her. He watches her,
and adds, pitilessly.*] It's rather scanty, eh? [*She turns
to the ottoman. He raises his pistol instantly, and
cries.*] Stop! [*She stops.*] Where are you going?

Raina [*with dignified patience*]. Only to get my cloak.

Man [*darting to the ottoman and snatching the cloak*]. A
good idea. No: I'll keep the cloak: and you will take
care that nobody comes in and sees you without it.
This is a better weapon than the pistol. [*He throws
the pistol down on the ottoman.*]

Raina [*revolted*]. It is not the weapon of a gentleman!

Man. It's good enough for a man with only you to stand
between him and death. [*As they look at one another
for a moment, Raina hardly able to believe that even
a Servian officer can be so cynically and selfishly un-
chivalrous, they are startled by a sharp fusillade in
the street. The chill of imminent death hushes the
man's voice as he adds*] Do you hear? If you are going
to bring those scoundrels in on me you shall receive
them as you are. [*Raina meets his eye with unflinch-
ing scorn. Suddenly he starts, listening. There is a
step outside. Someone tries the door, and then knocks
hurriedly and urgently at it. Raina looks at the man,
breathless. He throws up his head with the gesture
of a man who sees that it is all over with him, and,*

dropping the manner which he has been assuming to intimidate her, flings the cloak to her, exclaiming, sincerely and kindly] No use: I'm done for. Quick! wrap yourself up: they're coming!

Raina [*catching the cloak eagerly*]. Oh, thank you. [*She wraps herself up with great relief. He draws his sabre and turns to the door, waiting.*]

Louka [*outside, knocking*]. My lady, my lady! Get up, quick, and open the door.

Raina [*anxiously*]. What will you do?

Man [*grimly*]. Never mind. Keep out of the way. It will not last long.

Raina [*impulsively*]. I'll help you. Hide yourself, oh, hide yourself, quick, behind the curtain. [*She seizes him by a torn strip of his sleeve, and pulls him towards the window.*]

Man [*yielding to her*]. There is just half a chance, if you keep your head. Remember: nine soldiers out of ten are born fools. [*He hides behind the curtain, looking out for a moment to say, finally*] If they find me, I promise you a fight—a devil of a fight! [*He disappears. Raina takes off the cloak and throws it across the foot of the bed. Then with a sleepy, disturbed air, she opens the door. Louka enters excitedly.*]

Louka. A man has been seen climbing up the water-pipe to your balcony—a Servian. The soldiers want to search for him; and they are so wild and drunk and furious. My lady says you are to dress at once.

Raina [*as if annoyed at being disturbed*]. They shall not search here. Why have they been let in?

Catherine [*coming in hastily*]. Raina, darling, are you safe? Have you seen anyone or heard anything?

Raina. I heard the shooting. Surely the soldiers will not dare come in here?

Catherine. I have found a Russian officer, thank Heaven: he knows Sergius. [*Speaking through the door to someone outside.*] Sir, will you come in now! My daughter is ready.

[*A young Russian officer, in Bulgarian uniform, enters, sword in hand.*]

The Officer [*with soft, feline politeness and stiff military carriage*]. Good evening, gracious lady; I am sorry to intrude, but there is a fugitive hiding on the balcony. Will you and the gracious lady your mother please to withdraw whilst we search?

Raina [*petulantly*]. Nonsense, sir, you can see that there is no one on the balcony. [*She throws the shutters wide open and stands with her back to the curtain where the man is hidden, pointing to the moonlit balcony. A couple of shots are fired right under the window, and a bullet shatters the glass opposite Raina, who winks and gasps, but stands her ground, whilst Catherine screams, and the officer rushes to the balcony.*]

The Officer [*on the balcony, shouting savagely down to the street*]. Cease firing there, you fools: do you hear? Cease firing, damn you. [*He glares down for a moment; then turns to Raina, trying to resume his polite manner.*] Could anyone have got in without your knowledge? Were you asleep?

Raina. No, I have not been to bed.

The Officer [*impatiently, coming back into the room*]. Your neighbours have their heads so full of runaway Servians that they see them everywhere. [*Politely.*] Gracious lady, a thousand pardons. Good-night. [*Military bow, which Raina returns coldly. Another to Catherine, who follows him out. Raina closes the shutters. She turns and sees Louka, who has been watching the scene curiously.*]

Raina. Don't leave my mother, Louka, whilst the soldiers are here. [*Louka glances at Raina, at the ottoman, at the curtain; then purses her lips secretively, laughs to herself, and goes out. Raina follows her to the door, shuts it behind her with a slam, and locks it violently. The man immediately steps out from behind the curtain, sheathing his sabre, and dismissing the danger from his mind in a businesslike way.*]

Man. A narrow shave; but a miss is as good as a mile. Dear young lady, your servant until death. I wish for your sake I had joined the Bulgarian army instead of the Servian. I am not a native Servian.

Raina [*haughtily*]. No, you are one of the Austrians who set the Servians on to rob us of our national liberty, and who officer their army for them. We hate them!

Man. Austrian! not I. Don't hate me, dear young lady. I am only a Swiss, fighting merely as a professional soldier. I joined Servia because it was nearest to me. Be generous: you've beaten us hollow.

Raina. Have I not been generous?

Man. Noble!—heroic! But I'm not saved yet. This particular rush will soon pass through; but the pursuit will go on all night by fits and starts. I must take my chance to get off during a quiet interval. You don't mind my waiting just a minute or two, do you?

Raina. Oh, no: I am sorry you will have to go into danger again. [*Motioning towards ottoman.*] Won't you sit— [*She breaks off with an irrepressible cry of alarm as she catches sight of the pistol. The man, all nerves, shies like a frightened horse.*]

Man [*irritably*]. Don't frighten me like that. What is it?

Raina. Your pistol! It was staring that officer in the face all the time. What an escape!

Man [*vexed at being unnecessarily terrified*]. Oh, is that all?

Raina [*staring at him rather superciliously, conceiving a poorer and poorer opinion of him, and feeling proportionately more and more at her ease with him*]. I am sorry I frightened you. [*She takes up the pistol and hands it to him.*] Pray take it to protect yourself against me.

Man [*grinning wearily at the sarcasm as he takes the pistol*]. No use, dear young lady: there's nothing in it. It's not loaded. [*He make a grimace at it, and drops it disparagingly into his revolver case.*]

Raina. Load it by all means.

Man. I've no ammunition. What use are cartridges in battle? I always carry chocolate instead; and I finished the last cake of that yesterday.

Raina [*outraged in her most cherished ideals of manhood*]. Chocolate! Do you stuff your pockets with sweets—like a schoolboy—even in the field?

Man. Yes. Isn't it contemptible?

[*Raina stares at him, unable to utter her feelings. Then she sails away scornfully to the chest of drawers, and returns with the box of confectionery in her hand.*]

Raina. Allow me. I am sorry I have eaten them all except these. [*She offers him the box.*]

Man [*ravenously*]. You're an angel! [*He gobbles the com-*

fits.] Creams! Delicious! [*He looks anxiously to see whether there are any more. There are none. He accepts the inevitable with pathetic goodhumor, and says, with grateful emotion*] Bless you, dear lady. You can always tell an old soldier by the inside of his holsters and cartridge boxes. The young ones carry pistols and cartridges; the old ones, grub. Thank you. [*He hands back the box. She snatches it contemptuously from him and throws it away. This impatient action is so sudden that he shies again.*] Ugh! Don't do things so suddenly, gracious lady. Don't revenge yourself because I frightened you just now.

Raina [*superbly*]. Frighten me! Do you know, sir, that though I am only a woman, I think I am at heart as brave as you.

Man. I should think so. You haven't been under fire for three days as I have. I can stand two days without shewing it much; but no man can stand three days: I'm as nervous as a mouse. [*He sits down on the ottoman, and takes his head in his hands.*] Would you like to see me cry?

Raina [*quickly*]. No.

Man. If you would, all you have to do is to scold me just as if I were a little boy and you my nurse. If I were in camp now they'd play all sorts of tricks on me.

Raina [*a little moved*]. I'm sorry. I won't scold you. [*Touched by the sympathy in her tone, he raises his head and looks gratefully at her: she immediately draws back and says stiffly*] You must excuse me: our soldiers are not like that. [*She moves away from the ottoman.*]

Man. Oh, yes, they are. There are only two sorts of soldiers: old ones and young ones. I've served fourteen years: half of your fellows never smelt powder before. Why, how is it that you've just beaten us? Sheer ignorance of the art of war, nothing else. [*Indignantly.*] I never saw anything so unprofessional.

Raina [*ironically*]. Oh, was it unprofessional to beat you?

Man. Well, come, is it professional to throw a regiment of cavalry on a battery of machine guns, with the dead certainty that if the guns go off not a horse or man will ever get within fifty yards of the fire? I couldn't believe my eyes when I saw it.

Raina [*eagerly turning to him, as all her enthusiasm and her dream of glory rush back on her*]. Did you see the great cavalry charge? Oh, tell me about it. Describe it to me.

Man. You never saw a cavalry charge, did you?

Raina. How could I?

Man. Ah, perhaps not—of course. Well, it's a funny sight. It's like slinging a handful of peas against a window pane: first one comes; then two or three close behind him; and then all the rest in a lump.

Raina [*her eyes dilating as she raises her clasped hands ecstatically*]. Yes, first One!—the bravest of the brave!

Man [*prosaically*]. Hm! you should see the poor devil pulling at his horse.

Raina. Why should he pull at his horse?

Man [*impatient of so stupid a question*]. It's running away with him, of course: do you suppose the fellow wants to get there before the others and be killed? Then they all come. You can tell the young ones by their wildness and their slashing. The old ones come bunched up under the number one guard: they know that they are mere projectiles, and that it's no use trying to fight. The wounds are mostly broken knees, from the horses cannoning together.

Raina. Ugh! But I don't believe the first man is a coward. I believe he is a hero!

Man [*goodhumoredly*]. That's what you'd have said if you'd seen the first man in the charge to-day.

Raina [*breathless*]. Ah, I knew it! Tell me—tell me about him.

Man. He did it like an operatic tenor—a regular handsome fellow, with flashing eyes and lovely moustache, shouting a war-cry and charging like Don Quixote at the windmills. We nearly burst with laughter at him; but when the sergeant ran up as white as a sheet, and told us they'd sent us the wrong cartridges, and that we couldn't fire a shot for the next ten minutes, we laughed at the other side of our mouths. I never felt so sick in my life, though I've been in one or two very tight places. And I hadn't even a revolver cartridge—nothing but chocolate. We'd no bayonets—nothing. Of course, they just cut us to bits. And there

was Don Quixote flourishing like a drum major,
thinking he'd done the cleverest thing ever known,
whereas he ought to be courtmartialled for it. Of all
the fools ever let loose on a field of battle, that man
must be the very maddest. He and his regiment simply
committed suicide—only the pistol missed fire, that's
all.

Raina [*deeply wounded, but steadfastly loyal to her ideals*].
Indeed! Would you know him again if you saw him?

Man. Shall I ever forget him. [*She again goes to the chest
of drawers. He watches her with a vague hope that
she may have something else for him to eat. She takes
the portrait from its stand and brings it to him.*]

Raina. That is a photograph of the gentleman—the patriot
and hero—to whom I am betrothed.

Man [*looking at it*]. I'm really very sorry. [*Looking at
her.*] Was it fair to lead me on? [*He looks at the portrait again.*] Yes: that's him: not a doubt of it. [*He
stifles a laugh.*]

Raina [*quickly*]. Why do you laugh?

Man [*shamefacedly, but still greatly tickled*]. I didn't laugh,
I assure you. At least I didn't mean to. But when I
think of him charging the windmills and thinking he
was doing the finest thing—[*chokes with suppressed
laughter*].

Raina [*sternly*]. Give me back the portrait, sir.

Man [*with sincere remorse*]. Of course. Certainly. I'm
really very sorry. [*She deliberately kisses it, and looks
him straight in the face, before returning to the chest
of drawers to replace it. He follows her, apologizing.*]
Perhaps I'm quite wrong, you know: no doubt I am.
Most likely he had got wind of the cartridge business
somehow, and knew it was a safe job.

Raina. That is to say, he was a pretender and a coward!
You did not dare say that before.

Man [*with a comic gesture of despair*]. It's no use, dear
lady: I can't make you see it from the professional
point of view. [*As he turns away to get back to the
ottoman, the firing begins again in the distance.*]

Raina [*sternly, as she sees him listening to the shots*]. So
much the better for you.

Man [*turning*]. How?

Raina. You are my enemy; and you are at my mercy.

What would I do if I were a professional soldier?

Man. Ah, true, dear young lady: you're always right. I know how good you have been to me: to my last hour I shall remember those three chocolate creams. It was unsoldierly; but it was angelic.

Raina [*coldly*]. Thank you. And now I will do a soldierly thing. You cannot stay here after what you have just said about my future husband; but I will go out on the balcony and see whether it is safe for you to climb down into the street. [*She turns to the window.*]

Man [*changing countenance*]. Down that waterpipe! Stop! Wait! I can't! I daren't! The very thought of it makes me giddy. I came up it fast enough with death behind me. But to face it now in cold blood!—[*He sinks on the ottoman.*] It's no use: I give up: I'm beaten. Give the alarm. [*He drops his head in his hands in the deepest dejection.*]

Raina [*disarmed by pity*]. Come, don't be disheartened. [*She stoops over him almost maternally: he shakes his head.*] Oh, you are a very poor soldier—a chocolate cream soldier. Come, cheer up: it takes less courage to climb down than to face capture—remember that.

Man [*dreamily, lulled by her voice*]. No, capture only means death; and death is sleep—oh, sleep, sleep, sleep, undisturbed sleep! Climbing down the pipe means doing something—exerting myself—thinking! Death ten times over first.

Raina [*softly and wonderingly, catching the rhythm of his weariness*]. Are you so sleepy as that?

Man. I've not had two hours undisturbed sleep since the war began. I'm on the staff: you don't know what that means. I haven't closed my eyes for thirty-six hours.

Raina [*desperately*]. But what am I to do with you.

Man [*staggering up*]. Of course I must do something. [*He shakes himself; pulls himself together; and speaks with rallied vigour and courage.*] You see, sleep or no sleep, hunger or no hunger, tired or not tired, you can always do a thing when you know it must be done. Well, that pipe must be got down—[*He hits himself on the chest, and adds*]—Do you hear that, you chocolate cream soldier? [*He turns to the window.*]

Raina [*anxiously*]. But if you fall?

Man. I shall sleep as if the stones were a feather bed.
Good-bye. [*He makes boldly for the window, and his
hand is on the shutter when there is a terrible burst
of firing in the street beneath.*]

Raina [*rushing to him*]. Stop! [*She catches him by the
shoulder, and turns him quite round.*] They'll kill you.

Man [*coolly, but attentively*]. Never mind: this sort of
thing is all in my day's work. I'm bound to take my
chance. [*Decisively.*] Now do what I tell you. Put out
the candles, so that they shan't see the light when I
open the shutters. And keep away from the window,
whatever you do. If they see me, they're sure to have
a shot at me.

Raina [*clinging to him*]. They're sure to see you: it's
bright moonlight. I'll save you—oh, how can you be
so indifferent? You want me to save you, don't you?

Man. I really don't want to be troublesome. [*She shakes
him in her impatience.*] I am not indifferent, dear
young lady, I assure you. But how is it to be done?

Raina. Come away from the window—please. [*She coaxes
him back to the middle of the room. He submits
humbly. She releases him, and addresses him patroniz-
ingly.*] Now listen. You must trust to our hospitality.
You do not yet know in whose house you are. I am a
Petkoff.

Man. What's that?

Raina [*rather indignantly*]. I mean that I belong to the
family of the Petkoffs, the richest and best known in
our country.

Man. Oh, yes, of course. I beg your pardon. The Petkoffs,
to be sure. How stupid of me!

Raina. You know you never heard of them until this
minute. How can you stoop to pretend?

Man. Forgive me: I'm too tired to think; and the change
of subject was too much for me. Don't scold me.

Raina. I forgot. It might make you cry. [*He nods, quite
seriously. She pouts and then resumes her patronizing
tone.*] I must tell you that my father holds the highest
command of any Bulgarian in our army. He is
[*proudly*] a Major.

Man [*pretending to be deeply impressed*]. A Major! Bless
me! Think of that!

Raina. You shewed great ignorance in thinking that it

was necessary to climb up to the balcony, because ours is the only private house that has two rows of windows. There is a flight of stairs inside to get up and down by.

Man. Stairs! How grand! You live in great luxury indeed, dear young lady.

Raina. Do you know what a library is?

Man. A library? A roomful of books.

Raina. Yes, we have one, the only one in Bulgaria.

Man. Actually a real library! I should like to see that.

Raina [*affectedly*]. I tell you these things to shew you that you are not in the house of ignorant country folk who would kill you the moment they saw your Servian uniform, but among civilized people. We go to Bucharest every year for the opera season; and I have spent a whole month in Vienna.

Man. I saw that, dear young lady. I saw at once that you knew the world.

Raina. Have you ever seen the opera of Ernani?

Man. Is that the one with the devil in it in red velvet, and a soldier's chorus?

Raina [*contemptuously*]. No!

Man [*stifling a heavy sigh of weariness*]. Then I don't know it.

Raina. I thought you might have remembered the great scene where Ernani, flying from his foes just as you are tonight, takes refuge in the castle of his bitterest enemy, an old Castilian noble. The noble refuses to give him up. His guest is sacred to him.

Man [*quickly waking up a little*]. Have your people got that notion?

Raina [*with dignity*]. My mother and I can understand that notion, as you call it. And if instead of threatening me with your pistol as you did, you had simply thrown yourself as a fugitive on our hospitality, you would have been as safe as in your father's house.

Man. Quite sure?

Raina [*turning her back on him in disgust*]. Oh, it is useless to try and make you understand.

Man. Don't be angry: you see how awkward it would be for me if there was any mistake. My father is a very hospitable man: he keeps six hotels; but I couldn't trust him as far as that. What about your father?

Raina. He is away at Slivnitza fighting for his country. I answer for your safety. There is my hand in pledge of it. Will that reassure you? [*She offers him her hand.*]

Man [*looking dubiously at his own hand*]. Better not touch my hand, dear young lady. I must have a wash first.

Raina [*touched*]. That is very nice of you. I see that you are a gentleman.

Man [*puzzled*]. Eh?

Raina. You must not think I am surprised. Bulgarians of really good standing—people in our position—wash their hands nearly every day. But I appreciate your delicacy. You may take my hand. [*She offers it again.*]

Man [*kissing it with his hands behind his back*]. Thanks, gracious young lady: I feel safe at last. And now would you mind breaking the news to your mother? I had better not stay here secretly longer than is necessary.

Raina. If you will be so good as to keep perfectly still whilst I am away.

Man. Certainly. [*He sits down on the ottoman.*]

[*Raina goes to the bed and wraps herself in the fur cloak. His eyes close. She goes to the door, but on turning for a last look at him, sees that he is dropping off to sleep.*]

Raina [*at the door*]. You are not going asleep, are you? [*He murmurs inarticulately: she runs to him and shakes him.*] Do you hear? Wake up: you are falling asleep.

Man. Eh? Falling aslee—? Oh, no, not the least in the world: I was only thinking. It's all right: I'm wide awake.

Raina [*severely*]. Will you please stand up while I am away. [*He rises reluctantly.*] All the time, mind.

Man [*standing unsteadily*]. Certainly—certainly: you may depend on me.

[*Raina looks doubtfully at him. He smiles foolishly. She goes reluctantly, turning again at the door, and almost catching him in the act of yawning. She goes out.*]

Man [*drowsily*]. Sleep, sleep, sleep, sleep, slee—[*The words trail off into a murmur. He wakes again with a shock on the point of falling.*] Where am I? That's what I want to know: where am I? Must keep awake. Nothing keeps me awake except danger—remember that—[*intently*] danger, danger, danger, dan— Where's danger? Must find it. [*He starts off vaguely around the room in search of it.*] What am I looking for? Sleep—danger—don't know. [*He stumbles against the bed.*] Ah, yes: now I know. All right now. I'm to go to bed, but not to sleep—be sure not to sleep—because of danger. Not to lie down, either, only sit down. [*He sits on the bed. A blissful expression comes into his face.*] Ah! [*With a happy sigh he sinks back at full length; lifts his boots into the bed with a final effort; and falls fast asleep instantly. Catherine comes in, followed by Raina.*]

Raina [*looking at the ottoman*]. He's gone! I left him here.

Catherine. Here! Then he must have climbed down from the—

Raina [*seeing him*]. Oh! [*She points.*]

Catherine [*scandalized*]. Well! [*She strides to the left side of the bed, Raina following and standing opposite her on the right.*] He's fast asleep. The brute!

Raina [*anxiously*]. Sh!

Catherine [*shaking him*]. Sir! [*Shaking him again, harder.*] Sir!! [*Vehemently shaking very hard.*] Sir!!!

Raina [*catching her arm*]. Don't, mamma: the poor dear is worn out. Let him sleep.

Catherine [*letting him go and turning amazed to Raina*]. The poor dear! Raina!!! [*She looks sternly at her daughter. The man sleeps profoundly.*]

*The sixth of March, 1886. In the garden of Major Petkoff's
house. It is a fine spring morning; and the garden looks
fresh and pretty. Beyond the paling the tops of a couple
of minarets can be seen, shewing that there is a valley
there, with the little town in it. A few miles further the Balkan mountains rise and shut in the view. Within the garden
the side of the house is seen on the right, with a garden door
reached by a little flight of steps. On the left the stable yard,
with its gateway, encroaches on the garden. There are fruit
bushes along the paling and house, covered with washing
hung out to dry. A path runs by the house, and rises by
two steps at the corner where it turns out of the sight along
the front. In the middle a small table, with two bent wood
chairs at it, is laid for breakfast with Turkish coffee pot,
cups, rolls, etc.; but the cups have been used and the bread
broken. There is a wooden garden seat against the wall on
the left.*

*Louka, smoking a cigaret, is standing between the table
and the house, turning her back with angry disdain on a
manservant who is lecturing her. He is a middle-aged man
of cool temperament and low but clear and keen intelligence, with the complacency of the servant who values
himself on his rank in servility, and the imperturbability of
the accurate calculator who has no illusions. He wears a
white Bulgarian costume jacket with decorated border,
sash, wide knickerbockers, and decorated gaiters. His head
is shaved up to the crown, giving him a high Japanese forehead. His name is Nicola.*

Nicola. Be warned in time, Louka: mend your manners.
 I know the mistress. She is so grand that she never
 dreams that any servant could dare to be disrespectful

to her; but if she once suspects that you are defying her, out you go.

Louka. I do defy her. I will defy her. What do I care for her?

Nicola. If you quarrel with the family, I never can marry you. It's the same as if you quarrelled with me!

Louka. You take her part against me, do you?

Nicola [*sedately*]. I shall always be dependent on the good will of the family. When I leave their service and start a shop in Sofea, their custom will be half my capital: their bad word would ruin me.

Louka. You have no spirit. I should like to see them dare say a word against me!

Nicola [*pityingly*]. I should have expected more sense from you, Louka. But you're young, you're young!

Louka. Yes; and you like me the better for it, don't you? But I know some family secrets they wouldn't care to have told, young as I am. Let them quarrel with me if they dare!

Nicola [*with compassionate superiority*]. Do you know what they would do if they heard you talk like that?

Louka. What could they do?

Nicola. Discharge you for untruthfulness. Who would believe any stories you told after that? Who would give you another situation? Who in this house would dare be seen speaking to you ever again? How long would your father be left on his little farm? [*She impatiently throws away the end of her cigaret, and stamps on it.*] Child, you don't know the power such high people have over the like of you and me when we try to rise out of our poverty against them. [*He goes close to her and lowers his voice.*] Look at me, ten years in their service. Do you think I know no secrets? I know things about the mistress that she wouldn't have the master know for a thousand levas. I know things about him that she wouldn't let him hear the last of for six months if I blabbed them to her. I know things about Raina that would break off her match with Sergius if—

Louka [*turning on him quickly*]. How do you know? I never told you!

Nicola [*opening his eyes cunningly*]. So that's your little secret, is it? I thought it might be something like that. Well, you take my advice, and be respectful; and make the mistress feel that no matter what you know or don't know, they can depend on you to hold your tongue and serve the family faithfully. That's what they like; and that's how you'll make most out of them.

Louka [*with searching scorn*]. You have the soul of a servant, Nicola.

Nicola [*complacently*]. Yes: that's the secret of success in service.

[*A loud knocking with a whip handle on a wooden door, outside on the left, is heard.*]

Male Voice Outside. Hollo! Hollo there! Nicola!

Louka. Master! back from the war!

Nicola [*quickly*]. My word for it, Louka, the war's over. Off with you and get some fresh coffee. [*He runs out into the stable yard.*]

Louka [*as she puts the coffee pot and the cups upon the tray, and carries it into the house*]. You'll never put the soul of a servant into me.

[*Major Petkoff comes from the stable yard, followed by Nicola. He is a cheerful, excitable, insignificant, unpolished man of about 50, naturally unambitious except as to his income and his importance in local society, but just now greatly pleased with the military rank which the war has thrust on him as a man of consequence in his town. The fever of plucky patriotism which the Servian attack roused in all the Bulgarians has pulled him through the war; but he is obviously glad to be home again.*]

Petkoff [*pointing to the table with his whip*]. Breakfast out here, eh?

Nicola. Yes, sir. The mistress and Miss Raina have just gone in.

Petkoff [*sitting down and taking a roll*]. Go in and say I've come; and get me some fresh coffee.

Nicola. It's coming, sir. [*He goes to the house door. Louka, with fresh coffee, a clean cup, and a brandy bottle on her tray meets him.*] Have you told the mistress?

Louka. Yes: she's coming.

[*Nicola goes into the house. Louka brings the coffee to the table.*]

Petkoff. Well, the Servians haven't run away with you, have they?

Louka. No, sir.

Petkoff. That's right. Have you brought me some cognac?

Louka [*putting the bottle on the table*]. Here, sir.

Petkoff. That's right. [*He pours some into his coffee. Catherine who has at this early hour made only a very perfunctory toilet, and wears a Bulgarian apron over a once brilliant, but now half worn out red dressing gown, and a colored handkerchief tied over her thick black hair, with Turkish slippers on her bare feet, comes from the house, looking astonishingly handsome and stately under all the circumstances. Louka goes into the house.*]

Catherine. My dear Paul, what a surprise for us. [*She stoops over the back of his chair to kiss him.*] Have they brought you fresh coffee?

Petkoff. Yes, Louka's been looking after me. The war's over. The treaty was signed three days ago at Bucharest; and the decree for our army to demobilize was issued yesterday.

Catherine [*springing erect, with flashing eyes*]. The war over! Paul: have you let the Austrians force you to make peace?

Petkoff [*submissively*]. My dear: they didn't consult me. What could *I* do? [*She sits down and turns away from him.*] But of course we saw to it that the treaty was an honorable one. It declares peace—

Catherine [*outraged*]. Peace!

Petkoff [*appeasing her*].—but not friendly relations: remember that. They wanted to put that in; but I insisted on its being struck out. What more could I do?

Catherine. You could have annexed Servia and made Prince Alexander Emperor of the Balkans. That's what I would have done.

Petkoff. I don't doubt it in the least, my dear. But I should have had to subdue the whole Austrian Empire first; and that would have kept me too long away from you. I missed you greatly.

Catherine [*relenting*]. Ah! [*Stretches her hand affectionately across the table to squeeze his.*]

Petkoff. And how have you been, my dear?

Catherine. Oh, my usual sore throats, that's all.

Petkoff [*with conviction*]. That comes from washing your
neck every day. I've often told you so.

Catherine. Nonsense, Paul!

Petkoff [*over his coffee and cigaret*]. I don't believe in
going too far with these modern customs. All this
washing can't be good for the health: it's not natural.
There was an Englishman at Phillipopolis who used
to wet himself all over with cold water every morning
when he got up. Disgusting! It all comes from the
English: their climate makes them so dirty that they
have to be perpetually washing themselves. Look at
my father: he never had a bath in his life; and he
lived to be ninety-eight, the healthiest man in Bulgaria.
I don't mind a good wash once a week to keep up my
position; but once a day is carrying the thing to a
ridiculous extreme.

Catherine. You are a barbarian at heart still, Paul. I hope
you behaved yourself before all those Russian officers.

Petkoff. I did my best. I took care to let them know that
we had a library.

Catherine. Ah; but you didn't tell them that we have an
electric bell in it? I have had one put up.

Petkoff. What's an electric bell?

Catherine. You touch a button; something tinkles in the
kitchen; and then Nicola comes up.

Petkoff. Why not shout for him?

Catherine. Civilized people never shout for their servants.
I've learnt that while you were away.

Petkoff. Well, I'll tell you something I've learnt, too.
Civilized people don't hang out their washing to dry
where visitors can see it; so you'd better have all that
[*indicating the clothes on the bushes*] put somewhere
else.

Catherine. Oh, that's absurd, Paul: I don't believe really
refined people notice such things.

[*Someone is heard knocking at the stable gates.*]

Petkoff. There's Sergius. [*Shouting.*] Hollo, Nicola!

Catherine. Oh, don't shout, Paul: it really isn't nice.

Petkoff. Bosh! [*He shouts louder than before.*] Nicola!

Nicola [*appearing at the house door*]. Yes, sir.

Petkoff. If that is Major Saranoff, bring him round this
way. [*He pronounces the name with the stress on the
second syllable—Sarah noff.*]

Nicola. Yes, sir. [*He goes into the stable yard.*]

Petkoff. You must talk to him, my dear, until Raina takes him off our hands. He bores my life out about our not promoting him—over my head, mind you.

Catherine. He certainly ought to be promoted when he marries Raina. Besides, the country should insist on having at least one native general.

Petkoff. Yes, so that he could throw away whole brigades instead of regiments. It's no use, my dear: he has not the slightest chance of promotion until we are quite sure that the peace will be a lasting one.

Nicola [*at the gate, announcing*]. Major Sergius Saranoff!

[*He goes into the house and returns presently with a third chair, which he places at the table. He then withdraws. Major Sergius Saranoff, the original of the portrait in Raina's room, is a tall, romantically handsome man, with the physical hardihood, the high spirit, and the susceptible imagination of an untamed mountaineer chieftain. But his remarkable personal distinction is of a characteristically civilized type. The ridges of his eyebrows, curving with a ram's-horn twist round the marked projections at the outer corners, his jealously observant eye, his nose, thin, keen, and apprehensive in spite of the pugnacious high bridge and large nostril, his assertive chin, would not be out of place in a Paris salon. In short, the clever, imaginative barbarian has an acute critical faculty which has been thrown into intense activity by the arrival of western civilization in the Balkans; and the result is precisely what the advent of nineteenth century thought first produced in England: to-wit, Byronism. By his brooding on the perpetual failure, not only of others, but of himself, to live up to his imaginative ideals, his consequent cynical scorn for humanity, the jejune credulity as to the absolute validity of his ideals and the unworthiness of the world in disregarding them, his wincings and mockeries under the sting of the petty disillusions which every hour spent among men brings to his infallibly quick observation, he has acquired the half tragic, half ironic air, the mysterious moodiness, the suggestion of a strange and terrible history that has left him nothing but undying remorse, by which Childe Harold fascinated the grandmothers of his*

English contemporaries. Altogether it is clear that here or nowhere is Raina's ideal hero. Catherine is hardly less enthusiastic, and much less reserved in shewing her enthusiasm. As he enters from the stable gate, she rises effusively to greet him. Petkoff is distinctly less disposed to make a fuss about him.]

Petkoff. Here already, Sergius. Glad to see you!

Catherine. My dear Sergius! [*She holds out both her hands.*]

Sergius [*kissing them with scrupulous gallantry*]. My dear mother, if I may call you so.

Petkoff [*drily*]. Mother-in-law, Sergius; mother-in-law! Sit down, and have some coffee.

Sergius. Thank you, none for me. [*He gets away from the table with a certain distaste for Petkoff's enjoyment of it, and posts himself with conscious grace against the rail of the steps leading to the house.*]

Catherine. You look superb—splendid. The campaign has improved you. Everybody here is mad about you. We were all wild with enthusiasm about that magnificent cavalry charge.

Sergius [*with grave irony*]. Madam: it was the cradle and the grave of my military reputation.

Catherine. How so?

Sergius. I won the battle the wrong way when our worthy Russian generals were losing it the right way. That upset their plans, and wounded their self-esteem. Two of their colonels got their regiments driven back on the correct principles of scientific warfare. Two major-generals got killed strictly according to military etiquette. Those two colonels are now major-generals; and I am still a simple major.

Catherine. You shall not remain so, Sergius. The women are on your side; and they will see that justice is done you.

Sergius. It is too late. I have only waited for the peace to send in my resignation.

Petkoff [*dropping his cup in his amazement*]. Your resignation!

Catherine. Oh, you must withdraw it!

Sergius [*with resolute, measured emphasis, folding his arms*]. I never withdraw!

Petkoff [*vexed*]. Now who could have supposed you were going to do such a thing?

Sergius [*with fire*]. Everyone that knew me. But enough of myself and my affairs. How is Raina; and where is Raina?

Raina [*suddenly coming round the corner of the house and standing at the top of the steps in the path*]. Raina is here. [*She makes a charming picture as they all turn to look at her. She wears an underdress of pale green silk, draped with an overdress of thin ecru canvas embroidered with gold. On her head she wears a pretty Phrygian cap of gold tinsel. Sergius, with an exclamation of pleasure, goes impulsively to meet her. She stretches out her hand: he drops chivalrously on one knee and kisses it.*]

Petkoff [*aside to Catherine, beaming with parental pride*]. Pretty, isn't it? She always appears at the right moment.

Catherine [*impatiently*]. Yes: she listens for it. It is an abominable habit.

[*Sergius leads Raina forward with splendid gallantry, as if she were a queen. When they come to the table, she turns to him with a bend of the head; he bows; and thus they separate, he coming to his place, and she going behind her father's chair.*]

Raina [*stooping and kissing her father*]. Dear father! Welcome home!

Petkoff [*patting her cheek*]. My little pet girl. [*He kisses her; she goes to the chair left by Nicola for Sergius, and sits down.*]

Catherine. And so you're no longer a soldier, Sergius.

Sergius. I am no longer a soldier. Soldiering, my dear madam, is the coward's art of attacking mercilessly when you are strong, and keeping out of harm's way when you are weak. That is the whole secret of successful fighting. Get your enemy at a disadvantage; and never, on any account, fight him on equal terms. Eh, Major!

Petkoff. They wouldn't let us make a fair stand-up fight of it. However, I suppose soldiering has to be a trade like any other trade.

Sergius. Precisely. But I have no ambition to succeed as a tradesman; so I have taken the advice of that bagman of a captain that settled the exchange of prisoners with us at Peerot, and given it up.

Petkoff. What, that Swiss fellow? Sergius: I've often thought of that exchange since. He over-reached us about those horses.

Sergius. Of course he over-reached us. His father was a hotel and livery stable keeper; and he owed his first step to his knowledge of horse-dealing. [*With mock enthusiasm.*] Ah, he was a soldier—every inch a soldier! If only I had bought the horses for my regiment instead of foolishly leading it into danger, I should have been a field-marshal now!

Catherine. A Swiss? What was he doing in the Servian army?

Petkoff. A volunteer of course—keen on picking up his profession. [*Chuckling.*] We shouldn't have been able to begin fighting if these foreigners hadn't shewn us how to do it: we knew nothing about it; and neither did the Servians. Egad, there'd have been no war without them.

Raina. Are there many Swiss officers in the Servian Army?

Petkoff. No—all Austrians, just as our officers were all Russians. This was the only Swiss I came across. I'll never trust a Swiss again. He cheated us—humbugged us into giving him fifty able bodied men for two hundred confounded worn out chargers. They weren't even eatable!

Sergius. We were two children in the hands of that consummate soldier, Major: simply two innocent little children.

Raina. What was he like?

Catherine. Oh, Raina, what a silly question!

Sergius. He was like a commercial traveller in uniform. Bourgeois to his boots.

Petkoff [*grinning*]. Sergius: tell Catherine that queer story his friend told us about him—how he escaped after Slivnitza. You remember?—about his being hid by two women.

Sergius [*with bitter irony*]. Oh, yes, quite a romance. He was serving in the very battery I so unprofessionally charged. Being a thorough soldier, he ran away like the rest of them, with our cavalry at his heels. To escape their attentions, he had the good taste to take refuge in the chamber of some patriotic young Bulgarian lady. The young lady was enchanted by his persuasive commercial traveller's manners. She very modestly entertained him for an hour or so and then called in her mother lest her conduct should appear unmaidenly. The old lady was equally fascinated; and the fugitive was sent on his way in the morning, disguised in an old coat belonging to the master of the house, who was away at the war.

Raina [*rising with marked stateliness*]. Your life in the camp has made you coarse, Sergius. I did not think you would have repeated such a story before me. [*She turns away coldly.*]

Catherine [*also rising*]. She is right, Sergius. If such women exist, we should be spared the knowledge of them.

Petkoff. Pooh! nonsense! what does it matter?

Sergius [*ashamed*]. No, Petkoff: I was wrong. [*To Raina, with earnest humility.*] I beg your pardon. I have behaved abominably. Forgive me, Raina. [*She bows reservedly.*] And you, too, madam. [*Catherine bows graciously and sits down. He proceeds solemnly, again addressing Raina.*] The glimpses I have had of the seamy side of life during the last few months have made me cynical; but I should not have brought my cynicism here—least of all into your presence, Raina. I—[*Here, turning to the others, he is evidently about to begin a long speech when the Major interrupts him.*]

Petkoff. Stuff and nonsense, Sergius. That's quite enough fuss about nothing: a soldier's daughter should be able to stand up without flinching to a little strong conversation. [*He rises.*] Come: it's time for us to get to business. We have to make up our minds how those three regiments are to get back to Phillipopolis:— there's no forage for them on the Sophia route. [*He goes towards the house.*] Come along. [*Sergius is about to follow him when Catherine rises and intervenes.*]

Catherine. Oh, Paul, can't you spare Sergius for a few moments? Raina has hardly seen him yet. Perhaps I can help you to settle about the regiments.

Sergius [*protesting*]. My dear madam, impossible: you—

Catherine [*stopping him playfully*]. You stay here, my dear Sergius: there's no hurry. I have a word or two to say to Paul. [*Sergius instantly bows and steps back.*] Now, dear [*taking Petkoff's arm*], come and see the electric bell.

Petkoff. Oh, very well, very well. [*They go into the house together affectionately. Sergius, left alone with Raina, looks anxiously at her, fearing that she may be still offended. She smiles, and stretches out her arms to him.*]

Sergius [*hastening to her, but refraining from touching her without express permission*]. Am I forgiven?

Raina [*placing her hands on his shoulder as she looks up at him with admiration and worship*]. My hero! My king.

Sergius. My queen! [*He kisses her on the forehead with holy awe.*]

Raina. How I have envied you, Sergius! You have been out in the world, on the field of battle, able to prove yourself there worthy of any woman in the world; whilst I have had to sit at home inactive—dreaming —useless—doing nothing that could give me the right to call myself worthy of any man.

Sergius. Dearest, all my deeds have been yours. You inspired me. I have gone through the war like a knight in a tournament with his lady looking on at him!

Raina. And you have never been absent from my thoughts for a moment. [*Very solemnly.*] Sergius: I think we two have found the higher love. When I think of you, I feel that I could never do a base deed, or think an ignoble thought.

Sergius. My lady, and my saint! [*Clasping her reverently.*]

Raina [*returning his embrace*]. My lord and my g—

Sergius. Sh—sh! Let me be the worshipper, dear. You little know how unworthy even the best man is of a girl's pure passion!

Raina. I trust you. I love you. You will never disappoint me, Sergius. [*Louka is heard singing within the house. They quickly release each other.*] Hush! I can't pretend to talk indifferently before her: my heart is too full. [*Louka comes from the house with her tray. She goes to the table, and begins to clear it, with her back turned to them.*] I will go and get my hat; and then we can go out until lunch time. Wouldn't you like that?

Sergius. Be quick. If you are away five minutes, it will seem five hours. [*Raina runs to the top of the steps and turns there to exchange a look with him and wave him a kiss with both hands. He looks after her with emotion for a moment, then turns slowly away, his face radiant with the exultation of the scene which has just passed. The movement shifts his field of vision, into the corner of which there now comes the tail of Louka's double apron. His eye gleams at once. He takes a stealthy look at her, and begins to twirl his moustache nervously, with his left hand akimbo on his hip. Finally, striking the ground with his heels in something of a cavalry swagger, he strolls over to the left of the table, opposite her, and says*] Louka: do you know what the higher love is?

Louka [*astonished*]. No, sir.

Sergius. Very fatiguing thing to keep up for any length of time, Louka. One feels the need of some relief after it.

Louka [*innocently*]. Perhaps you would like some coffee, sir? [*She stretches her hand across the table for the coffee pot.*]

Sergius [*taking her hand*]. Thank you, Louka.

Louka [*pretending to pull*]. Oh, sir, you know I didn't mean that. I'm surprised at you!

Sergius [*coming clear of the table and drawing her with him*]. I am surprised at myself, Louka. What would Sergius, the hero of Slivnitza, say if he saw me now? What would Sergius, the apostle of the higher love, say if he saw me now? What would the half dozen Sergiuses who keep popping in and out of this handsome figure of mine say if they caught us here? [*Letting go her hand and slipping his arm dexterously round her waist.*] Do you consider my figure handsome, Louka?

Louka. Let me go, sir. I shall be disgraced. [*She struggles: he holds her inexorably.*] Oh, will you let go?

Sergius [*looking straight into her eyes*]. No.

Louka. Then stand back where we can't be seen. Have you no common sense?

Sergius. Ah, that's reasonable. [*He takes her into the stableyard gateway, where they are hidden from the house.*]

Louka [*complaining*]. I may have been seen from the

windows: Miss Raina is sure to be spying about after
you.

Sergius [*stung—letting her go*]. Take care, Louka. I may
be worthless enough to betray the higher love; but do
not you insult it.

Louka [*demurely*]. Not for the world, sir, I'm sure. May
I go on with my work please, now?

Sergius [*again putting his arm round her*]. You are a
provoking little witch, Louka. If you were in love with
me, would you spy out of windows on me?

Louka. Well, you see, sir, since you say you are half a
dozen different gentlemen all at once, I should have a
great deal to look after.

Sergius [*charmed*]. Witty as well as pretty. [*He tries to
kiss her.*]

Louka [*avoiding him*]. No, I don't want your kisses.
Gentlefolk are all alike—you making love to me behind Miss Raina's back, and she doing the same
behind yours.

Sergius [*recoiling a step*]. Louka!

Louka. It shews how little you really care!

Sergius [*dropping his familiarity and speaking with freezing
politeness*]. If our conversation is to continue, Louka,
you will please remember that a gentleman does not
discuss the conduct of the lady he is engaged to with
her maid.

Louka. It's so hard to know what a gentleman considers
right. I thought from your trying to kiss me that you
had given up being so particular.

Sergius [*turning from her and striking his forehead as he
comes back into the garden from the gateway*]. Devil!
devil!

Louka. Ha! ha! I expect one of the six of you is very like
me, sir, though I am only Miss Raina's maid. [*She
goes back to her work at the table, taking no further
notice of him.*]

Sergius [*speaking to himself*]. Which of the six is the real
man?—that's the question that torments me. One of
them is a hero, another a buffoon, another a humbug,
another perhaps a bit of a blackguard. [*He pauses and
looks furtively at Louka, as he adds with deep bitter-
ness*] And one, at least, is a coward—jealous, like all
cowards. [*He goes to the table.*] Louka.

Louka. Yes?

Sergius. Who is my rival?

Louka. You shall never get that out of me, for love or money.

Sergius. Why?

Louka. Never mind why. Besides, you would tell that I told you; and I should lose my place.

Sergius [*holding out his right hand in affirmation*]. No; on the honor of a—[*He checks himself, and his hand drops nerveless as he concludes, sardonically*]—of a man capable of behaving as I have been behaving for the last five minutes. Who is he?

Louka. I don't know. I never saw him. I only heard his voice through the door of her room.

Sergius. Damnation! How dare you?

Louka [*retreating*]. Oh, I mean no harm: you've no right to take up my words like that. The mistress knows all about it. And I tell you that if that gentleman ever comes here again, Miss Raina will marry him, whether he likes it or not. I know the difference between the sort of manner you and she put on before one another and the real manner. [*Sergius shivers as if she had stabbed him. Then, setting his face like iron, he strides grimly to her, and grips her above the elbows with both hands.*]

Sergius. Now listen you to me!

Louka [*wincing*]. Not so tight: you're hurting me!

Sergius. That doesn't matter. You have stained my honor by making me a party to your eavesdropping. And you have betrayed your mistress—

Louka [*writhing*]. Please—

Sergius. That shews that you are an abominable little clod of common clay, with the soul of a servant. [*He lets her go as if she were an unclean thing, and turns away, dusting his hands of her, to the bench by the wall, where he sits down with averted head, meditating gloomily.*]

Louka [*whimpering angrily with her hands up her sleeves, feeling her bruised arms*]. You know how to hurt with your tongue as well as with your hands. But I don't care, now I've found out that whatever clay I'm made of, you're made of the same. As for her, she's a liar; and her fine airs are a cheat; and I'm worth six of

her. [*She shakes the pain off hardily; tosses her head;
and sets to work to put the things on the tray. He
looks doubtfully at her once or twice. She finishes
packing the tray, and laps the cloth over the edges,
so as to carry all out together. As she stoops to lift
it, he rises.*]

Sergius. Louka! [*She stops and looks defiantly at him with
the tray in her hands.*] A gentleman has no right to
hurt a woman under any circumstances. [*With profound humility, uncovering his head.*] I beg your
pardon.

Louka. That sort of apology may satisfy a lady. Of what
use is it to a servant?

Sergius [*thus rudely crossed in his chivalry, throws it off
with a bitter laugh and says slightingly*]. Oh, you wish
to be paid for the hurt? [*He puts on his shako, and
takes some money from his pocket.*]

Louka [*her eyes filling with tears in spite of herself*]. No,
I want my hurt made well.

Sergius [*sobered by her tone*]. How?

[*She rolls up her left sleeve; clasps her arm with the thumb
and fingers of her right hand; and looks down at the
bruise. Then she raises her head and looks straight at
him. Finally, with a superb gesture she presents her
arm to be kissed. Amazed, he looks at her; at the arm;
at her again; hesitates; and then, with shuddering intensity, exclaims*] Never! [*and gets away as far as
possible from her. Her arm drops. Without a word,
and with unaffected dignity, she takes her tray, and is
approaching the house when Raina returns wearing a
hat and jacket in the height of the Vienna fashion of
the previous year, 1885. Louka makes way proudly
for her, and then goes into the house.*]

Raina. I'm ready! What's the matter? [*Gaily.*] Have you
been flirting with Louka?

Sergius [*hastily*]. No, no. How can you think such a thing?

Raina [*ashamed of herself*]. Forgive me, dear: it was only
a jest. I am so happy to-day.

[*He goes quickly to her, and kisses her hand remorsefully.
Catherine comes out and calls to them from the top of
the steps.*]

Catherine [*coming down to them*]. I am sorry to disturb
you, children; but Paul is distracted over those three

regiments. He does not know how to get them to Phillipopolis; and he objects to every suggestion of mine. You must go and help him, Sergius. He is in the library.

Raina [*disappointed*]. But we are just going out for a walk.

Sergius. I shall not be long. Wait for me just five minutes. [*He runs up the steps to the door.*]

Raina [*following him to the foot of the steps and looking up at him with timid coquetry*]. I shall go round and wait in full view of the library windows. Be sure you draw father's attention to me. If you are a moment longer than five minutes, I shall go in and fetch you, regiments or no regiments.

Sergius [*laughing*]. Very well. [*He goes in. Raina watches him until he is out of her sight. Then, with a perceptible relaxation of manner, she begins to pace up and down about the garden in a brown study.*]

Catherine. Imagine their meeting that Swiss and hearing the whole story! The very first thing your father asked for was the old coat we sent him off in. A nice mess you have got us into!

Raina [*gazing thoughtfully at the gravel as she walks*]. The little beast!

Catherine. Little beast! What little beast?

Raina. To go and tell! Oh, if I had him here, I'd stuff him with chocolate creams till he couldn't ever speak again!

Catherine. Don't talk nonsense. Tell me the truth, Raina. How long was he in your room before you came to me?

Raina [*whisking round and recommencing her march in the opposite direction*]. Oh, I forget.

Catherine. You cannot forget! Did he really climb up after the soldiers were gone, or was he there when that officer searched the room?

Raina. No. Yes, I think he must have been there then.

Catherine. You think! Oh, Raina, Raina! Will anything ever make you straightforward? If Sergius finds out, it is all over between you.

Raina [*with cool impertinence*]. Oh, I know Sergius is your pet. I sometimes wish you could marry him instead of me. You would just suit him. You would pet him, and spoil him, and mother him to perfection.

Catherine [*opening her eyes very widely indeed*]. Well,
upon my word!

Raina [*capriciously—half to herself*]. I always feel a
longing to do or say something dreadful to him—to
shock his propriety—to scandalize the five senses out
of him! [*To Catherine perversely*.] I don't care whether
he finds out about the chocolate cream soldier or not. I
half hope he may. [*She again turns flippantly away
and strolls up the path to the corner of the house*.]

Catherine. And what should I be able to say to your father,
pray?

Raina [*over her shoulder, from the top of the two steps*].
Oh, poor father! As if he could help himself! [*She
turns the corner and passes out of sight*.]

Catherine [*looking after her, her fingers itching*]. Oh,
if you were only ten years younger! [*Louka comes
from the house with a salver, which she carries hanging down by her side*.] Well?

Louka. There's a gentleman just called, madam—a Servian
officer—

Catherine [*flaming*]. A Servian! How dare he—[*Checking
herself bitterly*.] Oh, I forgot. We are at peace now. I
suppose we shall have them calling every day to pay
their compliments. Well, if he is an officer why don't
you tell your master? He is in the library with Major
Saranoff. Why do you come to me?

Louka. But he asks for you, madam. And I don't think
he knows who you are: he said the lady of the house.
He gave me this little ticket for you. [*She takes a
card out of her bosom; puts it on the salver and offers
it to Catherine*.]

Catherine [*reading*]. "Captain Bluntschli!" That's a German name.

Louka. Swiss, madam, I think.

Catherine [*with a bound that makes Louka jump back*].
Swiss! What is he like?

Louka [*timidly*]. He has a big carpet bag, madam.

Catherine. Oh, Heavens, he's come to return the coat!
Send him away—say we're not at home—ask him to
leave his address and I'll write to him—Oh, stop: that
will never do. Wait! [*She throws herself into a chair
to think it out. Louka waits*.] The master and Major
Saranoff are busy in the library, aren't they?

Louka. Yes, madam.

Catherine [*decisively*]. Bring the gentleman out here at once. [*Imperatively.*] And be very polite to him. Don't delay. Here [*impatiently snatching the salver from her*]: leave that here; and go straight back to him.

Louka. Yes, madam. [*Going.*]

Catherine. Louka!

Louka [*stopping*]. Yes, madam.

Catherine. Is the library door shut?

Louka. I think so, madam.

Catherine. If not, shut it as you pass through.

Louka. Yes, madam. [*Going.*]

Catherine. Stop! [*Louka stops.*] He will have to go out that way [*indicating the gate of the stable yard*]. Tell Nicola to bring his bag here after him. Don't forget.

Louka [*surprised*]. His bag?

Catherine. Yes, here, as soon as possible. [*Vehemently.*] Be quick! [*Louka runs into the house. Catherine snatches her apron off and throws it behind a bush. She then takes up the salver and uses it as a mirror, with the result that the handkerchief tied round her head follows the apron. A touch to her hair and a shake to her dressing gown makes her presentable.*] Oh, how—how—how can a man be such a fool! Such a moment to select! [*Louka appears at the door of the house, announcing "Captain Bluntschli;" and standing aside at the top of the steps to let him pass before she goes in again. He is the man of the adventure in Raina's room. He is now clean, well brushed, smartly uniformed, and out of trouble, but still unmistakably the same man. The moment Louka's back is turned, Catherine swoops on him with hurried, urgent, coaxing appeal.*] Captain Bluntschli, I am very glad to see you; but you must leave this house at once. [*He raises his eyebrows.*] My husband has just returned, with my future son-in-law; and they know nothing. If they did, the consequences would be terrible. You are a foreigner: you do not feel our national animosities as we do. We still hate the Servians: the only effect of the peace on my husband is to make him feel like a lion baulked of his prey. If he discovered our secret, he would never forgive me; and my daughter's life would hardly be safe. Will you, like the chivalrous gentleman and soldier you are, leave at once before he finds you here?

Bluntschli [*disappointed, but philosophical*]. At once, gracious lady. I only came to thank you and return the coat you lent me. If you will allow me to take it out of my bag and leave it with your servant as I pass out, I need detain you no further. [*He turns to go into the house.*]

Catherine [*catching him by the sleeve*]. Oh, you must not think of going back that way. [*Coaxing him across to the stable gates.*] This is the shortest way out. Many thanks. So glad to have been of service to you. Good-bye.

Bluntschli. But my bag?

Catherine. It will be sent on. You will leave me your address.

Bluntschli. True. Allow me. [*He takes out his card-case, and stops to write his address, keeping Catherine in an agony of impatience. As he hands her the card, Petkoff, hatless, rushes from the house in a fluster of hospitality, followed by Sergius.*]

Petkoff [*as he hurries down the steps*]. My dear Captain Bluntschli—

Catherine. Oh Heavens! [*She sinks on the seat against the wall.*]

Petkoff [*too preoccupied to notice her as he shakes Bluntschli's hand heartily*]. Those stupid people of mine thought I was out here, instead of in the—haw! —library. [*He cannot mention the library without betraying how proud he is of it.*] I saw you through the window. I was wondering why you didn't come in. Saranoff is with me: you remember him, don't you?

Sergius [*saluting humorously, and then offering his hand with great charm of manner*]. Welcome, our friend the enemy!

Petkoff. No longer the enemy, happily. [*Rather anxiously.*] I hope you've come as a friend, and not on business.

Catherine. Oh, quite as a friend, Paul. I was just asking Captain Bluntschli to stay to lunch; but he declares he must go at once.

Sergius [*sardonically*]. Impossible, Bluntschli. We want you here badly. We have to send on three cavalry regiments to Phillipopolis; and we don't in the least know how to do it.

Bluntschli [*suddenly attentive and business-like*]. Phillipopolis! The forage is the trouble, eh?

Petkoff [*eagerly*]. Yes, that's it. [*To Sergius.*] He sees the whole thing at once.

Bluntschli. I think I can shew you how to manage that.

Sergius. Invaluable man! Come along! [*Towering over Bluntschli, he puts his hand on his shoulder and takes him to the steps, Petkoff following. As Bluntschli puts his foot on the first step, Raina comes out of the house.*]

Raina [*completely losing her presence of mind*]. Oh, the chocolate cream soldier!

[*Bluntschli stands rigid. Sergius, amazed, looks at Raina, then at Petkoff, who looks back at him and then at his wife.*]

Catherine [*with commanding presence of mind*]. My dear Raina, don't you see that we have a guest here—Captain Bluntschli, one of our new Servian friends?

[*Raina bows; Bluntschli bows.*]

Raina. How silly of me! [*She comes down into the centre of the group, between Bluntschli and Petkoff.*] I made a beautiful ornament this morning for the ice pudding; and that stupid Nicola has just put down a pile of plates on it and spoiled it. [*To Bluntschli, winningly.*] I hope you didn't think that you were the chocolate cream soldier, Captain Bluntschli.

Bluntschli [*laughing*]. I assure you I did. [*Stealing a whimsical glance at her.*] Your explanation was a relief.

Petkoff [*suspiciously, to Raina*]. And since when, pray, have you taken to cooking?

Catherine. Oh, whilst you were away. It is her latest fancy.

Petkoff [*testily*]. And has Nicola taken to drinking? He used to be careful enough. First he shews Captain Bluntschli out here when he knew quite well I was in the—hum!—library; and then he goes downstairs and breaks Raina's chocolate soldier. He must—[*At this moment Nicola appears at the top of the steps R., with a carpet bag. He descends; places it respectfully before Bluntschli; and waits for further orders.*

*General amazement. Nicola, unconscious of the effect
he is producing, looks perfectly satisfied with himself.
When Petkoff recovers his power of speech, he breaks
out at him with]* Are you mad, Nicola?

Nicola [taken aback]. Sir?

Petkoff. What have you brought that for?

Nicola. My lady's orders, sir. Louka told me that—

Catherine [interrupting him]. My orders! Why should I
order you to bring Captain Bluntschli's luggage out
here? What are you thinking of, Nicola?

*Nicola [after a moment's bewilderment, picking up the
bag as he addresses Bluntschli with the very perfection
of servile discretion].* I beg your pardon, sir, I am
sure. *[To Catherine.]* My fault, madam! I hope you'll
overlook it! *[He bows, and is going to the steps with
the bag, when Petkoff addresses him angrily.]*

Petkoff. You'd better go and slam that bag, too, down
on Miss Raina's ice pudding! *[This is too much for
Nicola. The bag drops from his hands on Petkoff's
corns, eliciting a roar of anguish from him.]* Begone,
you butter-fingered donkey.

Nicola [snatching up the bag, and escaping into the house].
Yes, sir.

Catherine. Oh, never mind, Paul, don't be angry!

Petkoff [muttering]. Scoundrel. He's got out of hand while
I was away. I'll teach him. *[Recollecting his guest.]* Oh,
well, never mind. Come, Bluntschli, let's have no more
nonsense about you having to go away. You know
very well you're not going back to Switzerland yet.
Until you do go back you'll stay with us.

Raina. Oh, do, Captain Bluntschli.

Petkoff [to Catherine]. Now, Catherine, it's of you that
he's afraid. Press him and he'll stay.

Catherine. Of course I shall be only too delighted if *[ap-
pealingly]* Captain Bluntschli really wishes to stay.
He knows my wishes.

Bluntschli [in his driest military manner]. I am at madame's
orders.

Sergius [cordially]. That settles it!

Petkoff [heartily]. Of course!

Raina. You see, you must stay!

Bluntschli [smiling]. Well, if I must, I must!

[Gesture of despair from Catherine.]

In the library after lunch. It is not much of a library, its literary equipment consisting of a single fixed shelf stocked with old paper covered novels, broken backed, coffee stained, torn and thumbed, and a couple of little hanging shelves with a few gift books on them, the rest of the wall space being occupied by trophies of war and the chase. But it is a most comfortable sitting-room. A row of three large windows in the front of the house shew a mountain panorama, which is just now seen in one of its softest aspects in the mellowing afternoon light. In the left hand corner, a square earthenware stove, a perfect tower of colored pottery, rises nearly to the ceiling and guarantees plenty of warmth. The ottoman in the middle is a circular bank of decorated cushions, and the window seats are well upholstered divans. Little Turkish tables, one of them with an elaborate hookah on it, and a screen to match them, complete the handsome effect of the furnishing. There is one object, however, which is hopelessly out of keeping with its surroundings. This is a small kitchen table, much the worse for wear, fitted as a writing table with an old canister full of pens, an eggcup filled with ink, and a deplorable scrap of severely used pink blotting paper.

At the side of this table, which stands on the right, Bluntschli is hard at work, with a couple of maps before him, writing orders. At the head of it sits Sergius, who is also supposed to be at work, but who is actually gnawing the feather of a pen, and contemplating Bluntschli's quick, sure, business-like progress with a mixture of envious irritation at his own incapacity, and awestruck wonder at an ability which seems to him almost miraculous, though its prosaic character forbids him to esteem it. The major is comfortably established on the ottoman, with a newspaper in his hand and the tube of the hookah within his reach.

Catherine sits at the stove, with her back to them, embroidering. Raina, reclining on the divan under the left hand window, is gazing in a daydream out at the Balkan landscape, with a neglected novel in her lap.

The door is on the left. The button of the electric bell is between the door and the fireplace.

Petkoff [*looking up from his paper to watch how they are getting on at the table*]. Are you sure I can't help you in any way, Bluntschli?

Bluntschli [*without interrupting his writing or looking up*]. Quite sure, thank you. Saranoff and I will manage it.

Sergius [*grimly*]. Yes: we'll manage it. He finds out what to do; draws up the orders; and I sign 'em. Division of labour, Major. [*Bluntschli passes him a paper.*] Another one? Thank you. [*He plants the papers squarely before him; sets his chair carefully parallel to them; and signs with the air of a man resolutely performing a difficult and dangerous feat.*] This hand is more accustomed to the sword than to the pen.

Petkoff. It's very good of you, Bluntschli, it is indeed, to let yourself be put upon in this way. Now are you quite sure I can do nothing?

Catherine [*in a low, warning tone*]. You can stop interrupting, Paul.

Petkoff [*starting and looking round at her*]. Eh? Oh! Quite right, my love, quite right. [*He takes his newspaper up, but lets it drop again.*] Ah, you haven't been campaigning, Catherine: you don't know how pleasant it is for us to sit here, after a good lunch, with nothing to do but enjoy ourselves. There's only one thing I want to make me thoroughly comfortable.

Catherine. What is that?

Petkoff. My old coat. I'm not at home in this one: I feel as if I were on parade.

Catherine. My dear Paul, how absurd you are about that old coat! It must be hanging in the blue closet where you left it.

Petkoff. My dear Catherine, I tell you I've looked there. Am I to believe my own eyes or not? [*Catherine quietly rises and presses the button of the electric bell by the fireplace.*] What are you shewing off that bell for? [*She looks at him majestically, and silently re-*

sumes her chair and her needlework.] My dear: if
you think the obstinacy of your sex can make a coat
out of two old dressing gowns of Raina's, your water-
proof, and my mackintosh, you're mistaken. That's
exactly what the blue closet contains at present.
[*Nicola presents himself.*]

Catherine [*unmoved by Petkoff's sally.*] Nicola: go to the
blue closet and bring your master's old coat here—
the braided one he usually wears in the house.

Nicola. Yes, madam. [*Nicola goes out.*] ·

Petkoff. Catherine.

Catherine. Yes, Paul?

Petkoff. I bet you any piece of jewellery you like to order
from Sophia against a week's housekeeping money,
that the coat isn't there.

Catherine. Done, Paul.

Petkoff [*excited by the prospect of a gamble*]. Come:
here's an opportunity for some sport. Who'll bet on it?
Bluntschli: I'll give you six to one.

Bluntschli [*imperturbably*]. It would be robbing you, Major.
Madame is sure to be right. [*Without looking up, he
passes another batch of papers to Sergius.*]

Sergius [*also excited*]. Bravo, Switzerland! Major: I bet
my best charger against an Arab mare for Raina that
Nicola finds the coat in the blue closet.

Petkoff [*eagerly*]. Your best char—

Catherine [*hastily interrupting him*]. Don't be foolish,
Paul. An Arabian mare will cost you 50,000 levas.

Raina [*suddenly coming out of her picturesque revery*].
Really, mother, if you are going to take the jewellery,
I don't see why you should grudge me my Arab.

[*Nicola comes back with the coat and brings it to Petkoff,
who can hardly believe his eyes.*]

Catherine. Where was it, Nicola?

Nicola. Hanging in the blue closet, madam.

Petkoff. Well, I am d—

Catherine [*stopping him*]. Paul!

Petkoff. I could have sworn it wasn't there. Age is beginning to tell on me. I'm getting hallucinations. [*To
Nicola.*] Here: help me to change. Excuse me, Bluntschli. [*He begins changing coats, Nicola acting as
valet.*] Remember: I didn't take that bet of yours,
Sergius. You'd better give Raina that Arab steed your-

self, since you've roused her expectations. Eh, Raina?
[*He looks round at her; but she is again rapt in the
landscape. With a little gush of paternal affection and
pride, he points her out to them and says*] She's dreaming, as usual.

Sergius. Assuredly she shall not be the loser.

Petkoff. So much the better for her. *I* shan't come off so
cheap, I expect. [*The change is now complete. Nicola
goes out with the discarded coat.*] Ah, now I feel at
home at last. [*He sits down and takes his newspaper
with a grunt of relief.*]

Bluntschli [*to Sergius, handing a paper*]. That's the last
order.

Petkoff [*jumping up*]. What! finished?

Bluntschli. Finished. [*Petkoff goes beside Sergius; looks
curiously over his left shoulder as he signs; and says
with childlike envy*] Haven't you anything for me to
sign?

Bluntschli. Not necessary. His signature will do.

Petkoff. Ah, well, I think we've done a thundering good
day's work. [*He goes away from the table.*] Can I do
anything more?

Bluntschli. You had better both see the fellows that are to
take these. [*To Sergius.*] Pack them off at once; and
shew them that I've marked on the orders the time
they should hand them in by. Tell them that if they
stop to drink or tell stories—if they're five minutes
late, they'll have the skin taken off their backs.

Sergius [*rising indignantly*]. I'll say so. And if one of them
is man enough to spit in my face for insulting him,
I'll buy his discharge and give him a pension. [*He
strides out, his humanity deeply outraged.*]

Bluntschli [*confidentially*]. Just see that he talks to them
properly, Major, will you?

Petkoff [*officiously*]. Quite right, Bluntschli, quite right.
I'll see to it. [*He goes to the door importantly, but
hesitates on the threshold.*] By the bye, Catherine,
you may as well come, too. They'll be far more
frightened of you than of me.

Catherine [*putting down her embroidery*]. I daresay I had
better. You will only splutter at them. [*She goes out,
Petkoff holding the door for her and following her.*]

Bluntschli. What a country! They make cannons out of

cherry trees; and the officers send for their wives to keep discipline! [*He begins to fold and docket the papers. Raina, who has risen from the divan, strolls down the room with her hands clasped behind her, and looks mischievously at him.*]

Raina. You look ever so much nicer than when we last met. [*He looks up, surprised.*] What have you done to yourself?

Bluntschli. Washed; brushed; good night's sleep and breakfast. That's all.

Raina. Did you get back safely that morning?

Bluntschli. Quite, thanks.

Raina. Were they angry with you for running away from Sergius's charge?

Bluntschli. No, they were glad; because they'd all just run away themselves.

Raina [*going to the table, and leaning over it towards him*]. It must have made a lovely story for them—all that about me and my room.

Bluntschli. Capital story. But I only told it to one of them —a particular friend.

Raina. On whose discretion you could absolutely rely?

Bluntschli. Absolutely.

Raina. Hm! He told it all to my father and Sergius the day you exchanged the prisoners. [*She turns away and strolls carelessly across to the other side of the room.*]

Bluntschli [*deeply concerned and half incredulous*]. No! you don't mean that, do you?

Raina [*turning, with sudden earnestness*]. I do indeed. But they don't know that it was in this house that you hid. If Sergius knew, he would challenge you and kill you in a duel.

Bluntschli. Bless me! then don't tell him.

Raina [*full of reproach for his levity*]. Can you realize what it is to me to deceive him? I want to be quite perfect with Sergius—no meanness, no smallness, no deceit. My relation to him is the one really beautiful and noble part of my life. I hope you can understand that.

Bluntschli [*sceptically*]. You mean that you wouldn't like him to find out that the story about the ice pudding was a—a—a—You know.

Raina [*wincing*]. Ah, don't talk of it in that flippant way.
I lied: I know it. But I did it to save your life. He
would have killed you. That was the second time I
ever uttered a falsehood. [*Bluntschli rises quickly and
looks doubtfully and somewhat severely at her.*] Do
you remember the first time?

Bluntschli. I! No. Was I present?

Raina. Yes; and I told the officer who was searching for
you that you were not present.

Bluntschli. True. I should have remembered it.

Raina [*greatly encouraged*]. Ah, it is natural that you
should forget it first. It cost you nothing: it cost me
a lie!—a lie!! [*She sits down on the ottoman, looking
straight before her with her hands clasped on her
knee. Bluntschli, quite touched, goes to the ottoman
with a particularly reassuring and considerate air, and
sits down beside her.*]

Bluntschli. My dear young lady, don't let this worry you.
Remember: I'm a soldier. Now what are the two
things that happen to a soldier so often that he comes
to think nothing of them? One is hearing people tell
lies [*Raina recoils*]: the other is getting his life saved
in all sorts of ways by all sorts of people.

Raina [*rising in indignant protest*]. And so he becomes a
creature incapable of faith and of gratitude.

Bluntschli [*making a wry face*]. Do you like gratitude?
I don't. If pity is akin to love, gratitude is akin to the
other thing.

Raina. Gratitude! [*Turning on him.*] If you are incapable
of gratitude you are incapable of any noble sentiment.
Even animals are grateful. Oh, I see now exactly
what you think of me! You were not surprised to
hear me lie. To you it was something I probably did
every day—every hour. That is how men think of
women. [*She walks up the room melodramatically.*]

Bluntschli [*dubiously*]. There's reason in everything. You
said you'd told only two lies in your whole life. Dear
young lady: isn't that rather a short allowance? I'm
quite a straightforward man myself; but it wouldn't
last me a whole morning.

Raina [*staring haughtily at him*]. Do you know, sir, that
you are insulting me?

Bluntschli. I can't help it. When you get into that noble attitude and speak in that thrilling voice, I admire you; but I find it impossible to believe a single word you say.

Raina [*superbly*]. Captain Bluntschli!

Bluntschli [*unmoved*]. Yes?

Raina [*coming a little towards him, as if she could not believe her senses*]. Do you mean what you said just now? Do you know what you said just now?

Bluntschli. I do.

Raina [*gasping*]. I! I!!! [*She points to herself incredulously, meaning "I, Raina Petkoff, tell lies!" He meets her gaze unflinchingly. She suddenly sits down beside him, and adds, with a complete change of manner from the heroic to the familiar*] How did you find me out?

Bluntschli [*promptly*]. Instinct, dear young lady. Instinct, and experience of the world.

Raina [*wonderingly*]. Do you know, you are the first man I ever met who did not take me seriously?

Bluntschli. You mean, don't you, that I am the first man that has ever taken you quite seriously?

Raina. Yes, I suppose I do mean that. [*Cosily, quite at her ease with him.*] How strange it is to be talked to in such a way! You know, I've always gone on like that —I mean the noble attitude and the thrilling voice. I did it when I was a tiny child to my nurse. She believed in it. I do it before my parents. They believe in it. I do it before Sergius. He believes in it.

Bluntschli. Yes: he's a little in that line himself, isn't he?

Raina [*startled*]. Do you think so?

Bluntschli. You know him better than I do.

Raina. I wonder—I wonder is he? If I thought that—! [*Discouraged.*] Ah, well, what does it matter? I suppose, now that you've found me out, you despise me.

Bluntschli [*warmly, rising*]. No, my dear young lady, no, no, no a thousand times. It's part of your youth—part of your charm. I'm like all the rest of them—the nurse —your parents—Sergius: I'm your infatuated admirer.

Raina [*pleased*]. Really?

Bluntschli [*slapping his breast smartly with his hand, German fashion*]. Hand aufs Herz! Really and truly.

Raina [*very happy*]. But what did you think of me for giving you my portrait?

Bluntschli [*astonished*]. Your portrait! You never gave me your portrait.

Raina [*quickly*]. Do you mean to say you never got it?

Bluntschli. No. [*He sits down beside her, with renewed interest, and says, with some complacency*] When did you send it to me?

Raina [*indignantly*]. I did not send it to you. [*She turns her head away, and adds, reluctantly*] It was in the pocket of that coat.

Bluntschli [*pursing his lips and rounding his eyes*]. Oh-o-oh! I never found it. It must be there still.

Raina [*springing up*]. There still!—for my father to find the first time he puts his hand in his pocket! Oh, how could you be so stupid?

Bluntschli [*rising also*]. It doesn't matter: it's only a photograph: how can he tell who it was intended for? Tell him he put it there himself.

Raina [*impatiently*]. Yes, that is so clever—so clever! What shall I do?

Bluntschli. Ah, I see. You wrote something on it. That was rash!

Raina [*annoyed almost to tears*]. Oh, to have done such a thing for you, who care no more—except to laugh at me—oh! Are you sure nobody has touched it?

Bluntschli. Well, I can't be quite sure. You see I couldn't carry it about with me all the time: one can't take much luggage on active service.

Raina. What did you do with it?

Bluntschli. When I got through to Peerot I had to put it in safe keeping somehow. I thought of the railway cloak room; but that's the surest place to get looted in modern warfare. So I pawned it.

Raina. Pawned it!!!

Bluntschli. I know it doesn't sound nice; but it was much the safest plan. I redeemed it the day before yesterday. Heaven only knows whether the pawnbroker cleared out the pockets or not.

Raina [*furious—throwing the words right into his face*]. You have a low, shopkeeping mind. You think of things that would never come into a gentleman's head.

Bluntschli [*phlegmatically*]. That's the Swiss national character, dear lady.

Raina. Oh, I wish I had never met you. [*She flounces away and sits at the window fuming.*]

[*Louka comes in with a heap of letters and telegrams on her salver, and crosses, with her bold, free gait, to the table. Her left sleeve is looped up to the shoulder with a brooch, shewing her naked arm, with a broad gilt bracelet covering the bruise.*]

Louka [*to Bluntschli*]. For you. [*She empties the salver recklessly on the table.*] The messenger is waiting. [*She is determined not to be civil to a Servian, even if she must bring him his letters.*]

Bluntschli [*to Raina*]. Will you excuse me: the last postal delivery that reached me was three weeks ago. These are the subsequent accumulations. Four telegrams—a week old. [*He opens one.*] Oho! Bad news!

Raina [*rising and advancing a little remorsefully*]. Bad news?

Bluntschli. My father's dead. [*He looks at the telegram with his lips pursed, musing on the unexpected change in his arrangements.*]

Raina. Oh, how very sad!

Bluntschli. Yes: I shall have to start for home in an hour. He has left a lot of big hotels behind him to be looked after. [*Takes up a heavy letter in a long blue envelope.*] Here's a whacking letter from the family solicitor. [*He pulls out the enclosures and glances over them.*] Great Heavens! Seventy! Two hundred! [*In a crescendo of dismay.*] Four hundred! Four thousand!! Nine thousand six hundred!!! What on earth shall I do with them all?

Raina [*timidly*]. Nine thousand hotels?

Bluntschli. Hotels! Nonsense. If you only knew!—oh, it's too ridiculous! Excuse me: I must give my fellow orders about starting. [*He leaves the room hastily, with the documents in his hand.*]

Louka [*tauntingly*]. He has not much heart, that Swiss, though he is so fond of the Servians. He has not a word of grief for his poor father.

Raina [*bitterly*]. Grief!—a man who has been doing nothing but killing people for years! What does he care? What does any soldier care? [*She goes to the door, evidently restraining her tears with difficulty.*]

Louka. Major Saranoff has been fighting, too; and he has

plenty of heart left. [*Raina, at the door, looks haughtily at her and goes out.*] Aha! I thought you wouldn't get much feeling out of your soldier. [*She is following Raina when Nicola enters with an armful of logs for the fire.*]

Nicola [*grinning amorously at her*]. I've been trying all the afternoon to get a minute alone with you, my girl. [*His countenance changes as he notices her arm.*] Why, what fashion is that of wearing your sleeve, child?

Louka [*proudly*]. My own fashion.

Nicola. Indeed! If the mistress catches you, she'll talk to you. [*He throws the logs down on the ottoman, and sits comfortably beside them.*]

Louka. Is that any reason why you should take it on yourself to talk to me?

Nicola. Come: don't be so contrary with me. I've some good news for you. [*He takes out some paper money. Louka, with an eager gleam in her eyes, comes close to look at it.*] See, a twenty leva bill! Sergius gave me that out of pure swagger. A fool and his money are soon parted. There's ten levas more. The Swiss gave me that for backing up the mistress's and Raina's lies about him. He's no fool, he isn't. You should have heard old Catherine downstairs as polite as you please to me, telling me not to mind the Major being a little impatient; for they knew what a good servant I was—after making a fool and a liar of me before them all! The twenty will go to our savings; and you shall have the ten to spend if you'll only talk to me so as to remind me I'm a human being. I get tired of being a servant occasionally.

Louka [*scornfully*]. Yes: sell your manhood for thirty levas, and buy me for ten! Keep your money. You were born to be a servant. I was not. When you set up your shop you will only be everybody's servant instead of somebody's servant.

Nicola [*picking up his logs, and going to the stove*]. Ah, wait till you see. We shall have our evenings to ourselves; and I shall be master in my own house, I promise you. [*He throws the logs down and kneels at the stove.*]

Louka. You shall never be master in mine. [*She sits down on Sergius's chair.*]

Nicola [*turning, still on his knees, and squatting down rather forlornly, on his calves, daunted by her implacable disdain*]. You have a great ambition in you, Louka. Remember: if any luck comes to you, it was I that made a woman of you.

Louka. You!

Nicola [*with dogged self-assertion*]. Yes, me. Who was it made you give up wearing a couple of pounds of false black hair on your head and reddening your lips and cheeks like any other Bulgarian girl? I did. Who taught you to trim your nails, and keep your hands clean, and be dainty about yourself, like a fine Russian lady? Me! do you hear that? me! [*She tosses her head defiantly; and he rises, ill-humoredly, adding more coolly*] I've often thought that if Raina were out of the way, and you just a little less of a fool and Sergius just a little more of one, you might come to be one of my grandest customers, instead of only being my wife and costing me money.

Louka. I believe you would rather be my servant than my husband. You would make more out of me. Oh, I know that soul of yours.

Nicola [*going up close to her for greater emphasis*]. Never you mind my soul; but just listen to my advice. If you want to be a lady, your present behaviour to me won't do at all, unless when we're alone. It's too sharp and impudent; and impudence is a sort of familiarity: it shews affection for me. And don't you try being high and mighty with me either. You're like all country girls: you think it's genteel to treat a servant the way I treat a stable-boy. That's only your ignorance; and don't you forget it. And don't be so ready to defy everybody. Act as if you expected to have your own way, not as if you expected to be ordered about. The way to get on as a lady is the same as the way to get on as a servant: you've got to know your place; that's the secret of it. And you may depend on me to know my place if you get promoted. Think over it, my girl. I'll stand by you: one servant should always stand by another.

Louka [*rising impatiently*]. Oh, I must behave in my own way. You take all the courage out of me with your cold-blooded wisdom. Go and put those logs on the fire: that's the sort of thing you understand. [*Before Nicola can retort, Sergius comes in. He checks himself a moment on seeing Louka; then goes to the stove.*]

Sergius [*to Nicola*]. I am not in the way of your work, I hope.

Nicola [*in a smooth, elderly manner*]. Oh, no, sir, thank you kindly. I was only speaking to this foolish girl about her habit of running up here to the library whenever she gets a chance, to look at the books. That's the worst of her education, sir: it gives her habits above her station. [*To Louka.*] Make that table tidy, Louka, for the Major. [*He goes out sedately.*]

[*Louka, without looking at Sergius, begins to arrange the papers on the table. He crosses slowly to her, and studies the arrangement of her sleeve reflectively.*]

Sergius. Let me see: is there a mark there? [*He turns up the bracelet and sees the bruise made by his grasp. She stands motionless, not looking at him: fascinated, but on her guard.*] Ffff! Does it hurt?

Louka. Yes.

Sergius. Shall I cure it?

Louka [*instantly withdrawing herself proudly, but still not looking at him*]. No. You cannot cure it now.

Sergius [*masterfully*]. Quite sure? [*He makes a movement as if to take her in his arms.*]

Louka. Don't trifle with me, please. An officer should not trifle with a servant.

Sergius [*touching the arm with a merciless stroke of his forefinger*]. That was no trifle, Louka.

Louka. No. [*Looking at him for the first time.*] Are you sorry?

Sergius [*with measured emphasis, folding his arms*]. I am never sorry.

Louka [*wistfully*]. I wish I could believe a man could be so unlike a woman as that. I wonder are you really a brave man?

Sergius [*unaffectedly, relaxing his attitude*]. Yes: I am a brave man. My heart jumped like a woman's at the

first shot; but in the charge I found that I was brave.
Yes: that at least is real about me.

Louka. Did you find in the charge that the men whose
fathers are poor like mine were any less brave than
the men who are rich like you?

Sergius [*with bitter levity*]. Not a bit. They all slashed
and cursed and yelled like heroes. Psha! the courage
to rage and kill is cheap. I have an English bull ter-
rier who has as much of that sort of courage as the
whole Bulgarian nation, and the whole Russian nation
at its back. But he lets my groom thrash him, all the
same. That's your soldier all over! No, Louka, your
poor men can cut throats; but they are afraid of their
officers; they put up with insults and blows; they stand
by and see one another punished like children—aye,
and help to do it when they are ordered. And the
officers!—well [*with a short, bitter laugh*] I am an
officer. Oh [*fervently*] give me the man who will defy
to the death any power on earth or in heaven that sets
itself up against his own will and conscience: he alone
is the brave man.

Louka. How easy it is to talk! Men never seem to me to
grow up: they all have schoolboy's ideas. You don't
know what true courage is.

Sergius [*ironically*]. Indeed! I am willing to be instructed.

Louka. Look at me! how much am I allowed to have my
own will? I have to get your room ready for you—to
sweep and dust, to fetch and carry. How could that
degrade me if it did not degrade you to have it done
for you? But [*with subdued passion*] if I were Empress of Russia, above everyone in the world, then—
ah, then, though according to you I could shew no
courage at all; you should see, you should see.

Sergius. What would you do, most noble Empress?

Louka. I would marry the man I loved, which no other
queen in Europe has the courage to do. If I loved
you, though you would be as far beneath me as I am
beneath you, I would dare to be the equal of my
inferior. Would you dare as much if you loved me?
No: if you felt the beginnings of love for me you
would not let it grow. You dare not: you would marry
a rich man's daughter because you would be afraid
of what other people would say of you.

Sergius [*carried away*]. You lie: it is not so, by all the stars! If I loved you, and I were the Czar himself, I would set you on the throne by my side. You know that I love another woman, a woman as high above you as heaven is above earth. And you are jealous of her.

Louka. I have no reason to be. She will never marry you now. The man I told you of has come back. She will marry the Swiss.

Sergius [*recoiling*]. The Swiss!

Louka. A man worth ten of you. Then you can come to me; and I will refuse you. You are not good enough for me. [*She turns to the door.*]

Sergius [*springing after her and catching her fiercely in his arms*]. I will kill the Swiss; and afterwards I will do as I please with you.

Louka [*in his arms, passive and steadfast*]. The Swiss will kill you, perhaps. He has beaten you in love. He may beat you in war.

Sergius [*tormentedly*]. Do you think I believe that she —she! whose worst thoughts are higher than your best ones, is capable of trifling with another man behind my back?

Louka. Do you think she would believe the Swiss if he told her now that I am in your arms?

Sergius [*releasing her in despair*]. Damnation! Oh, damnation! Mockery, mockery everywhere: everything I think is mocked by everything I do. [*He strikes himself frantically on the breast.*] Coward, liar, fool! Shall I kill myself like a man, or live and pretend to laugh at myself? [*She again turns to go.*] Louka! [*She stops near the door.*] Remember: you belong to me.

Louka [*quietly*]. What does that mean—an insult?

Sergius [*commandingly*]. It means that you love me, and that I have had you here in my arms, and will perhaps have you there again. Whether that is an insult I neither know nor care: take it as you please. But [*vehemently*] I will not be a coward and a trifler. If I choose to love you, I dare marry you, in spite of all Bulgaria. If these hands ever touch you again, they shall touch my affianced bride.

Louka. We shall see whether you dare keep your word. But take care. I will not wait long.

Sergius [*again folding his arms and standing motionless in the middle of the room*]. Yes, we shall see. And you shall wait my pleasure.

[*Bluntschli, much preoccupied, with his papers still in his hand, enters, leaving the door open for Louka to go out. He goes across to the table, glancing at her as he passes. Sergius, without altering his resolute attitude, watches him steadily. Louka goes out, leaving the door open.*]

Bluntschli [*absently, sitting at the table as before, and putting down his papers*]. That's a remarkable looking young woman.

Sergius [*gravely, without moving*]. Captain Bluntschli.

Bluntschli. Eh?

Sergius. You have deceived me. You are my rival. I brook no rivals. At six o'clock I shall be in the drilling-ground on the Klissoura road, alone, on horseback, with my sabre. Do you understand?

Bluntschli [*staring, but sitting quite at his ease*]. Oh, thank you: that's a cavalry man's proposal. I'm in the artillery; and I have the choice of weapons. If I go, I shall take a machine gun. And there shall be no mistake about the cartridges this time.

Sergius [*flushing, but with deadly coldness*]. Take care, sir. It is not our custom in Bulgaria to allow invitations of that kind to be trifled with.

Bluntschli [*warmly*]. Pooh! don't talk to me about Bulgaria. You don't know what fighting is. But have it your own way. Bring your sabre along. I'll meet you.

Sergius [*fiercely delighted to find his opponent a man of spirit*]. Well said, Switzer. Shall I lend you my best horse?

Bluntschli. No: damn your horse!—thank you all the same, my dear fellow. [*Raina comes in, and hears the next sentence.*] I shall fight you on foot. Horseback's too dangerous: I don't want to kill you if I can help it.

Raina [*hurrying forward anxiously*]. I have heard what Captain Bluntschli said, Sergius. You are going to fight. Why? [*Sergius turns away in silence, and goes to the stove, where he stands watching her as she continues, to Bluntschli*] What about?

Bluntschli. I don't know: he hasn't told me. Better not interfere, dear young lady. No harm will be done: I've often acted as sword instructor. He won't be able to touch me; and I'll not hurt him. It will save explanations. In the morning I shall be off home; and you'll never see me or hear of me again. You and he will then make it up and live happily ever after.

Raina [*turning away deeply hurt, almost with a sob in her voice*]. I never said I wanted to see you again.

Sergius [*striding forward*]. Ha! That is a confession.

Raina [*haughtily*]. What do you mean?

Sergius. You love that man!

Raina [*scandalized*]. Sergius!

Sergius. You allow him to make love to you behind my back, just as you accept me as your affianced husband behind his. Bluntschli: you knew our relations; and you deceived me. It is for that that I call you to account, not for having received favours that I never enjoyed.

Bluntschli [*jumping up indignantly*]. Stuff! Rubbish! I have received no favours. Why, the young lady doesn't even know whether I'm married or not.

Raina [*forgetting herself*]. Oh! [*Collapsing on the ottoman.*] Are you?

Sergius. You see the young lady's concern, Captain Bluntschli. Denial is useless. You have enjoyed the privilege of being received in her own room, late at night—

Bluntschli [*interrupting him pepperily*]. Yes; you blockhead! She received me with a pistol at her head. Your cavalry were at my heels. I'd have blown out her brains if she'd uttered a cry.

Sergius [*taken aback*]. Bluntschli! Raina: is this true?

Raina [*rising in wrathful majesty*]. Oh, how dare you, how dare you?

Bluntschli. Apologize, man, apologize! [*He resumes his seat at the table.*]

Sergius [*with the old measured emphasis, folding his arms*]. I never apologize.

Raina [*passionately*]. This is the doing of that friend of yours, Captain Bluntschli. It is he who is spreading this horrible story about me. [*She walks about excitedly.*]

Bluntschli. No: he's dead—burnt alive.

Raina [*stopping, shocked*]. Burnt alive!

Bluntschli. Shot in the hip in a wood-yard. Couldn't drag himself out. Your fellows' shells set the timber on fire and burnt him, with half a dozen other poor devils in the same predicament.

Raina. How horrible!

Sergius. And how ridiculous! Oh, war! war! the dream of patriots and heroes! A fraud, Bluntschli, a hollow sham, like love.

Raina [*outraged*]. Like love! You say that before me.

Bluntschli. Come, Saranoff: that matter is explained.

Sergius. A hollow sham, I say. Would you have come back here if nothing had passed between you, except at the muzzle of your pistol? Raina is mistaken about our friend who was burnt. He was not my informant.

Raina. Who then? [*Suddenly guessing the truth.*] Ah, Louka! my maid, my servant! You were with her this morning all that time after—after—Oh, what sort of god is this I have been worshipping! [*He meets her gaze with sardonic enjoyment of her disenchantment. Angered all the more, she goes closer to him, and says, in a lower, intenser tone*] Do you know that I looked out of the window as I went upstairs, to have another sight of my hero; and I saw something that I did not understand then. I know now that you were making love to her.

Sergius [*with grim humor*]. You saw that?

Raina. Only too well. [*She turns away, and throws herself on the divan under the centre window, quite overcome.*]

Sergius [*cynically*]. Raina: our romance is shattered. Life's a farce.

Bluntschli [*to Raina, goodhumoredly*]. You see: he's found himself out now.

Sergius. Bluntschli: I have allowed you to call me a blockhead. You may now call me a coward as well. I refuse to fight you. Do you know why?

Bluntschli. No; but it doesn't matter. I didn't ask the reason when you cried on; and I don't ask the reason now that you cry off. I'm a professional soldier. I fight when I have to, and am very glad to get out of it when I haven't to. You're only an amateur: you think fighting's an amusement.

Sergius. You shall hear the reason all the same, my pro-

fessional. The reason is that it takes two men—real
men—men of heart, blood and honor—to make a
genuine combat. I could no more fight with you
than I could make love to an ugly woman. You've no
magnetism: you're not a man, you're a machine.

Bluntschli [*apologetically*]. Quite true, quite true. I always
was that sort of chap. I'm very sorry. But now that
you've found that life isn't a farce, but something
quite sensible and serious, what further obstacle is
there to your happiness?

Raina [*rising*]. You are very solicitous about my happiness
and his. Do you forget his new love—Louka? It is not
you that he must fight now, but his rival, Nicola.

Sergius. Rival!! [*Striking his forehead.*]

Raina. Did you not know that they are engaged?

Sergius. Nicola! Are fresh abysses opening! Nicola!!

Raina [*sarcastically*]. A shocking sacrifice, isn't it? Such
beauty, such intellect, such modesty, wasted on a
middle-aged servant man! Really, Sergius, you cannot
stand by and allow such a thing. It would be unworthy of your chivalry.

Sergius [*losing all self-control*]. Viper! Viper! [*He rushes
to and fro, raging.*]

Bluntschli. Look here, Saranoff; you're getting the worst of
this.

Raina [*getting angrier*]. Do you realize what he has done,
Captain Bluntschli? He has set this girl as a spy on
us; and her reward is that he makes love to her.

Sergius. False! Monstrous!

Raina. Monstrous! [*Confronting him.*] Do you deny that
she told you about Captain Bluntschli being in my
room?

Sergius. No; but—

Raina [*interrupting*]. Do you deny that you were making
love to her when she told you?

Sergius. No; but I tell you—

Raina [*cutting him short contemptuously*]. It is unnecessary to tell us anything more. That is quite enough for
us. [*She turns her back on him and sweeps majestically
back to the window.*]

Bluntschli [*quietly, as Sergius, in an agony of mortification,
sinks on the ottoman, clutching his averted head be-*

tween his fists]. I told you you were getting the worst
of it, Saranoff.

Sergius. Tiger cat!

Raina [*running excitedly to Bluntschli*]. You hear this man
calling me names, Captain Bluntschli?

Bluntschli. What else can he do, dear lady? He must
defend himself somehow. Come [*very persuasively*],
don't quarrel. What good does it do? [*Raina, with a
gasp, sits down on the ottoman, and after a vain effort
to look vexedly at Bluntschli, she falls a victim to her
sense of humor, and is attacked with a disposition to
laugh.*]

Sergius. Engaged to Nicola! [*He rises.*] Ha! ha! [*Going to
the stove and standing with his back to it.*] Ah, well,
Bluntschli, you are right to take this huge imposture
of a world coolly.

Raina [*to Bluntschli with an intuitive guess at his state of
mind*]. I daresay you think us a couple of grown up
babies, don't you?

Sergius [*grinning a little*]. He does, he does. Swiss civilization nursetending Bulgarian barbarism, eh?

Bluntschli [*blushing*]. Not at all, I assure you. I'm only
very glad to get you two quieted. There now, let's be
pleasant and talk it over in a friendly way. Where
is this other young lady?

Raina. Listening at the door, probably.

Serguis [*shivering as if a bullet had struck him, and speaking with quiet but deep indignation*]. I will prove that
that, at least, is a calumny. [*He goes with dignity to
the door and opens it. A yell of fury bursts from him
as he looks out. He darts into the passage, and returns
dragging in Louka, whom he flings against the table,
R., as he cries*] Judge her, Bluntschli—you, the moderate, cautious man: judge the eavesdropper.

[*Louka stands her ground, proud and silent.*]

Bluntschli [*shaking his head*]. I mustn't judge her. I once
listened myself outside a tent when there was a mu-
tiny brewing. It's all a question of the degree of prov-
ocation. My life was at stake.

Louka. My love was at stake. [*Sergius flinches, ashamed of
her in spite of himself.*] I am not ashamed.

Raina [*contemptuously*]. Your love! Your curiosity, you
mean.

Louka [*facing her and retorting her contempt with interest*]. My love, stronger than anything you can feel, even for your chocolate cream soldier.

Sergius [*with quick suspicion—to Louka*]. What does that mean?

Louka [*fiercely*]. It means—

Sergius [*interrupting her slightingly*]. Oh, I remember, the ice pudding. A paltry taunt, girl.

[*Major Petkoff enters, in his shirtsleeves.*]

Petkoff. Excuse my shirtsleeves, gentlemen. Raina: somebody has been wearing that coat of mine: I'll swear it —somebody with bigger shoulders than mine. It's all burst open at the back. Your mother is mending it. I wish she'd make haste. I shall catch cold. [*He looks more attentively at them.*] Is anything the matter?

Raina. No. [*She sits down at the stove with a tranquil air.*]

Sergius. Oh, no! [*He sits down at the end of the table, as at first.*]

Bluntschli [*who is already seated*]. Nothing, nothing.

Petkoff [*sitting down on the ottoman in his old place*]. That's all right. [*He notices Louka.*] Anything the matter, Louka?

Louka. No, sir.

Petkoff [*genially*]. That's all right. [*He sneezes.*] Go and ask your mistress for my coat, like a good girl, will you? [*She turns to obey; but Nicola enters with the coat; and she makes a pretence of having business in the room by taking the little table with the hookah away to the wall near the windows.*]

Raina [*rising quickly, as she sees the coat on Nicola's arm*]. Here it is, papa. Give it to me, Nicola; and do you puts some more wood on the fire. [*She takes the coat, and brings it to the Major, who stands up to put it on. Nicola attends to the fire.*]

Petkoff [*to Raina, teasing her affectionately*]. Aha! Going to be very good to poor old papa just for one day after his return from the wars, eh?

Raina [*with solemn reproach*]. Ah, how can you say that to me, father?

Petkoff. Well, well, only a joke, little one. Come, give me a kiss. [*She kisses him.*] Now give me the coat.

Raina. Now, I am going to put it on for you. Turn your back. [*He turns his back and feels behind him with his arms for the sleeves. She dexterously takes the photograph from the pocket and throws it on the table before Bluntschli, who covers it with a sheet of paper under the very nose of Sergius, who looks on amazed, with his suspicions roused in the highest degree. She then helps Petkoff on with his coat.*] There, dear! Now are you comfortable?

Petkoff. Quite, little love. Thanks. [*He sits down; and Raina returns to her seat near the stove.*] Oh, by the bye, I've found something funny. What's the meaning of this? [*He puts his hand into the picked pocket.*] Eh? Hallo! [*He tries the other pocket.*] Well, I could have sworn—[*Much puzzled, he tries the breast pocket.*] I wonder—[*Tries the original pocket.*] Where can it—[*A light flashes on him; he rises, exclaiming*] Your mother's taken it.

Raina [*very red*]. Taken what?

Petkoff. Your photograph, with the inscription: "Raina, to her Chocolate Cream Soldier—a souvenir." Now you know there's something more in this than meets the eye; and I'm going to find it out. [*Shouting*] Nicola!

Nicola [*dropping a log, and turning*]. Sir!

Petkoff. Did you spoil any pastry of Miss Raina's this morning?

Nicola. You heard Miss Raina say that I did, sir.

Petkoff. I know that, you idiot. Was it true?

Nicola. I am sure Miss Raina is incapable of saying anything that is not true, sir.

Petkoff. Are you? Then I'm not. [*Turning to the others.*] Come: do you think I don't see it all? [*Goes to Sergius, and slaps him on the shoulder.*] Sergius: you're the chocolate cream soldier, aren't you?

Sergius [*starting up*]. I! a chocolate cream soldier! Certainly not.

Petkoff. Not! [*He looks at them. They are all very serious and very conscious.*] Do you mean to tell me that Raina sends photographic souvenirs to other men?

Sergius [*enigmatically*]. The world is not such an innocent place as we used to think, Petkoff.

Bluntschli [*rising*]. It's all right, Major. I'm the chocolate cream soldier. [*Petkoff and Sergius are equally
astonished.*] The gracious young lady saved my life
by giving me chocolate creams when I was starving—
shall I ever forget their flavour! My late friend Stolz
told you the story at Peerot. I was the fugitive.

Petkoff. You! [*He gasps.*] Sergius: do you remember how
those two women went on this morning when we
mentioned it? [*Sergius smiles cynically. Petkoff con-
fronts Raina severely.*] You're a nice young woman,
aren't you?

Raina [*bitterly*]. Major Saranoff has changed his mind.
And when I wrote that on the photograph, I did not
know that Captain Bluntschli was married.

Bluntschli [*much startled—protesting vehemently*]. I'm not
married.

Raina [*with deep reproach*]. You said you were.

Bluntschli. I did not. I positively did not. I never was
married in my life.

Petkoff [*exasperated*]. Raina: will you kindly inform me,
if I am not asking too much, which gentleman you
are engaged to?

Raina. To neither of them. This young lady [*introducing
Louka, who faces them all proudly*] is the object of
Major Saranoff's affections at present.

Petkoff. Louka! Are you mad, Sergius? Why, this girl's
engaged to Nicola.

Nicola [*coming forward*]. I beg your pardon sir. There
is a mistake. Louka is not engaged to me.

Petkoff. Not engaged to you, you scoundrel! Why, you
had twenty-five levas from me on the day of your betrothal; and she had that gilt bracelet from Miss Raina.

Nicola [*with cool unction*]. We gave it out so, sir. But
it was only to give Louka protection. She had a soul
above her station; and I have been no more than her
confidential servant. I intend, as you know, sir, to set
up a shop later on in Sofea; and I look forward to her
custom and recommendation should she marry into
the nobility. [*He goes out with impressive discretion,
leaving them all staring after him.*]

Petkoff [*breaking the silence*]. Well, I am—hm!

Sergius. This is either the finest heroism or the most crawl-
ing baseness. Which is it, Bluntschli?

Bluntschli. Never mind whether it's heroism or baseness. Nicola's the ablest man I've met in Bulgaria. I'll make him manager of a hotel if he can speak French and German.

Louka [*suddenly breaking out at Sergius*]. I have been insulted by everyone here. You set them the example. You owe me an apology. [*Sergius immediately, like a repeating clock of which the spring has been touched, begins to fold his arms.*]

Bluntschli [*before he can speak*]. It's no use. He never apologizes.

Louka. Not to you, his equal and his enemy. To me, his poor servant, he will not refuse to apologize.

Sergius [*approvingly*]. You are right. [*He bends his knee in his grandest manner.*] Forgive me!

Louka. I forgive you. [*She timidly gives him her hand, which he kisses.*] That touch makes me your affianced wife.

Sergius [*springing up*]. Ah, I forgot that!

Louka [*coldly*]. You can withdraw if you like.

Sergius. Withdraw! Never! You belong to me! [*He puts his arm about her and draws her to him.*]

[*Catherine comes in and finds Louka in Sergius's arms, and all the rest gazing at them in bewildered astonishment.*]

Catherine. What does this mean? [*Sergius releases Louka.*]

Petkoff. Well, my dear, it appears that Sergius is going to marry Louka instead of Raina. [*She is about to break out indignantly at him: he stops her by exclaiming testily*] Don't blame me: I've nothing to do with it. [*He retreats to the stove.*]

Catherine. Marry Louka! Sergius: you are bound by your word to us!

Sergius [*folding his arms*]. Nothing binds me.

Bluntschli [*much pleased by this piece of common sense*]. Saranoff: your hand. My congratulations. These heroics of yours have their practical side after all. [*To Louka.*] Gracious young lady: the best wishes of a good Republican! [*He kisses her hand, to Raina's great disgust.*]

Catherine [*threateningly*]. Louka: you have been telling stories.

Louka. I have done Raina no harm.

Catherine [*haughtily*]. Raina! [*Raina is equally indignant at the liberty.*]

Louka. I have a right to call her Raina: she calls me Louka. I told Major Saranoff she would never marry him if the Swiss gentleman came back.

Bluntschli [*surprised*]. Hallo!

Louka [*turning to Raina*]. I thought you were fonder of him than of Sergius. You know best whether I was right.

Bluntschli. What nonsense! I assure you, my dear Major, my dear Madame, the gracious young lady simply saved my life, nothing else. She never cared two straws for me. Why, bless my heart and soul, look at the young lady and look at me. She, rich, young, beautiful, with her imagination full of fairy princes and noble natures and cavalry charges and goodness knows what! And I, a commonplace Swiss soldier who hardly knows what a decent life is after fifteen years of barracks and battles—a vagabond—a man who has spoiled all his chances in life through an incurably romantic disposition—a man—

Sergius [*starting as if a needle had pricked him and interrupting Bluntschli in incredulous amazement*]. Excuse me, Bluntschli: what did you say had spoiled your chances in life?

Bluntschli [*promptly*]. An incurably romantic disposition. I ran away from home twice when I was a boy. I went into the army instead of into my father's business. I climbed the balcony of this house when a man of sense would have dived into the nearest cellar. I came sneaking back here to have another look at the young lady when any other man of my age would have sent the coat back—

Petkoff. My coat!

Bluntschli.—Yes: that's the coat I mean—would have sent it back and gone quietly home. Do you suppose I am the sort of fellow a young girl falls in love with? Why, look at our ages! I'm thirty-four: I don't suppose the young lady is much over seventeen. [*This estimate produces a marked sensation, all the rest turning and staring at one another. He proceeds innocently.*] All that adventure which was life or death to me, was only a schoolgirl's game to her—chocolate creams and hide and seek. Here's the proof! [*He takes the photograph from the table.*] Now, I ask you, would a woman who took the affair seriously have sent me this and written on it: "Raina, to her chocolate cream soldier—a souvenir"? [*He exhibits the photograph triumphantly, as if it settled the matter beyond all possibility of refutation.*]

Petkoff. That's what I was looking for. How the deuce did it get there?

Bluntschli [*to Raina complacently*]. I have put everything right, I hope, gracious young lady!

Raina [*in uncontrollable vexation*]. I quite agree with your account of yourself. You are a romantic idiot. [*Bluntschli is unspeakably taken aback.*] Next time I hope you will know the difference between a schoolgirl of seventeen and a woman of twenty-three.

Bluntschli [*stupefied*]. Twenty-three! [*She snaps the photograph contemptuously from his hand; tears it across; and throws the pieces at his feet.*]

Sergius [*with grim enjoyment of Bluntschli's discomfiture*]. Bluntschli: my one last belief is gone. Your sagacity is a fraud, like all the other things. You have less sense than even I have.

Bluntschli [*overwhelmed*]. Twenty-three! Twenty-three!! [*He considers.*] Hm! [*Swiftly making up his mind.*] In that case, Major Petkoff, I beg to propose formally to become a suitor for your daughter's hand, in place of Major Saranoff retired.

Raina. You dare!

Bluntschli. If you were twenty-three when you said those things to me this afternoon, I shall take them seriously.

Catherine [*loftily polite*]. I doubt, sir, whether you quite realize either my daughter's position or that of Major Sergius Saranoff, whose place you propose to take. The Petkoffs and the Saranoffs are known as the richest and most important families in the country. Our position is almost historical: we can go back for nearly twenty years.

Petkoff. Oh, never mind that, Catherine. [*To Bluntschli.*] We should be most happy, Bluntschli, if it were only a question of your position; but hang it, you know, Raina is accustomed to a very comfortable establishment. Sergius keeps twenty horses.

Bluntschli. But what on earth is the use of twenty horses?
Why, it's a circus.

Catherine [*severely*]. My daughter, sir, is accustomed to a
first-rate stable.

Raina. Hush, mother, you're making me ridiculous.

Bluntschli. Oh, well, if it comes to a question of an establishment, here goes! [*He goes impetuously to the
table and seizes the papers in the blue envelope.*] How
many horses did you say?

Sergius. Twenty, noble Switzer!

Bluntschli. I have two hundred horses. [*They are amazed.*]
How many carriages?

Sergius. Three.

Bluntschli. I have seventy. Twenty-four of them will hold
twelve inside, besides two on the box, without counting the driver and conductor. How many tablecloths
have you?

Sergius. How the deuce do I know?

Bluntschli. Have you four thousand?

Sergius. No.

Bluntschli. I have. I have nine thousand six hundred pairs
of sheets and blankets, with two thousand four hundred eider-down quilts. I have ten thousand knives
and forks, and the same quantity of dessert spoons. I
have six hundred servants. I have six palatial establish-
ments, besides two livery stables, a tea garden and a
private house. I have four medals for distinguished
services; I have the rank of an officer and the standing of a gentleman; and I have three native languages.
Show me any man in Bulgaria that can offer as much.

Petkoff [*with childish awe*]. Are you Emperor of Switzerland?

Bluntschli. My rank is the highest known in Switzerland:
I'm a free citizen.

Catherine. Then Captain Bluntschli, since you are my
daughter's choice, I shall not stand in the way of her
happiness. [*Petkoff is about to speak.*] That is Major
Petkoff's feeling also.

Petkoff. Oh, I shall be only too glad. Two hundred horses!
Whew!

Sergius. What says the lady?

Raina [*pretending to sulk*]. The lady says that he can keep his tablecloths and his omnibuses. I am not here to be sold to the highest bidder.

Bluntschli. I won't take that answer. I appealed to you as a fugitive, a beggar, and a starving man. You accepted me. You gave me your hand to kiss, your bed to sleep in, and your roof to shelter me—

Raina [*interrupting him*]. I did not give them to the Emperor of Switzerland!

Bluntschli. That's just what I say. [*He catches her hand quickly and looks her straight in the face as he adds, with confident mastery*] Now tell us who you did give them to.

Raina [*succumbing with a shy smile*]. To my chocolate cream soldier!

Bluntschli [*with a boyish laugh of delight*]. That'll do. Thank you. [*Looks at his watch and suddenly becomes businesslike.*] Time's up, Major. You've managed those regiments so well that you are sure to be asked to get rid of some of the Infantry of the Teemok division. Send them home by way of Lom Palanka. Saranoff: don't get married until I come back: I shall be here punctually at five in the evening on Tuesday fortnight. Gracious ladies—good evening. [*He makes them a military bow, and goes.*]

Sergius. What a man! What a man!

Oscar Wilde (1854–1900)
The Importance of Being Earnest

The Unimportance of Being Oscar

BY MARY MC CARTHY

One of Oscar Wilde's acquaintances wrote of him that he could never be quite a gentleman because he dressed too well and his manners were too polished. The same criticism can be made of his art. There is something *outré* in all of Wilde's work that makes one sympathize to a degree with the Marquess of Queensberry; this fellow is really insufferable. Oscar's real sin (and the one for which society punished him, homosexuality being merely the blotter charge) was making himself too much at home. This is as readily seen in his comedies as in his epigrammatic indorsement of socialism or his call on a Colorado coal mine. He was overly familiar with his subjects. Shaw said of him that he did not know enough about art to justify his parade of aestheticism. Certainly, he was not intimate enough with poverty to style himself an enemy of riches. In this light, the Marquess of Queensberry's libel, that he went about "posing" as a sodomist, speaks, in the plain man's language, the true word of damnation. In his comedies, it is his audience whose acquaintance he presumes on. Where the usual work of art invites the spectator into its world, already furnished and habitable, Wilde's plays do just the opposite: the author invites himself and his fast opinions into the world of the spectator. He ensconces himself with intolerable freedom and always outstays his sufferance—the trouble with Wilde's wit is that it does not recognize when the party is over. The effect of this effrontery is provoking in both senses; the outrageous has its own monotony, and insolence can only strike once.

In *The Importance of Being Earnest* (Royal Theatre), the tedium is concentrated in the second act, where two young ladies are rude to each other over tea and cake, and two young gentlemen follow them being selfish about

the muffins. The joke of gluttony and the joke of rude-
ness (which are really the same one, for heartlessness is
the basic pleasantry) have been exhausted in the first act:
nothing can be said by the muffin that has not already
been said by the cucumber sandwich. The thin little joke
that remains, the importance of the name Ernest for
matrimony, is in its visible aspects insufficiently entertaining. That the joke about the name Ernest is doubtless
a private one makes it less endurable to the audience, which
is pointedly left out of the fun. To the bisexual man, it
was perhaps deliciously comic that a man should have one
name, the tamest in English, for his wife and female relations, and another for his male friends, for trips and
"lost" weekends; but Wilde was a prude—he went to law
to clear his character—and the antisocial jibe dwindles
on the stage to a refined and incomprehensible titter.

Yet, in spite of the exhausting triviality of the second
act, *The Importance of Being Earnest* is Wilde's most
original play. It has the character of a ferocious idyl.
Here, for the first time, the subject of Wilde's comedy
coincides with its climate; there is no more pretense of
emotion. The unwed mother, his stock "serious" heroine,
here becomes a stock joke—"shall there be a different
standard for women than for men?" cries Mr. Jack Worthing, flinging himself on the governess, Miss Prism, who
had checked him accidentally in a valise at a railroad
station twenty-five years before. In *The Importance of
Being Earnest* the title is a *blague,* and virtue disappears
from the Wilde stage, as though jerked off by one of those
hooks that were used in the old days of vaudeville to remove an unsuccessful performer. Depravity is the hero
and the only character, the people on the stage embodying various shades of it. It is deepest dyed in the pastoral
region of respectability and innocence. The London *roué*
is artless simplicity itself beside the dreadnought society
dowager, and she, in her turn, is out-brazened by her deb-
utante daughter, and she by the country miss, and she
by her spectacled governess, till finally the village rector
with his clerical clothes, his vow of celibacy, and his sermon on the manna, adjustable to all occasions, slithers
noiselessly into the rose garden, specious as the Serpent
Himself.

The formula of this humor is the same as that of the

detective story: the culprit is the man with the most guile-less appearance. Normal expectations are methodically inverted, and the structure of the play is the simple structure of the paradox. Like the detective story, like the paradox, this play is a shocker. It is pure sport of the mind, and hence very nearly "English." The clergyman is the fox; the governess the vixen; and the young bloods are out for the kill. Humanitarian considerations are out of place here; they belong to the middle class. Insensibility is the comic "vice" of the characters; it is also their charm and badge of prestige. Selfishness and servility are the moral alternatives presented; the sinister impression made by the governess and the rector comes partly from their rectitude and partly from their menial demeanor. Algernon Moncrieff and Cecily Cardew are, taken by themselves, unendurable; the meeching Dr. Chasuble, however, justifies their way of life by affording a comparison—it is better to be cruel than craven.

Written on the brink of his fall, *The Importance of Being Earnest* is Wilde's true *De Profundis;* the other was false sentiment. This is hell, and if a great deal of it is tiresome, eternity is, as M. Sartre says, a bore. The tone of the Wilde dialogue, inappropriate to the problem drama, perfectly reflects conditions in this infernal Arcadia; peevish, fretful, valetudinarian, it is the tone of an elderly recluse who lives imprisoned by his comforts; it combines the finicky and the greedy, like a piggish old lady.

Fortunately, however, for everyone, there is a goddess in the play. The great lumbering dowager, Lady Augusta Bracknell, traveling to the country in a luggage-train, is the only character thick and rudimentary enough to be genuinely well-born. Possibly because of her birth, she has a certain Olympian freedom. When she is on the stage—during the first and the third acts—the play opens up. The epigram, which might be defined as the *desire* to say something witty, falters before her majesty. Her own rumbling speech is unpredictable; anything may come out of her. Where the other characters are hard as nails, Lady Augusta is rock. She is so insensitive that the spoken word reaches her slowly, from an immeasurable distance, as if she were deaf. Into this splendid creation, Wilde surely put all the feelings of admiration and despair aroused in him by Respectability. This citadel of the arbitrary was for him the Castle; he remarked, in his later years, that he would have been glad to marry Queen Victoria. Lady Augusta is the one character he could ever really imagine, partly, no doubt, because she could not imagine *him*. Her effrontery surpasses his by being perfectly unconscious; she cannot impose on the audience for she does not know they are there. She is named, oddly enough, after Bracknell, the country address of the Marchioness of Queensberry, where Wilde, as it turned out, was less at home than he fancied. The irony of the pastoral setting was apparently not lost on the Marquess of Queensberry, who arrived at the first night with a bunch of turnips and carrots.

First produced at the St. James' Theatre, February 14, 1895

CHARACTERS

John Worthington, J.P.
Algernon Moncrieff
Rev. Canon Chasuble, D.D.
Merriman, butler
Lane, manservant
Lady Bracknell
Hon. Gwendolen Fairfax
Cecily Cardew
Miss Prism, governess

*Morning-room in Algernon's flat in Half-Moon Street. The
room is luxuriously and artistically furnished. The sound
of a piano is heard in the adjoining room.*

[*Lane is arranging afternoon tea on the table, and after
the music has ceased, Algernon enters.*]

Algernon. Did you hear what I was playing, Lane?

Lane. I didn't think it polite to listen, sir.

Algernon. I'm sorry for that, for your sake. I don't play
accurately—any one can play accurately—but I play
with wonderful expression. As far as the piano is
concerned, sentiment is my forte. I keep science for
Life.

Lane. Yes, sir.

Algernon. And, speaking of the science of Life, have you
got the cucumber sandwiches cut for Lady Bracknell?

Lane. Yes, sir. [*Hands them on a salver.*]

Algernon [*Inspects them, takes two, and sits down on the
sofa.*] Oh! . . . by the way, Lane, I see from your
book that on Thursday night, when Lord Shoreman
and Mr. Worthing were dining with me, eight bottles
of champagne are entered as having been consumed.

Lane. Yes, sir; eight bottles and a pint.

Algernon. Why is it that at a bachelor's establishment the
servants invariably drink the champagne? I ask merely
for information.

Lane. I attribute it to the superior quality of the wine, sir.
I have often observed that in married households the
champagne is rarely of a first-rate brand.

Algernon. Good heavens! Is marriage so demoralizing as
that?

Lane. I believe it *is* a very pleasant state, sir. I have had very little experience of it myself up to the present. I have only been married once. That was in consequence of a misunderstanding between myself and a young person.

Algernon [*languidly*]. I don't know that I am much interested in your family life, Lane.

Lane. No, sir; it is not a very interesting subject. I never think of it myself.

Algernon. Very natural, I am sure. That will do, Lane, thank you.

Lane. Thank you, sir. [*Lane goes out.*]

Algernon. Lane's views on marriage seem somewhat lax. Really, if the lower orders don't set us a good example, what on earth is the use of them? They seem, as a class, to have absolutely no sense of moral responsibility.

[*Enter Lane.*]

Lane. Mr. Ernest Worthing.

[*Enter Jack. Lane goes out.*]

Algernon. How are you, my dear Ernest? What brings you up to town?

Jack. Oh, pleasure, pleasure! What else should bring one anywhere? Eating as usual, I see, Algy!

Algernon [*stiffly*]. I believe it is customary in good society to take some slight refreshment at five o'clock. Where have you been since last Thursday?

Jack [*sitting down on the sofa*]. In the country.

Algernon. What on earth do you do there?

Jack [*pulling off his gloves*]. When one is in town one amuses oneself. When one is in the country one amuses other people. It is excessively boring.

Algernon. And who are the people you amuse?

Jack [*airily*]. Oh, neighbours, neighbours.

Algernon. Got nice neighbours in your part of Shropshire?

Jack. Perfectly horrid! Never speak to one of them.

Algernon. How immensely you must amuse them! [*Goes over and takes sandwich.*] By the way, Shropshire is your county, is it not?

Jack. Eh? Shropshire? Yes, of course. Hallo! Why all these cups? Why cucumber sandwiches? Why such reckless extravagance in one so young? Who is coming to tea?

Algernon. Oh! merely Aunt Augusta and Gwendolen.

Jack. How perfectly delightful!

Algernon. Yes, that is all very well; but I am afraid Aunt
    Augusta won't quite approve of your being here.

Jack. May I ask why?

Algernon. My dear fellow, the way you flirt with Gwen-
    dolen is perfectly disgraceful. It is almost as bad as
    the way Gwendolen flirts with you.

Jack. I am in love with Gwendolen. I have come up to
    town expressly to propose to her.

Algernon. I thought you had come up for pleasure? . . . I
    call that business.

Jack. How utterly unromantic you are!

Algernon. I really don't see anything romantic in propos-
    ing. It is very romantic to be in love. But there is
    nothing romantic about a definite proposal. Why,
    one may be accepted. One usually is, I believe. Then
    the excitement is all over. The very essence of ro-
    mance is uncertainty. If ever I get married, I'll cer-
    tainly try to forget the fact.

Jack. I have no doubt about that, dear Algy. The Divorce
    Court was specially invented for people whose mem-
    ories are so curiously constituted.

Algernon. Oh! there is no use speculating on that subject.
    Divorces are made in Heaven—[*Jack puts out his
    hand to take a sandwich. Algernon at once interferes.*]
    Please don't touch the cucumber sandwiches. They are
    ordered specially for Aunt Augusta. [*Takes one and
    eats it.*]

Jack. Well, you have been eating them all the time.

Algernon. That is quite a different matter. She is my aunt.
    [*Takes plate from below.*] Have some bread and but-
    ter. The bread and butter is for Gwendolen. Gwen-
    dolen is devoted to bread and butter.

Jack [*advancing to table and helping himself*]. And very
    good bread and butter it is too.

Algernon. Well, my dear fellow, you need not eat as if you
    were going to eat it all. You behave as if you were
    married to her already. You are not married to her
    already, and I don't think you ever will be.

Jack. Why on earth do you say that?

Algernon. Well, in the first place, girls never marry the
    men they flirt with. Girls don't think it right.

Jack. Oh, that is nonsense!

Algernon. It isn't. It is a great truth. It accounts for the extraordinary number of bachelors that one sees all over the place. In the second place, I don't give my consent.

Jack. Your consent!

Algernon. My dear fellow, Gwendolen is my first cousin. And before I allow you to marry her, you will have to clear up the whole question of Cecily. [*Rings bell.*]

Jack. Cecily! What on earth do you mean? What do you mean, Algy, by Cecily? I don't know any one of the name of Cecily.

[*Enter Lane.*]

Algernon. Bring me that cigarette case Mr. Worthing left in the smoking-room the last time he dined here.

Lane. Yes, sir. [*Lane goes out.*]

Jack. Do you mean to say you have had my cigarette case all this time? I wish to goodness you had let me know. I have been writing frantic letters to Scotland Yard about it. I was very nearly offering a large reward.

Algernon. Well, I wish you would offer one. I happen to be more than usually hard up.

Jack. There is no good offering a large reward now that the thing is found.

[*Enter Lane with the cigarette case on a salver. Algernon takes it at once. Lane goes out.*]

Algernon. I think that is rather mean of you, Ernest, I must say. [*Opens case and examines it.*] However, it makes no matter, for, now that I look at the inscription inside, I find that the thing isn't yours after all.

Jack. Of course it's mine. [*Moving to him.*] You have seen me with it a hundred times, and you have no right whatsoever to read what is written inside. It is a very ungentlemanly thing to read a private cigarette case.

Algernon. Oh! it is absurd to have a hard and fast rule about what one should read and what one shouldn't. More than half of modern culture depends on what one shouldn't read.

Jack. I am quite aware of the fact, and I don't propose to discuss modern culture. It isn't the sort of thing one should talk of in private. I simply want my cigarette case back.

Algernon. Yes; but this isn't your cigarette case. This cigarette case is a present from someone of the name

of Cecily, and you said you didn't know anyone of
that name.

Jack. Well, if you want to know, Cecily happens to be my
aunt.

Algernon. Your aunt!

Jack. Yes. Charming old lady she is, too. Lives at Tunbridge Wells. Just give it back to me, Algy.

Algernon [*retreating to back of sofa*]. But why does she
call herself little Cecily if she is your aunt and lives
at Tunbridge Wells. [*Reading.*] "From little Cecily
with her fondest love."

Jack [*moving to sofa and kneeling upon it*]. My dear fellow,
what on earth is there in that? Some aunts are tall,
some aunts are not tall. That is a matter that surely an
aunt may be allowed to decide for herself. You seem
to think that every aunt should be exactly like your
aunt! That is absurd. For Heaven's sake give me back
my cigarette case. [*Follows Algernon round the room.*]

Algernon. Yes. But why does your aunt call you her
uncle? "From little Cecily, with her fondest love to
her dear Uncle Jack." There is no objection, I admit,
to an aunt being a small aunt, but why an aunt, no
matter what her size may be, should call her own
nephew her uncle, I can't quite make out. Besides,
your name isn't Jack at all; it is Ernest.

Jack. It isn't Ernest; it's Jack.

Algernon. You have always told me it was Ernest. I have
introduced you to every one as Ernest. You answer to
the name of Ernest. You look as if your name was
Ernest. You are the most earnest-looking person I ever
saw in my life. It is perfectly absurd your saying that
your name isn't Ernest. It's on your cards. Here is
one of them [*taking it from case*]. "Mr. Ernest Worthing, B.4, The Albany." I'll keep this as a proof that
your name is Ernest if ever you attempt to deny it to
me, or to Gwendolen, or to any one else. [*Puts the
card in his pocket.*]

Jack. Well, my name is Ernest in town and Jack in the
country, and the cigarette case was given to me in the
country.

Algernon. Yes, but that does not account for the fact that
your small Aunt Cecily, who lives at Tunbridge Wells,

calls you her dear uncle. Come, old boy, you had much better have the thing out at once.

Jack. My dear Algy, you talk exactly as if you were a dentist. It is very vulgar to talk like a dentist when one isn't a dentist. It produces a false impression.

Algernon. Well, that is exactly what dentists always do. Now, go on! Tell me the whole thing. I may mention that I have always suspected you of being a confirmed and secret Bunburyist, and I am quite sure of it now.

Jack. Bunburyist? What on earth do you mean by a Bunburyist?

Algernon. I'll reveal to you the meaning of that incomparable expression as soon as you are kind enough to inform me why you are Ernest in town and Jack in the country.

Jack. Well, produce my cigarette case first.

Algernon. Here it is. [*Hands cigarette case.*] Now produce your explanation, and pray make it improbable. [*Sits on sofa.*]

Jack. My dear fellow, there is nothing improbable about my explanation at all. In fact it's perfectly ordinary. Old Mr. Thomas Cardew, who adopted me when I was a little boy, made me in his will guardian to his granddaughter, Miss Cecily Cardew. Cecily, who addresses me as her uncle from motives of respect that you could not possibly appreciate, lives at my place in the country under the charge of her admirable governess, Miss Prism.

Algernon. Where is that place in the country, by the way?

Jack. That is nothing to you, dear boy. You are not going to be invited. . . . I may tell you candidly that the place is not in Shropshire.

Algernon. I suspected that, my dear fellow! I have Bunburyed all over Shropshire on two separate occasions. Now, go on. Why are you Ernest in town and Jack in the country?

Jack. My dear Algy, I don't know whether you will be able to understand my real motives. You are hardly serious enough. When one is placed in the position of guardian, one has to adopt a very high moral tone on all subjects. It's one's duty to do so. And as a high moral tone can hardly be said to conduce very much to either one's health or one's happiness, in order to get up to town I have always pretended to have a younger brother of the name of Ernest, who lives in the Albany, and gets into the most dreadful scrapes. That, my dear Algy, is the whole truth pure and simple.

Algernon. The truth is rarely pure and never simple. Modern life would be very tedious if it were either, and modern literature a complete impossibility!

Jack. That wouldn't be at all a bad thing.

Algernon. Literary criticism is not your forte, my dear fellow. Don't try it. You should leave that to people who haven't been at a University. They do it so well in the daily papers. What you really are is a Bunburyist. I was quite right in saying you were a Bunburyist. You are one of the most advanced Bunburyists I know.

Jack. What on earth do you mean?

Algernon. You have invented a very useful younger brother called Ernest, in order that you may be able to come up to town as often as you like. I have invented an invaluable permanent invalid called Bunbury, in order that I may be able to go down into the country whenever I choose. Bunbury is perfectly invaluable. If it wasn't for Bunbury's extraordinary bad health, for instance, I wouldn't be able to dine with you at Willis's tonight, for I have been really engaged to Aunt Augusta for more than a week.

Jack. I haven't asked you to dine with me anywhere tonight.

Algernon. I know. You are absurdly careless about sending out invitations. It is very foolish of you. Nothing annoys people so much as not receiving invitations.

Jack. You had much better dine with your Aunt Augusta.

Algernon. I haven't the smallest intention of doing anything of the kind. To begin with, I dined there on Monday, and once a week is quite enough to dine with one's own relations. In the second place, whenever I do dine there I am always treated as a member of the family, and sent down with either no woman at all, or two. In the third place, I know perfectly well whom she will place me next to, tonight. She will place me next to Mary Farquhar, who always flirts with her own husband across the dinner table. That is not very pleasant. Indeed, it is not even decent . . . and that sort of thing is enormously on the increase. The amount of women in London who flirt with their own husbands is perfectly scandalous. It looks so bad. It is simply washing one's clean linen in public. Besides, now that I know you to be a confirmed Bunburyist I naturally want to talk to you about Bunburying. I want to tell you the rules.

Jack. I'm not a Bunburyist at all. If Gwendolen accepts me, I am going to kill my brother, indeed I think I'll kill him in any case. Cecily is a little too much interested in him. It is rather a bore. So I am going to get rid of Ernest. And I strongly advise you to do the same with Mr. . . . with your invalid friend who has the absurd name.

Algernon. Nothing will induce me to part with Bunbury, and if you ever get married, which seems to me extremely problematic, you will be very glad to know Bunbury. A man who marries without knowing Bunbury has a very tedious time of it.

Jack. That is nonsense. If I marry a charming girl like Gwendolen, and she is the only girl I ever saw in my life that I would marry, I certainly won't want to know Bunbury.

Algernon. Then your wife will. You don't seem to realize, that in married life three is company and two is none.

Jack [*sententiously*]. That, my dear young friend, is the theory that the corrupt French Drama has been propounding for the last fifty years.

Algernon. Yes! and that the happy English home has proved in half the time.

Jack. For heaven's sake, don't try to be cynical. It's perfectly easy to be cynical.

Algernon. My dear fellow, it isn't easy to be anything nowadays. There's such a lot of beastly competition about. [*The sound of an electric bell is heard.*] Ah! that must be Aunt Augusta. Only relatives, or creditors, ever ring in that Wagnerian manner. Now, if I get her out of the way for ten minutes, so that you can have an opportunity for proposing to Gwendolen, may I dine with you tonight at Willis's?

Jack. I suppose so, if you want to.

Algernon. Yes, but you must be serious about it. I hate

people who are not serious about meals. It is so shallow of them.

[*Enter Lane*]

Lane. Lady Bracknell and Miss Fairfax.

[*Algernon goes forward to meet them. Enter Lady Bracknell and Gwendolen.*]

Lady Bracknell. Good afternoon, dear Algernon, I hope you are behaving very well.

Algernon. I'm feeling very well, Aunt Augusta.

Lady Bracknell. That's not quite the same thing. In fact the two things rarely go together. [*Sees Jack and bows to him with icy coldness.*]

Algernon [*to Gwendolen*]. Dear me, you are smart!

Gwendolen. I am always smart! Am I not, Mr. Worthing?

Jack. You're quite perfect, Miss Fairfax.

Gwendolen. Oh! I hope I am not that. It would leave no room for developments, and I intend to develop in many directions. [*Gwendolen and Jack sit down together in the corner.*]

Lady Bracknell. I'm sorry if we are a little late, Algernon, but I was obliged to call on dear Lady Harbury. I hadn't been there since her poor husband's death. I never saw a woman so altered; she looks quite twenty years younger. And now I'll have a cup of tea and one of those nice cucumber sandwiches you promised me.

Algernon. Certainly, Aunt Augusta. [*Goes over to teatable.*]

Lady Bracknell. Won't you come and sit here, Gwendolen?

Gwendolen. Thanks, mamma, I'm quite comfortable where I am.

Algernon [*picking up empty plate in horror*]. Good heavens! Lane! Why are there no cucumber sandwiches? I ordered them specially.

Lane [*gravely*]. There were no cucumbers in the market this morning, sir. I went down twice.

Algernon. No cucumbers!

Lane. No, sir. Not even for ready money.

Algernon. That will do, Lane, thank you.

Lane. Thank you, sir. [*Goes out.*]

Algernon. I am greatly distressed, Aunt Augusta, about there being no cucumbers, not even for ready money.

Lady Bracknell. It really makes no matter, Algernon. I had some crumpets with Lady Harbury, who seems to me to be living entirely for pleasure now.

Algernon. I hear her hair has turned quite gold from grief.

Lady Bracknell. It certainly has changed its colour. From what cause I, of course, cannot say. [*Algernon crosses and hands tea.*] Thank you. I've quite a treat for you tonight, Algernon. I am going to send you down with Mary Farquhar. She is such a nice woman, and so attentive to her husband. It's delightful to watch them.

Algernon. I am afraid, Aunt Augusta, I shall have to give up the pleasure of dining with you tonight after all.

Lady Bracknell [*frowning*]. I hope not, Algernon. It would put my table completely out. Your uncle would have to dine upstairs. Fortunately he is accustomed to that.

Algernon. It is a great bore, and, I need hardly say, a terrible disappointment to me, but the fact is I have just had a telegram to say that my poor friend Bunbury is very ill again. [*Exchanges glances with Jack.*] They seem to think I should be with him.

Lady Bracknell. It is very strange. This Mr. Bunbury seems to suffer from curiously bad health.

Algernon. Yes; poor Bunbury is a dreadful invalid.

Lady Bracknell. Well, I must say, Algernon, that I think it is high time that Mr. Bunbury made up his mind whether he was going to live or to die. This shilly-shallying with the question is absurd. Nor do I in any way approve of the modern sympathy with invalids. I consider it morbid. Illness of any kind is hardly a thing to be encouraged in others. Health is the primary duty of life. I am always telling that to your poor uncle, but he never seems to take much notice . . . as far as any improvement in his ailments goes. I should be much obliged if you would ask Mr. Bunbury, from me, to be kind enough not to have a relapse on Saturday, for I rely on you to arrange my music for me. It is my last reception, and one wants something that will encourage conversation, particularly at the end of the season when every one has practically said whatever they had to say, which, in most cases, was probably not much.

Algernon. I'll speak to Bunbury, Aunt Augusta, if he is still conscious, and I think I can promise you he'll be all right by Saturday. Of course the music is a great difficulty. You see, if one plays good music, people don't listen, and if one plays bad music, people don't talk. But I'll run over the programme I've draw out, if you will kindly come into the next room for a moment.

Lady Bracknell. Thank you, Algernon. It is very thoughtful of you. [*Rising, and following Algernon.*] I'm sure the programme will be delightful, after a few expurgations. French songs I cannot possibly allow. People always seem to think that they are improper, and either look shocked, which is vulgar, or laugh, which is worse. But German sounds a thoroughly respectable language, and, indeed I believe is so. Gwendolen, you will accompany me.

Gwendolen. Certainly, mamma.

[*Lady Bracknell and Algernon go into the music-room; Gwendolen remains behind.*]

Jack. Charming day it has been, Miss Fairfax.

Gwendolen. Pray don't talk to me about the weather, Mr. Worthing. Whenever people talk to me about the weather, I always feel quite certain that they mean something else. And that makes me so nervous.

Jack. I do mean something else.

Gwendolen. I thought so. In fact, I am never wrong.

Jack. And I would like to be allowed to take advantage of Lady Bracknell's temporary absence. . . .

Gwendolen. I would certainly advise you to do so. Mamma has a way of coming back suddenly into a room that I have often had to speak to her about.

Jack [*nervously*]. Miss Fairfax, ever since I met you I have admired you more than any girl . . . I have ever met since . . . I met you.

Gwendolen. Yes, I am quite aware of the fact. And I often wish that in public, at any rate, you had been more demonstrative. For me you have always had an irresistible fascination. Even before I met you I was far from indifferent to you. [*Jack looks at her in amazement.*] We live, as I hope you know, Mr. Worthing, in an age of ideals. The fact is constantly mentioned in the more expensive monthly magazines, and has reached the provincial pulpits, I am told; and my ideal has always been to love some one of the name of Ernest. There is something in that name that in-spires absolute confidence. The moment Algernon first mentioned to me that he had a friend called Ernest, I knew I was destined to love you.

Jack. You really love me, Gwendolen?

Gwendolen. Passionately!

Jack. Darling! You don't know how happy you've made me.

Gwendolen. My own Ernest!

Jack. But you don't really mean to say that you couldn't love me if my name wasn't Ernest?

Gwendolen. But your name is Ernest.

Jack. Yes, I know it is. But supposing it was something else? Do you mean to say you couldn't love me then?

Gwendolen [*glibly*]. Ah! that is clearly a metaphysical speculation, and like most metaphysical speculations has very little reference at all to the actual facts of real life, as we know them.

Jack. Personally, darling, to speak quite candidly, I don't much care about the name of Ernest. . . . I don't think the name suits me at all.

Gwendolen. It suits you perfectly. It is a divine name. It has a music of its own. It produces vibrations.

Jack. Well, really, Gwendolen, I must say that I think there are lots of other much nicer names. I think Jack, for instance, a charming name.

Gwendolen. Jack? . . . No, there is very little music in the name Jack, if any at all, indeed. It does not thrill. It produces absolutely no vibrations. . . . I have known several Jacks, and they all, without exception, were more than usually plain. Besides, Jack is a notorious domesticity for John! And I pity any woman who is married to a man called John. She would probably never be allowed to know the entrancing pleasure of a single moment's solitude. The only really safe name is Ernest.

Jack. Gwendolen, I must get christened at once—I mean we must get married at once. There is no time to be lost.

Gwendolen. Married, Mr. Worthing?

Jack [*astounded*]. Well . . . surely. You know that I love you, and you led me to believe, Miss Fairfax, that you were not absolutely indifferent to me.

Gwendolen. I adore you. But you haven't proposed to me yet. Nothing has been said at all about marriage. The subject has not even been touched on.

Jack. Well . . . may I propose to you now?

Gwendolen. I think it would be an admirable opportunity. And to spare you any possible disappointment, Mr. Worthing, I think it only fair to tell you quite frankly beforehand that I am fully determined to accept you.

Jack. Gwendolen!

Gwendolen. Yes, Mr. Worthing, what have you got to say to me?

Jack. You know what I have got to say to you.

Gwendolen. Yes, but you don't say it.

Jack. Gwendolen, will you marry me? [*Goes on his knees.*]

Gwendolen. Of course I will, darling. How long you have been about it! I am afraid you have had very little experience in how to propose.

Jack. My own one, I have never loved any one in the world but you.

Gwendolen. Yes, but men often propose for practice. I know my brother Gerald does. All my girl-friends tell me so. What wonderfully blue eyes you have, Ernest! They are quite, quite blue. I hope you will always look at me just like that, especially when there are other people present.

[*Enter Lady Bracknell.*]

Lady Bracknell. Mr. Worthing! Rise sir, from this semi-recumbent posture. It is most indecorous.

Gwendolen. Mamma! [*He tries to rise; she restrains him.*] I must beg you to retire. This is no place for you. Besides, Mr. Worthing is not quite finished yet.

Lady Bracknell. Finished what, may I ask?

Gwendolen. I am engaged to Mr. Worthing, mamma. [*They rise together.*]

Lady Bracknell. Pardon me, you are not engaged to any one. When you do become engaged to some one, I, or your father, should his health permit him, will inform you of the fact. An engagement should come on a young girl as a surprise, pleasant or unpleasant, as the case may be. It is hardly a matter that she could be allowed to arrange for herself. . . . And now I have a few questions to put to you, Mr. Worthing.

While I am making these inquiries, you, Gwendolen, will wait for me below in the carriage.

Gwendolen [*reproachfully*]. Mamma!

Lady Bracknell. In the carriage, Gwendolen! [*Gwendolen goes to the door. She and Jack blow kisses to each other behind Lady Bracknell's back. Lady Bracknell looks vaguely about as if she could not understand what the noise was. Finally turns round.*] Gwendolen, the carriage!

Gwendolen. Yes, mamma. [*Goes out, looking back at Jack.*]

Lady Bracknell [*sitting down*]. You can take a seat, Mr. Worthing. [*Looks in her pocket for notebook and pencil.*]

Jack. Thank you, Lady Bracknell, I prefer standing.

Lady Bracknell [*pencil and notebook in hand*]. I feel bound to tell you that you are not down on my list of eligible young men, although I have the same list as the dear Duchess of Bolton has. We work together, in fact. However, I am quite ready to enter your name, should your answers be what a really affectionate mother requires. Do you smoke?

Jack. Well, yes, I must admit I smoke.

Lady Bracknell. I am glad to hear it. A man should always have an occupation of some kind. There are far too many idle men in London as it is. How old are you?

Jack. Twenty-nine.

Lady Bracknell. A very good age to be married at. I have always been of opinion that a man who desires to get married should know either everything or nothing. Which do you know?

Jack [*after some hesitation*]. I know nothing, Lady Bracknell.

Lady Bracknell. I am pleased to hear it. I do not approve of anything that tampers with natural ignorance. Ignorance is like a delicate exotic fruit; touch it and the bloom is gone. The whole theory of modern education is radically unsound. Fortunately in England, at any rate, education produces no effect whatsoever. If it did, it would prove a serious danger to the upper classes, and probably lead to acts of violence in Grosvenor Square. What is your income?

Jack. Between seven and eight thousand a year.

Lady Bracknell [*makes a note in her book*]. In land, or in investments?

Jack. In investments, chiefly.

Lady Bracknell. That is satisfactory. What between the duties expected of one during one's lifetime, and the duties exacted from one after one's death, land has ceased to be either a profit or a pleasure. It gives one position, and prevents one from keeping it up. That's all that can be said about land.

Jack. I have a country house with some land, of course, attached to it, about fifteen hundred acres, I believe; but I don't depend on that for my real income. In fact, as far as I can make out, the poachers are the only people who make anything out of it.

Lady Bracknell. A country house! How many bedrooms? Well, that point can be cleared up afterwards. You have a town house, I hope? A girl with a simple, unspoiled nature, like Gwendolen, could hardly be expected to reside in the country.

Jack. Well, I own a house in Belgrave Square, but it is let by the year to Lady Bloxham. Of course, I can get it back whenever I like, at six months' notice.

Lady Bracknell. Lady Bloxham? I don't know her.

Jack. Oh, she goes about very little. She is a lady considerably advanced in years.

Lady Bracknell. Ah, nowadays that is no guarantee of respectability of character. What number in Belgrave Square?

Jack. 149.

Lady Bracknell [*shaking her head*]. The unfashionable side. I thought there was something. However, that could easily be altered.

Jack. Do you mean the fashion, or the side?

Lady Bracknell [*sternly*]. Both, if necessary, I presume. What are your politics?

Jack. Well, I am afraid I really have none. I am a Liberal Unionist.

Lady Bracknell. Oh, they count as Tories. They dine with us. Or come in the evening, at any rate. Now to minor matters. Are your parents living?

Jack. I have lost both my parents.

Lady Bracknell. To lose one parent, Mr. Worthing, may be regarded as a misfortune; to lose both looks like carelessness. Who was your father? He was evidently a man of some wealth. Was he born in what the Radical papers call the purple of commerce, or did he rise from the ranks of the aristocracy?

Jack. I am afraid I really don't know. The fact is, Lady Bracknell, I said I had lost my parents. It would be nearer the truth to say that my parents seem to have lost me. . . . I don't actually know who I am by birth. I was . . . well, I was found.

Lady Bracknell. Found!

Jack. The late Mr. Thomas Cardew, an old gentleman of a very charitable and kindly disposition, found me, and gave me the name of Worthing, because he happened to have a first-class ticket for Worthing in his pocket at the time. Worthing is a place in Sussex. It is a sea-side resort.

Lady Bracknell. Where did the charitable gentleman who had a first-class ticket for this seaside resort find you?

Jack [*gravely*]. In a handbag.

Lady Bracknell. A handbag?

Jack [*very seriously*]. Yes, Lady Bracknell. I was in a handbag—a somewhat large, black leather handbag, with handles to it—an ordinary handbag in fact.

Lady Bracknell. In what locality did this Mr. James, or Thomas, Cardew come across this ordinary handbag?

Jack. In the cloakroom at Victoria Station. It was given to him in mistake for his own.

Lady Bracknell. The cloakroom at Victoria Station?

Jack. Yes. The Brighton line.

Lady Bracknell. The line is immaterial, Mr. Worthing, I confess I feel somewhat bewildered by what you have just told me. To be born, or at any rate bred, in a handbag, whether it had handles or not, seems to me to display a contempt for the ordinary decencies of family life that reminds one of the worst excesses of the French Revolution. And I presume you know what that unfortunate movement led to? As for the particular locality in which the handbag was found, a cloakroom at a railway station might serve to conceal a social indiscretion—has probably, indeed, been used for that purpose before now—but it could hardly be regarded as an assured basis for a recognized position in good society.

Jack. May I ask you then what you would advise me to do? I need hardly say I would do anything in the world to ensure Gwendolen's happiness.

Lady Bracknell. I would strongly advise you, Mr. Worthing, to try and acquire some relations as soon as possible, and to make a definite effort to produce at any rate one parent, of either sex, before the season is quite over.

Jack. Well, I don't see how I could possibly manage to do that. I can produce the handbag at any moment. It is in my dressing-room at home. I really think that should satisfy you, Lady Bracknell.

Lady Bracknell. Me, sir! What has it to do with me? You can hardly imagine that I and Lord Bracknell would dream of allowing our only daughter—a girl brought up with the utmost care—to marry into a cloakroom, and form an alliance with a parcel. Good morning, Mr. Worthing! [*Lady Bracknell sweeps out in majestic indignation.*]

Jack. Good morning! [*Algernon, from the other room, strikes up the Wedding March. Jack looks perfectly furious, and goes to the door.*] For goodness' sake don't play that ghastly tune, Algy! How idiotic you are!

[*The music stops and Algernon enters cheerily.*]

Algernon. Didn't it go off all right, old boy? You don't mean to say Gwendolen refused you? I know it is a way she has. She is always refusing people. I think it is most ill-natured of her.

Jack. Oh, Gwendolen is as right as a trivet. As far as she is concerned, we are engaged. Her mother is perfectly unbearable. Never met such a Gorgon. . . . I don't really know what a Gorgon is like, but I am quite sure that Lady Bracknell is one. In any case, she is a monster, without being a myth, which is rather unfair. . . . I beg your pardon, Algy, I suppose I shouldn't talk about your own aunt in that way before you.

Algernon. My dear boy, I love hearing my relations abused. It is the only thing that makes me put up with them at all. Relations are simply a tedious pack of people, who haven't got the remotest knowledge of how to live, nor the smallest instinct about when to die.

Jack. Oh, that is nonsense!

Algernon. It isn't!

Jack. Well, I won't argue about the matter. You always want to argue about things.

Algernon. That is exactly what things were originally made for.

Jack. Upon my word, if I thought that, I'd shoot myself. . . . [*A pause.*] You don't think there is any chance of Gwendolen becoming like her mother in about a hundred and fifty years, do you, Algy?

Algernon. All women become like their mothers. That is their tragedy. No man does. That's his.

Jack. Is that clever?

Algernon. It is perfectly phrased! and quite as true as any observation in civilized life should be.

Jack. I am sick to death of cleverness. Everybody is clever nowadays. You can't go anywhere without meeting clever people. The thing has become an absolute public nuisance. I wish to goodness we had a few fools left.

Algernon. We have.

Jack. I should extremely like to meet them. What do they talk about?

Algernon. The fools? Oh! about the clever people, of course.

Jack. What fools.

Algernon. By the way, did you tell Gwendolen the truth about your being Ernest in town, and Jack in the country?

Jack [*in a very patronizing manner*]. My dear fellow, the truth isn't quite the sort of thing one tells to a nice, sweet, refined girl. What extraordinary ideas you have about the way to behave to a woman!

Algernon. The only way to behave to a woman is to make love to her, if she is pretty, and to someone else, if she is plain.

Jack. Oh, that is nonsense.

Algernon. What about your brother? What about the profligate Ernest?

Jack. Oh, before the end of the week I shall have got rid of him. I'll say he died in Paris of apoplexy. Lots of people die of apoplexy, quite suddenly, don't they?

Algernon. Yes, but it's hereditary, my dear fellow. It's a
    sort of thing that runs in families. You had much
    better say a severe chill.

Jack. You are sure a severe chill isn't hereditary, or any-
    thing of that kind?

Algernon. Of course it isn't!

Jack. Very well, then. My poor brother Ernest is carried
    off suddenly, in Paris, by a severe chill. That gets rid
    of him.

Algernon. But I thought you said that . . . Miss Cardew
    was a little too much interested in your poor brother
    Ernest? Won't she feel his loss a good deal?

Jack. Oh, that is all right. Cecily is not a silly romantic girl,
    I am glad to say. She has got a capital appetite, goes
    on long walks, and pays no attention at all to her les-
    sons.

Algernon. I would rather like to see Cecily.

Jack. I will take very good care you never do. She is exces-
    sively pretty, and she is only just eighteen.

Algernon. Have you told Gwendolen yet that you have an
    excessively pretty ward who is only just eighteen?

Jack. Oh! one doesn't blurt these things out to people.
    Cecily and Gwendolen are perfectly certain to be ex-
    tremely great friends. I'll bet you anything you like
    that half an hour after they have met, they will be
    calling each other sister.

Algernon. Women only do that when they have called each
    other a lot of other things first. Now, my dear boy,
    if we want to get a good table at Willis's, we really
    must go and dress. Do you know it is nearly seven?

Jack [*irritably*]. Oh! it always is nearly seven.

Algernon. Well, I'm hungry.

Jack. I never knew you when you weren't. . . .

Algernon. What shall we do after dinner? Go to a theatre?

Jack. Oh no! I loathe listening.

Algernon. Well, let us go to the Club?

Jack. Oh, no! I hate talking.

Algernon. Well, we might trot round to the Empire at ten?

Jack. Oh, no! I can't bear looking at things. It is so silly.

Algernon. Well, what shall we do?

Jack. Nothing!

Algernon. It is awfully hard work doing nothing. However,

I don't mind hard work where there is no definite object of any kind.

[*Enter Lane.*]

Lane. Miss Fairfax.

[*Enter Gwendolen. Lane goes out.*]

Algernon. Gwendolen, upon my word!

Gwendolen. Algy, kindly turn your back. I have something very particular to say to Mr. Worthing.

Algernon. Really, Gwendolen, I don't think I can allow this at all.

Gwendolen. Algy, you always adopt a strictly immoral attitude towards life. You are not quite old enough to do that.

[*Algernon retires to the fireplace.*]

Jack. My own darling!

Gwendolen. Ernest, we may never be married. From the expression on mamma's face I fear we never shall. Few parents nowadays pay any regard to what their children say to them. The old-fashioned respect for the young is fast dying out. Whatever influence I ever had over mamma, I lost at the age of three. But although she may prevent us from becoming man and wife, and I may marry someone else, and marry often, nothing that she can possibly do can alter my eternal devotion to you.

Jack. Dear Gwendolen!

Gwendolen. The story of your romantic origin, as related to me by mamma, with unpleasing comments, has naturally stirred the deeper fibres of my nature. Your Christian name has an irresistible fascination. The simplicity of your character makes you exquisitely incomprehensible to me. Your town address at the Albany I have. What is your address in the country?

Jack. The Manor House, Woolton, Hertfordshire.

[*Algernon, who has been carefully listening, smiles to himself, and writes the address on his shirt-cuff. Then picks up the Railway Guide.*]

Gwendolen. There is a good postal service, I suppose? It may be necessary to do something desperate. That of course will require serious consideration. I will communicate with you daily.

Jack. My own one!

Gwendolen. How long do you remain in town?

Jack. Till Monday.

Gwendolen. Good! Algy, you may turn round now.

Algernon. Thanks, I've turned round already.

Gwendolen. You may also ring the bell.

Jack. You will let me see you to your carriage, my own darling?

Gwendolen. Certainly.

Jack [*to Lane, who now enters*]. I will see Miss Fairfax out.

Lane. Yes, sir.

[*Jack and Gwendolen go off. Lane presents several letters on a salver to Algernon. It is to be surmised that they are bills, as Algernon, after looking at the envelopes, tears them up.*]

Algernon. A glass of sherry, Lane.

Lane. Yes, sir.

Algernon. Tomorrow, Lane, I'm going Bunburying.

Lane. Yes, sir.

Algernon. I shall probably not be back till Monday. You can put up my dress clothes, my smoking jacket, and all the Bunbury suits. . . .

Lane. Yes, sir. [*Handing sherry.*]

Algernon. I hope tomorrow will be a fine day, Lane.

Lane. It never is, sir.

Algernon. Lane, you're a perfect pessimist.

Lane. I do my best to give satisfaction, sir.

[*Enter Jack. Lane goes off.*]

Jack. There's a sensible, intellectual girl! the only girl I ever cared for in my life. [*Algernon is laughing immoderately.*] What on earth are you so amused at?

Algernon. Oh, I'm a little anxious about poor Bunbury, that is all.

Jack. If you don't take care, your friend Bunbury will get you into a serious scrape some day.

Algernon. I love scrapes. They are the only things that are never serious.

Jack. Oh, that's nonsense, Algy. You never talk anything but nonsense.

Algernon. Nobody ever does.

[*Jack looks indignantly at him, and leaves the room. Algernon lights a cigarette, reads his shirt-cuff, and smiles.*]

act 2

Garden at the Manor House. A flight of grey stone steps leads up to the house. The garden, an old-fashioned one, full of roses. Time of year, July. Basket chairs, and a table covered with books, are set under a large yew-tree.

[*Miss Prism discovered seated at the table. Cecily is at the back, watering flowers.*]

Miss Prism [*calling*]. Cecily, Cecily! Surely such a utilitarian occupation as the watering of flowers is rather Moulton's duty than yours? Especially at a moment when intellectual pleasures await you. Your German grammar is on the table. Pray open it at page fifteen. We will repeat yesterday's lesson.

Cecily [*coming over very slowly*]. But I don't like German. It isn't at all a becoming language. I know perfectly well that I look quite plain after my German lesson.

Miss Prism. Child, you know how anxious your guardian is that you should improve yourself in every way. He laid particular stress on your German, as he was leaving for town yesterday. Indeed, he always lays stress on your German when he is leaving for town.

Cecily. Dear Uncle Jack is so very serious! Sometimes he is so serious that I think he cannot be quite well.

Miss Prism [*drawing herself up*]. Your guardian enjoys the best of health, and his gravity of demeanor is especially to be commended in one so comparatively young as he is. I know no one who has a higher sense of duty and responsibility.

Cecily. I suppose that is why he often looks a little bored when we three are together.

Miss Prism. Cecily! I am surprised at you. Mr. Worthing has many troubles in his life. Idle merriment and triviality would be out of place in his conversation.

You must remember his constant anxiety about that
unfortunate young man his brother.

Cecily. I wish Uncle Jack would allow that unfortunate
young man, his brother, to come down here sometimes. We might have a good influence over him, Miss
Prism. I am sure you certainly would. You know
German, and geology, and things of that kind influence a man very much. [*Cecily begins to write in
her diary.*]

Miss Prism [*shaking her head*]. I do not think that even I
could produce any effect on a character that according
to his own brother's admission is irretrievably weak
and vacillating. Indeed I am not sure that I would
desire to reclaim him. I am not in favor of this modern
mania for turning bad people into good people at a
moment's notice. As a man sows so let him reap. You
must put away your diary, Cecily. I really don't see
why you should keep a diary at all.

Cecily. I keep a diary in order to enter the wonderful
secrets of my life. If I didn't write them down, I
I should probably forget all about them.

Miss Prism. Memory, my dear Cecily, is the diary that we
all carry about with us.

Cecily. Yes, but it usually chronicles the things that have
never happened, and couldn't possibly have happened.
I believe that Memory is responsible for nearly all
the three-volume novels that Mudie sends us.

Miss Prism. Do not speak slightingly of the three-volume
novel, Cecily. I wrote one myself in earlier days.

Cecily. Did you really, Miss Prism? How wonderfully
clever you are! I hope it did not end happily? I don't
like novels that end happily. They depress me so
much.

Miss Prism. The good ended happily, and the bad un-
happily. That is what Fiction means.

Cecily. I suppose so. But it seems very unfair. And was
your novel ever published?

Miss Prism. Alas! no. The manuscript unfortunately was
abandoned. [*Cecily starts.*] I used the word in the sense
of lost or mislaid. To your work, child, these speculations are profitless.

Cecily [*smiling*]. But I see dear Dr. Chasuble coming up
through the garden.

Miss Prism [*rising and advancing*]. Dr. Chasuble! This is indeed a pleasure.

[*Enter Canon Chasuble.*]

Chasuble. And how are we this morinng? Miss Prism, you are, I trust, well?

Cecily. Miss Prism has just been complaining of a slight headache. I think it would do her so much good to have a short stroll with you in the Park, Dr. Chasuble.

Miss Prism. Cecily, I have not mentioned anything about a headache.

Cecily. No, dear Miss Prism, I know that, but I felt instinctively that you had a headache. Indeed I was thinking about that, and not about my German lesson, when the Rector came in.

Chasuble. I hope, Cecily, you are not inattentive.

Cecily. Oh, I am afraid I am.

Chasuble. That is strange. Were I fortunate enough to be Miss Prism's pupil, I would hang upon her lips [*Miss Prism glares.*] I spoke metaphorically.—My metaphor was drawn from bees. Ahem! Mr. Worthing, I suppose, has not returned from town yet?

Miss Prism. We do not expect him till Monday afternoon.

Chasuble. Ah yes, he usually likes to spend his Sunday in London. He is not one of those whose sole aim is enjoyment, as, by all accounts, that unfortunate young man his brother seems to be. But I must not disturb Egeria and her pupil any longer.

Miss Prism. Egeria? My name is Laetitia, Doctor.

Chasuble [*bowing*]. A classical allusion merely, drawn from the Pagan authors. I shall see you both no doubt at Evensong?

Miss Prism. I think, dear Doctor, I will have a stroll with you. I find I have a headache after all, and a walk might do it good.

Chasuble. With pleasure, Miss Prism, with pleasure. We might go as far as the schools and back.

Miss Prism. That would be delightful. Cecily, you will read your Political Economy in my absence. The chapter on the Fall of the Rupee you may omit. It is somewhat too sensational. Even these metallic problems have their melodramatic side. [*Goes down the garden with Dr. Chasuble.*]

Cecily [*picks up books and throws them back on table*].

Horrid Political Economy! Horrid Geography! Horrid, horrid German!

[*Enter Merriman with a card on a salver.*]

Merriman. Mr. Ernest Worthing has just driven over from the station. He has brought his luggage with him.

Cecily [*takes the card and reads it*]. "Mr. Ernest Worthing, B.4, The Albany, W." Uncle Jack's brother! Did you tell him Mr. Worthing was in town?

Merriman. Yes, Miss. He seemed very much disappointed. I mentioned that you and Miss Prism were in the garden. He said he was anxious to speak to you privately for a moment.

Cecily. Ask Mr. Ernest Worthing to come here. I suppose you had better talk to the housekeeper about a room for him.

Merriman. Yes, Miss. [*Merriman goes off.*]

Cecily. I have never met any really wicked person before. I feel rather frightened. I am so afraid he will look just like every one else. [*Enter Algernon, very gay and debonnaire.*] He does!

Algernon [*raising his hat*]. You are my little cousin Cecily, I'm sure.

Cecily. You are under some strange mistake. I am not little. In fact, I believe I am more than usually tall for my age. [*Algernon is rather taken aback.*] But I am your cousin Cecily. You, I see from your card, are Uncle Jack's brother, my cousin Ernest, my wicked cousin Ernest.

Algernon. Oh! I am not really wicked at all, Cousin Cecily. You mustn't think that I am wicked.

Cecily. If you are not, then you have certainly been deceiving us all in a very inexcusable manner. I hope you have not been leading a double life, pretending to be wicked and being really good all the time. That would be hypocrisy.

Algernon [*looks at her in amazement*]. Oh! Of course I have been rather reckless.

Cecily. I am glad to hear it.

Algernon. In fact, now you mention the subject, I have been very bad in my own small way.

Cecily. I don't think you should be so proud of that, though I am sure it must have been very pleasant.

Algernon. It is much pleasanter being here with you.

Cecily. I can't understand how you are here at all. Uncle Jack won't be back till Monday afternoon.

Algernon. That is a great disappointment. I am obliged to go up by the first train on Monday morning. I have a business appointment that I am anxious . . . to miss!

Cecily. Couldn't you miss it anywhere but in London?

Algernon. No: the appointment is in London.

Cecily. Well, I know, of course, how important it is not to keep a business engagement, if one wants to retain any sense of the beauty of life, but still I think you had better wait till Uncle Jack arrives. I know he wants to speak to you about your emigrating.

Algernon. About my what?

Cecily. Your emigrating. He has gone up to buy your outfit.

Algernon. I certainly wouldn't let Jack buy my outfit. He has no taste in neckties at all.

Cecily. I don't think you will require neckties. Uncle Jack is sending you to Australia.

Algernon. Australia! I'd sooner die.

Cecily. Well, he said at dinner on Wednesday night, that you would have to choose between this world, the next world, and Australia.

Algernon. Oh, well! The accounts I have received of Australia and the next world are not particularly encouraging. This world is good enough for me, Cousin Cecily.

Cecily. Yes, but are you good enough for it?

Algernon. I'm afraid I'm not that. That is why I want you to reform me. You might make that your mission, if you don't mind, cousin Cecily.

Cecily. I'm afraid I've no time, this afternoon.

Algernon. Well, would you mind my reforming myself this afternoon?

Cecily. It is rather Quixotic of you. But I think you should try.

Algernon. I will. I feel better already.

Cecily. You are looking a little worse.

Algernon. That is because I am hungry.

Cecily. How thoughtless of me. I should have remembered that when one is going to lead an entirely new life, one requires regular and wholesome meals. Won't you come in?

Algernon. Thank you. Might I have a buttonhole first? I
never have any appetite unless I have a buttonhole
first.

Cecily. A Maréchal Niel? [*Picks up scissors.*]

Algernon. No, I'd sooner have a pink rose.

Cecily. Why? [*Cuts a flower.*]

Algernon. Because you are like a pink rose, Cousin Cecily.

Cecily. I don't think it can be right for you to talk to me
like that. Miss Prism never says such things to me.

Algernon. Then Miss Prism is a shortsighted old lady.
[*Cecily puts the rose in his buttonhole.*] You are the
prettiest girl I ever saw.

Cecily. Miss Prism says that all good looks are a snare.

Algernon. They are a snare that every sensible man would
like to be caught in.

Cecily. Oh, I don't think I would care to catch a sensible
man. I shouldn't know what to talk to him about.

[*They pass into the house. Miss Prism and Dr. Chasuble
return.*]

Miss Prism. You are too much alone, dear Dr. Chasuble.
You should get married. A misanthrope I can understand—a womanthrope, never!

Chasuble [*with a scholar's shudder*]. Believe me, I do not
deserve so neologistic a phrase. The precept as well
as the practice of the Primitive Church was distinctly
against matrimony.

Miss Prism [*sententiously*]. That is obviously the reason
why the Primitive Church has not lasted up to the
present day. And you do not seem to realize, dear
Doctor, that by persistently remaining single, a man
converts himself into a permanent public temptation.
Men should be more careful; this very celibacy leads
weaker vessels astray.

Chasuble. But is a man not equally attractive when
married?

Miss Prism. No married man is ever attractive except to
his wife.

Chasuble. And often, I've been told, not even to her.

Miss Prism. That depends on the intellectual sympathies of
the woman. Maturity can always be depended on.
Ripeness can be trusted. Young women are green.
[*Dr. Chasuble starts.*] I spoke horticulturally. My
metaphor was drawn from fruits. But where is Cecily?

Chasuble. Perhaps she followed us to the schools.

[*Enter Jack slowly from the back of the garden. He is dressed in the deepest mourning, with crepe hatband and black gloves.*]

Miss Prism. Mr. Worthing!

Chasuble. Mr. Worthing?

Miss Prism. This is indeed a surprise. We did not look for you till Monday afternoon.

Jack [*shakes Miss Prism's hand in a tragic manner*]. I have returned sooner than I expected. Dr. Chasuble, I hope you are well?

Chasuble. Dear Mr. Worthing, I trust this garb of woe does not betoken some terrible calamity?

Jack. My brother.

Miss Prism. More shameful debts and extravagance?

Chasuble. Still leading his life of pleasure?

Jack [*shaking his head*]. Dead!

Chasuble. Your brother Ernest dead?

Jack. Quite dead.

Miss Prism. What a lesson for him! I trust he will profit by it.

Chasuble. Mr. Worthing, I offer you my sincere condolence. You have at least the consolation of knowing that you were always the most generous and forgiving of brothers.

Jack. Poor Ernest! He had many faults, but it is a sad, sad blow.

Chasuble. Very sad indeed. Were you with him at the end?

Jack. No. He died abroad; in Paris, in fact. I had a telegram last night from the manager of the Grand Hotel.

Chasuble. Was the cause of death mentioned?

Jack. A severe chill, it seems.

Miss Prism. As a man sows, so shall he reap.

Chasuble [*raising his hand*]. Charity, dear Miss Prism, charity! None of us are perfect. I myself am peculiarly susceptible to draughts. Will the interment take place here?

Jack. No. He seems to have expressed a desire to be buried in Paris.

Chasuble. In Paris! [*Shakes his head.*] I fear that hardly points to any very serious state of mind at the last. You would no doubt wish me to make some slight allusion to this tragic domestic affliction next Sunday.

[*Jack pressed his hand convulsively.*] My sermon on the meaning of the manna in the wilderness can be adapted to almost any occasion, joyful, or, as in the present case, distressing. [*All sigh.*] I have preached it at harvest celebrations, christenings, confirmations, on days of humiliation and festal days. The last time I delivered it was in the Cathedral, as a charity sermon on behalf of the Society for the Prevention of Discontent among the Upper Orders. The Bishop, who was present, was much struck by some of the analogies I drew.

Jack. Ah! that reminds me, you mentioned christenings I think, Dr. Chasuble? I suppose you know how to christen all right? [*Dr. Chasuble looks astounded.*] I mean, of course, you are continually christening, aren't you?

Miss Prism. It is, I regret to say, one of the Rector's most constant duties in this parish. I have often spoken to the poorer classes on the subject. But they don't seem to know what thrift is.

Chasuble. But is there any particular infant in whom you are interested, Mr. Worthing? Your brother was, I believe, unmarried, was he not?

Jack. Oh yes.

Miss Prism [*bitterly*]. People who live entirely for pleasure usually are.

Jack. But it is not for any child, dear Doctor. I am very fond of children. No! the fact is, I would like to be christened myself, this afternoon, if you have nothing better to do.

Chasuble. But surely, Mr. Worthing, you have been christened already?

Jack. I don't remember anything about it.

Chasuble. But have you any grave doubts on the subject?

Jack. I certainly intend to have. Of course I don't know if the thing would bother you in any way, or if you think I am a little too old now.

Chasuble. Not at all. The sprinkling, and, indeed, the immersion of adults is a perfectly canonical practice.

Jack. Immersion!

Chasuble. You need have no apprehensions. Sprinkling is all that is necessary, or indeed I think advisable. Our weather is so changeable. At what hour would you wish the ceremony performed?

Jack. Oh, I might trot round about five if that would suit you.

Chasuble. Perfectly, perfectly! In fact I have two similar ceremonies to perform at that time. A case of twins that occurred recently in one of the outlying cottages on your own estate. Poor Jenkins the carter, a most hard-working man.

Jack. Oh! I don't see much fun in being christened along with other babies. It would be childish. Would half-past five do?

Chasuble. Admirably! Admirably! [*Takes out watch.*] And now, dear Mr. Worthing, I will not intrude any longer into a house of sorrow. I would merely beg you not to be too much bowed down by grief. What seem to us bitter trials are often blessings in disguise.

Miss Prism. This seems to me a blessing of an extremely obvious kind.

[*Enter Cecily from the house.*]

Cecily. Uncle Jack! Oh, I am pleased to see you back. But what horrid clothes you have got on. Do go and change them.

Miss Prism. Cecily!

Chasuble. My child! My child! [*Cecily goes towards Jack; he kisses her brow in a melancholy manner.*]

Cecily. What is the matter, Uncle Jack? Do look happy! You look as if you had toothache, and I have got such a surprise for you. Who do you think is in the dining-room? Your brother!

Jack. Who?

Cecily. Your brother Ernest. He arrived about half an hour ago.

Jack. What nonsense! I haven't got a brother.

Cecily. Oh, don't say that. However badly he may have behaved to you in the past he is still your brother. You couldn't be so heartless as to disown him. I'll tell him to come out. And you will shake hands with him, won't you, Uncle Jack? [*Runs back into the house.*]

Chasuble. These are very joyful tidings.

Miss Prism. After we had all been resigned to his loss, his sudden return seems to me peculiarly distressing.

Jack. My brother is in the dining-room? I don't know what it all means. I think it is perfectly absurd.

[*Enter Algernon and Cecily hand in hand. They come slowly up to Jack.*]

Jack. Good heavens! [*Motions Algernon away.*]

Algernon. Brother John, I have come down from town to tell you that I am very sorry for all the trouble I have given you, and that I intend to lead a better life in the future. [*Jack glares at him and does not take his hand.*]

Cecily. Uncle Jack, you are not going to refuse your own brother's hand?

Jack. Nothing will induce me to take his hand. I think his coming down here disgraceful. He knows perfectly well why.

Cecily. Uncle Jack, do be nice. There is some good in everyone. Ernest has just been telling me about his poor invalid friend Mr. Bunbury whom he goes to visit so often. And surely there must be much good in one who is kind to an invalid, and leaves the pleasures of London to sit by a bed of pain.

Jack. Oh! he has been talking about Bunbury, has he?

Cecily. Yes, he has told me all about poor Mr. Bunbury, and his terrible state of health.

Jack. Bunbury! Well, I won't have him talk to you about Bunbury or about anything else. It is enough to drive one perfectly frantic.

Algernon. Of course I admit that the faults were all on my side. But I must say that I think that Brother John's coldness to me is peculiarly painful. I expected a more enthusiastic welcome, especially considering it is the first time I have come here.

Cecily. Uncle Jack, if you don't shake hands with Ernest I will never forgive you.

Jack. Never forgive me?

Cecily. Never, never, never!

Jack. Well, this is the last time I shall ever do it. [*Shakes hands with Algernon and glares.*]

Chasuble. It's pleasant, is it not, to see so perfect a reconciliation? I think we might leave the two brothers together.

Miss Prism. Cecily, you will come with us.

Cecily. Certainly, Miss Prism. My little task of reconciliation is over.

Chasuble. You have done a beautiful action today, dear child.

Miss Prism. We must not be premature in our judgements.

Cecily. I feel very happy. [*They all go off except Jack and Algernon.*]

Jack. You young scoundrel, Algy, you must get out of this place as soon as possible. I don't allow any Bunburying here.

[*Enter Merriman.*]

Merriman. I have put Mr. Ernest's things in the room next to yours, sir. I suppose that is all right?

Jack. What?

Merriman. Mr. Ernest's luggage, sir. I have unpacked it and put it in the room next to your own.

Jack. His luggage?

Merriman. Yes sir. Three portmanteaus, a dressing-case, two hatboxes, and a large luncheon-basket.

Algernon. I am afraid I can't stay more than a week this time.

Jack. Merriman, order the dogcart at once. Mr. Ernest has been suddenly called back to town.

Merriman. Yes, sir. [*Goes back into the house.*]

Algernon. What a fearful liar you are, Jack. I have not been called back to town at all.

Jack. Yes, you have.

Algernon. I haven't heard any one call me.

Jack. Your duty as a gentleman calls you back.

Algernon. My duty as a gentleman has never interfered with my pleasures in the smallest degree.

Jack. I can quite understand that.

Algernon. Well, Cecily is a darling.

Jack. You are not to talk of Miss Cardew like that. I don't like it.

Algernon. Well, I don't like your clothes. You look perfectly ridiculous in them. Why on earth don't you go up and change? It is perfectly childish to be in deep mourning for a man who is actually staying for a whole week with you in your house as a guest. I call it grotesque.

Jack. You are certainly not staying with me for a whole

week as a guest or anything else. You have got to
leave . . . by the four-five train.

Algernon. I certainly won't leave you so long as you are in
mourning. It would be most unfriendly. If I were in
mourning you would stay with me, I suppose. I
should think it very unkind if you didn't.

Jack. Well, will you go if I change my clothes?

Algernon. Yes, if you are not too long. I never saw anybody take so long to dress, and with such little result.

Jack. Well, at any rate, that is better than being always
overdressed as you are.

Algernon. If I am occasionally a little overdressed, I make
up for it by being always immensely overeducated.

Jack. Your vanity is ridiculous, your conduct an outrage,
and your presence in my garden utterly absurd.
However, you have got to catch the four-five, and I
hope you will have a pleasant journey back to town.
This Bunburying, as you call it, has not been a great
success for you. [*Goes into the house.*]

Algernon. I think it has been a great success. I'm in love
with Cecily, and that is everything. [*Enter Cecily at
the back of the garden. She picks up the can and
begins to water the flowers.*] But I must see her before
I go, and make arrangements for another Bunbury.
Ah, there she is.

Cecily. Oh, I merely came back to water the roses. I
thought you were with Uncle Jack.

Algernon. He's gone to order the dogcart for me.

Cecily. Oh, is he going to take you for a nice drive?

Algernon. He's going to send me away.

Cecily. Then have we got to part?

Algernon. I am afraid so. It's a very painful parting.

Cecily. It is always painful to part from people whom one
has known for a very brief space of time. The absence
of old friends one can endure with equanimity. But
even a momentary separation from any one to whom
one has just been introduced is almost unbearable.

Algernon. Thank you.

[*Enter Merriman.*]

Merriman. The dogcart is at the door, sir.

[*Algernon looks appealingly at Cecily.*]

Cecily. It can wait, Merriman . . . for . . . five minutes.

Merriman. Yes, miss. [*Exit Merriman.*]

Algernon. I hope, Cecily, I shall not offend you if I state quite frankly and openly that you seem to me to be in every way the visible personification of absolute perfection.

Cecily. I think your frankness does you great credit, Ernest. If you will allow me, I will copy your remarks into my diary. [*Goes over to table and begins writing in diary.*]

Algernon. Do you really keep a diary? I'd give anything to look at it. May I?

Cecily. Oh no. [*Puts her hand over it.*] You see, it is simply a very young girl's record of her own thoughts and impressions, and consequently meant for publication. When it appears in volume form I hope you will order a copy. But pray, Ernest, don't stop. I delight in taking down from dictation. I have reached "absolute perfection." You can go on. I am quite ready for more.

Algernon [*somewhat taken aback*]. Ahem! Ahem!

Cecily. Oh, don't cough, Ernest. When one is dictating one should speak fluently and not cough. Besides, I don't know how to spell a cough. [*Writes as Algernon speaks.*]

Algernon [*speaking very rapidly*]. Cecily, ever since I first looked upon your wonderful and incomparable beauty, I have dared to love you wildly, passionately, devotedly, hopelessly.

Cecily. I don't think that you should tell me that you love me wildly, passionately, devotedly, hopelessly. Hopelessly doesn't seem to make much sense, does it?

Algernon. Cecily.

[*Enter Merriman.*]

Merriman. The dogcart is waiting, sir.

Algernon. Tell it to come round next week, at the same hour.

Merriman [*looks at Cecily, who makes no sign*]. Yes, sir. [*Merriman retires.*]

Cecily. Uncle Jack would be very much annoyed if he knew you were staying on till next week, at the same hour.

Algernon. Oh, I don't care about Jack. I don't care for anybody in the whole world but you. I love you, Cecily. You will marry me, won't you?

Cecily. You silly boy! Of course. Why, we have been
    engaged for the last three months.

Algernon. For the last three months?

Cecily. Yes, it will be exactly three months on Thursday.

Algernon. But how did we become engaged?

Cecily. Well, ever since dear Uncle Jack first confessed to
    us that he had a younger brother who was very wicked
    and bad, you of course have formed the chief topic of
    conversation between myself and Miss Prism. And
    of course a man who is much talked about is always
    very attractive. One feels there must be something in
    him, after all. I daresay it was foolish of me, but I
    fell in love with you, Ernest.

Algernon. Darling. And when was the engagement actually
    settled?

Cecily. On the 14th of February last. Worn out by your
    entire ignorance of my existence, I determined to end
    the matter one way or the other, and after a long
    struggle with myself I accepted you under this dear
    old tree here. The next day I bought this little ring
    in your name, and this is the little bangle with the
    true lovers' knot I promised you always to wear.

Algernon. Did I give you this? It's very pretty, isn't it?

Cecily. Yes, you've wonderfully good taste, Ernest. It's
    the excuse I've always given for your leading such a
    bad life. And this is the box in which I keep all your
    dear letters. [*Kneels at table, opens box, and produces
    letters tied up with blue ribbon.*]

Algernon. My letters! But, my own sweet Cecily, I have
    never written you any letters.

Cecily. You need hardly remind me of that, Ernest. I
    remember only too well that I was forced to write your
    letters for you. I wrote always three times a week, and
    sometimes oftener.

Algernon. Oh, do let me read them, Cecily?

Cecily. Oh, I couldn't possibly. They would make you far
    too conceited. [*Replaces box.*] The three you wrote me
    after I had broken off the engagement are so beautiful,
    and so badly spelled, that even now I can hardly
    read them without crying a little.

Algernon. But was our engagement ever broken off?

Cecily. Of course it was. On the 22nd of last March. You

can see the entry if you like. [*Shows diary.*] "Today I broke off my engagement with Ernest. I feel it is better to do so. The weather still continues charming."

Algernon. But why on earth did you break it off? What had I done? I had done nothing at all. Cecily, I am very much hurt indeed to hear you broke it off. Particularly when the weather was so charming.

Cecily. It would hardly have been a really serious engagement if it hadn't been broken off at least once. But I forgave you before the week was out.

Algernon [*crossing to her, and kneeling*]. What a perfect angel you are, Cecily.

Cecily. You dear romantic boy. [*He kisses her, she puts her fingers through his hair.*] I hope your hair curls naturally, does it?

Algernon. Yes darling, with a little help from others.

Cecily. I am so glad.

Algernon. You'll never break off our engagement again, Cecily?

Cecily. I don't think I could break it off now that I have actually met you. Besides, of course, there is the question of your name.

Algernon. Yes, of course. [*Nervously.*]

Cecily. You must not laugh at me, darling, but it had always been a girlish dream of mine to love some one whose name was Ernest. [*Algernon rises, Cecily also.*] There is something in that name that seems to inspire absolute confidence. I pity any poor married woman whose husband is not called Ernest.

Algernon. But, my dear child, do you mean to say you could not love me if I had some other name?

Cecily. But what name?

Algernon. Oh, any name you like—Algernon—for instance . . .

Cecily. But I don't like the name of Algernon.

Algernon. Well, my own dear, sweet, loving little darling, I really can't see why you should object to the name of Algernon. It is not at all a bad name. In fact, it is rather an aristocratic name. Half of the chaps who get into the Bankruptcy Court are called Algernon. But seriously, Cecily . . . [*moving to her*] if my name was Algy, couldn't you love me?

Cecily [*rising*]. I might respect you, Ernest, I might admire your character, but I fear that I should not be
able to give you my undivided attention.

Algernon. Ahem! Cecily! [*Picking up hat.*] Your Rector
here is, I suppose, thoroughly experienced in the practice of all the rites and ceremonials of the Church?

Cecily. Oh, yes. Dr. Chasuble is a most learned man. He
has never written a single book, so you can imagine
how much he knows.

Algernon. I must see him at once on a most important
christening—I mean on most important business.

Cecily. Oh!

Algernon. I shan't be away more than half an hour.

Cecily. Considering that we have been engaged since February the 14th, and that I only met you today for the
first time, I think it is rather hard that you should
leave me for so long a period as half an hour. Couldn't
you make it twenty minutes?

Algernon. I'll be back in no time. [*Kisses her and rushes
down the garden.*]

Cecily. What an impetuous boy he is! I like his hair so
much. I must enter his proposal in my diary.

[*Enter Merriman.*]

Merriman. A Miss Fairfax just called to see Mr. Worthing.
On very important business, Miss Fairfax states.

Cecily. Isn't Mr. Worthing in his library?

Merriman. Mr. Worthing went over in the direction of the
Rectory some time ago.

Cecily. Pray ask the lady to come out here; Mr. Worthing
is sure to be back soon. And you can bring tea.

Merriman. Yes, Miss. [*Goes out.*]

Cecily. Miss Fairfax! I suppose one of the many good
elderly women who are associated with Uncle Jack
in some of his philanthropic work in London. I
don't quite like women who are interested in philanthropic work. I think it is so forward of them.

[*Enter Merriman.*]

Merriman. Miss Fairfax.

[*Enter Gwendolen. Exit Merriman.*]

Cecily [*advancing to meet her*]. Pray let me introduce
myself to you. My name is Cecily Cardew.

Gwendolen. Cecily Cardew? [*Moving to her and shaking
hands.*] What a very sweet name! Something tells me

that we are going to be great friends. I like you already more than I can say. My first impressions of people are never wrong.

Cecily. How nice of you to like me so much after we have known each other such a comparatively short time. Pray sit down.

Gwendolen [*still standing up*]. I may call you Cecily, may I not?

Cecily. With pleasure!

Gwendolen. And you will always call me Gwendolen, won't you?

Cecily. If you wish.

Gwendolen. Then that is all quite settled, is it not?

Cecily. I hope so. [*A pause. They both sit down together.*]

Gwendolen. Perhaps this might be a favorable opportunity for my mentioning who I am. My father is Lord Bracknell. You have never heard of papa, I suppose?

Cecily. I don't think so.

Gwendolen. Outside the family circle, papa, I am glad to say, is entirely unknown. I think that is quite as it should be. The home seems to me to be the proper sphere for the man. And certainly once a man begins to neglect his domestic duties he becomes painfully effeminate, does he not? And I don't like that. It makes men so very attractive. Cecily, mamma, whose views on education are remarkably strict, has brought me up to be extremely shortsighted; it is part of her system; so do you mind my looking at you through my glasses?

Cecily. Oh, not at all, Gwendolen. I am very fond of being looked at.

Gwendolen [*after examining Cecily carefully through a lorgnette*]. You are here on a short visit, I suppose.

Cecily. Oh no! I live here.

Gwendolen [*severely*]. Really? Your mother, no doubt, or some female relative of advanced years, resides here also?

Cecily. Oh no! I have no mother, nor, in fact, any relations.

Gwendolen. Indeed?

Cecily. My dear guardian, with the assistance of Miss Prism, has the arduous task of looking after me.

Gwendolen. Your guardian?

Cecily. Yes, I am Mr. Worthing's ward.

Gwendolen. Oh! It is strange he never mentioned to me
that he had a ward. How secretive of him! He grows
more interesting hourly. I am not sure, however, that
the news inspires me with feelings of unmixed delight. [*Rising and going to her.*] I am very fond of
you, Cecily; I have liked you ever since I met you!
But I am bound to state that now that I know that
you are Mr. Worthing's ward, I cannot help expressing
a wish you were—well, just a little older than you
seem to be—and not quite so very alluring in appearance. In fact, if I may speak candidly—

Cecily. Pray do! I think that whenever one has anything unpleasant to say, one should always be quite candid.

Gwendolen. Well, to speak with perfect candor, Cecily, I
wish that you were fully forty-two, and more than
usually plain for your age. Ernest has a strong up-
right nature. He is the very soul of truth and honor.
Disloyalty would be as impossible to him as deception.
But even men of the noblest possible moral character
are extremely susceptible to the influence of the
physical charms of others. Modern, no less than
Ancient History, supplies us with many most painful
examples of what I refer to. If it were not so, indeed,
History would be quite unreadable.

Cecily. I beg your pardon, Gwendolen, did you say Ernest?

Gwendolen. Yes.

Cecily. Oh, but it is not Mr. Ernest Worthing who is my
guardian. It is his brother—his elder brother.

Gwendolen [*sitting down again*]. Ernest never mentioned
to me that he had a brother.

Cecily. I am sorry to say they have not been on good terms
for a long time.

Gwendolen. Ah! that accounts for it. And now that I think
of it I have never heard any man mention his brother.
The subject seems distasteful to most men. Cecily, you
have lifted a load from my mind. I was growing almost anxious. It would have been terrible if any
cloud had come across a friendship like ours, would
it not? Of course you are quite, quite sure that it is
not Mr. Ernest Worthing who is your guardian?

Cecily. Quite sure. [*A pause.*] In fact, I am going to be his.

Gwendolen [*inquiringly*]. I beg your pardon?

Cecily [*rather shy and confidingly*]. Dearest Gwendolen,

there is no reason why I should make a secret of it to you. Our little country newspaper is sure to chronicle the fact next week. Mr. Ernest Worthing and I are engaged to be married.

Gwendolen [*quite politely, rising*]. My darling Cecily, I think there must be some slight error. Mr. Ernest Worthing is engaged to me. The announcement will appear in the *Morning Post* on Saturday at the latest.

Cecily [*very politely, rising*]. I am afraid you must be under some misconception. Ernest proposed to me exactly ten minutes ago. [*Shows diary.*]

Gwendolen [*examines diary through her lorgnette carefully*]. It is very curious, for he asked me to be his wife yesterday afternoon at 5:30. If you would care to verify the incident, pray do so. [*Produces diary of her own.*] I never travel without my diary. One should always have something sensational to read in the train. I am so sorry, dear Cecily, if it is any disappointment to you, but I am afraid I have the prior claim.

Cecily. It would distress me more than I can tell you, dear Gwendolen, if it caused you any mental or physical anguish, but I feel bound to point out that since Ernest proposed to you he clearly has changed his mind.

Gwendolen [*meditatively*]. If the poor fellow has been entrapped into any foolish promise I shall consider it my duty to rescue him at once, and with a firm hand.

Cecily [*thoughtfully and sadly*]. Whatever unfortunate entanglement my dear boy may have got into, I will never reproach him with it after we are married.

Gwendolen. Do you allude to me, Miss Cardew, as an entanglement? You are presumptuous. On an occasion of this kind it becomes more than a moral duty to speak one's mind. It becomes a pleasure.

Cecily. Do you suggest, Miss Fairfax, that I entrapped Ernest into an engagement? How dare you? This is no time for wearing the shallow mask of manners. When I see a spade I call it a spade.

Gwendolen [*satirically*]. I am glad to say that I have never seen a spade. It is obvious that our social spheres have been widely different.

[*Enter Merriman, followed by the footman. He carries a salver, table cloth, and plate stand. Cecily is about to retort. The presence of the servants exercises a re-*

straining influence, under which both girls chafe.]

Merriman. Shall I lay tea here as usual, Miss?

Cecily [*sternly, in a calm voice*]. Yes, as usual. [*Merriman begins to clear table and lay cloth. A long pause. Cecily and Gwendolen glare at each other.*]

Gwendolen. Are there many interesting walks in the vicinity, Miss Cardew?

Cecily. Oh! yes! a great many. From the top of one of the hills quite close one can see five counties.

Gwendolen. Five counties! I don't think I should like that; I hate crowds.

Cecily [*sweetly*]. I suppose that is why you live in town? [*Gwendolen bites her lip, and beats her foot nervously with her parasol.*]

Gwendolen [*looking round*]. Quite a well-kept garden this is, Miss Cardew.

Cecily. So glad you like it, Miss Fairfax.

Gwendolen. I had no idea there were any flowers in the country.

Cecily. Oh, flowers are as common here, Miss Fairfax, as people are in London.

Gwendolen. Personally I cannot understand how anybody manages to exist in the country, if anybody who is anybody does. The country always bores me to death.

Cecily. Ah! This is what the newspapers call agricultural depression, is it not? I believe the aristocracy are suffering very much from it just at present. It is almost an epidemic amongst them, I have been told. May I offer you some tea, Miss Fairfax?

Gwendolen [*with elaborate politeness*]. Thank you. [*Aside.*] Detestable girl! But I require tea!

Cecily [*sweetly*]. Sugar?

Gwendolen [*superciliously*]. No, thank you. Sugar is not fashionable any more. [*Cecily looks angrily at her, takes up the tongs and puts four lumps of sugar into the cup.*]

Cecily [*severely*]. Cake or bread and butter?

Gwendolen [*in a bored manner*]. Bread and butter, please. Cake is rarely seen at the best houses nowadays.

Cecily [*cuts a very large slice of cake and puts it on the tray*]. Hand that to Miss Fairfax.

[*Merriman does so, and goes out with footman. Gwendolen*

drinks the tea and makes a grimace. Puts down cup at once, reaches out her hand to the bread and butter, looks at it, and finds it is cake. Rises in indignation.]

Gwendolen. You have filled my tea with lumps of sugar, and though I asked most distinctly for bread and butter, you have given me cake. I am known for the gentleness of my disposition, and the extraordinary sweetness of my nature, but I warn you, Miss Cardew, you may go too far.

Cecily [*rising*]. To save my poor, innocent, trusting boy from the machinations of any other girl there are no lengths to which I would not go.

Gwendolen. From the moment I saw you I distrusted you. I felt that you were false and deceitful. I am never deceived in such matters. My first impressions of people are invariably right.

Cecily. It seems to me, Miss Fairfax, that I am trespassing on your valuable time. No doubt you have many other calls of a similar character to make in the neighbourhood.

[*Enter Jack.*]

Gwendolen [*catching sight of him*]. Ernest! My own Ernest!

Jack. Gwendolen! Darling! [*Offers to kiss her.*]

Gwendolen [*drawing back*]. A moment! May I ask if you are engaged to be married to this young lady? [*Points to Cecily.*]

Jack [*laughing*]. To dear little Cecily! Of course not! What could have put such an idea into your pretty little head?

Gwendolen. Thank you. You may! [*Offers her cheek.*]

Cecily [*very sweetly*]. I knew there must be some misunderstanding, Miss Fairfax. The gentleman whose arm is at present round your waist is my dear guardian, Mr. John Worthing.

Gwendolen. I beg your pardon?

Cecily. This is Uncle Jack.

Gwendolen [*receding*]. Jack! Oh!

[*Enter Algernon.*]

Cecily. Here is Ernest.

Algernon [*goes straight over to Cecily without noticing anyone else*]. My own love! [*Offers to kiss her.*]

Cecily [*drawing back*]. A moment, Ernest! May I ask you

—are you engaged to be married to this young lady?

Algernon [*looking round*]. To what young lady? Good heavens! Gwendolen!

Cecily. Yes: to good heavens, Gwendolen, I mean to Gwendolen.

Algernon [*laughing*]. Of course not! What could have put such an idea into your pretty little head?

Cecily. Thank you. [*Presenting her cheek to be kissed.*] You may. [*Algernon kisses her.*]

Gwendolen. I felt there was some slight error, Miss Cardew. The gentleman who is now embracing you is my cousin, Mr. Algernon Moncrieff.

Cecily [*breaking away from Algernon*]. Algernon Moncrieff! Oh! [*The two girls move towards each other and put their arms round each other's waists as if for protection.*]

Cecily. Are you called Algernon?

Algernon. I cannot deny it.

Cecily. Oh!

Gwendolen. Is your name really John?

Jack [*standing rather proudly*]. I could deny it if I liked. I could deny anything if I liked. But my name certainly is John. It has been John for years.

Cecily [*to Gwendolen*]. A gross deception has been practised on both of us.

Gwendolen. My poor wounded Cecily!

Cecily. My sweet wronged Gwendolen!

Gwendolen [*slowly and seriously*]. You will call me sister, will you not? [*They embrace. Jack and Algernon groan and walk up and down.*]

Cecily [*rather brightly*]. There is just one question I would like to be allowed to ask my guardian.

Gwendolen. An admirable idea! Mr. Worthing, there is just one question I would like to be permitted to put to you. Where is your brother Ernest? We are both engaged to be married to your brother Ernest, so it is a matter of some importance to us to know where your brother Ernest is at present.

Jack [*slowly and hesitatingly*]. Gwendolen—Cecily—it is very painful for me to be forced to speak the truth. It is the first time in my life that I have ever been reduced to such a painful position, and I am really quite inexperienced in doing anything of the kind. However,

I will tell you quite frankly that I have no brother
Ernest. I have no brother at all. I never had a brother
in my life, and I certainly have not the smallest intention of ever having one in the future.

Cecily [*surprised*]. No brother at all?

Jack [*cheerily*]. None!

Gwendolen [*severely*]. Had you never a brother of any
kind?

Jack [*pleasantly*]. Never. Not even of any kind.

Gwendolen. I am afraid it is quite clear, Cecily, that neither
of us is engaged to be married to anyone.

Cecily. It is not a very pleasant position for a young girl
suddenly to find herself in. Is it?

Gwendolen. Let us go into the house. They will hardly
venture to come after us there.

Cecily. No, men are so cowardly, aren't they?

[*They retire into the house with scornful looks.*]

Jack. This ghastly state of things is what you call Bunburying, I suppose?

Algernon. Yes, and a perfectly wonderful Bunbury it is.
The most wonderful Bunbury I have ever had in my
life.

Jack. Well, you've no right whatsoever to Bunbury here.

Algernon. That is absurd. One has a right to Bunbury anywhere one chooses. Every serious Bunburyist knows
that.

Jack. Serious Bunburyist? Good heavens!

Algernon. Well, one must be serious about something, if
one wants to have any amusement in life. I happen to
be serious about Bunburying. What on earth you are
serious about I haven't got the remotest idea. About
everything, I should fancy. You have such an absolutely trivial nature.

Jack. Well, the only small satisfaction I have in the whole
of this wretched business is that your friend Bunbury
is quite exploded. You won't be able to run down to
the country quite so often as you used to do, dear
Algy. And a very good thing too.

Algernon. Your brother is a little off color, isn't he, dear
Jack? You won't be able to disappear to London quite
so frequently as your wicked custom was. And not a
bad thing either.

Jack. As for your conduct towards Miss Cardew, I must

say that your taking in a sweet, simple, innocent girl like that is quite inexcusable. To say nothing of the fact that she is my ward.

Algernon. I can see no possible defence at all for your deceiving a brilliant, clever, thoroughly experienced young lady like Miss Fairfax. To say nothing of the fact that she is my cousin.

Jack. I wanted to be engaged to Gwendolen, that is all. I love her.

Algernon. Well, I simply wanted to be engaged to Cecily. I adore her.

Jack. There is certainly no chance of your marrying Miss Cardew.

Algernon. I don't think there is much likelihood, Jack. of you and Miss Fairfax being united.

Jack. Well, that is no business of yours.

Algernon. If it was my business, I wouldn't talk about it. [*Begins to eat muffins.*] It is very vulgar to talk about one's business. Only people like stockbrokers do that, and then merely at dinner parties.

Jack. How you can sit there, calmly eating muffins when we are in this horrible trouble, I can't make out. You seem to me to be perfectly heartless.

Algernon. Well, I can't eat muffins in an agitated manner. The butter would probably get on my cuffs. One should always eat muffins quite calmly. It is the only way to eat them.

Jack. I say it's perfectly heartless your eating muffins at all, under the circumstances.

Algernon. When I am in trouble, eating is the only thing that consoles me. Indeed, when I am in really great trouble, as any one who knows me intimately will tell you, I refuse everything except food and drink. At the present moment I am eating muffins because I am unhappy. Besides, I am particularly fond of muffins. [*Rising.*]

Jack [*rising*]. Well, there is no reason why you should eat them all in that greedy way. [*Takes muffins from Algernon.*]

Algernon [*offering tea-cake*]. I wish you would have tea-cake instead. I don't like tea-cake.

Jack. Good heavens! I suppose a man may eat his own muffins in his own garden.

Algernon. But you have just said it was perfectly heartless to eat muffins.

Jack. I said it was perfectly heartless of you, under the circumstances. That is a very different thing.

Algernon. That may be. But the muffins are the same. [*He seizes the muffin-dish from Jack.*]

Jack. Algy, I wish to goodness you would go.

Algernon. You can't possibly ask me to go without having some dinner. It's absurd. I never go without my dinner. No one ever does, except vegetarians and people like that. Besides I have just made arrangements with Dr. Chasuble to be christened at a quarter to six under the name of Ernest.

Jack. My dear fellow, the sooner you give up that nonsense the better. I made arrangements this morning with Dr. Chasuble to be christened myself at 5:30, and I naturally will take the name of Ernest. Gwendolen would wish it. We can't both be christened Ernest. It's absurd. Besides, I have a perfect right to be christened if I like. There is no evidence at all that I have ever been christened by anybody. I should think it extremely probable I never was, and so does Dr. Chasuble. It is entirely different in your case. You have been christened already.

Algernon. Yes, but I have not been christened for years.

Jack. Yes, but you have been christened. That is the important thing.

Algernon. Quite so. So I know my constitution can stand it. If you are not quite sure about your ever having been christened, I must say I think it rather dangerous your venturing on it now. It might make you very unwell. You can hardly have forgotten that someone very closely connected with you was very nearly carried off this week in Paris by a severe chill.

Jack. Yes, but you said yourself that a severe chill was not hereditary.

Algernon. It usen't to be, I know—but I daresay it is now. Science is always making wonderful improvements in things.

Jack [*picking up the muffin-dish*]. Oh, that is nonsense; you are always talking nonsense.

Algernon. Jack, you are at the muffins again! I wish you

wouldn't. There are only two left. [*Takes them.*] I told you I was particularly fond of muffins.

Jack. But I hate tea-cake.

Algernon. Why on earth then do you allow tea-cake to be served up for your guests? What ideas you have of hospitality!

Jack. Algernon! I have already told you to go. I don't want you here. Why don't you go!

Algernon. I haven't quite finished my tea yet! and there is still one muffin left. [*Jack groans, and sinks into a chair. Algernon still continues eating.*]

act 3

Morning-room at the Manor House. Gwendolen and Cecily are at the window, looking out into the garden.

Gwendolen. The fact that they did not follow us at once into the house, as any one else would have done, seems to me to show that they have some sense of shame left.

Cecily. They have been eating muffins. That looks like repentence.

Gwendolen [*after a pause*]. They don't seem to notice us at all. Couldn't you cough?

Cecily. But I haven't got a cough.

Gwendolen. They're looking at us. What effrontery!

Cecily. They're approaching. That's very forward of them.

Gwendolen. Let us preserve a dignified silence.

Cecily. Certainly. It's the only thing to do now.

[*Enter Jack followed by Algernon. They whistle some dreadful popular air from a British Opera.*]

Gwendolen. This dignified silence seems to produce an unpleasant effect.

Cecily. A most distasteful one.

Gwendolen. But we will not be the first to speak.

Cecily. Certainly not.

Gwendolen. Mr. Worthing, I have something very particular to ask you. Much depends on your reply.

Cecily. Gwendolen, your common sense is invaluable. Mr. Moncrieff, kindly answer me the following question. Why did you pretend to be my guardian's brother?

Algernon. In order that I might have an opportunity of meeting you.

Cecily [*to Gwendolen*]. That certainly seems a satisfactory explanation, does it not?

Gwendolen. Yes, dear, if you can believe him.

Cecily. I don't. But that does not affect the wonderful beauty of his answer.

Gwendolen. True. In matters of grave importance, style, not sincerity, is the vital thing. Mr. Worthing, what explanation can you offer to me for pretending to have a brother? Was it in order that you might have an opportunity of coming up to town to see me as often as possible?

Jack. Can you doubt it, Miss Fairfax?

Gwendolen. I have the gravest doubts upon the subject. But I intend to crush them. This is not the moment for German scepticism. [*Moving to Cecily.*] Their explanations appear to be quite satisfactory, especially Mr. Worthing's. That seems to me to have the stamp of truth upon it.

Cecily. I am more than content with what Mr. Moncrieff said. His voice alone inspires one with absolute credulity.

Gwendolen. Then you think we should forgive them?

Cecily. Yes. I mean no.

Gwendolen. True! I had forgotten. There are principles at stake that one cannot surrender. Which of us should tell them? The task is not a pleasant one.

Cecily. Could we not both speak at the same time?

Gwendolen. An excellent idea! I nearly always speak at the same time as other people. Will you take the time from me?

Cecily. Certainly. [*Gwendolen beats time with uplifted finger.*]

Gwendolen and *Cecily* [*speaking together*]. Your Christian names are still an insuperable barrier. That is all!

Jack and *Algernon* [*speaking together*]. Our Christian names! Is that all? But we are going to be christened this afternoon.

Gwendolen [*to Jack*]. For my sake you are prepared to do this terrible thing?

Jack. I am.

Cecily [*to Algernon*]. To please me you are ready to face this fearful ordeal?

Algernon. I am!

Gwendolen. How absurd to talk of the equality of the sexes! Where questions of self-sacrifice are concerned, men are infinitely beyond us.

Jack. We are. [*Clasps hands with Algernon.*]

Cecily. They have moments of physical courage of which we women know absolutely nothing.

Gwendolen [*to Jack*]. Darling!

Algernon [*to Cecily*]. Darling! [*They fall into each other's arms.*]

[*Enter Merriman. When he enters he coughs loudly, seeing the situation.*]

Merriman. Ahem! Ahem! Lady Bracknell.

Jack. Good heavens!

[*Enter Lady Bracknell. The couples separate in alarm. Exit Merriman.*]

Lady Bracknell. Gwendolen! What does this mean?

Gwendolen. Merely that I am engaged to be married to Mr. Worthing, mamma.

Lady Bracknell. Come here. Sit down. Sit down immediately. Hesitation of any kind is a sign of mental decay in the young, of physical weakness in the old. [*Turns to Jack.*] Apprised, sir, of my daughter's sudden flight by her trusty maid, whose confidence I purchased by means of a small coin, I followed her at once by a luggage train. Her unhappy father is, I am glad to say, under the impression that she is attending a more than usually lengthy lecture by the University Extension Scheme on the Influence of a Permanent Income on Thought. I do not propose to undeceive him. Indeed I have never undeceived him on any question. I would consider it wrong. But of course, you will clearly understand that all communication between yourself and my daughter must cease immediately from this moment. On this point, as indeed on all points, I am firm.

Jack. I am engaged to be married to Gwendolen, Lady Bracknell!

Lady Bracknell. You are nothing of the kind, sir. And now as regards Algernon! . . . Algernon!

Algernon. Yes, Aunt Augusta.

Lady Bracknell. May I ask if it is in this house that your invalid friend Mr. Bunbury resides?

Algernon [*stammering*]. Oh! No! Bunbury doesn't live here. Bunbury is somewhere else at present. In fact, Bunbury is dead.

Lady Bracknell. Dead! When did Mr. Bunbury die? His death must have been extremely sudden.

Algernon [*airily*]. Oh! I killed Bunbury this afternoon. I mean poor Bunbury died this afternoon.

Lady Bracknell. What did he die of?

Algernon. Bunbury? Oh, he was quite exploded.

Lady Bracknell. Exploded! Was he the victim of a revolutionary outrage? I was not aware that Mr. Bunbury was interested in social legislation. If so, he is well punished for his morbidity.

Algernon. My dear Aunt Augusta, I mean he was found out! The doctors found out that Bunbury could not live, that is what I mean—so Bunbury died.

Lady Bracknell. He seems to have had great confidence in the opinion of his physicians. I am glad, however, that he made up his mind at the last to some definite course of action, and acted under proper medical advice. And now that we have finally got rid of this Mr. Bunbury, may I ask, Mr. Worthing, who is that young person whose hand my nephew Algernon is now holding in what seems to me a peculiarly unnecessary manner?

Jack. That lady is Miss Cecily Cardew, my ward.

[*Lady Bracknell bows coldly to Cecily.*]

Algernon. I am engaged to be married to Cecily, Aunt Augusta.

Lady Bracknell. I beg your pardon?

Cecily. Mr. Moncrieff and I are engaged to be married, Lady Bracknell.

Lady Bracknell [*with a shiver, crossing to the sofa and sitting down*]. I do not know whether there is anything peculiarly exciting in the air of this particular part of Hertfordshire, but the number of engagements that go on seems to me considerably above the proper average that statistics have laid down for our guidance. I think some preliminary inquiry on my part would not be out of place. Mr. Worthing, is Miss Cardew at all connected with any of the larger railway stations in London? I merely desire information. Until yesterday I had no idea that there were any families or persons whose origin was a Terminus.

[*Jack looks perfectly furious, but restrains himself.*]

Jack [*in a cold, clear voice*]. Miss Cardew is the granddaughter of the late Mr. Thomas Cardew of 149 Belgrave Square, S.W.; Gervase Park, Dorking, Surrey; and the Sporran, Fifeshire, N.B.

Lady Bracknell. That sounds not unsatisfactory. Three addresses always inspire confidence, even in tradesmen. But what proof have I of their authenticity?

Jack. I have carefully preserved the Court Guides of the period. They are open to your inspection, Lady Bracknell.

Lady Bracknell [*grimly*]. I have known strange errors in that publication.

Jack. Miss Cardew's family solicitors are Messrs. Markby, Markby, and Markby.

Lady Bracknell. Markby, Markby, and Markby? A firm of the very highest position in their profession. Indeed I am told that one of the Mr. Markby's is occasionally to be seen at dinner parties. So far I am satisfied.

Jack [*very irritably*]. How extremely kind of you, Lady Bracknell! I have also in my possession, you will be pleased to hear, certificates of Miss Cardew's birth, baptism, whooping cough, registration, vaccination, confirmation, and the measles; both the German and the English variety.

Lady Bracknell. Ah! A life crowded with incident, I see; though perhaps somewhat too exciting for a young girl. I am not myself in favor of premature experiences. [*Rises, looks at her watch.*] Gwendolen! the time approaches for our departure. We have not a moment to lose. As a matter of form, Mr. Worthing, I had better ask you if Miss Cardew has any little fortune?

Jack. Oh! about a hundred and thirty thousand pounds in the Funds. That is all. Good-bye, Lady Bracknell. So pleased to have seen you.

Lady Bracknell [*sitting down again*]. A moment, Mr. Worthing. A hundred and thirty thousand pounds! And in the Funds! Miss Cardew seems to me a most attractive young lady, now that I look at her. Few girls of the present day have any really solid qualities, any of the qualities that last, and improve with time. We live, I regret to say, in an age of surfaces. [*To Cecily.*] Come over here, dear. [*Cecily goes across.*]

Pretty child! your dress is sadly simple, and your hair seems almost as Nature might have left it. But we can soon alter all that. A thoroughly experienced French maid produces a really marvellous result in a very brief space of time. I remember recommending one to young Lady Lancing, and after three months her own husband did not know her.

Jack. And after six months nobody knew her.

Lady Bracknell [*glares at Jack for a few moments. Then bends, with a practised smile, to Cecily*]. Kindly turn round, sweet child. [*Cecily turns completely round.*] No, the side view is what I want. [*Cecily presents her profile.*] Yes, quite as I expected. There are distinct social possibilities in your profile. The two weak points in our age are its want of principle and its want of profile. The chin a little higher, dear. Style largely depends on the way the chin is worn. They are worn very high, just at present. Algernon!

Algernon. Yes, Aunt Augusta!

Lady Bracknell. There are distinct social possibilities in Miss Cardew's profile.

Algernon. Cecily is the sweetest, dearest, prettiest girl in the whole world. And I don't care twopence about social possibilities.

Lady Bracknell. Never speak disrespectfully of Society, Algernon. Only people who can't get into it do that. [*To Cecily.*] Dear child, of course you know that Algernon has nothing but his debts to depend upon. But I do not approve of mercenary marriages. When I married Lord Bracknell I had no fortune of any kind. But I never dreamed for a moment of allowing that to stand in my way. Well, I suppose I must give my consent.

Algernon. Thank you, Aunt Augusta.

Lady Bracknell. Cecily, you may kiss me!

Cecily [*kisses her*]. Thank you, Lady Bracknell.

Lady Bracknell. You may also address me as Aunt Augusta for the future.

Cecily. Thank you, Aunt Augusta.

Lady Bracknell. The marriage, I think, had better take place quite soon.

Algernon. Thank you, Aunt Augusta.

Cecily. Thank you, Aunt Augusta.

Lady Bracknell. To speak frankly, I am not in favor of long engagements. They give people the opportunity of finding out each other's character before marriage, which I think is never advisable.

Jack. I beg your pardon for interrupting you, Lady Bracknell, but this engagement is quite out of the question. I am Miss Cardew's guardian, and she cannot marry without my consent until she comes of age. That consent I absolutely decline to give.

Lady Bracknell. Upon what grounds, may I ask? Algernon is an extremely, I may almost say an ostentatiously, eligible young man. He has nothing, but he looks everything. What more can one desire?

Jack. It pains me very much to have to speak frankly to you, Lady Bracknell, about your nephew, but the fact is that I do not approve at all of his moral character. I suspect him of being untruthful. [*Algernon and Cecily look at him in indignant amazement.*]

Lady Bracknell. Untruthful! My nephew Algernon? Impossible! He is an Oxonian.

Jack. I fear there can be no possible doubt about the matter. This afternoon during my temporary absence in London on an important question of romance, he obtained admission to my house by means of the false pretence of being my brother. Under an assumed name he drank, I've just been informed by my butler, an entire pint bottle of my Perrier-Jouet, Brut, '89; wine I was specially reserving for myself. Continuing his disgraceful deception, he succeeded in the course of the afternoon in alienating the affections of my only ward. He subsequently stayed to tea, and devoured every single muffin. And what makes his conduct all the more heartless is, that he was perfectly well aware from the first that I have no brother, that I never had a brother, and that I don't intend to have a brother, not even of any kind. I distinctly told him so myself yesterday afternoon.

Lady Bracknell. Ahem! Mr. Worthing, after careful consideration I have decided entirely to overlook my nephew's conduct to you.

Jack. That is very generous of you, Lady Bracknell. My own decision, however, is unalterable. I decline to give my consent.

Lady Bracknell [*to Cecily*]. Come here, sweet child. [*Cecily goes over.*] How old are you, dear?

Cecily. Well, I am really only eighteen, but I always admit to twenty when I go to evening parties.

Lady Bracknell. You are perfectly right in making some slight alteration. Indeed, no woman should ever be quite accurate about her age. It looks so calculating. . . . [*In a meditative manner.*] Eighteen, but admitting to twenty at evening parties. Well, it will not be very long before you are of age and free from the restraints of tutelage. So I don't think your guardian's consent is, after all, a matter of any importance.

Jack. Pray excuse me, Lady Bracknell, for interrupting you again, but it is only fair to tell you that according to the terms of her grandfather's will Miss Cardew does not come legally of age till she is thirty-five.

Lady Bracknell. That does not seem to me to be a grave objection. Thirty-five is a very attractive age. London society is full of women of the very highest birth who have, of their own free choice, remained thirty-five for years. Lady Dumbleton is an instance in point. To my own knowledge she has been thirty-five ever since she arrived at the age of forty, which was many years ago now. I see no reason why our dear Cecily should not be even still more attractive at the age you mention than she is at present. There will be a large accumulation of property.

Cecily. Algy, could you wait for me till I was thirty-five?

Algernon. Of course I could, Cecily. You know I could.

Cecily. Yes, I felt it instinctively, but I couldn't wait all that time. I hate waiting even five minutes for anybody. It always makes me rather cross. I am not punctual myself, I know, but I do like punctuality in others, and waiting, even to be married, is quite out of the question.

Algernon. Then what is to be done, Cecily?

Cecily. I don't know, Mr. Moncrieff.

Lady Bracknell. My dear Mr. Worthing, as Miss Cardew states positively that she cannot wait till she is thirty-five—a remark which I am bound to say seems to me to show a somewhat impatient nature—I would beg of you to reconsider your decision.

Jack. But my dear Lady Bracknell, the matter is entirely

in your own hands. The moment you consent to my marriage with Gwendolen, I will most gladly allow your nephew to form an alliance with my ward.

Lady Bracknell [*rising and drawing herself up*]. You must be quite aware that what you propose is out of the question.

Jack. Then a passionate celibacy is all that any of us can look forward to.

Lady Bracknell. That is not the destiny I propose for Gwendolen. Algernon, of course, can choose for himself. [*Pulls out her watch.*] Come, dear [*Gwendolen rises*], we have already missed five, if not six, trains. To miss any more might expose us to comment on the platform.

[*Enter Dr. Chasuble.*]

Chasuble. Everything is quite ready for the christenings.

Lady Bracknell. The christenings, sir! Is not that somewhat premature?

Chasuble [*looking rather puzzled, and pointing to Jack and Algernon*]. Both these gentlemen have expressed a desire for immediate baptism.

Lady Bracknell. At their age? The idea is grotesque and irreligious! Algernon, I forbid you to be baptized. I will not hear of such excesses. Lord Bracknell would be highly displeased if he learned that that was the way in which you wasted your time and money.

Chasuble. Am I to understand then that there are to be no christenings at all this afternoon?

Jack. I don't think that, as things are now, it would be of much practical value to either of us, Dr. Chasuble.

Chasuble. I am grieved to hear such sentiments from you, Mr. Worthing. They savour of the heretical views of the Anabaptists, views that I have completely refuted in four of my unpublished sermons. However, as your present mood seems to be one peculiarly secular, I will return to the church at once. Indeed, I have just been informed by the pew-opener that for the last hour and a half Miss Prism has been waiting for me in the vestry.

Lady Bracknell [*starting*]. Miss Prism! Did I hear you mention a Miss Prism?

Chasuble. Yes, Lady Bracknell. I am on my way to join her.

Lady Bracknell. Pray allow me to detain you for a moment. This matter may prove to be one of vital importance to Lord Bracknell and myself. Is this Miss Prism a female of repellent aspect, remotely connected with education?

Chasuble [*somewhat indignantly*]. She is the most cultivated of ladies, and the very picture of respectability.

Lady Bracknell. It is obviously the same person. May I ask what position she holds in your household?

Chasuble [*severely*]. I am a celibate, madam.

Jack [*interposing*]. Miss Prism, Lady Bracknell, has been for the last three years Miss Cardew's esteemed governess and valued companion.

Lady Bracknell. In spite of what I hear of her, I must see her at once. Let her be sent for.

Chasuble [*looking off*]. She approaches; she is nigh.

[*Enter Miss Prism hurriedly.*]

Miss Prism. I was told you expected me in the vestry, dear Canon. I have been waiting for you there for an hour and three-quarters. [*Catches sight of Lady Bracknell, who has fixed her with a stony glare. Miss Prism grows pale and quails. She looks anxiously round as if desirous to escape.*]

Lady Bracknell [*in a severe, judicial voice*]. Prism! [*Miss Prism bows her head in shame.*] Come here, Prism! [*Miss Prism approaches in a humble manner.*] Prism! Where is that baby? [*General consternation. The Canon starts back in horror. Algernon and Jack pretend to be anxious to shield Cecily and Gwendolen from hearing the details of a terrible public scandal.*] Twenty-eight years ago, Prism, you left Lord Bracknell's house, Number 104, Upper Grosvenor Square, in charge of a perambulator that contained a baby of the male sex. You never returned. A few weeks later, through the elaborate investigations of the Metropolitan police, the perambulator was discovered at midnight standing by itself in a remote corner of Bayswater. It contained the manuscript of a three-volume novel of more than usually revolting sentimentality. [*Miss Prism starts in involuntary indignation.*] But the baby was not there. [*Every one looks at Miss Prism.*] Prism! Where is that baby? [*A pause.*]

Miss Prism. Lady Bracknell, I admit with shame that I do not know. I only wish I did. The plain facts of the case are these. On the morning of the day you mention, a day that is for ever branded on my memory, I prepared as usual to take the baby out in its perambulator. I had also with me a somewhat old, but capacious handbag in which I had intended to place the manuscript of a work of fiction that I had written during my few unoccupied hours. In a moment of mental abstraction, for which I can never forgive myself, I deposited the manuscript in the bassinette and placed the baby in the handbag.

Jack [*who has been listening attentively*]. But where did you deposit the handbag?

Miss Prism. Do not ask me, Mr. Worthing.

Jack. Miss Prism, this is a matter of no small importance to me. I insist on knowing where you deposited the handbag that contained that infant.

Miss Prism. I left it in the cloakroom of one of the larger railway stations in London.

Jack. What railway station?

Miss Prism [*quite crushed*]. Victoria. The Brighton line. [*Sinks into a chair.*]

Jack. I must retire to my room for a moment. Gwendolen, wait here for me.

Gwendolen. If you are not too long, I will wait here for you all my life. [*Exit Jack in great excitement.*]

Chasuble. What do you think this means, Lady Bracknell?

Lady Bracknell. I dare not even suspect, Dr. Chasuble. I need hardly tell you that in families of high position strange coincidences are not supposed to occur. They are hardly considered the thing.

[*Noises heard overhead as if some one was throwing trunks about. Every one looks up.*]

Cecily. Uncle Jack seems strangely agitated.

Chasuble. Your guardian has a very emotional nature.

Lady Bracknell. This noise is extremely unpleasant. It sounds as if he was having an argument. I dislike arguments of any kind. They are always vulgar, and often convincing.

Chasuble [*looking up*]. It has stopped now. [*The noise is redoubled.*]

Lady Bracknell. I wish he would arrive at some conclusion.

Gwendolen. This suspense is terrible. I hope it will last.

[*Enter Jack with a handbag of black leather in his hand.*]

Jack [*rushing over to Miss Prism*]. Is this the handbag, Miss
    Prism? Examine it carefully before you speak. The
    happiness of more than one life depends on your
    answer.

Miss Prism [*calmly*]. It seems to be mine. Yes, here is the
    injury it received through the upsetting of a Gower
    Street omnibus in younger and happier days. Here
    is the stain on the lining caused by the explosion of a
    temperance beverage, an incident that occurred at
    Leamington. And here, on the lock, are my initials. I
    had forgotten that in an extravagant mood I had had
    them placed there. The bag is undoubtedly mine. I am
    delighted to have it so unexpectedly restored to me.
    It has been a great inconvenience being without it all
    these years.

Jack [*in a pathetic voice*]. Miss Prism, more is restored to
    you than this handbag. I was the baby you placed in
    it.

Miss Prism [*amazed*]. You?

Jack [*embracing her*]. Yes . . . mother!

Miss Prism [*recoiling in indignant astonishment*]. Mr.
    Worthing, I am unmarried!

Jack. Unmarried! I do not deny that is a serious blow. But
    after all, who has the right to cast a stone against
    one who has suffered? Cannot repentance wipe out
    an act of folly? Why should there be one law for
    men, and another for women? Mother, I forgive you.
    [*Tries to embrace her again.*]

Miss Prism [*still more indignant*]. Mr. Worthing, there is
    some error. [*Pointing to Lady Bracknell.*] There is the
    lady who can tell you who you really are.

Jack [*after a pause*]. Lady Bracknell, I hate to seem in-
    quisitive, but would you kindly inform me who I am?

Lady Bracknell. I am afraid that the news I have to give
    you will not altogether please you. You are the son
    of my poor sister, Mrs. Moncrieff, and consequently
    Algernon's elder brother.

Jack. Algy's elder brother! Then I have a brother after all.
    I knew I had a brother! I always said I had a brother!
    Cecily—how could you have ever doubted that I had
    a brother? [*Seizes hold of Algernon.*] Dr. Chasuble,

my unfortunate brother. Miss Prism, my unfortunate
brother. Gwendolen, my unfortunate brother. Algy,
you young scoundrel, you will have to treat me with
more respect in the future. You have never behaved
to me like a brother in all your life.

Algernon. Well, not till today, old boy, I admit. I did my
best, however, though I was out of practice. [*Shakes
hands.*]

Gwendolen [*to Jack*]. My own! But what own are you?
What is your Christian name, now that you have
become some one else?

Jack. Good heavens! . . . I had quite forgotten that point.
Your decision on the subject of my name is irrevoc-
able, I suppose?

Gwendolen. I never change, except in my affections.

Cecily. What a noble nature you have, Gwendolen!

Jack. Then the question had better be cleared up at once.
Aunt Augusta, a moment. At the time when Miss
Prism left me in the handbag, had I been christened
already?

Lady Bracknell. Every luxury that money could buy, including christening, had been lavished on you by
your fond and doting parents.

Jack. Then I was christened! That is settled. Now, what
name was I given? Let me know the worst.

Lady Bracknell. Being the eldest son you were naturally
christened after your father.

Jack [*irritably*]. Yes, but what was my father's Christian
name?

Lady Bracknell [*meditatively*]. I cannot at the present
moment recall what the General's Christian name was.
But I have no doubt he had one. He was eccentric, I
admit. But only in later years. And that was the result
of the Indian climate, and marriage, and indigestion,
and other things of that kind.

Jack. Algy! Can't you recollect what our father's Christian
name was?

Algernon. My dear boy, we were never even on speaking
terms. He died before I was a year old.

Jack. His name would appear in the Army Lists of the
period, I suppose, Aunt Augusta?

Lady Bracknell. The General was essentially a man of
peace, except in his domestic life. But I have no doubt

his name would appear in any military directory.

Jack. The Army Lists of the last forty years are here. These delightful records should have been my constant study. [*Rushes to bookcase and tears the books out*]. M. Generals . . . Mallam, Maxbohm, Magley—what ghastly names they have—Markby, Migsby, Mobbs, Moncrieff! Lieutenant 1840, Captain, Lieutenant-Colonel, Colonel, General 1869, Christian names, Ernest John. [*Puts book very quietly down and speaks quite calmly*.] I always told you, Gwendolen, my name was Ernest, didn't I? Well, it is Ernest after all. I mean it naturally is Ernest.

Lady Bracknell. Yes, I remember now that the General was called Ernest. I knew I had some particular reason for disliking the name.

Gwendolen. Ernest! My own Ernest! I felt from the first that you could have no other name!

Jack. Gwendolen, it is terrible thing for a man to find out suddenly that all his life he has been speaking nothing but the truth. Can you forgive me?

Gwendolen. I can. For I feel that you are sure to change.

Jack. My own one!

Chasuble [*to Miss Prism*]. Laetitia! [*Embraces her.*]

Miss Prism [*enthusiastically*]. Frederick! At last!

Algernon. Cecily! [*Embraces her*]. At last!

Jack. Gwendolyn! [*Embraces her*]. At last!

Lady Bracknell. My nephew, you seem to be displaying signs of triviality.

Jack. On the contrary, Aunt Augusta, I've now realized for the first time in my life the vital Importance of Being Earnest.